Die Schönheit des Augenblicks

Frauen im japanischen Holzdruck

The Beauty of the Moment

Women in Japanese Woodblock Prints

HERAUSGEGEBEN VON
EDITED BY

Katharina Epprecht

ESSAYS VON
ESSAYS BY

Shawn Eichman
Katharina Epprecht
Marie Kakinuma
Andreas Marks
John D. Szostak

Museum Rietberg Zürich
Scheidegger & Spiess

In Zusammenarbeit mit dem Honolulu Museum of Art
In collaboration with the Honolulu Museum of Art

Konservierung ermöglicht durch die Robert F. Lange Stiftung
Conservation funded by the Robert F. Lange Foundation

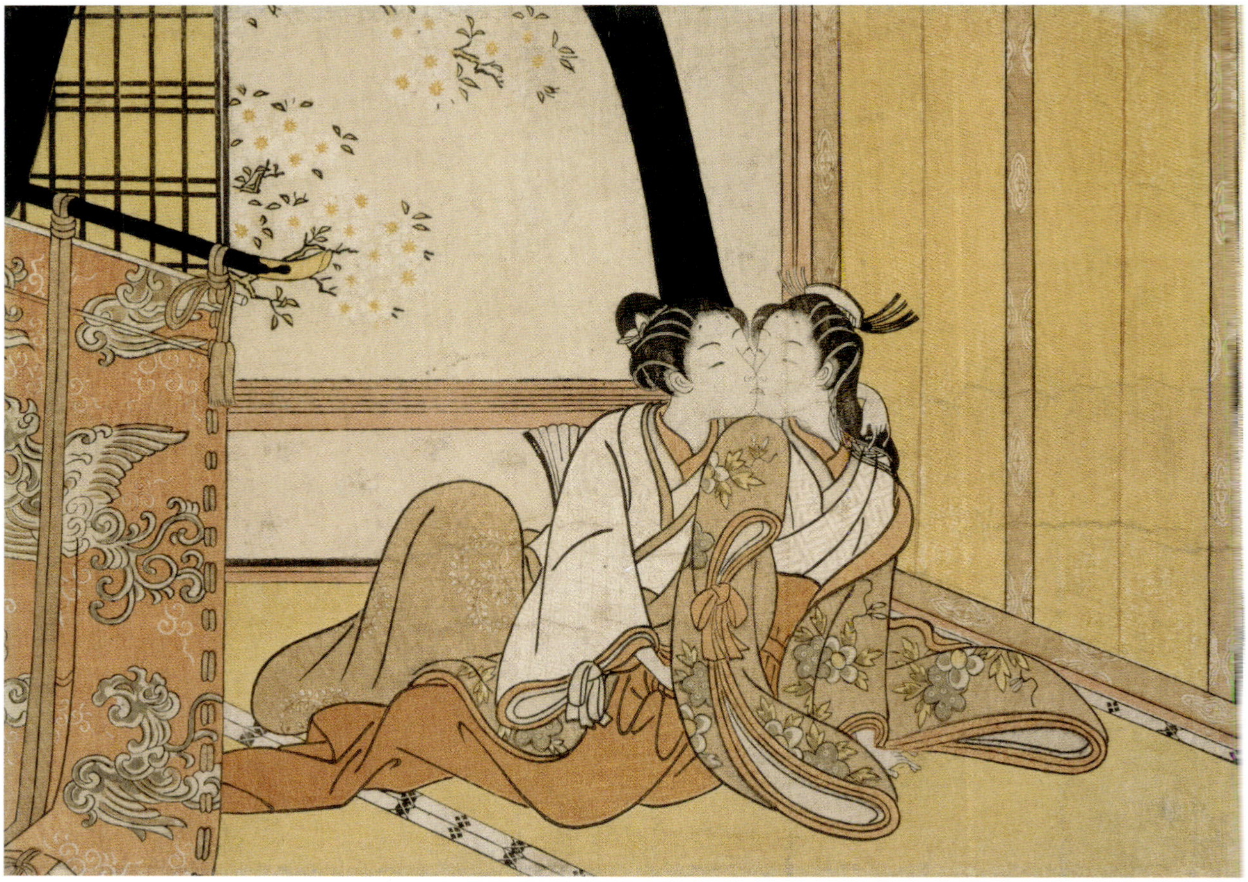

FIG. 1

Dank
Acknowledgments

KATHARINA EPPRECHT

Die Vorbereitungen zur Ausstellung *Die Schönheit des Augenblicks* standen von Anfang an unter einem günstigen Stern. Es begann damit, dass sich die Eröffnung exakt auf *tanabata,* das «Sternenfest», festlegen liess, welches jedes Jahr am 7. Juli in Japan gefeiert wird. Nur an diesem Tag im Jahr, so will es die geläufigste Version der Geschichte, ist es der Weberin Orihime und dem Rinderhirten Hikoboshi vergönnt, sich zu treffen, bevor die beiden Sterne Wega und Altair, die die beiden Liebenden repräsentieren, wieder durch die Milchstrasse getrennt werden.

Die Zusammenarbeit zwischen dem Honolulu Museum of Art (bis Anfang 2012 bekannt als Honolulu Academy of Arts) und dem Museum Rietberg Zürich gestaltete sich bezüglich Überquerung grosser Distanzen und bezüglich Geschwindigkeit der Konzeptentwicklung und -realisierung wie eine Nachahmung der *tanabata*-Geschichte. Bei einem einzigen Treffen in Honolulu mit Shawn Eichman, Sawako Chang und Carol Morland bestimmten wir in wenigen Tagen die Auswahl der Drucke und das Katalogkonzept. Shawn Eichman und Carol Morland erklärten sich sogleich bereit, in kürzester Zeit die Katalogeinträge zu verfassen. Als eine Unklarheit zu einem der Sujets auftauchte, reagierte der Direktor des Clark Centre of Japanese Art and Culture, Andreas Marks, umgehend auf die in den Äther gesandte Frage. Ausserdem liess sich Andreas Marks für einen grösseren Beitrag gewinnen, der die Entwicklung des Sujets «Bilder schöner Frauen», *bijinga,* bis in die Mitte des 19. Jahrhunderts aufzeigt. Nicole Coolidge Rousmaniere, Gründungsdirektorin des Sainsbury Institute for the Study of Japanese Arts and Cultures, verdanken wir den wertvollen Tipp, uns an John D. Szostak zu wenden, der an der University of Hawaii unterrichtet. Er erfüllte rasch unseren Wunsch, auch die weniger schönen Seiten des *ukiyo-e,* «Bilder der fliessenden, vergänglichen Welt», zu thematisieren und dem Leser eine Vorstellung von den realen Verhältnissen in den Freudenvierteln zu vermitteln. Jeanne Egloff steuerte die Künstlerbiografien bei, und Marie Kakinuma vermittelte nicht nur zwischen Tokio und Zürich rund um die Videoinstallationen der zeitgenössischen Künstlerin Tabaimo, sondern verfasste auch die dazugehörenden Texte. Tabaimos vielschichtige Anspielungen auf traditionelle Holzdrucke in ihrer ganz und gar eigenständigen und gegenwartsbezogenen Kunst öffnen uns ein wichtiges Fenster zur heutigen japanischen Gesellschaft.

Right from the start, a lucky star shone on the preparations for the *The Beauty of the Moment* exhibition. To begin with, the opening coincided with *tanabata,* the "star festival," which is celebrated every year in Japan on July 7th. According to the most familiar version of the story, Orihime, a weaver, and Hikoboshi, a cattle herd, are allowed to meet only on this day of the year, before the stars that represent the two lovers, Vega and Altair, are again separated by the Milky Way.

In terms of conquering great distances and with regard to the speed with which a concept was developed and realized, the collaboration between the Honolulu Museum of Art (known as the Honolulu Academy of Arts until 2012) and the Museum Rietberg Zürich seemed like a reenactment of the *tanabata* story. At a single meeting in Honolulu involving Shawn Eichman, Sawako Chang, and Carol Morland, the selection of prints and the catalogue concept were established in just a few days time. Shawn Eichman and Carol Morland immediately declared their willingness to compose catalogue entries with an extremely short deadline. And when something was unclear about one of the subjects, the director of the Clark Centre of Japanese Art and Culture, Andreas Marks, reacted promptly to the question sent through the airwaves. Andreas Marks could also be convinced to write a longer contribution outlining the development of the subject "images of beautiful women," *bijinga,* through the mid-nineteenth century. Nicole Coolidge Rousmaniere, founding director of the Sainsbury Institute for the Study of Japanese Arts and Cultures, gave us the valuable tip to contact John D. Szostak, who teaches at the University of Hawaii. He quickly agreed to our request to thematize the less beautiful side of *ukiyo-e,* "pictures of the floating world," and provide readers with an impression of the real conditions in the Geisha quarter. Jeanne Egloff contributed the artists' biographies, and Marie Kakinuma not only mediated between Tokyo and Zürich on the video installations of the contemporary artist Tabaimo, but also wrote the accompanying texts. Tabaimo's complex references to traditional woodblock prints in her thoroughly independent, topically relevant art, open a crucial window to contemporary Japanese society.

It was almost as if the above-mentioned *tanabata* story's love theme provided the framework for the whole project: thanks to the fortunate circumstance of being able to view one work from Honolulu and another from

Es schien fast, als ob die anfangs erwähnte Liebesthematik der *tanabata*-Geschichte der Nährboden für das ganze Projekt gewesen sei, denn dank des glücklichen Zusammentreffens von einem Werk aus Honolulu und einem anderen aus Zürich konnte sogar ein bis anhin nicht näher bestimmbares Sujet aus der Sammlung des Museums Rietberg genauer identifiziert werden. Dies war deshalb möglich, weil die beiden Drucke bezüglich des generellen Stils, der Farbgebung, des spezifischen Gewandtypus und der Details des Interieurs bis hin zu den Abschlussbändern der Tatami-Matten und Bambusvorhänge einander verblüffend ähnlich sind (KAT. 24 UND FIG. 1). Dasjenige in Honolulu trägt die Signatur Harunobus, dasjenige in Zürich ist nicht signiert. Zwar bestand aufgrund des Stils nie ein Zweifel, dass das Blatt im Museum Rietberg ein Entwurf Harunobus sei, doch wusste man nicht, dass es sich bei der innig von einem jungen Mann geküssten Frau um dieselbe handeln muss wie auf dem Blatt in Honolulu, nämlich um die dritte Prinzessin, Onna Sannomiya, aus der *Geschichte vom Prinzen Genji.* Dementsprechend muss der junge Mann Prinz Genji sein. In der Ausstellung können die beiden Blätter nebeneinander betrachtet werden, bevor sie wieder durch den halben Globus getrennt voneinander aufbewahrt werden.

Als wir für die Gestaltung des Katalogs nach einer geeigneten Person suchten, fiel die Grafikerin Hitomi Murai sprichwörtlich vom Himmel und beglückte uns mit ihrer einfühlsamen Gestaltung und ihrer höchst kooperativen Arbeitsweise. Die szenografische Inszenierung der Holzdrucke und die Gestaltung des Plakats und des Flyers lagen in den verlässlichen Händen von Martin Sollberger und Jacqueline Schöb aus unserem Team für Corporate Design. Diese Zusammenarbeit ist seit jeher höchst erfreulich und kreativ. Christof von Waldkirch hielt, unterstützt von Laura Beyer, die Fäden des Projekts in vorbildlicher Weise zusammen und kümmerte sich auch um die rechtzeitige Einbindung der internen Abteilungen Marketing, Events und Kunstvermittlung. Da nicht alle an der Ausstellung und dem Katalog beteiligten Personen namentlich genannt sein können, gilt mein Dank allen Mitarbeiterinnen und Mitarbeitern des Museums Rietberg, die sich von meiner Begeisterung für die wunderbaren Holzdrucke aus Hawaii anstecken liessen und alles daran setzten, dass die Ausstellung ein Erfolg werden sollte.

Wir sind dem Unternehmen JTI Schweiz zu grösstem Dank verpflichtet. Nachdem uns JTI bereits die Finanzierung des permanent im Museum Rietberg eingebauten japanischen Teezimmers ermöglicht hatte, übernahm JTI diesmal das Hauptsponsoring für die Ausstellung *Die Schönheit des Augenblicks.* Die Realisierung der aufwendigen Einbauten für die Installation von Tabaimos Arbeiten und die Möglichkeit, zur Ausstellungseröffnung ein unvergessliches und stimmungsvolles *tanabata*-Fest zu veranstalten, verdanken wir dem unverhofften und grosszügigen Engagement der seit vielen Jahren mit unserem Haus verbundenen Gönnerin Regula Brunner.

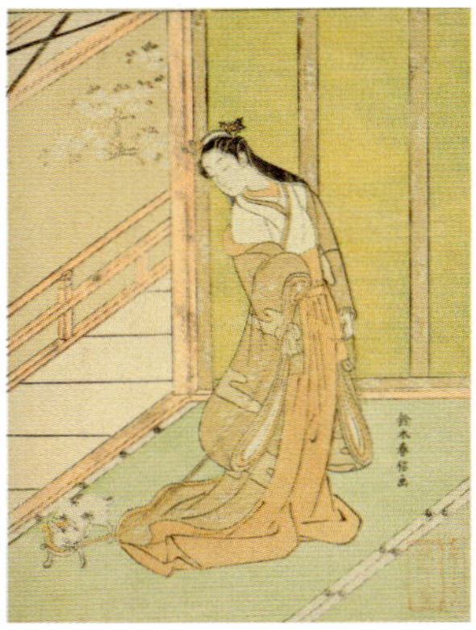

24

Zurich side by side, it was possible to identify a subject from the Museum Rietberg that had previously evaded precise definition. It was possible to link the two prints, since they display amazing similarities with regard to general style, coloring, specific type of clothing, and details of the interiors, through to the finishing bands of the *tatami* mats, and bamboo curtains (CAT. 24 AND FIG. 1). The work in Honolulu was signed by Harunobu; the one in Zürich is unsigned. Based on the style, there was, indeed, never a doubt that the sheet in the Museum Rietberg was a design by Harunobu, yet it was not clear that the woman being intimately kissed by a young man is the same as the one on the sheet in Honolulu, namely, the third princess, Onna Sannomiya, from the *Tale of Genji.* Accordingly, the young man must be Prince Genji. During the exhibition, the two works can be viewed next to each other, before they return to their separate homes half a world apart.

In our search for someone suitable to design the catalogue, graphic designer Hitomi Murai literally fell from the sky and honored us with her sensitive design and extremely cooperative working method. The scenographic staging of the woodblock prints and the design of the poster and flyer were in the capable hands of Martin Sollberger and Jacqueline Schöb from our corporate design team. Our collaboration with them has always been extremely pleasurable and creative. Christof von Waldkirch held the strings of the project together in a commendable way, with the support of Laura Beyer, and attended to the timely inclusion of our internal departments for marketing, events, and art education. Since not everyone involved in the exhibition and catalogue can be named individually, my thanks go to the entire staff at the Museum Rietberg who let themselves be inspired by my enthusiasm for the wonderful woodblock prints from Hawaii, and did everything in their power to make the exhibition a success.

We owe our utmost thanks to the firm JTI Switzerland. After already financing the Japanese tea room installed as a permanent facility at the Museum Rietberg, this time, JTI took on the main sponsorship of the exhibition *The Beauty of the Moment.* For the realization of the elaborate fixtures for the installation of Tabaimo's works and the possibility to host an unforgettable and atmospheric *tanabata* festival for the exhibition opening we thank the unexpected and generous involvement of benefactor Regula Brunner who has been allied with our museum for many years.

Japanische Holzschnitte im Honolulu Museum of Art
Japanese Woodblock Prints at the Honolulu Museum of Art

SHAWN EICHMAN

Das Honolulu Museum of Art (ehemals Honolulu Academy of Arts) ist das einzige akkreditierte umfassende Kunstmuseum auf Hawaii. Es besitzt eine Sammlung, bestehend aus über 50 000 Kunstwerken und 30 permanenten Ausstellungsbereichen, die sich der Kunst aus Hawaii, Europa, den Amerikas, Ozeanien, den Philippinen, Indonesien, Süd- und Südostasien, China, Korea und Japan widmet. Das HMA fusionierte 2011 mit The Contemporary Museum und konnte so seine Bestände und seine Programmgestaltung im Bereich der zeitgenössischen Kunst erheblich erweitern. Mit dem Spalding House entstand darüber hinaus ein zweiter Campus.

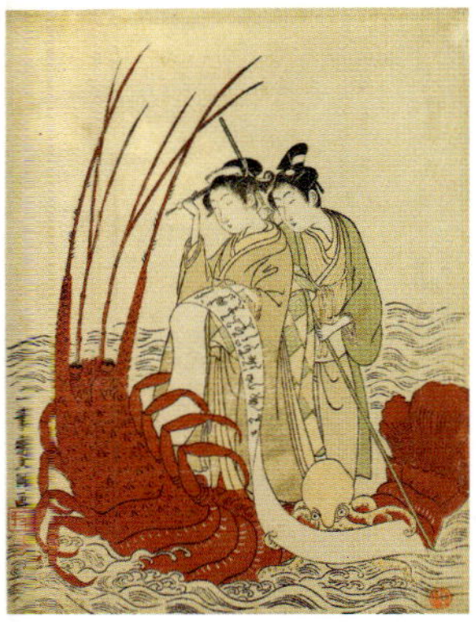

28

Das Museum wurde 1922 auf private Initiative von Anna Rice Cooke (1853–1934), der Tochter einer Missionarsfamilie, gegründet und 1927 eröffnet. Ihre Absicht sei, so erklärte Cooke in einer Rede zur Eröffnung des Hauses, die Menschen Hawaiis mit Kunst in Berührung zu bringen, auch wenn sie leider «weit von den Kunstzentren entfernt» seien; «über das Medium der Kunst sollen sie mit jenen tiefen Vorstellungen in Kontakt kommen, die uns allen gemeinsam sind. Und dadurch erhalten sie eine Grundlage für die Entwicklung einer neuen Identität auf diesen Inseln, bereichert durch die tradierten Stammeskulturen.» Japanische Kunst war von Anfang an Teil von Cookes Museumskonzept – die Gründerin erwarb die ersten «Bilder der fliessenden Welt» *(ukiyo-e)* für das Museum, darunter den seltenen Druck *Parodie des 7. Aktes des «Chûshingura»* von Ippitsusai Bunchô (KAT. 28).

Das Honolulu Museum of Art konnte seine Sammlung japanischer Holzschnitte dank der Unterstützung von James A. Michener (1907–1997) erheblich erweitern. Michener hatte während seines Militärdienstes in der US-amerikanischen Marine im Zweiten Weltkrieg ein Interesse an Asien und der Pazifikregion entwickelt; später verfasste er verschiedene Populärromane, die in der Region spielen, insbesondere *Tales of the South Pacific* (1947), das als Musical am Broadway Erfolge feierte und 1958 verfilmt wurde. Michener machte sich durch die Veröffentlichung eines Buches mit dem Titel *The Floating World* (1955) auch als Wissenschaftler einen Namen. Eine Sammlerin mit einer kleinen, aber feinen Sammlung japanischer Drucke, Georgia Forman aus Buffalo aus dem Bundesstaat New York, war von Micheners Einblicken so beeindruckt, dass sie ihm ihre Sammlung vermachte. Wenig später erwarb Michener die bedeutende Sammlung des in Evanston im

The Honolulu Museum of Art (formerly the Honolulu Academy of Arts) is Hawaii's only accredited comprehensive art museum. With a collection of more than 50,000 works, the museum has thirty permanent galleries dedicated to the arts of Hawaii, Europe, the Americas, Oceania, the Philippines, Indonesia, South and Southeast Asia, China, Korea, and Japan. In addition, in 2011 the HMA merged with The Contemporary Museum, significantly expanding its holdings and programming in contemporary art, and adding a second campus, now known as Spalding House.

The museum was privately established by Anna Rice Cooke (1853–1934), daughter of a missionary family, in 1922, and opened to the public in 1927. As Cooke stated in her speech commemorating the opening, it was her intention to provide exposure to the arts for the Hawaii community, despite their disadvantage in "being far from the centres of Art," so that "contacting through the channel of art those deep intuitions common to all, [they] may perceive a foundation on which a new culture, enriched by the old strains, may be built in these islands." From the start, Cooke included Japanese art in her vision for the museum, and she made the Museum's first acquisitions of *ukiyo-e,* including *Parody of Act 7 of the "Chûshingura"* by Ippitsusai Bunchô (CAT. 28).

The Honolulu Museum of Art's collection of Japanese woodblock prints expanded significantly through the patronage of James A. Michener (1907–1997). Michener developed an interest in Asia and the Pacific when he served in the navy during World War II, and later wrote several popular novels that took place in the region, most notably *Tales of the South Pacific* (1947), which was adapted into a successful Broadway musical and feature film (1958). Michener also established a reputation as a scholar of Japanese prints through the publication of his first book on the subject, *The Floating World,* in 1955. A collector with a small but fine group of Japanese prints, Mrs. Georgia Forman of Buffalo, New York, was so impressed with Michener's insights that she bequeathed her collection to him, and soon afterward he acquired the major collection of Evanston, Illinois-based Charles H. Chandler, with more than 4,500 prints, including one of the world's most complete assemblages of prints by Hiroshige (through Michener's support, the Museum now has the largest collection of Hiroshige prints in the world, the core of which came from Chandler). However, Michener's own interests were more focused on the

Bundesstaat Illinois lebenden Charles H. Chandler, die aus über 4500 Drucken bestand. Darunter befand sich eine der vollständigsten Sammlungen von Hiroshige-Drucken weltweit (dank Michener besitzt das Museum heute die grösste Sammlung von Hiroshige-Drucken auf der ganzen Welt; ihr Grundbestand geht auf Chandler zurück). Michener persönlich interessierte sich jedoch mehr für die sogenannte «primitive» Periode vom Anfang bis zur Mitte des 18. Jahrhunderts, etwa für die wunderbare *Kurtisane* von Kaigetsudô Dohan (KAT. 1). Michener erweiterte und vervollständigte die Sammlung der von Forman und Chandler erworbenen Holzschnitte und schenkte dem Museum ab dem Ende der 1950er-Jahre bis 1991 insgesamt über 5000 Drucke.

Michener wurde in seiner Sammeltätigkeit schon früh von Richard D. Lane (1926–2002), einem namhaften Literatur- und Kunstwissenschaftler für die Edo-Zeit, beraten; dieser besass ebenfalls enge Verbindungen zum Honolulu Museum of Art und hatte an der University of Hawaii Japanisch studiert. 2003 erwarb das HMA Lanes Sammlung, darunter schätzungsweise 10 000 Bände japanischer Holzschnittbücher, die häufig von denselben Künstlern stammten, die auch die von Michener geschenkten Einzelblätter kreiert hatten. Durch den Ankauf der Lane-Sammlung konnte das HMA seine *ukiyo-e*-Bestände massgeblich erweitern und die Objekte zur Buchgestaltung der Edo-Zeit vervollständigen. Die Buchgestaltung dieser Zeit sei von entscheidender Bedeutung – so erklärte Lane leidenschaftlich im Laufe seiner gesamten Karriere –, um die Entwicklung von Holzschnitten in Japan wirklich zu verstehen. Weitere Ergänzungen der Sammlung sind Philip H. Roach Jr. zu verdanken, der dem Museum mehr als 1000 Drucke schenkte und so die Bestände im Bereich des 20. Jahrhunderts, insbesondere aus der Meiji-Zeit (1868–1912) und der Taishô-Zeit (1912–1926), erweiterte.

Seit 1991 wird die Sammlung japanischer Drucke des Museums permanent durch die in Hawaii ansässige Robert F. Lange Stiftung unterstützt. Dies ermöglichte zum einen die Konservierung von Tausenden Drucken und ihren Fortbestand für zukünftige Generationen. Zum anderen konnte eine neue digitale Datenbank der Sammlung eingerichtet werden, die künftig Online-Zugang zu Bildern und Informationen der über 10 000 Einzelblattdrucke des Museums und den gesamten Fotografien von Holzschnittbüchern aus der Sammlung Lane geben wird. Aufgrund der grosszügigen Unterstützung wurde die Museumsgalerie, die eine permanente Ausstellung japanischer Holzschnitte zeigt, 2008 nach der Robert F. Lange Stiftung benannt.

Dank des Engagements dieser und anderer Förderer ist das Honolulu Museum of Art zu einem wichtigen internationalen Zentrum für das Sammeln, Konservieren, Ausstellen und Erforschen japanischer Holzschnitte und Holzschnittbücher geworden. Es verfügt zudem über eines der dynamischsten museumspädagogischen Angebote der Welt, um ein tieferes Verständnis für Japans Beitrag zur Weltkunst und Weltkultur zu wecken.

so-called "primitive" period of the early to mid-eighteenth century, such as the marvelous *Courtesan* by Kaigetsudô Dohan (CAT. 1), and he continued to expand upon and refine the prints acquired from Forman and Chandler, ultimately donating more than 5,000 prints to the museum over more than three decades, from the late 1950s through 1991.

Early on in his collecting Michener was advised by noted Edo-period literature and art scholar Richard D. Lane (1926–2002), who also had close ties to the Honolulu Museum of Art, and studied Japanese at the University of Hawaii. In 2003, the HMA acquired Lane's collection, including an estimated 10,000 volumes of Japanese woodblock-printed books, many with illustrations by the same artists represented by the single-sheet prints Michener donated. The acquisition of the Lane Collection has significantly augmented the HMA's holdings in *ukiyo-e,* adding depth in Edo-period book design, which Lane himself passionately advocated throughout his career, and which was essential to a proper understanding of the development of woodblock printing in Japan. Further additions have been made to the collection by Philip H. Roach, Jr., who has given more than 1,000 prints, strengthening the museum's holdings in twentieth-century works, especially from the Meiji (1868–1912) and Taishô (1912–1926) periods.

Since 1991, the Museum's collection of Japanese prints has received ongoing support from the Hawaii-based Robert F. Lange Foundation, which has enabled not only the conservation of thousands of prints, preserving them for future generations, but has also made possible a new digital collection database that will eventually provide online access to images and information for the museum's entire collection of more than 10,000 single-sheet prints, and complete photography of the woodblock-printed books in the Lane Collection. In recognition of this relationship, in 2008 the museum's permanent gallery for the display of Japanese prints was named after the Lange Foundation.

Through the assistance of these and other patrons, the Honolulu Museum of Art has become an important international center for the collection, preservation, display and study of Japanese woodblock prints and woodblock-printed books, with one of the world's most dynamic programs promoting a deeper awareness of Japan's contributions to world art and culture.

Einleitung
Introduction

KATHARINA EPPRECHT

Das Honolulu Museum of Art besitzt eine der qualitativ hervorragendsten und am besten erhaltenen Sammlungen japanischer Holzdrucke weltweit. Dank der künstlerischen und thematischen Breite sowie der schieren Fülle der heute mehr als 10 000 Einzelblätter umfassenden Sammlung war es nicht nur möglich, sondern auch höchst interessant, ein Thema herauszulösen, das den bekannten Sammler und Romancier James A. Michener, aus dessen vormaligem Besitz die meisten Drucke stammen, besonders begeistert hat: «Bilder schöner Frauen», *bijinga.* In seinem 1959 erschienenen Überblickswerk *Japanese Prints: From the Early Masters to the Modern* meint Michener, der sich auch als kenntnisreicher Autor verschiedener Bücher zum Holzdruck hervorgetan hat, zum Porträt der berühmten Kurtisane Hanaôgi von Kitagawa Utamaro (KAT. 72): «It was from my account of this haunting woman that I was able to afford most of the prints shown here, so in a very real sense she can be called the patron saint of this collection, except that the word saint is one which hardly applies to this remarkable woman.»[1] Michener spielt hier auf seinen Bestsellerroman *Sayonara* an, in dem einer modernen Hanaôgi die Hauptrolle zukommt. Diese Romanfigur, die Michener offenbar finanziellen Wohlstand bescherte, entstand eindeutig inspiriert durch die gleichnamige Schönheit, die im 18. Jahrhundert gelebt hatte und in zahlreichen Holzdrucken verewigt worden war.

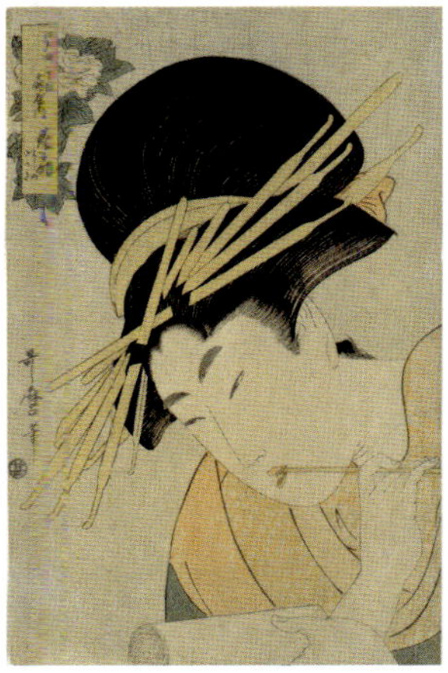

72

Das Betrachten von japanischen Holzdrucken, insbesondere was das Genre der «Bilder schöner Frauen» betrifft, soll in erster Linie das Auge erfreuen. Dies bestätigt bezeichnenderweise der Titel *Designed for Pleasure* gerade jenes kürzlich in New York erschienenen Ausstellungskatalogs, der in paradigmatischer Weise die kunsthistorische Diskussion um den Holzdruck über die traditionell vorwiegend ästhetische Betrachtungsweise hinausführt.[2] Im Japanischen verwendet man den Begriff *ukiyo-e,* «Bilder der fliessenden, vergänglichen Welt», als Synonym für Holzdruck. David Pollack interpretiert *ukiyo* als Welt der Mode, die sich ihrerseits ständig verändert und vergänglich ist.[3] Tatsächlich scheinen die stark verallgemeinerten Körperumrisse der Frauen primär dazu eingesetzt zu werden, Flächen zu definieren, die mit einem unglaublichen Reichtum an wechselnden Stoffmustern und Farbkombinationen bedeckt sind. Kleider, Frisuren und Haarkämme sind die eigentlichen Blickfänge. Das sich wandelnde Schönheitsideal manifestiert sich dementsprechend in den «Bildern schöner Frauen»

The Honolulu Museum of Art is home to one of the highest quality and best preserved collections of Japanese woodblock prints in the world. Due to its artistic and thematic breadth as well as the sheer abundance of the collection, which currently consists of more than 10,000 individual sheets, it was not only possible but also extremely interesting to extract a theme that would stir the interest of the renowned collector and novelist James A. Michener, former owner of most of the *bijinga* "images of beautiful women" prints. In his overview work *Japanese Prints: From the Early Masters to the Modern* published in 1959, Michener, who as a well-known author, also distinguished himself as a knowledgeable author of various books on woodblock prints, said of the portrait of renowned courtesan Hanaôgi by Kitagawa Utamaro (CAT. 72): "It was from my account of this haunting woman that I was able to afford most of the prints shown here, so in a very real sense she can be called the patron saint of this collection, except that the word saint is one which hardly applies to this remarkable woman."[1] Michener refers to his bestseller *Sayonara,* in which the main role is played by Hanaôgi, a modern woman. The character in the novel, who apparently brought financial wealth for Michener, was clearly inspired by the eponymous eighteenth-century beauty eternalized in numerous woodblock prints.

Viewing Japanese woodblock prints should first and foremost be pleasing to the eye, which is particularly applicable to the "images of beautiful women" genre. This is tellingly confirmed by the title of an exhibition catalogue recently published in New York, *Designed for Pleasure,* which paradigmatically leads art-historical discussion of woodblock prints beyond a traditional, primarily aesthetic perspective.[2] In Japanese, one uses the term *ukiyo-e,* "images of the floating world," as synonym for woodblock print. David Pollack interprets *ukiyo* as the world of fashion, which for its part, is constantly changing and ephemeral.[3] In fact, the highly generalized body outlines of the women seem to function primarily to define surfaces covered with an unbelievable wealth of changing patterns and color combinations. Clothes, hairstyles, and hair combs are the actual eye catchers. In "images of beautiful women," the changing ideal of beauty thus clearly manifests itself with regard to fashion rather than physiognomic preferences.

The idealized beauties are elegant and desirable women who appear as courtesans (including various

offensichtlicher in Bezug auf die Mode und weniger in Bezug auf physiognomische Präferenzen.

Die idealisierten Schönheiten sind elegante und begehrenswerte Frauen, die auftreten als Kurtisanen (dazu gehören Prostituierte verschiedenen Ranges), als vornehmlich in Musik, Tanz und Konversation gut ausgebildete Geishas (wörtlich «Kunstpersonen»), als Angestellte in Teehäusern, Verkäuferinnen oder auch als ganz gewöhnliche Bürgersfrauen. Wären da nicht unmissverständliche Anspielungen mittels Attributen, Requisiten oder klärenden Aufschriften, man könnte die Frauen weder bezüglich ihrer gesellschaftlichen Stellung noch ihrer physiognomischen Eigenart unterscheiden. So kann es durchaus vorkommen, dass trotz verschiedener Physiognomie anhand von Aufschriften ein und dieselbe Schönheit identifiziert werden kann oder ein identisches Gesichtsmodell für unterschiedliche Personen verwendet wird, indem lediglich die Aufschrift und die Requisiten vertauscht werden. Man sucht also in diesen Darstellungen vergeblich nach individuellen Zügen realer Frauen.

Dennoch ist es gerade die modellhafte Typisierung der Gesichter, die zum genauen Betrachten anregt. Mit geübtem Auge ist es sehr wohl möglich, anhand der Gesichter die Handschrift der einzelnen Künstler zu erkennen. Und man staunt, wie wenig Abweichung in Gesichtsumriss, den Proportionen zwischen Augenbrauen, Augen, Mund und Nase oder in dem Schwung und der Ausformung der Details es bedarf, um ein unschuldiges Jungmädchengesicht einem Harunobu oder eine reife Schönheit einem Utamaro zuzuschreiben. Der Schönheitswettbewerb wird demzufolge mehr zwischen den Künstlern und den von ihnen geschaffenen, ziemlich einheitlichen Modellen ausgetragen als zwischen den dargestellten Schönheiten selbst. Was die Frauendarstellungen unterscheidet, ist in erster Linie die künstlerische Eigenart des jeweiligen Entwerfers oder aber die Entwicklung des Genres selbst, insbesondere was Zeitstil und Druckverfahren betrifft.

Nur sehr wenige Holzschnittkünstler interessierten sich für stärker ausgeprägte Individualgesichter. Das Individuelle zeigt sich aber auch dann primär in Bezug auf psychologisch festlegbare Charaktere. In diesem Zusammenhang muss die aussergewöhnliche Fähigkeit von Kitagawa Utamaro herausgestrichen werden, der es verstand, seinen Frauengesichtern mit minimalen Mitteln unterschiedliche Emotionen einzuschreiben. Darin sind seine Frauengesichter den japanischen *No*-Masken verwandt, denn auch dort sind die verschiedenen Frauentypen nur durch Nuancen voneinander unterscheidbar, und Gefühle sind an eine überindividuelle, allgemeingültige Form gebunden.

Die starke Stilisierung und Typisierung ihrer Gesichter hebt die Frauen in eine Art Traumwelt. Ihre Schönheit hat beinahe etwas Unheimliches. Japan besitzt eine weit zurückreichende Tradition von Geschichten, in denen sich schöne Frauen als Geister und Dämonen entpuppen.[4] Noch in der jüngeren Vergangenheit lässt der Nobelpreisträger Yasunari Kawabata

ranks of prostitutes); as geishas especially well educated in music, dance, and conversation (literally "art people"); as employees at tea houses; as salesgirls, and also as entirely common middle-class housewives. Were it not for the unmistakable allusions by means of attributes, props, and explanatory inscriptions, one would not be able to differentiate the women with regard to their social position or distinct facial features. It is thus entirely likely that despite different countenances, on the basis of the inscriptions, one and the same beautiful woman can be identified; or that an identical face model can be used to represent different persons by merely changing the inscriptions and props. One thus seeks in vain for individual traits of real women in these depictions.

However, it is precisely the model-like typecasting of the faces that incites precise viewing. With a well-trained eye, it is entirely possible to recognize the signature of the different artists based on the faces. It is amazing how little deviation is required in the outlines of the faces, the proportions between the eyebrows, eyes, mouth, and nose; or in the buoyancy and shaping of the details, to attribute an innocent young girl's face to Harunobu or a mature beauty to Utamaro. The beauty contest is hence one among the artists and the rather uniform models they have created rather than the represented beauties themselves. What distinguishes the depictions of the women is mainly the particular designer's artistic uniqueness, and also the development of the genre as such, especially with regard to period style and printing methods.

Only a very few woodblock artists were interested in more strongly pronounced individualized faces. In such cases, however, the individual nature showed itself mainly with reference to psychologically definable characters. In this context, it is necessary to emphasize the exceptional skill of Kitagawa Utamaro, who was able to inscribe his women's faces using minimal means. His women's faces are herewith related to Japanese *No* masks as there, too, the various women's types can be differentiated only through nuances, and feelings are bound to a supra-individual, generally valid form.

The heavy stylization and typifying of their faces elevates the women to a type of dream world. Their beauty has something almost uncanny about it. Japan has a long-standing tradition of stories in which beautiful women turn out to be ghosts or demons.[4] Even in the recent past, Nobel prize winner Yasunari Kawabata (1899–1972), in his love story *Beauty and Mourning,* had Mr. Oki say to his beautiful but slightly crazy lover, "A young girl who thinks like that is haunted by the ghosts of the past. Maybe that's why your neck is so slender and wraithlike. Beautiful slender of course."[5]

The connection between beauty and demonic possession might provide at least part of the answer to the question of why no real beauties with strong, individually embossed traits were depicted. Flawless beauty is not of this world, yet should it nonetheless surface, there is reason to fear it or offer unbridled devotion. It is no

(1899–1972) in seinem Liebesroman *Schönheit und Trauer* Herrn Oki zu seiner wunderschönen, aber leicht irrsinnigen Geliebten sagen: «Ein junges Mädchen, das so denkt, ist von den Geistern der Vergangenheit besessen. Vielleicht ist deshalb dein Hals so wunderbar schlank, so geisterhaft schön [...]»[5]

Der Zusammenhang zwischen Schönheit und Dämonenhaftigkeit beantwortet vielleicht ansatzweise die Frage, weshalb keine realen Schönheiten mit stärker individuell geprägten Zügen dargestellt wurden. Makellose Schönheit ist nicht von dieser Welt, und bricht sie dennoch hervor, besteht Grund zum Fürchten oder zu hemmungsloser Hingabe. Nicht von ungefähr gibt der weibliche Nacken, der in Japan als weitaus erotischster Körperteil der Frau angesehen wird, immer wieder zu ambivalenten Äusserungen Anlass. Bezeichnenderweise ist derselbe als geisterhaft erlebte Jungmädchennacken in Kawabatas Geschichte an anderer Stelle einer Tötungsfantasie ausgesetzt. Der traditionelle japanische Kimono als nur scheinbar züchtige Verhüllung des weiblichen Körpers ist im Prinzip ein aufwendig inszenierter Rahmen für den bezaubernden Nacken schöner Frauen, auf den sich animalischer Trieb und ängstliche Bewunderung richten.

Das Thema «Bilder schöner Frauen» mit japanischen Holzdrucken aus dem Honolulu Museum of Art wurde vor einigen Jahren bereits für eine von Kobayashi Tadashi für Japan konzipierte Ausstellung gewählt.[6] Die Zürcher Ausstellung beschränkt sich aber nicht wie jene auf Drucke aus der ursprünglich von James A. Michener zusammengetragenen Sammlung. Das wichtigste Auswahlkriterium war die Qualität und Einzigartigkeit jedes einzelnen Blattes. Dementsprechend liegt der Schwerpunkt auch bei den Stardesignern des goldenen Zeitalters des Holzdrucks im 18. und 19. Jahrhundert: Harunobu, Kiyonaga, Utamaro und Kunisada. Diese Künstler hatten bestimmte Vorlieben für Themen und Kompositionen, in denen schöne Frauen die Hauptrolle spielen. So setzte Harunobu seine zarten Mädchenfiguren etwa gerne in einen poetischen Kontext, während Utamaro sich als Meister des sogenannten «Grosskopfbildes», *ôkubi-e,* hervortat.

Aus der vergleichsweise bescheidenen Holzdrucksammlung des Museums Rietberg stellen wir in der Ausstellung nur wenige Werke an die Seite der Leihgaben aus Hawaii. Darunter soll aber unser bedeutendstes Werk von Kitagawa Utamaro, *Szenen aus den «Erzählungen von Ise»,* auf keinen Fall fehlen (FIG. 2, S. 10). In Japan selbst ist kein Exemplar dieses Triptychons erhalten. Die einzige bekannte und vollständig mit allen drei Blättern erhaltene Version befindet sich im Besitz des Musée Guimet in Paris.

mere coincidence that women's necks, which in Japan are considered a woman's far most erotic body part, are constant cause for ambivalent utterances. Characteristically, in another passage of Kawabata's story, the same young girl's neck that is experienced as ghostly, is subjected to murder fantasies. The traditional Japanese kimono, an only seemingly modest covering of the female body, is basically an elaborately staged framework for the enchanting necks of beautiful women toward which animalistic drives and timid admiration are directed.

The "images of beautiful women" theme in Japanese woodblock prints from the Honolulu Museum of Art was already selected several years ago for an exhibition planned by Kobayashi Tadashi for Japan.[6] However, the Zurich exhibition is not limited to prints from the James A. Michener collection, as that one was. The most important selection criterion was the quality and uniqueness of each individual sheet. Accordingly, emphasis is on star designers from the golden age of woodblock printing in the eighteenth and nineteenth centuries: Harunobu, Kiyonaga, Utamaro, and Kunisada. These artists had certain preferences in terms of themes and composition in which beautiful women played the main role. For example, Harunobu liked to place his delicate girls' figures in a poetic context, whereas Utamaro emerged as master of the so-called "large-head picture" or bust portrait.

In the exhibition, we have put only a few works from the relatively modest woodblock print collection of the Museum Rietberg alongside the loans from Hawaii. Among them, however, is our most significant work by Kitagawa Utamaro, *Scene from "Tales of Ise"* (FIG. 2, P. 10). In Japan, no copy of this triptych has been preserved. The only known version complete with all three sheets is owned by the Musée Guimet in Paris.

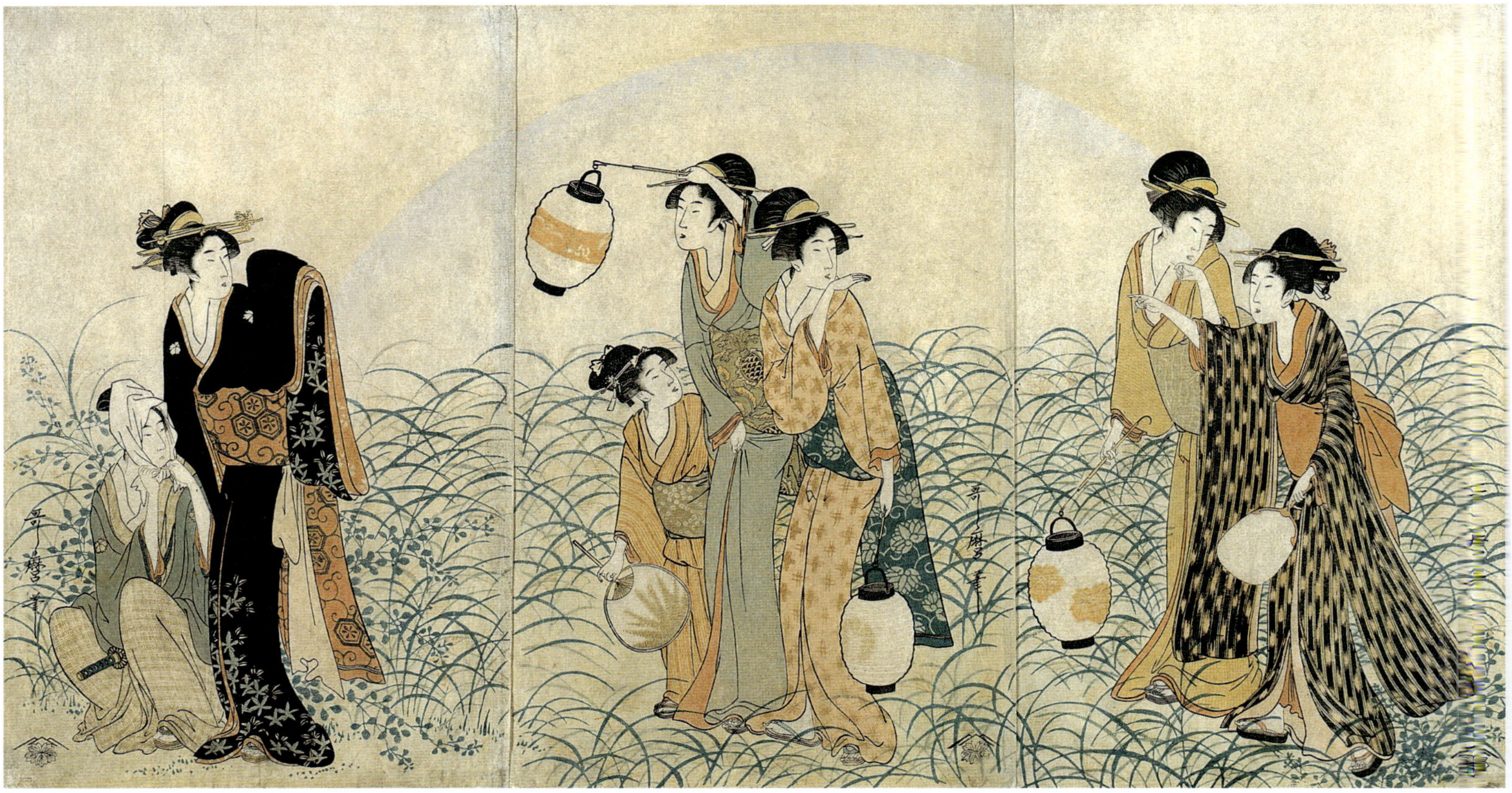

FIG. 2

1 Michener 1959, S. 142.
2 Meech und Oliver 2008. Dieser Katalog thematisiert u. a. das Verhältnis zwischen Malerei, illustrierten Büchern und Holzdruck und untersucht, welche Holzschnittkünstler sich in welcher Weise in verschiedenen Gattungen ausdrückten. Ebenso werden das Verhältnis und die Einflussmöglichkeiten zwischen Designern und Verlegern zur Sprache gebracht oder die Bedeutung der Käufer. Dies sind wertvolle Untersuchungen zu weiterreichenden Aspekten der Holzschnittkunst. Sie ändern aber nichts daran, dass der Holzdruck primär dazu da war, eine in ästhetischer Hinsicht ideale Welt zu beschreiben.
3 Ebd., S. 169.
4 Lewinsky-Sträuli 1989.
5 Kawabata 1990, S. 142.
6 Kobayashi und Link 1994.

1 Michener 1959, p. 142.
2 Meech and Oliver 2008. This catalogue treats, among other things the relationship among painting, illustrated books, and woodblock prints, and examines how woodblock artists expressed themselves in different ways in various genres. Also discussed is the relationship between editors and designers, and the possibilities for influencing one another, and the significance of the buyer. These are valuable investigations on wide-ranging aspects of woodblock art. But they do not change the fact that the woodblock was primarily there to describe a world that was, in an aesthetic perspective, an ideal one.
3 Ibid., p. 169.
4 Lewinsky-Sträuli 1989.
5 Kawabata 1975, p. 157.
6 Kobayashi and Link 1994.

Die Entwicklung von *Bijinga* bis in die Mitte des 19. Jahrhunderts*
The Development of *Bijinga* until the Mid-Nineteenth Century*

ANDREAS MARKS

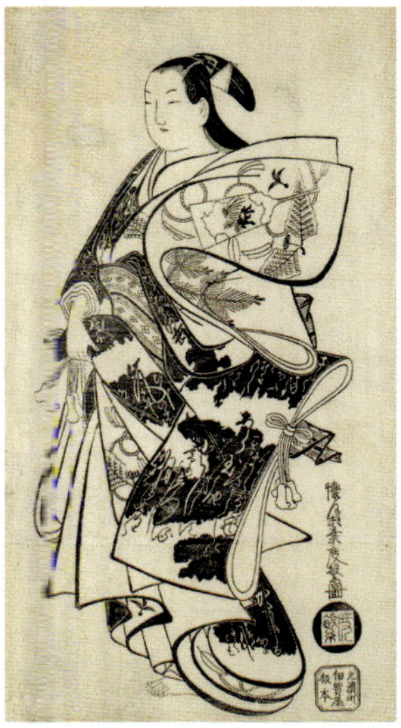

1

Bis in die Mitte des 19. Jahrhunderts führte das Japan der frühen Neuzeit, insbesondere seine Hauptstadt Edo (heute Tokio), eine friedliche Existenz. Von der Aussenwelt grösstenteils abgeschnitten, entfaltete sich ein reges gesellschaftliches, kulturelles und intellektuelles Leben. Während des Tokugawa-Shogunats (1603–1868) florierten die Künste, und neue Kunstformen entwickelten sich zu allseits beliebten Vergnügungen. Zu diesen zählen Holzschnitte, besser bekannt als *ukiyo-e* (wörtlich: «Bilder der fliessenden Welt»), die meist *kabuki*-Darsteller, schöne Frauen oder Krieger zeigen. Von Künstlern gestaltet und von Verlegern herausgegeben, richteten sich *ukiyo-e* vor allem an die Edokko (Bewohner Edos), aber auch an Besucher aus der Ferne.

Holzschnitte wurden vom Verleger direkt an die Allgemeinheit verkauft. Die Verleger übernahmen die Herstellung der Drucke, die sie mit einem Drucker, einem Zuschneider von Holzblöcken und einem Künstler abstimmten; Letzterer wurde mit der Gestaltung des Motivs beauftragt. Die Drucke waren erschwinglich und sollten unmittelbar erfreuen. Als Papierarbeiten waren sie vergänglich und daher nicht für langfristige Zwecke vorgesehen. Einige Formate wie *hashira-e* («Pfostenbilder») waren ausdrücklich zur Ausstattung des Hauses vorgesehen. Ihre Käufer waren daher nicht unbedingt Sammler, die ihre Schätze der Nachwelt vermachen wollten. Die meisten Käufer erfreuten sich nur vorübergehend an einem Holzschnitt und ersetzten ihn dann durch ein anderes ansprechendes Motiv, wobei sie jeden Monat unter Hunderten neuer Bilder wählen konnten.

Holzschnitte waren keine Luxusgüter, sondern preisgünstige Objekte, die hohe Umsätze erzielen sollten. In einer meiner jüngsten Publikationen habe ich die Beziehungen zwischen Druckherstellung und Verkauf anhand der wenigen in zeitgenössischen Quellen verfügbaren Zahlen untersucht.[1] Damit sich die Investitionen für den Verleger amortisierten und ein Druck profitabel war, musste er etwa 600 Exemplare verkaufen. Im Unterschied zu früheren und späteren Quellen beziffert ein Edikt aus dem Jahr 1842 den Preis für einen Einzeldruck auf nur 16 *mon,* was dem damaligen Preis einer Schüssel Buchweizennudeln entsprach. Ende der 1830er-Jahre hatten sich die Preise zwischen 32 und 48 *mon* bewegt. In späteren Quellen ist von preislichen Abweichungen die Rede, die Einnahmen und Ausgaben genauer widerspiegeln; der Preis hing demnach vom Motiv und insbesondere der Qualität des Drucks ab.

Until the mid-nineteenth century, early modern Japan and particularly its capital Edo (today Tokyo) was peaceful and largely separated from the outside world while enjoying a vivid social, cultural, and intellectual life. During the reign of the Tokugawa shogunate (1603–1868) the arts flourished with new forms developing into vastly popular enjoyments. Among these are woodblock prints, better known as *ukiyo-e* (lit. “pictures of the floating world”), which depict mostly kabuki actors, beauties, or warriors. *Ukiyo-e* were designed by artists and issued by publishers predominantly for Edoites (residents of Edo) but also for visitors from afar.

Prints were sold directly from the publisher to the public. Publishers were responsible for the production of prints, which was coordinated with a printer, a woodblock cutter, and an artist who was commissioned to create a design. Prints were affordable and intended to be immediately enjoyed. As works on paper, they were perishable and therefore were not created for the long term. Some formats, like *hashira-e* (“pillar prints”), were specifically designed as decorations for a house. Consumers were therefore not necessarily collectors who put their treasures away for posterity. The majority enjoyed a print for a limited time before replacing it with the next appealing design, which they could choose from hundreds of new images every month.

Prints were not luxury goods but were affordably priced in order to reach a high sales volume. In a recent study I have detailed the economics of print production and sales based on the few figures we find in contemporary sources.[1] For a publisher to recoup his investment and make a profit, around 600 copies had to be sold. Compared to earlier and later sources, an edict from 1842 set the price for a single-sheet print to a rather low 16 *mon,* which was the same price as a bowl of buckwheat noodles at that time. In the late 1830s, prices fluctuated between 32 and 48 *mon.* Later sources describe price variations that reflect revenue and expense more accurately and depend on motif but especially on the quality of the print. Therefore, in 1852, an actor bust print by the most popular artists would range from 66 *mon* for a standard quality to 133 *mon* for a luxury edition.

Consumed by a highly demanding urban society, these prints developed over time from rather primitive, monochromatic images to multi-colored depictions that were produced with sophisticated printing techniques.

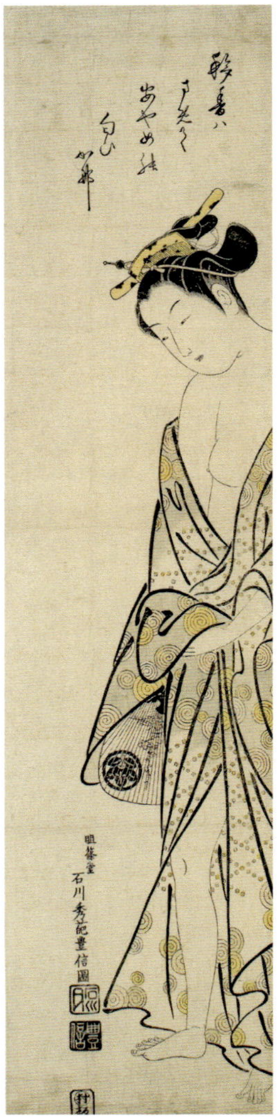

3

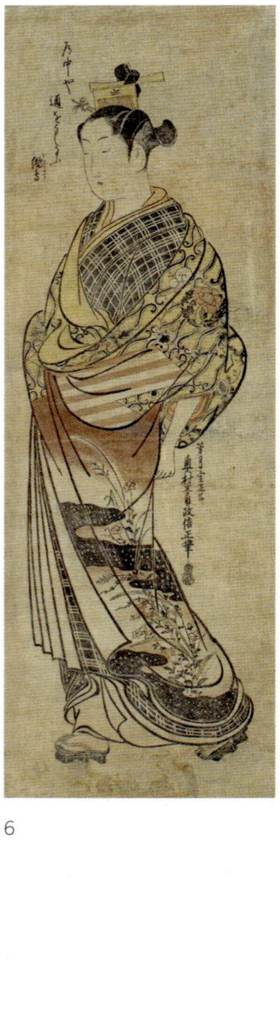

6

1852 schwankte der Preis für den Druck eines Schauspieler-Halbfigurenbildes der beliebtesten Künstler zwischen 66 *mon* für eine Standardausgabe und 133 *mon* für eine Luxusausgabe.

Goutiert von einer höchst anspruchsvollen urbanen Klientel, entwickelten sich diese Drucke mit der Zeit von eher primitiven, monochromen Bildern hin zu mehrfarbigen Darstellungen, die mithilfe anspruchsvoller Drucktechniken hergestellt wurden. Die vielen Tausende dieser erschwinglichen, massenproduzierten Kunstwerke, die die unterschiedlichsten Geschmäcker zufriedenstellten, spiegeln so die Trends und Gepflogenheiten ihrer Zeit wider. Eins der Hauptgenres ist *bijinga,* ein Begriff für sinnliche, aber nicht explizit sexuelle Bilder von männlichen und weiblichen Schönheiten, in denen Figuren idealisiert dargestellt wurden ohne jegliche Absicht, die Realität darzustellen.

Einblatt-Holzschnitte schöner Frauen wurden ab dem frühen 18. Jahrhundert hergestellt, gestaltet von Künstlern der Kaigetsudô-Schule wie Dohan (tätig ca. in den 1710er- bis 1730er-Jahren) (KAT. 1). *Bijinga* traten im Vergleich zu Schauspielerdrucken eher selten auf, bis die Drucke von Suzuki Harunobu (1725?–1770) in den 1760er-Jahren ein neues Niveau technischer Reife erreichten und das Interesse an *bijinga* sprunghaft anstieg. Im Laufe der Jahrzehnte reagierten Künstler auf die sich rasch wandelnden Käuferinteressen, hielten jedoch an dem Gebrauch unpersönlicher Stereotype als Stilmerkmal fest. Als Reaktion auf die Käufernachfrage wurden Kleidungsstücke, Ornamentik und Ausstattung aufwendiger, die Farben kräftiger. *Bijinga* wurden bis in die erste Hälfte des 20. Jahrhunderts hergestellt. Sie spiegeln dann auch den Einfluss westlicher Malerei, insbesondere den des bildhaften Realismus, wider.

Bijinga sollten dem femininen Ideal Ausdruck verleihen und Aspekte von Schönheit, Raffinesse, Gewandtheit und Romantik einfangen. Mit der Zeit reichte es nicht mehr aus, dass ein Druck einfach nur ästhetisch ansprechend war; die Figuren mussten mit Humor, Geist und Fantasie dargestellt sein. Schöne Frauen waren in allen erdenklichen Situationen, typischen und untypischen, zu sehen, so etwa bei der Hausarbeit, bei der Herstellung von Seide oder Drucken, bei einer Samurai-Prozession, als Krieger oder im Kontext von Literatur.

Gegenstand von *bijinga* waren vornehmlich die Schönheiten, die man im Idealfall in den Vergnügungsvierteln *(yûkaku)* der grossen Städte antraf, allen voran in Yoshiwara in Edo, dem grössten Vergnügungsviertel des Landes. Das auf einem Schilfmoor angelegte Vergnügungsviertel wurde 1618 eröffnet und 1657 in der Nähe des berühmten Asakusa-Tempels neu errichtet, nachdem es einem verheerenden Brand zum Opfer gefallen war. Nur in den Vergnügungsvierteln war Prostitution legal, entsprechend bewacht waren die Zonen, die es auch in anderen Städten gab: Shinmachi in Osaka, Shimabara in Kyoto, Miyosaki in Yokohama, Maruyama in Nagasaki.

Die «Unterhaltungsdamen» *(yûjo)*, die in den Bordellen oder «grünen Häusern» *(seirô)* dieser Viertel

Satisfying a range of particular tastes, the many thousands of these affordable, mass-produced artworks mirror the trends and customs of their time. One of the main genres is *bijinga,* a term encompassing alluring but not explicitly sexual images of beauties, both male and female, that were captured in an idealized fashion with no intention to reflect reality.

Single-sheet woodblock prints of beauties began to be produced in the early eighteenth century, designed by artists of the Kaigetsudô School such as Dohan (act. ca. 1710s–1730s) (CAT. 1). *Bijinga* remain scarce relative to actor prints until the 1760s when the prints of Suzuki Harunobu (1725?–1770) achieved a new level of technical sophistication and the interest in *bijinga* skyrocketed. Decade after decade, new artists responded to consumers' rapidly changing interests, but persisted with the use of impersonal stereotypes as representations of their style. Reflecting the market's demands, garments, ornaments, and accoutrements became more elaborate and colors became bolder. *Bijinga* continued to be produced into the first half of the twentieth century, showing the influences of Western painting, particularly pictorial realism.

Bijinga are meant to convey the feminine ideal, capturing aspects of beauty, refinement, accomplishments, and romance. Over time, it became insufficient for a print to simply be aesthetically pleasing; the figures had to be represented with humor, wit, and imagination. Beauties were presented in all kinds of situations, likely and unlikely, such as while doing housework, manufacturing silk, producing prints, performing a samurai procession, as warriors, or within the context of literature.

The subject of *bijinga* was predominantly the beauties that could ideally be found in the pleasure districts *(yûkaku)* of all the major cities, and foremost the largest in the nation, Edo's Yoshiwara. Opened in 1618 at a rush-moor site, it was rebuilt in 1657 in the vicinity of the famous Asakusa Temple after a devastating fire had caused its destruction. Only in the pleasure districts was prostitution legal and other cities had such guarded areas as well: Shinmachi in Osaka, Shimabara in Kyoto, Miyosaki in Yokohama, Maruyama in Nagasaki.

The "entertainment women" *(yûjo)* working in the brothels or "green houses" *(seirô)* of these districts were mostly sold there at a young age by poor families into the lower ranks of the brothel hierarchy, at the top of which were *oiran,* a generic term for all grades of high-ranking, fashionable, and expensive courtesans since the mid-eighteenth century. Regulations during the Edo period allowed prostitution at age seventeen but records exist of prostitutes as young as thirteen.[2]

Oiran can be easily distinguished in the prints through their dress and hair. They are typically shown wearing voluminous garments and their sash *(obi)* tied to the front rather than at the back. Their intricately styled hair was adorned with decorative accoutrements like hairpins. A striking appearance was essential to their trade.

Elaborate garments can already be seen in the earliest beauty prints like those of Kaigetsudô Dohan

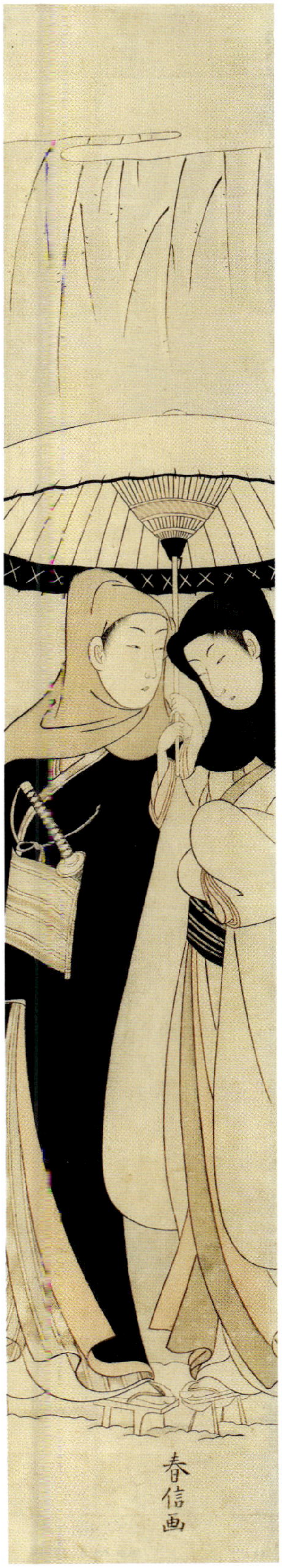

25

arbeiteten, stammten zumeist aus ärmlichen Verhältnissen und wurden von ihren Familien in jungen Jahren an ein Bordell verkauft, wo sie den niedrigsten Rang in der Hierarchie einnahmen. An der Spitze standen *oiran,* seit der Mitte des 18. Jahrhunderts ein Oberbegriff für hochrangige, modische und teure Kurtisanen. Prostitution war in der Edo-Zeit erst ab dem Alter von 17 Jahren erlaubt – Quellen belegen jedoch, dass manche Prostituierte gerade einmal 13 Jahre alt waren.[2]

Oiran sind auf Holzschnitten leicht durch ihre Gewänder und ihre Frisuren zu erkennen. Sie tragen in der Regel voluminöse Kleider, ihre Bauchschärpe *(obi)* ist vorne statt hinten gebunden. Das kunstvoll frisierte Haar wurde mit dekorativen Accessoires wie Haarnadeln geschmückt. Eine markante Erscheinung war in ihrem Gewerbe unerlässlich.

Kunstvolle Gewänder sind bereits auf den frühesten «Bildern schöner Frauen» zu sehen. Auf einem Druck von Kaigetsudô Dohan aus der Zeit um 1714, der im grossen *ôôban*-Format (KAT. 1) erschien, hebt eine stehende Kurtisane den vorderen Teil ihrer prunkvollen Gewänder zum Gehen. Ein «Pfostenbild» *(hashira-e)* einer spazierenden Kurtisane von Okumura Masanobu (1686–1764) aus der zweiten Hälfte der 1740er-Jahre zeigt eine ähnliche, jedoch etwas laszivere Pose mit entblösstem Arm (KAT. 6). Die Aufschrift verweist auf die Kurtisanen, die durch die Strassen von Yoshiwara stolzierten und die Männer mit ihrer Eleganz betörten:

Sieht man die Kurtisane beim Defilee,
verliert man die Kraft zu widerstehen
– wie ein Kuckuck,
der mitten im Flug abstürzt.[3]

Normalerweise gehen *bijinga* nicht über sexuelle Anspielungen hinaus. Sie unterscheiden sich damit von *warai-e* («Bilder zum Lachen»), besser bekannt als *shunga* («Frühlingsbilder») – erotische Bilder, die explizit sexuelle Handlungen darstellen. In *bijinga* sollen ein tiefer Ausschnitt, vielleicht sogar eine entblösste Schulter, eine vorne freizügig geöffnete Robe, nackte Füsse und Knöchel die Sinnlichkeit einer Schönheit zur Geltung bringen, ohne jedoch allzu anzüglich zu sein. In den 1740er- und 1750er-Jahren zeigt Ishikawa Toyonobu (1711–1785) eine Frau, die aus dem Bad kommt, mit einer gewagteren erotischen Note, denn sie entblösst sowohl Bein als auch Brust (KAT. 3).

Mit Suzuki Harunobu (1725?–1770) setzten zu Beginn der zweiten Hälfte des 18. Jahrhunderts nicht nur technische Innovationen im Produktionsprozess ein, die zum Mehrfarbendruck führten, nun machte sich auch eine subtile lyrische Interpretation von Schönheit bemerkbar. Harunobu scheint in seiner Gestaltung von schlanken, kindlich aussehenden Figuren auf chinesische Frauendarstellungen zurückzugreifen. Exemplarisch für seinen Stil ist das Meisterwerk *Liebespaar unter einem*

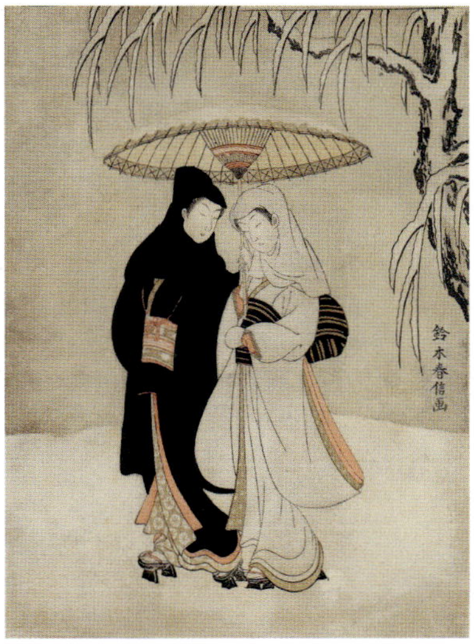

26

(act. ca. 1710s–1730s) from around 1714 of a standing courtesan hitching up the front of her ornate robes to walk, executed in the large *ôôban* format (CAT. 1). A *hashira-e* of a walking courtesan from the second half of the 1740s by Okumura Masanobu (1686–1764) shows a similar but slightly more lascivious pose with exposed arm (CAT. 6). The inscription refers to the spectacle of courtesans parading through the streets of the Yoshiwara, tantalizing the men with their elegance:

Seeing the courtesan on parade
one loses power to resist
—like a cuckoo falling in mid-flight.[3]

As a rule, *bijinga* do not go beyond innuendos, unlike *warai-e* ("laughing pictures"), better known under the term *shunga* ("spring pictures"), erotic images that are sexually explicit in nature. In *bijinga,* an elongated neckline, maybe even a shoulder, the robe opened suggestively at the front, bare feet and ankles, are all meant to enhance a beauty's sensuality without being too permissive. In the 1740s/50s, Ishikawa Toyonobu (1711–1785) designed a woman emerging from the bath with a bolder erotic touch, showing leg and exposing a breast (CAT. 3).

With Suzuki Harunobu (1725?–1770) in the beginning of the second half of the eighteenth century came not only technical innovations in the production process of prints leading to multi-color printing, but also a subtle, lyrical approach to beauty. Harunobu seems to be drawing from Chinese representations of women by creating slender, child-like statures. Exemplary for this style is his masterpiece *Lovers Sharing an Umbrella* (CAT. 26) from ca. 1766/1767. A man in a black robe and a woman in a white robe walk slowly through the snow, together holding an umbrella. This work seems to have been popular at the time of its publication as its motif was revisited by Harunobu in a "pillar print" *(hashira-e)* from the late 1760s in which the couple snuggle together

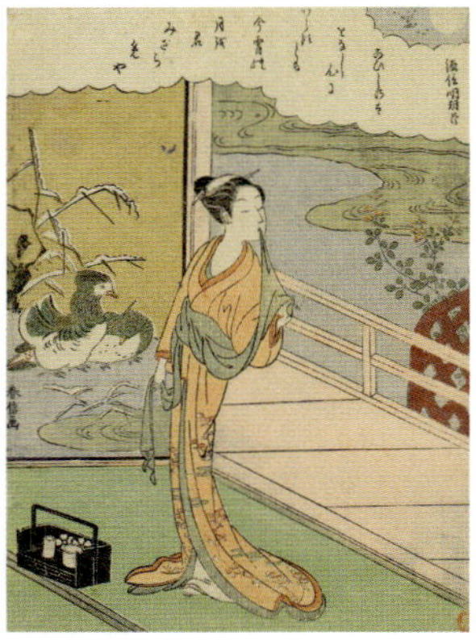

18

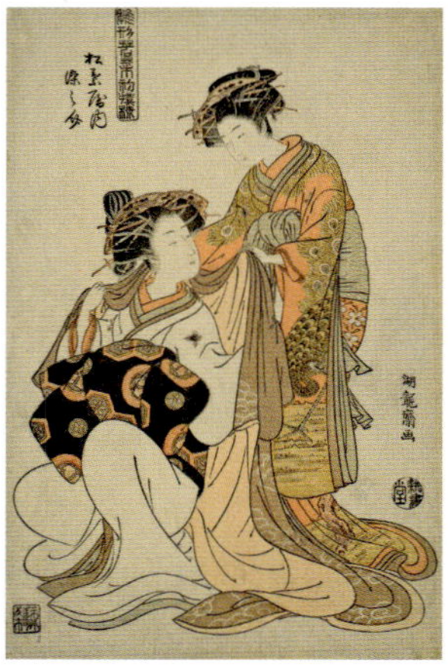

32

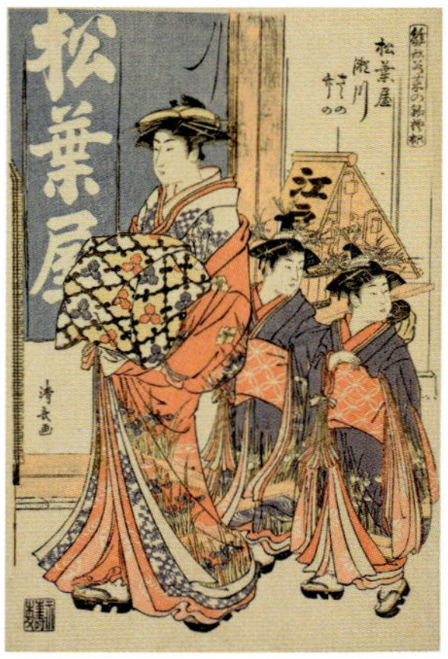

48

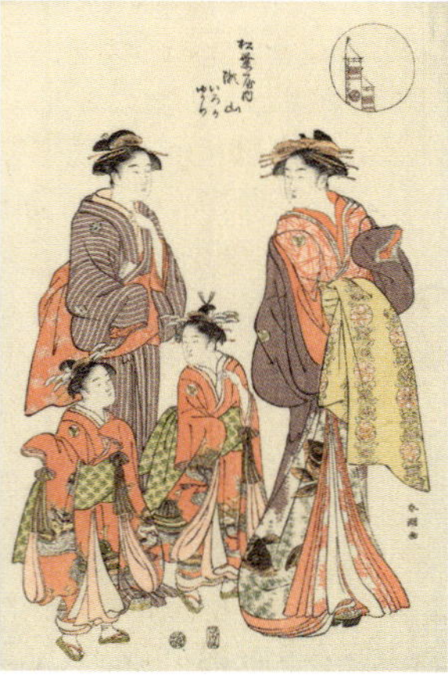

49

Schirm (KAT. 26) von ca. 1766/1767. Ein Mann in schwarzem Gewand und eine Frau in weisser Robe wandeln gemeinsam einen Schirm haltend langsam durch den Schnee. Das Werk muss bei Erscheinen überaus beliebt gewesen sein, denn Harunobu nahm das Motiv in einem «Pfostenbild» *(hashira-e)* aus den späten 1760er-Jahren wieder auf. In der späteren Version schmiegt sich das Paar nur noch enger aneinander (KAT. 25). *Hashira-e* waren im 18. Jahrhundert beliebt, fielen im 19. Jahrhundert jedoch anscheinend einem veränderten Publikumsgeschmack zum Opfer und verschwanden praktisch von der Bildfläche.

Viele von Harunobus Motiven wurden im damals vorherrschenden mittelgrossen *chûban*-Format ausgeführt und mithilfe von kulturellen Ereignissen, jahreszeitlichen Nuancen oder literarischen Anspielungen in Fortsetzungen veröffentlicht. Die jungen Frauen sind nun in Szenen eingebunden und in der Natur oder in faszinierenden Interieurs zu sehen, häufig begleitet von einem Gedicht. Auf einem Bild aus einer titellosen Serie über die «Sechsunddreissig Unsterblichen der Dichtkunst», auf dem der Vers von Minamoto no Saneakira (910–970) zu lesen ist, steht eine junge Frau vor einer bemalten Schiebetür mit Vögeln im Schnee (KAT. 18). Die fragile Schönheit, die sich nach einem Liebsten sehnt und den fernen Herbstmond anblickt, ist das perfekte Sinnbild des Begleitverses:

Was für eine Verschwendung,
dieser Mond und diese Blüten,
in solch einer Nacht;
wenn ich sie nur mit jemandem teilen könnte,
der sie so schätzt wie ich.[4]

Keine der bislang erwähnten *bijinga* nennt den Namen einer Person. Die Frauen bleiben anonym und geben so zu Spekulationen Anlass, ob die Vision des Künstlers auf allgemeinen Beobachtungen beruhte oder ob er eine konkrete Person im Sinn hatte, die ihn inspirierte. Mitte der 1770er-Jahre erscheinen jedoch *bijinga* von Ippitsusai Bunchô (aktiv ca. 1755–1790) und Isoda Koryûsai (1735–1790), die die Namen der porträtierten Kurtisanen aus Yoshiwara nennen – nach dem Tod von Harunobu 1770 hatten sich diese beiden zu den führenden Künstlern von «Bildern schöner Frauen» entwickelt.

Koryûsais frühe Drucke lehnen sich an Harunobus Stil an, und doch zeigt sich in der Serie *Modelle für die Mode: Neue Muster, so frisch wie junge Blätter (Hinagata wakana no hatsu moyô)* eine Neuorientierung hin zu weiblicheren Porträts mit fliessender Kleidung. Die Serie, die im Frühjahr 1776 erstmals erschien, zeigt eine Kurtisane und ihre Begleiterinnen, die in der neuesten Mode gekleidet sind. Derart beliebt war die Serie, dass der Künstler bis 1781 mindestens 140 verschiedene Motive kreierte.[5] Auf einem der ersten ist die Kurtisane Somenosuke aus dem Matsubaya-Freudenviertel zu

even closer (CAT. 25). *Hashira-e* were popular in the eighteenth century but, apparently a casualty of shifting taste, they virtually disappeared in the nineteenth.

Many of Harunobu's designs were executed in the *chûban* (mid-size) format that was predominant at that time and were serialized using cultural events, seasonal nuances or literary allusions. The young women are now integrated in a scene and shown either in a natural setting or within an intriguing interior space, often accompanied by a poem. In a design from an untitled series on the "Thirty-six Immortal Poets" that provides the verse of Minamoto no Saneakira (910–970), a young woman stands in front of a painted sliding door with birds in snow (CAT. 18). The fragile beauty, gazing at the distant autumn moon, longing for her lover, is matched perfectly to the accompanying verse:

What a waste,
this moon and these blossoms,
on such a night;
if only I could share them
with one who appreciates them as I do.[4]

None of the *bijinga* encountered so far in this essay have provided an individual's name and thus the women remain anonymous, leaving room for speculation regarding whether the artist's vision was based on general observations or if he had someone specific in mind that inspired him. In the mid-1770s, *bijinga* by Bunchô (act. ca. 1755–1790) and Isoda Koryûsai (1735–1790) who succeeded Harunobu after his death in 1770 as the foremost designer of beauty prints, carry the names of the Yoshiwara courtesans they depict.

Koryûsai's early prints are in the style of Harunobu, but a change of direction to more womanly portraits with flowing clothes is evident in the series *Models for Fashion: New Designs as Fresh as Young Leaves (Hinagata wakana no hatsu moyô)*, which depicts a courtesan together with her attendant(s) dressed in the latest fashion, issued from spring 1776. The series was so popular that by 1781 he had drawn at least 140 designs for it.[5] One of the designs from the beginning of this series features the courtesan Somenosuke from the Matsubaya brothel who is being helped into the outer garment *(uchikake)* of her five robes (CAT. 32).

The biannual guidebooks on the Yoshiwara, the *Yoshiwara saiken,* record a decline in appearance of elite, forbiddingly expensive courtesans by the mid-eighteenth century, a result of changes made by the brothels to cater for the broadening clientele that frequented the Yoshiwara. The Matsubaya was long counted among the most prestigious brothels and its decline did not begin until the first decade of the nineteenth century.[6] One reason for its long success was the outstanding beauty of the courtesan Segawa, for which the 1754 *Yoshiwara saiken* included her among the «Four Devas» *(shi tennô)*, the best four of

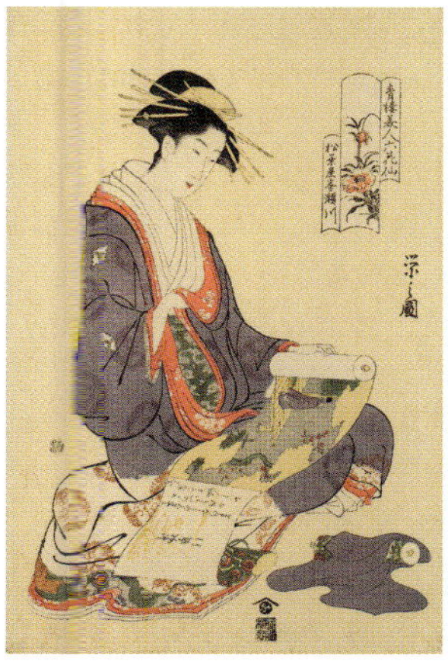

77

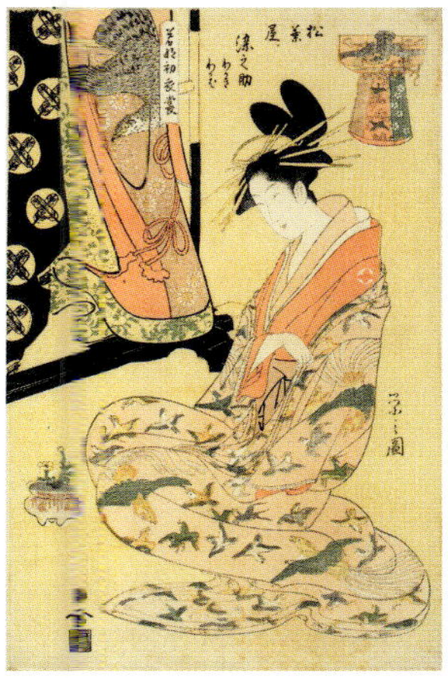

78

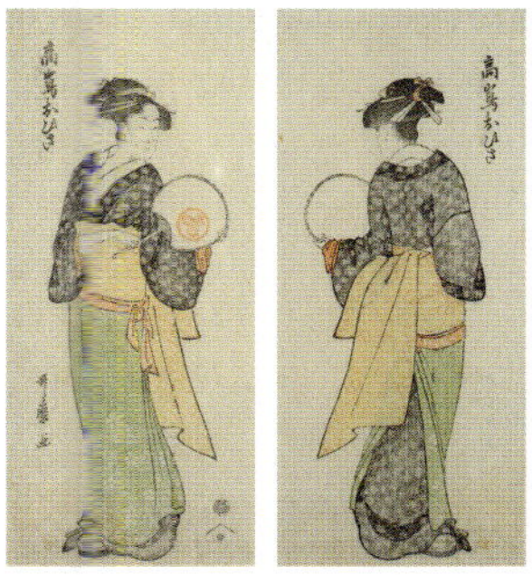

71

sehen, der eine Bedienstete in das Oberkleid *(uchikake)* ihrer fünf Gewänder hilft (KAT. 32).

Die halbjährlich erscheinenden Freudenhausführer durch Yoshiwara, die *Yoshiwara saiken,* verzeichnen Mitte des 18. Jahrhunderts einen Verfall im Erscheinungsbild elitärer, exorbitant teurer Kurtisanen – ein Ergebnis der neuen Regelungen von Bordellen, die eine immer grösser werdende Klientel in Yoshiwara bedienen wollten. Das Matsubaya zählte lange Zeit zu den angesehensten Freudenhäusern, sein Niedergang setzte erst im ersten Jahrzehnt des 19. Jahrhunderts ein.[6] Ein Grund für seinen langjährigen Erfolg war die aussergewöhnliche Schönheit der Kurtisane Segawa, die als eine der vier erfolgreichsten Kurtisanen von Yoshiwara im *Yoshiwara saiken* aus dem Jahr 1754 zu den «Vier Himmelsgöttern» *(shi tennô)* gezählt wurde.[7] Es war ein verbreiteter Brauch, die Namen der ranghöchsten Kurtisanen innerhalb eines Hauses zu vererben, und die neunte und letzte Segawa ist für das Jahr 1803 verzeichnet.[8]

Torii Kiyonaga (1752–1815) war der führende *bijinga*-Künstler der 1780er-Jahre. Die von ihm porträtierten Schönheiten wirken aussergewöhnlich gross, ihre Köpfe machen beinahe ein Neuntel ihrer Gesamtstatur aus.[9] 1782 führte Kiyonaga für kurze Zeit Koryûsais Meisterwerk-Reigen *Modelle für die Mode: Neue Muster, so frisch wie junge Blätter* fort. Auf einem Druck dieser Serie stellt er eine Segawa und ihre zwei Dienstmädchen *(kamuro)* Sasano und Takeno dar (KAT. 48). Angesichts des Erscheinungsdatums darf man vermuten, dass es sich bei dieser Segawa wahrscheinlich um Segawa VI handelt, die im Herbst 1783 aus dem Bordell freigekauft wurde, als ein Kaufmann des Kimonogeschäfts Echigoya dem Bordellbesitzer eine Ablösesumme zahlte.

Künstler porträtierten auch Kurtisanen mittleren Ranges aus Bordellen wie dem Matsubaya. Katsukawa Shunchô (tätig ca. 1781–1801) etwa porträtierte in den späten 1780er-Jahren Seyama mit ihren jungen Begleiterinnen Iroka und Yukari (KAT. 49). In der zweiten Hälfte der 1790er-Jahre stellte Chôbunsai Eishi (1756–1829) Kisegawa (KAT. 77) und Somenosuke (eine andere als die in Verbindung mit KAT. 32 erwähnte) dar (KAT. 78).

Andere auf *bijinga* dargestellte Frauen sind Geishas – Unterhalterinnen, die sowohl innerhalb als auch ausserhalb der Vergnügungsviertel tätig waren und von denen keine sexuellen Dienste erwartet wurden, wie im

the Yoshiwara.[7] It became common practice to pass on the names of top-ranking courtesans within a house and the last, ninth, Segawa is listed in 1803.[8]

Torii Kiyonaga (1752–1815) was the leading designer of *bijinga* in the 1780s. His beauties give the impression of being exceptionally tall and their heads account for almost one-ninth of their total stature.[9] In 1782, for a short time, Kiyonaga continued Koryûsai's masterpiece series *Models for Fashion: New Designs as Fresh as Young Leaves.* In one print from this series he depicts a Segawa and her two child attendants *(kamuro)*, Sasano and Takeno (CAT. 48). Based on the time of publication, this Segawa is probably Segawa VI, who was released from the brothel in autumn of 1783 by a salesclerk from the kimono shop Echigoya who bought out her contract from the brothel owner.

Artists also depicted mid-ranking courtesans from brothels like the Matsubaya. Katsukawa Shunchô (act. ca. 1781–1801), for example, portrayed in the late 1780s Seyama with her child attendants, Iroka and Yukari (CAT. 49). In the second half of the 1790s, Chôbunsai Eishi (1756–1829) depicted Kisegawa (CAT. 77) and a different Somenosuke to that mentioned earlier (CAT. 78).

Other women portrayed in *bijinga* are geisha, entertainers that were active both within and outside the pleasure districts and were not expected to provide sexual services, as is still largely misunderstood in the West. Geisha were hired to dance and/or sing but also to facilitate the flow of conversation by telling jokes and stories. A select number of women working at shops became motifs as well; some were celebrated beauties. The teahouse waitresses Okita of the Naniwaya and Ohisa of the Takashimaya were most famous during the 1790s (CATS. 68, 69, 71), together with Toyohina, a geisha and celebrated singer of Tomimoto music (CAT. 56). The three women were often depicted by Kitagawa Utamaro (1753–1806), who replaced Kiyonaga as the foremost designer of *bijinga* at that time. He is especially praised for his remarkably sensual and graceful bust portraits *(ôkubi-e)* of individual women.

The public fascination with *ukiyo-e* at the end of the eighteenth century created concern within the government, which tried to regulate its production. To safeguard public morality, the representation of current events was forbidden, as was the use of extravagant

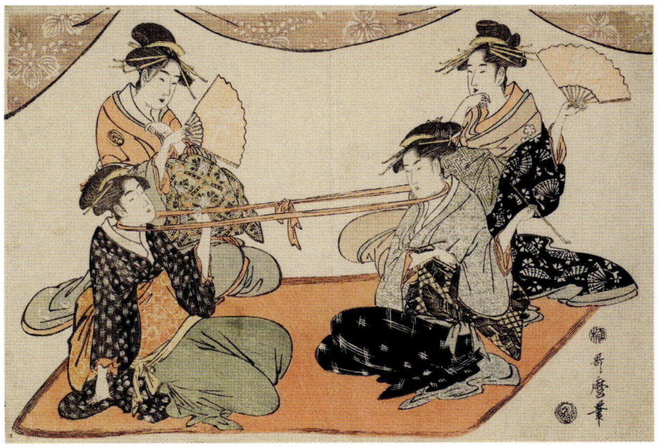

68

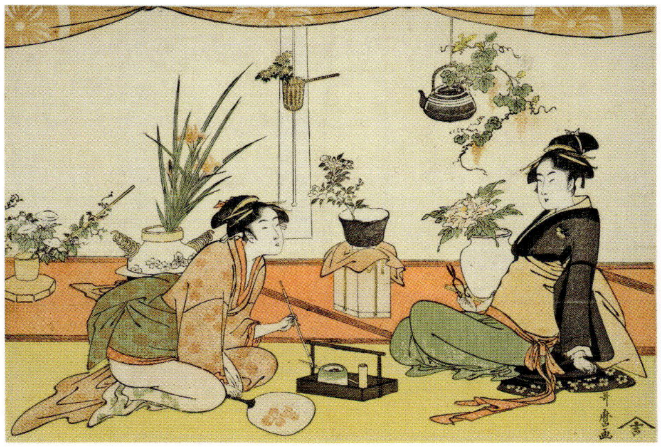

69

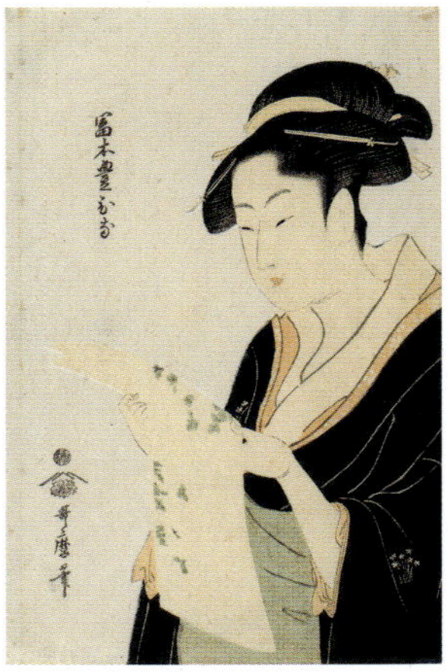

56

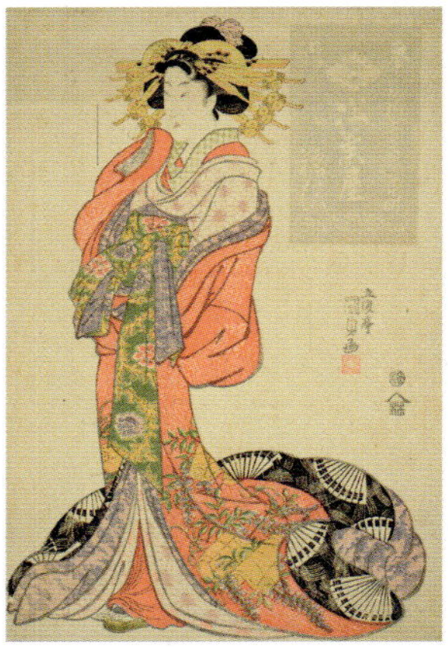

90

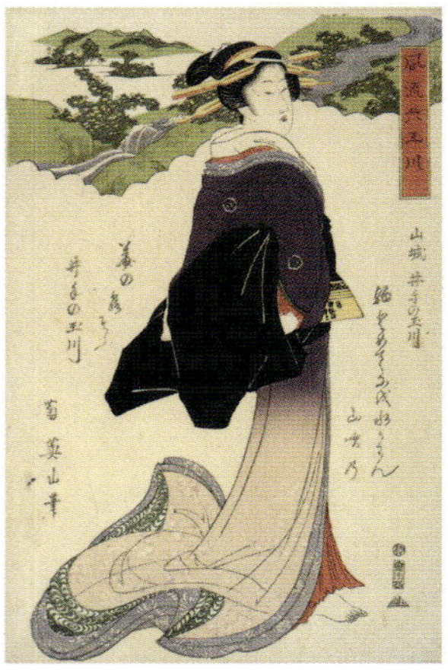

FIG. 3

Westen häufig noch immer fälschlicherweise geglaubt wird. Geishas wurden zum Tanzen und/oder Singen engagiert, aber auch, um Gespräche durch Witze und Geschichten in Gang zu halten. Eine gewisse Anzahl an Frauen, die in Geschäften arbeiteten, war ebenfalls auf *bijinga* zu sehen; manche waren gefeierte Schönheiten. Die Teehaus-Kellnerinnen Okita aus dem Naniwaya und Ohisa aus dem Takashimaya etwa waren in den 1790er-Jahren sehr berühmt (KAT. 68, 69, 71), zusammen mit Toyohina, einer Geisha und umjubelten Tomimoto-Sängerin (KAT. 56). Die drei Frauen wurden oft von Kitagawa Utamaro (1753–1806) porträtiert, der zu jener Zeit Kiyonaga als bekanntesten *bijinga*-Künstler ablöste. Er wird insbesondere für seine aussergewöhnlich sinnlichen und anmutigen Halbfigurenporträts *(ôkubi-e)* einzelner Damen gerühmt.

So gross war die öffentliche Begeisterung für *ukiyo-e,* dass die Regierung sich Ende des 18. Jahrhunderts alarmiert zeigte und die Herstellung zu kontrollieren versuchte. Um die öffentliche Moral zu wahren, wurde die Darstellung aktueller Ereignisse ebenso verboten wie der Gebrauch extravaganter Drucktechniken. Die Beschränkungen zielten insbesondere auf Bücher und Holzschnitte mit Texten, die – so befürchtete man – unorthodoxes Gedankengut förderten.[10] Ab 1791 mussten kommerziell erscheinende Drucke von einem Zensor genehmigt und mit einem runden *kiwame* oder «Zulassungs»-Siegel zertifiziert sein.[11] Einblatt-Holzschnitte wurden nicht so streng kontrolliert wie Bücher, was die Existenz vieler Drucke aus dieser Zeit erklärt, die im Hintergrund mit Glimmer versehen waren.

Die Bemühungen der Regierung, die Produktion zu beschränken, setzten sich 1793 und 1796 fort, als Dekrete die Nennung von Frauennamen mit Ausnahme der von Kurtisanen untersagten. Ein weiteres Edikt aus dem frühen 19. Jahrhundert verbot Porträts von Frauen mit der Begründung, diese seien «zu auffällig» *(medatsu)*.[12] Das Edikt hatte jedoch wenig Wirkung, wie verschiedene Erlasse der folgenden Jahre zeigten, die wiederholt dieselben Restriktionen anmahnten.

Zu Lebzeiten von Utamaro entwickelte sich Eishi zu seinem grössten Mitstreiter. Er war ursprünglich ein Samurai, der dem Shogun Tokugawa Ieharu (1737–1786) diente und von dem er seinen Künstlernamen Eishi erhielt. In den frühen 1780er-Jahren wandte sich Eishi dem Holzschnitt zu. Unter dem anfänglichen Einfluss von Kiyonaga wurde er zum Rivalen von Utamaro und begründete seine eigene Schule, die sich ebenfalls auf idealisierte Porträts schöner Frauen in elegantem und erhabenem Stil spezialisierte.

Künstler der in der zweiten Hälfte des 18. Jahrhunderts gegründeten Utagawa-Schule entwickelten sich zur treibenden Kraft von *bijinga* im 19. Jahrhundert. Die Bilder von Utagawa Toyokuni (1769–1825) haben etwas Feierliches und sind normalerweise keine Einzelporträts, sondern zeigen Landschaftsszenen oder andere Szenerien. Auf einem Triptychon, das Verkäuferinnen und Kundinnen in einem Fächergeschäft zeigt, tauchen

printing features. The restrictions were aimed particularly at books and prints with texts that were considered to promote unorthodox ideas.[10] From 1791 on, commercially published prints required the approval of a censor, certified by a round *kiwame* or "approval" seal.[11] Single-sheet prints were not as closely inspected as books, which explains the existence of many prints with mica applied to the background from this time period.

The government's efforts to restrict production continued with decrees announced in 1793 and again in 1796, when the inscription of names of women other than courtesans was prohibited. Another edict from early 1800 banned portraits of women for being "too conspicuous" *(medatsu)*.[12] That this edict had little effect can be seen in several subsequent edicts containing the same restrictions being issued in the following years.

During the time of Utamaro, Eishi emerged as his biggest contender. Originally a samurai who served the shogun Tokugawa Ieharu (1737–1786), from whom he received his artist name Eishi, he turned to printmaking in the early 1780s. Initially influenced by Kiyonaga, he became a rival to Utamaro and established his own school, also specializing in idealized portraits of beautiful women in an elegant and refined style.

Artists of the Utagawa School, founded in the second half of the eighteenth century, became the driving force of *bijinga* in the nineteenth century. Utagawa Toyokuni's (1769–1825) images have a solemn air and are usually set in landscapes or other settings rather than in the form of individual portraits. A triptych showing beauties working and shopping at a fan shop introduces elements of humor (CAT. 84). The name on the lantern to the left is "Eijudô"; however, this is the shop name of the publisher of this print, which was not really known for producing fan prints. The signboard in the shape of a giant fan overhead reveals the real name of the shop, Mieidô, a famous fan shop in Kyoto.

The foremost artist of *bijinga* in the nineteenth century was Toyokuni's master student, Kunisada (1786–1865). Kunisada continued in his teacher's style and created beauties with an emphasis on elaborate kimono designs and extravagant hairstyles, such as in the series known as *Votive Hand Towels (Hônô tenugui)* from ca. 1816. Each print portrays one courtesan in sumptuous garments; for example, Yosooi from the Matsubaya (CAT. 90). Kunisada's lavish portraits were executed with meticulous attention to detail and produced with state-of-the-art technical refinements like embossing, lacquering, and gradation. His popularity was such that a great many publishers commissioned designs by him; in total he created several hundred designs of beauties.

Kikugawa Eizan (1787–1867), studied under Katsushika Hokusai's (1760–1849) student Totoya Hokkei (1780–1850) among others. Published in the 1810s and 1820s, his images of beauties with slender figures, small eyes, and detached expressions recall those of Utamaro. In the series *Fashionable Views of the Six Tama Rivers (Fûryû mu tamagawa)* from ca. 1812–

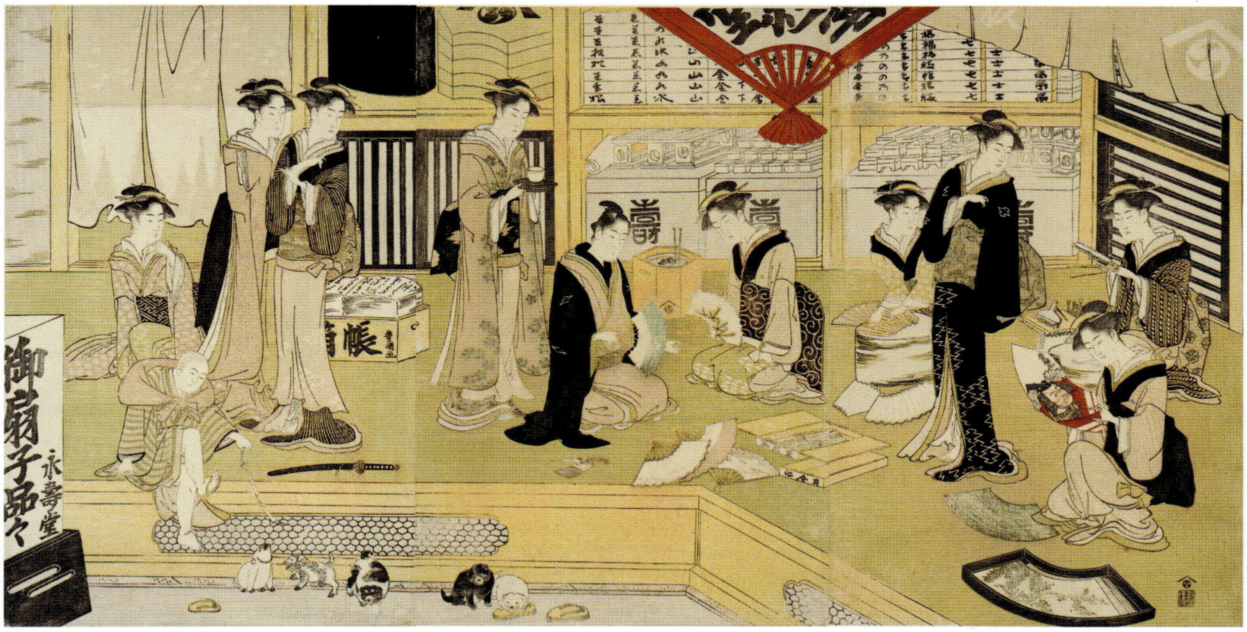

84

erstmals humoristische Elemente auf (KAT. 84). Der Name auf der Laterne links lautet Eijudô – dies ist allerdings der Name des Verlegers dieses Drucks, der für die Produktion von Fächerdrucken nicht unbedingt bekannt war. Das Ladenschild in Form eines riesigen Fächers verrät den wahren Namen des dargestellten Geschäfts: Mieidô, ein berühmter Fächerladen in Kyoto.

Der beliebteste *bijinga*-Künstler im 19. Jahrhundert war Toyokunis Meisterschüler Kunisada (1786–1865). Kunisada setzte den Stil seines Meisters fort und porträtierte Schönheiten, bei denen er den Akzent auf kunstvolle Kimono-Muster und extravagante Frisuren legte, beispielsweise in der Serie, die als *Votivhandtücher (Hônô tenugui)* von ca. 1816 bekannt ist. Jeder Druck zeigt eine andere Kurtisane in kostbaren Gewändern, so etwa Yosooi aus dem Matsubaya (KAT. 90). Kunisadas aufwendig gestaltete Porträts wurden mit grosser Liebe zum Detail und hochmodernen technischen Finessen wie Prägungen, Lackauftrag und Farbabstufungen hergestellt. Der Künstler genoss so grosse Popularität, dass zahlreiche Verleger Motive bei ihm in Auftrag gaben. Insgesamt stammen viele Hundert Darstellungen schöner Frauen von ihm.

Kikugawa Eizan (1787–1867) studierte unter anderem bei Totoya Hokkei (1780–1850), einem Schüler Katsushika Hokusais (1760–1849). Eizans Bilder zeigen Schönheiten von schlanker Gestalt mit kleinen Augen und distanziert wirkendem Gesichtsausdruck. Zwischen 1810 und 1830 veröffentlicht, erinnern sie an die Holzschnitte von Utamaro. In der Serie *Populäre Ansichten der sechs Tama-Flüsse (Fûryû mu tamagawa)* von ca. 1812–1813 verknüpft der Künstler typische Schönheiten mit dem seriellen Kunstgriff des Themas der sechs Tama-Flüsse (FIG. 3).

Eisen (1790–1848) studierte, so vermutet man, unter Eizan und spezialisierte sich ebenfalls auf die Darstellung schöner Frauen, an denen er vor allem von den

1813, he combines generic beauties with the serial device of the Six Jewel Rivers theme (FIG. 3).

Eisen (1790–1848) is believed to have studied under Eizan and also specialized in beauties that he mostly produced between the 1820s and 1840s. Eisen was a prolific writer and illustrator of popular and erotic books. He depicted his beauties in a lively style with a certain erotic realism, rivaling those of his contemporary Kunisada. Representations featuring detailed and sumptuous kimonos seem to be in fashion and great effort went into rendering the robes of Kunisada's and Eisen's beauties. Designers and publishers continually looked for new ways in which to present the beauties (CAT. 93). *Modern Pine Needles (Tôsei matsu no ha)* is a series of three prints, each featuring a beauty against a background of *jôruri* (a type of narrative music) texts of different kinds: *itchûbushi, shinnaibushi,* and *kiyomotobushi.* An inset of an opened folding fan contains the title of the play referred to in the text, here, *Yûkasumi Asamagadake* or *Mt. Asama in Evening Mist* (FIG. 4).

Bijinga and Japanese woodblock prints in general developed alongside technical innovations within their production process from simple, black and white pictures to intricate imagery in full color with various enhanced printing features. As consumer taste changed, new artists and new styles became fashionable, rendering previous ones obsolete. The early prints of artists like Harunobu, Utamaro, or Kiyonaga reflected established aesthetics, but they then soon began to assert slightly different notions of beauty and elegance. Realism was never the prime objective of the artists, their publishers, or the consumers. Beauty was conveyed as much through the woman's body as through the splendid costume in which she was dressed and the context in which she is depicted. Capturing an aesthetic ideal and expressing a more abstract sense of beauty kept this genre popular and alive into modern times.

1820er- bis in die 1840er-Jahre hinein arbeitete. Eisen war ein überaus produktiver Schriftsteller und Illustrator beliebter und erotischer Bücher. Er gestaltete seine Schönheiten in lebendigem Stil mit einem gewissen erotischen Realismus, der dem seines Zeitgenossen Kunisada in nichts nachstand. Darstellungen mit detailreichen und üppigen Kimonos scheinen en vogue zu sein, und auf die Gewänder von Kunisadas und Eisens Schönheiten wurden viel Mühe und Sorgfalt verwandt. Künstler und Verleger suchten beständig nach neuen Formen, die Schönheit von Frauen wiederzugeben (KAT. 93). Die Serie *Moderne Kiefernnadeln (Tôsei matsu no ha)* besteht aus drei Drucken, von denen jedes Bild eine Schönheit vor dem Hintergrund unterschiedlicher *jôruri*-Texte (einer Form von narrativer Musik) zeigt: *itchûbushi, shinnaibushi* und *kiyomotobushi.* Das Innere eines geöffneten Faltfächers nennt den Titel des Stücks, auf das der Text verweist: *Yûkasumi Asamagadake* oder *Der Berg Asama im Abendnebel* (FIG. 4).

Bijinga und japanische Holzschnitte im Allgemeinen entwickelten sich parallel zu technischen Innovationen im Produktionsprozess und wandelten sich von einfachen Schwarz-Weiss-Bildern hin zu einer vollfarbigen komplexen Bildsprache mit unterschiedlichen Spezialeffekten im Druck. Mit sich wandelndem Publikumsgeschmack kamen neue Künstler und Stile in Mode, die ihre Vorgänger ablösten. Die frühen Drucke von Künstlern wie Harunobu, Utamaro oder Kiyonaga spiegelten die etablierte Ästhetik wider, die späteren Werke manifestierten ein etwas anderes Verständnis von Schönheit und Eleganz. Realismus war nie das primäre Ziel von Künstlern, Verlegern oder Käufern. Schönheit vermittelte sich durch den weiblichen Körper, prächtige Gewänder und den Kontext der Darstellung. Eben weil *bijinga* ein ästhetisches Ideal einfingen und ein eher abstraktes Verständnis von Schönheit ausdrückten, blieb das Genre bis in die Moderne hinein beliebt.

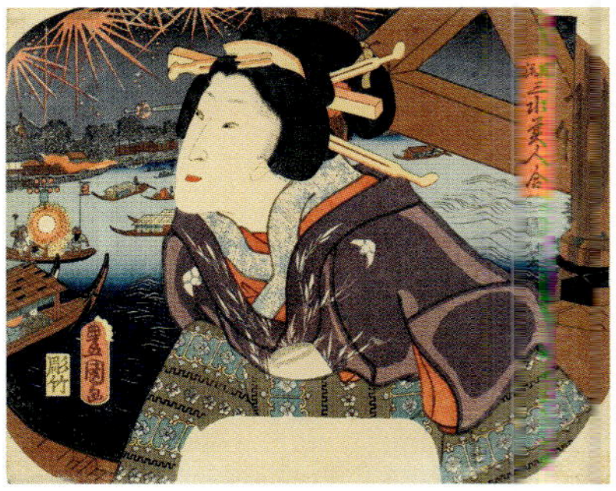

93

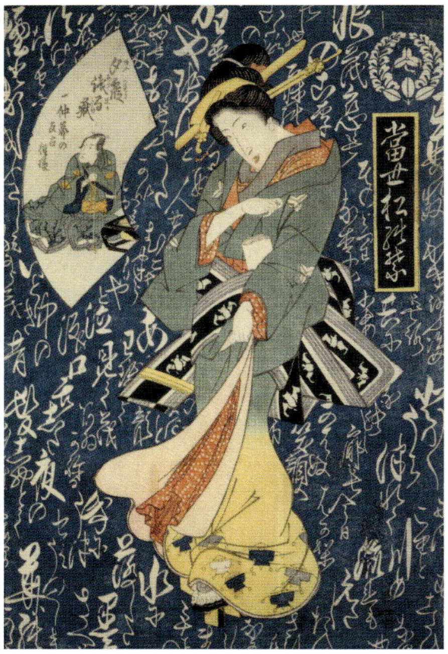

FIG. 4

* Ich danke Rhiannon Paget für ihre ausgezeichneten Kommentare und die redaktionelle Bearbeitung des Manuskripts. Dank ebenfalls an Katharina Epprecht für ihre äusserst wertvollen Anregungen, die ich übernommen habe.

1 Marks 2011, S. 22–26.
2 Seigle 1993, S. 34.
3 Clark 2001, Nr. 74. Übersetzung aus dem Englischen ins Deutsche: Claudia Kotte.
4 Übersetzung aus dem Englischen ins Deutsche: Claudia Kotte.
5 Eine ausführliche Analyse der Serie liefert Hockley 2003.
6 Seigle 1993, S. 207.
7 Ebd., S. 124 und ebd., S. 102–104, wo die Autorin die Geschichte einer treuen Segawa aus dem Jahr 1722 erzählt und dann erklärt, dass es keine Belege für die Richtigkeit der Geschichte gebe; der früheste Nachweis einer Segawa stammt aus dem Jahr 1728.
8 Ebd., S. 207.
9 Leonardo da Vinci (1452–1519) legte in seinem «vitruvianischen Menschen» die Vorgaben für die idealen menschlichen Proportionen fest; demnach sollte der Abstand von unterhalb des Kinns bis zum Scheitel ein Achtel der Gesamtgrösse betragen.
10 Thompson und Harootunian 1991 geben einen Überblick über die Zensurgesetze.
11 Eine Liste aller von 1791 bis 1875 verwendeten Siegel findet sich in Marks 2011, S. 469–493.
12 Clark 1995, S. 44.

* I am indebted to Rhiannon Paget for her excellent comments and for editing the manuscript. I am also grateful to Katharina Epprecht for her very useful suggestions that I have incorporated.

1 Marks 2011, pp. 22–26.
2 Seigle 1993, p. 34.
3 Translation from Clark 2001, no. 74.
4 Translation by John D. Szostak.
5 For an extensive analysis of this series, see Hockley 2003.
6 Seigle 1993, p. 207.
7 Ibid., p. 124. Ibid., pp. 102–104, retells the story of a loyal Segawa in 1722 and then explains that no record exists verifying it but the earliest record of a Segawa dates to 1728.
8 Ibid., p. 207.
9 According to the specifications for Leonardo da Vinci's (1452–1519) "Vitruvian Man," which exemplifies ideal human proportions, the distance from below the chin to the top of the head should be one-eighth of the total height.
10 For an overview of censorship laws, see Thompson and Harootunian 1991.
11 For a list of all seals in use from 1791 until 1875, see Marks 2011, pp. 469–493.
12 Clark 1995, p. 44.

Von idealisierten Visionen zu realistischen Impressionen: *Bijinga* im Wandel
From Idealized Visions to Realistic Impressions: The Changing Nature of *Bijinga*

JOHN D. SZOSTAK

Eines der beständigsten traditionellen Bildgenres in der Geschichte der japanischen Kunst ist *bijinga,* «Bilder schöner Frauen», die reizvolle Frauen aus allen Gesellschaftsschichten darstellen. Besonders prominente *bijinga*-Sujets in der Edo-Zeit (1603–1868) sind Kellnerinnen, Geishas, Prostituierte aus der Unterschicht und Kurtisanen aus der Oberschicht. Sie sind die Damen der «fliessenden Welt», eine euphemistische Bezeichnung für die lizenzierten Vergnügungsviertel Maruyama in Nagasaki, Shinmachi in Osaka, Shimabara in Kyoto und das berühmteste von allen, Yoshiwara in Edo. Doch so beliebt diese Darstellungen von Alltagsszenen aus den Vergnügungsvierteln damals auch waren und so sinnbildhaft sie heute für eine längst vergangene Ära der japanischen Geschichte stehen, so wenig sollten *bijinga* für bare Münze genommen werden. Eine realitätsnahe Darstellung war im Allgemeinen nicht der primäre Beweggrund der Künstler, die die Motive entwarfen, denn sie mieden in der Regel die unangenehmen Aspekte des Lebens in den Vergnügungsvierteln, ja des Lebens im Allgemeinen. Stattdessen betonten sie die positiven Zerstreuungen der «fliessenden Welt», bei denen Luxus, Kultiviertheit, Unterhaltung und sinnliche Vergnügungen im Vordergrund standen.

Die Kleidung, Frisuren, Kosmetika und Schmuckaccessoires der Frauen, die diese Welt bevölkerten, wurden in *ukiyo-e*-Drucken minutiös dokumentiert. Wie Kobayashi Tadashi allerdings bemerkt, «bekommen wir in diesen Bildern nicht die aussergewöhnlich individualisierten Merkmale bestimmter Frauen zu Gesicht. Die Kompositionen zeigen vielmehr die idealisierten und geschätzten Eigenschaften, die – so nahm man an – von Connaisseurs erwartet wurden.»[1] Diese Ansprüche konnten recht streng sein, wie *Geheime Lehren (Hidensho)*, ein Führer zu den Vergnügungsvierteln Kyotos aus dem 17. Jahrhundert, bestätigt. Darin wird die ideale Kurtisane wie folgt beschrieben:

> *Ihre Augen sollten etwas grösser sein, mit auffälligen schwarzen Pupillen. Die Augenbrauen sollten eng beieinander stehen, ähnlich wie Rauch. Das Gesicht sollte die Form eines Melonenkerns haben. Die Nase hängt von der Gesichtsform ab, ist jedoch wichtig. Finger und Zehen sollten zarte Nägel haben, die Finger sollten spitz zulaufen und geschmeidig sein, und sehr gelenkige Hände sind gut. Ihr Auftreten kann*

One of the most abiding traditional pictorial genres in the history of Japanese art is *bijinga,* "pictures of beauties" that feature attractive women from all walks of life. Especially prominent as subjects in the Edo period (1603–1868), *bijinga* are waitresses, geisha entertainers, lower-class prostitutes and high-ranked courtesans. These are the women of the "floating world," a euphemism for the licensed pleasure quarters of Maruyama in Nagasaki, Shinmachi in Osaka, Kyoto's Shimabara, and the most famous of all, the Yoshiwara district of Edo. But as popular as these depictions of life in the entertainment districts were in their day, and as emblematic as they are today of a period of Japanese history long since passed, *bijinga* should not be taken at face value. Generally speaking, verisimilitude was not the prime motivation of the artists who designed these prints, for they typically dispensed with the disagreeable aspects of life in the pleasure quarters, and indeed of life in general. Instead, they emphasized the positive, diverting qualities of the "floating world," with luxury, refinement, amusement, and sensual pleasure receiving the most frequent emphasis.

As for the women who occupied this world, their costumes, hairstyles, cosmetics and ornamental accessories were scrupulously documented in *ukiyo-e* prints, but as Kobayashi Tadashi notes, "we are not shown the uniquely individualized features of particular women in these pictures. Rather, these compositions depict the idealized and appreciated qualities associated with connoisseurial expectations."[1] These expectations could be quite strict, a fact affirmed in the *Hidensho (Secret Teachings)*, a seventeenth-century guidebook to Kyoto's pleasure quarters that describes the ideal courtesan as follows:

> *Her eyes should be a little large, with dominant black pupils. Eyebrows should be close together, on the smoky side. The face should have the shape of a melon seed. The nose depends on the shape of the face, but is important. Fingers and toes should have delicate nails, fingers tapered and supple, and double-jointed hands are good. Her demeanor can be improved by training. A small waist and legs that are long between the joints are good.*[2]

The guidebook's author, however, laments that it is a rare courtesan indeed who possesses all the desired characteristics. The only perfect beauties, it would seem, are to be found in the world of *bijinga.*

durch Ausbildung verbessert werden. Eine schlanke Taille und Beine, die zwischen den Gelenken lang sind, sind gut.[2]

Der Verfasser des Führers beklagt jedoch, dass es nur selten Kurtisanen gäbe, die über all die gewünschten Eigenschaften verfügten. Die einzig perfekten Schönheiten, so scheint es, sind in der Welt von *bijinga* zu finden.

Ein Beispiel für eine idealisierte Darstellung einer Schönheit aus der Edo-Zeit findet man auf einem Holzschnitt vom Ende des 18. Jahrhunderts, gestaltet von Chôbunsai Eishi (1756–1829). Er zeigt Utaura, eine Kurtisane aus dem Freudenhaus Kadotamaya (KAT. 50), die gerade mit ihrer Entourage eingetroffen ist, um den Abend mit einem Kunden zu verbringen. Eishi liefert verschiedene bildliche Anhaltspunkte, die Utaura als *oiran,* ein Oberbegriff für hochrangige Kurtisanen, ausweisen – dazu zählen die verschiedenen Schichten ihres Kimonos, ihr übergrosser Schildpattkamm sowie die kunstvollen Haarnadeln. Auch ihr Fortbewegungsmittel, eine teure schwarz lackierte Sänfte, die im Hintergrund zu sehen ist, verweist auf ihren elitären Status. Utaura wird von drei Frauen begleitet, zwei jungen *kamuro*-Bediensteten und ihrem *shinzô*-Lehrmädchen. Nach Einschätzung von Cecilia Segawa Seigle diente dieses Gefolge im 18. Jahrhundert als lebendiges «prunkvolles Beiwerk» der *oiran.*[3]

Eishi differenzierte die Figuren, indem er ihre Körpergrösse, die Art ihrer Kleidung und ihren Haarschmuck variierte; die Gesichtszüge der vier Frauen sind im Grunde jedoch austauschbar. Eishis einziges Zugeständnis bestand darin, die Gesichter der *kamuro* verkleinert darzustellen, damit sie besser zu ihrem kindlichen Körper passten. Ansonsten sind die Formen, Proportionen und Elemente ihrer Gesichter exakt gleich. Das wahre Thema von Eishis Holzschnitt, so darf man aus dieser Vereinheitlichung schliessen, ist nicht so sehr «Utaura von Kadotamaya» mit ihrem Gefolge als vielmehr die Vorstellung von «hochrangigen Kurtisanen», die sie verkörpert. Dazu gehören die nötigen Talente und Fertigkeiten, Glanz und gute Umgangsformen, die in idealisierter Form symbolisiert werden, um so die «Erwartungen kundiger Käufer» von Holzschnitten zu erfüllen. Es überrascht daher nicht, dass Eishi ausser dem Namen der Hauptfigur und ihrer Arbeitsstätte keine Auskunft über sein Motiv gibt. Der Holzschnitt verrät nichts über Utaura als Individuum, als Frau mit unverkennbaren Eigenschaften und unverwechselbarem Werdegang. Schriftliche Zeugnisse der Zeit und Historienliteratur liefern jedoch genügend Anhaltspunkte, um eine gute Vorstellung vom Leben einer Kurtisane zu gewinnen.

Wenn Utauras Lebensgeschichte denen anderer Frauen der Vergnügungsviertel ähnelt, dann begann ihr beruflicher Werdegang vermutlich im Alter von sechs oder sieben Jahren, womöglich sogar früher, als sie von mittellosen Eltern an ein Bordell verkauft wurde.[4] Ein solches Vorgehen scheint heute unvorstellbar; wie Seigle jedoch bemerkt, war die Entscheidung der Eltern, ihre Tochter auf diese Weise abzugeben, vielleicht auch dem

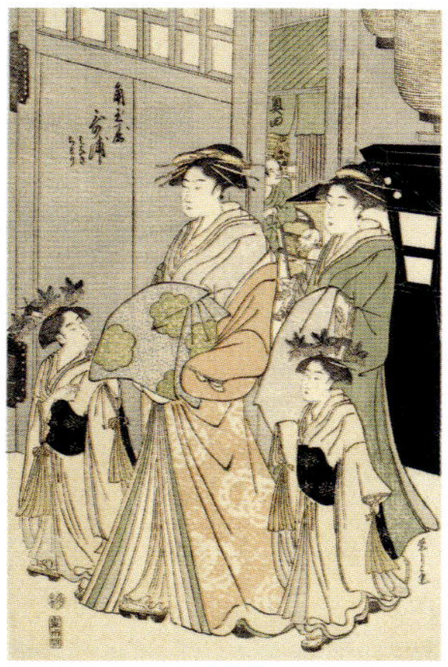

50

An example of an idealized vision of an Edo period beauty is found in a print dated to the late 1700s and designed by Chôbunsai Eishi (1756–1829). It features Utaura, a courtesan of the brothel Kadotamaya (CAT. 50), who has just arrived with her entourage to pass an evening with a client. Eishi offers many visual clues that allow us to identify Utaura as an *oiran,* a generic term for a highly ranked courtesan, including her multi-layered kimono, and her oversized tortoise shell comb and elaborate hairpins. Even her manner of conveyance, an expensive black lacquered palanquin seen in the background, suggests her elite status. Utaura is accompanied by three other figures, including two young *kamuro* servants and her *shinzô* apprentice. According to Cecilia Segawa Seigle, in the eighteenth century this retinue served as living "splendid accessories" for the *oiran.*[3]

Eishi differentiated these figures by varying their sizes and their manner of dress and hair ornamentation, yet the facial features of all four females are basically interchangeable. Eishi's only concession was to reduce the scale of the *kamuro* faces to better suit their child-sized bodies; otherwise he rendered the shapes, proportions, and components of their visages in precisely the same manner. This homogenization suggests that the true subject of Eishi's print is not, in fact, "Utaura of Kadotamaya" with her retinue per se, but rather the concept of "high-class courtesan" that she represents, including the requisite talents and skills, glamour and savoir faire, symbolized in an idealized form guaranteed to meet the print-buying public's "connoisseurial expectations." With such an aim in mind, it is no surprise that Eishi offers little salient information other than the primary subject's name and place of employment. We learn nothing from the print about Utaura the individual, a woman with distinctive qualities, characteristics, and a singular personal history. But enough information can be gleaned from contemporaneous written accounts and interpreted from period fiction to create an informed impression of what the life of a courtesan was like.

If Utaura's story was similar to that of other women of the pleasure quarters, then her professional life probably began around the age of six or seven, possibly even younger, when she was sold to a brothel by poverty-stricken parents.[4] Today such behavior seems unthinkable, but as Seigle notes, a parent's decision to sell a daughter off in this fashion may have been motivated in part by a desire to give her a better life. The lot of a poor farming family in Edo period Japan could be brutally hard, but if raised in a brothel, a daughter would at least be well fed and dressed, and would receive an education. Furthermore, there was a chance for her to achieve social betterment through marriage to a man of higher status. Once the purchase price passed hands, however, it fell on the daughter to repay her parents' debt, something that could take decades of employ in a profession that was not only strenuous but also often detrimental to a woman's health. "Most ordinary prostitutes completed their terms by the age of twenty-seven."

Wunsch geschuldet, ihr ein besseres Leben zu ermöglichen. Das Los einer armen Bauernfamilie im Japan der Edo-Zeit konnte gnadenlos sein, und in einem Bordell bekam die Tochter zumindest genug zu essen, erhielt Kleidung und eine Ausbildung. Ausserdem bestand die Chance auf sozialen Aufstieg, falls sie einen Mann aus der besseren Gesellschaft heiraten sollte. Sobald der Kauf vonstattengegangen war, war es an der Tochter, die Schulden ihrer Eltern zurückzuzahlen, und dies bedeutete oft jahrzehntelange Dienste in einem Beruf, der nicht nur anstrengend, sondern auch mit gesundheitlichen Risiken für die Frauen verbunden war. «Die meisten Prostituierten beendeten ihre Tätigkeit im Alter von 27 Jahren», schreibt Seigle. Zu dem Zeitpunkt waren jedoch meist zusätzliche persönliche Schulden angefallen, sodass sie noch mehrere Jahre weiterarbeiten mussten, bevor sie aus ihrem Lehrvertrag entlassen werden konnten.[5]

Nicht alle, die auf diese Weise in ein Bordell gerieten, sollten hochrangige Prostituierte werden, doch wenn ein neues Mädchen das Potenzial zur Schönheit besass und das nötige Temperament an den Tag legte, wurde sie eine *kamuro* und ging einer älteren Kurtisane als Bedienstete und Magd zur Hand. Wenn sie keinen Pflichten nachkommen musste, wurde eine *kamuro* in Kalligrafie, Dichtkunst, Tanz und anderen Künsten ausgebildet. Ebenso wichtiges Handwerkszeug im Gewerbe einer Kurtisane waren jedoch die Kunst der geistreichen Konversation, Koketterie, die Kunst der Überredung und Intrige, die eine *kamuro* erlernte, indem sie ihren «älteren Schwestern» im Umgang mit Kunden über die Schulter schaute. Da sie in so jungem Alter in diese Welt eintauchten, wurden die Mädchen schnell erwachsen; Seigle zufolge waren «*kamuro* in vielerlei Hinsicht kleine Erwachsene, die vorzeitig gezwungen waren, den Realitäten der Erwachsenen ins Auge zu sehen, da sie in jungem Alter in die Welt der Beziehungen und Sexualität von Erwachsenen hineingeworfen wurden».[6]

Im Alter von etwa zwölf Jahren änderte sich der Status der *kamuro,* und sie wurde in den Rang einer *shinzô* («neuen») oder auszubildenden Kurtisane erhoben; ab diesem Zeitpunkt erhielt sie eine intensivere Bildung in den Künsten, die Voraussetzung für die Unterhaltung männlicher Kunden war. Ihr Aufstieg zur vollwertigen Kurtisane erfolgte wenige Jahre später. Nun wurde ihr Benehmen strenger reglementiert, ihre Pflichten wurden härter. In *Der grosse Spiegel der Schönheit* (*Shoen Ôkagami,* 1684), einer Sammlung von Vignetten, die das Leben in der «fliessenden Welt» illustrieren, gibt der Autor Ihara Saikaku (1642–1693) bisweilen freimütig Einblick in das Leben von Prostituierten – und dies auf eine Art und Weise, die an das Mitgefühl des Lesers appelliert. Die Unterhaltung der Männer, so merkt Saikaku an, sei harte Arbeit, und sie werde dadurch noch erschwert, dass nicht ausreichend für das leibliche Wohl der Kurtisanen gesorgt würde, denn der Anblick einer essenden Frau galt als unschön.

writes Seigle, but by that time, most had incurred additional debt of their own, requiring several more years before they were free from the bonds of their indenture.[5]

Not all those who entered a brothel in this way were destined to be high-ranked prostitutes, but if a newly arrived girl showed potential for beauty and had the proper temperament, she would be made a *kamuro,* and assigned to an elder courtesan to act as her servant and handmaiden. When not immersed in these duties, *kamuro* received training in calligraphy, poetry composition, dance, and other cultural arts, but equally important tools in the courtesan's trade were the arts of witty banter, flirtation, persuasion, and guile, which *kamuro* learned by observing their "elder sisters" interacting with customers. Immersed in such a world at so young an age, the girls grew up quickly; indeed, according to Seigle, "*kamuro* were in many ways miniature grownups, forced to face certain adult realities prematurely by being thrown into the world of adult relationships and sexuality at an early age."[6]

Around the age of twelve years, the *kamuro*'s status would change to that of *shinzô* ("newly made") or apprentice courtesan, at which time she would be trained more intensely in the arts required to entertain male customers. Her promotion to fully fledged courtesan would occur within a few years of that, at which time her behavior would be more rigidly regulated and her duties more onerous. In *Great Mirror of Beauty* (*Shoen Ôkagami,* 1684), a collection of vignettes illustrating life in the "floating world," author Ihara Saikaku (1642–1693) offers occasional candid glimpses into the lives of prostitutes in a manner intended to evoke the reader's sympathy. Saikaku notes that entertaining men was hard work, made even harder by the fact that the courtesan was not allowed much in the way of sustenance, for the sight of a woman taking food was considered unappealing.

> *The most she might do is prod some boiled greens with her chopsticks, or sip a little clear soup. Even when she steals a moment to eat something in one of the back rooms, she has to make do with a few pickles over rice, and she knows the taste of certain foods only from the memories of her days as a* kamuro *… The only thing she is expected to consume is sake.*[7]

As for their financial affairs, courtesans operated in a system that seems to have been designed to keep them in perpetual debt. Saikaku outlines a few of their expenses, such as clothing for their attending *kamuro,* who at a certain age needed to exchange their girl's cotton quilt-lined kimono for adult-style silk-lined *awase* robes.[8] Quite often the courtesan's own garments and accessories needed replacing as well, for on any given night, Saikaku writes, "her combs might be stolen by a musician from town, or a customer of only slight acquaintance may decide to carry off her inner *obi* sash."[9]

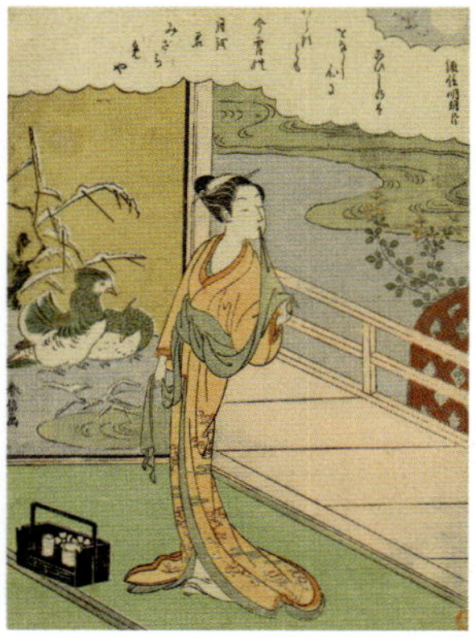

18

Im äussersten Fall darf sie mit ihren Stäbchen in etwas gekochtem Gemüse stochern oder an ein bisschen klarer Suppe nippen. Selbst wenn sie einen Moment verstohlen in einem der Hinterzimmer etwas isst, muss sie sich mit etwas eingelegtem Gemüse auf Reis begnügen, und sie kennt den Geschmack gewisser Lebensmittel nur aus Erinnerungen an ihre Zeit als kamuro *[...] Das Einzige, was sie konsumieren sollte, ist Sake.*[7]

Was finanzielle Angelegenheiten anging, so bewegten sich Kurtisanen in einem System, das anscheinend darauf angelegt war, sie in einen Schuldenkreislauf zu verstricken. Saikaku listet einige ihrer Ausgaben auf, darunter Kleidung für ihre *kamuro,* die ab einem gewissen Alter ihren baumwollgefütterten Mädchenkimono gegen seidengefütterte *awase*-Gewänder für Erwachsene tauschen mussten.[8] Auch die Kleidung und Accessoires der Kurtisane mussten des Öfteren ersetzt werden, denn nachts, so schreibt Saikaku, «raubte unter Umständen ein Musiker aus der Stadt ihre Kämme, oder ein flüchtig bekannter Kunde beschloss, ihre innere *obi*-Schärpe mit nach Hause zu nehmen».[9] Sie musste sich über aktuelle Ereignisse und Trends wie neue Theaterinszenierungen auf dem Laufenden halten und daher die Libretti aller neuen Stücke kaufen, ganz gleich, ob sie die Stücke zu besuchen gedachte oder nicht. Gelegentlich benötigte sie auch Geld für Geschenke, wenn zum Beispiel eine «Schwester»-Kurtisane im Bordell ein Kind bekam oder die Tochter ihres Meisters verheiratet wurde. Dies sind nur einige Beispiele für die unterschiedlichen Ausgaben, die eine Kurtisane von dem Geld bestreiten musste, das ihr blieb, nachdem die Bordellbesitzer ihren vertragsmässigen Anteil vom Verdienst abgezogen hatten. Angesichts der rauen Wirklichkeit hinter dem scheinbar glamourösen Leben kommt Saikaku zu dem Schluss: «Es gibt nichts Grösseres und zugleich nichts Traurigeres als das Leben einer Prostituierten.»[10]

Holzschnittkünstler wiesen selbstverständlich nicht auf die von Saikaku beschriebenen Schwierigkeiten hin, denn das hätte die Illusion einer «fliessenden Welt» frei von allen profanen Dingen zunichtegemacht. Dass *bijin* selten einen Gefühlsausdruck zeigen, der über ein sanftes, vieldeutiges Lächeln hinausgeht, könnte sogar darauf schliessen lassen, dass die Künstler der Edo-Zeit kein Interesse hatten, die Fähigkeit ihrer Sujets zu tieferen Gefühlen zu erkunden. Im Gegensatz dazu aber wurden derartige Gefühle regelmässig in *bijinga*-Drucken gepriesen und sogar idealisiert, und die hervorragendsten *ukiyo-e*-Künstler verliehen ihren Motiven durch intertextuelle Anspielungen, optische Effekte und überraschende Kombinationen häufig eine subtile emotionale und psychologische Note.

Ein Holzschnitt von Suzuki Harunobu (1725?–1770), der auf das Jahr 1767 zurückgeht, manifestiert diese Art indirekten Gefühlsausdrucks (KAT. 18). Die Teehausszene zeigt eine Kurtisane, die in einer Pause auf den nächtlichen Garten hinausblickt.

She needed to keep abreast of current events and trends, including new theater productions, which required her to purchase librettos for all the most recent plays, whether she expected to attend them or not. There was also the occasional need for gift money, such as when a sister courtesan in the brothel gave birth to a child, or when the master's daughter was married. This is just a sampling of the various expenditures a courtesan had to meet, using whatever earnings remained after the brothel owners took their share, according to the terms of her contract. Indeed, the hard realities behind her apparently glamorous life led Saikaku to conclude, "There is nothing grander and yet sadder than the life of a prostitute."[10]

Print artists, of course, made no reference to the kinds of difficulties Saikaku describes, for to do so would shatter the illusion of a "floating world" free from all mundane concerns. Indeed, the fact that *bijin* rarely show any emotional expression stronger than a gentle, ambiguous smile might suggest that Edo period artists were uninterested in exploring their subjects' capacity for deeper feelings. But, in fact, such sentiments were regularly celebrated and even idealized in *bijinga* prints, and the very best *ukiyo-e* artists regularly invested their designs with sophisticated emotional and psychological dimensions through intertextual references, visual puns, and unexpected pairings.

A print designed by Suzuki Harunobu (1725?–1770) and dated to 1767 demonstrates this kind of indirect emotional expression (CAT. 18). Set in a teahouse, the composition features a courtesan paused in her duties as she looks out over a night garden. Her face appears calm and composed, and only her unusual gesture of clenching her *obi* sash in her teeth indicates she is in the grip of strong feelings. It is only when we examine the verse inscribed in the cloud-shaped cartouche above her head that the nature of these feelings is clearly expressed. The verse was written by the Heian period courtier Minamoto no Saneakira (910–970), and is included in the famous tenth-century compendium *The Thirty-six Immortal Poets (Sanjû rokkasen)*. It translates as follows:

What a waste,
this moon and these blossoms,
on such a night;
if only I could share them
with one who appreciates them as I do.[11]

In the print, branches of blossoming camellia jut prominently into the courtesan's view, illuminated in the light of a glowing full moon. By reproducing the tableau described in Saneakira's poem, Harunobu links the sentiments of a Heian period aristocrat and those of a common Yoshiwara courtesan, lending nobility to her poignant longing for sympathetic companionship. Her sense of emotional isolation is further emphasized by the inclusion of a painted sliding *fusuma* panel featuring

Ihr Gesichtsausdruck scheint ruhig und gefasst, nur die ungewöhnliche Tatsache, dass sie ihre *obi*-Schärpe zwischen die Zähne klemmt, deutet auf ihre grosse emotionale Erregung hin. Erst der Vers, der in der wolkenförmigen Kartusche über ihrem Kopf geschrieben steht, gibt über die Art ihrer Gefühle Aufschluss. Er stammt von dem Höfling Minamoto no Saneakira (910–970) aus der Heian-Zeit und ist in dem berühmten Kompendium *Die Sechsunddreissig Unsterblichen der Dichtkunst (Sanjû rokkasen)* aus dem 10. Jahrhundert enthalten. Übersetzt lautet er:

Was für eine Verschwendung,
dieser Mond und diese Blüten,
in solch einer Nacht;
wenn ich sie nur mit jemandem teilen könnte,
der sie so schätzt wie ich.[11]

Im hellen Schein des Vollmondes ragen blühende Kamelienzweige auffällig ins Sichtfeld der Kurtisane. Harunobu verknüpft, indem er das in Saneakiras Gedicht beschriebene Tableau wiedergibt, die Gefühle eines Aristokraten aus der Heian-Zeit mit denen einer einfachen Kurtisane aus Yoshiwara und verleiht so ihrer schmerzlichen Sehnsucht nach verständnisvoller Gesellschaft etwas Nobles. Ihr Gefühl von emotionaler Isolation wird ausserdem durch die bemalte *fusuma*-Schiebewand betont, auf der männliche und weibliche Wasservögel zu sehen sind, die sich am Rand eines winterlichen Teiches aneinanderschmiegen und die Beständigkeit der Liebenden in einer kalten, lieblosen Welt repräsentieren. Harunobu gelingt es, den Gefühlen und der Unzufriedenheit der Kurtisane allein durch visuelle und textliche Anspielungen Ausdruck zu verleihen, sodass er das Gesicht der jungen Frau mit der emotionalen Neutralität

male and female waterfowl huddled together on the edge of a wintery pond, representing the constancy of lovers in a cold, uncaring world. In these ways, Harunobu manages to express the courtesan's desires and her dissatisfactions entirely through visual and textual allusions, leaving him free to render the young woman's face with the emotional neutrality and idealized features required of *bijin* images by popular convention.

Japan's woodblock print industry underwent drastic changes during the Meiji period (1868–1912), a time when imported graphic reproduction technologies, including copperplate etching, engraving, lithography, and photography, took a stronger foothold in Japan. Part of the attraction of these new technologies was their novelty, especially their exciting potential for realism, and for this reason woodblock print producers viewed them as a threat. Japan's fast-paced Westernization is the subject of a print design by Utagawa Yoshifuji (1828–1887), dated to the early 1870s and entitled *Imported and Domestic Goods: Playful Picture Comparing the Handiness of Tools and Means (Hakurai wamono tawamure dôgu chôhô kurabe zu)* (FIG. 5).[12] Yoshifuji's satirical image depicts newly imported Western systems and technologies paired against their traditional Japanese counterparts in a battle for survival. Among the contests Yoshifuji illustrates is a Western-style umbrella facing off against a Japanese bamboo-and-oiled-paper *kasa,* a wheeled *rikisha* passenger cart thrashing two Edo period palanquins, and a steamship faced off against a traditional sailed vessel.

In the lower left corner of Yoshifuji's image, we find one more battle in progress, a contest between a stack of *ukiyo-e* woodblock prints and a framed photograph, both of which display courtesans as their subject. As they fight, the two enemies exchange taunts and challenges. The photograph boasts, "I show only the truth. I dislike mistakes. No matter how many years pass, I am still interesting to look at," to which the bundle of *bijinga* prints retorts, "I make beautiful women and other things

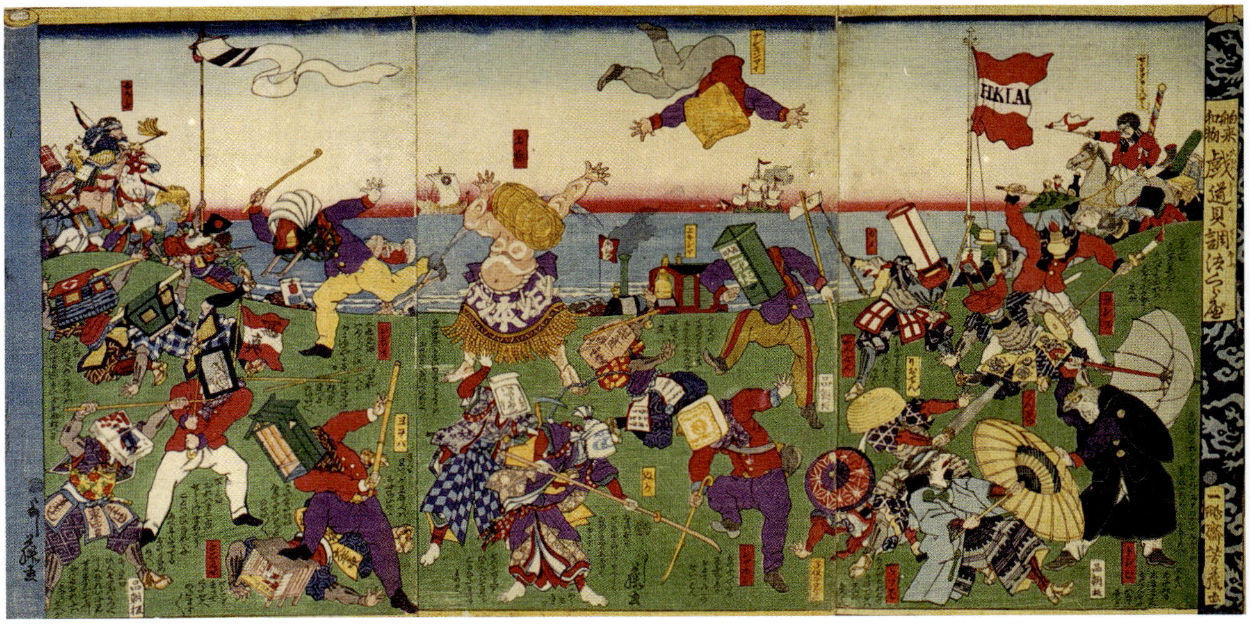

FIG. 5

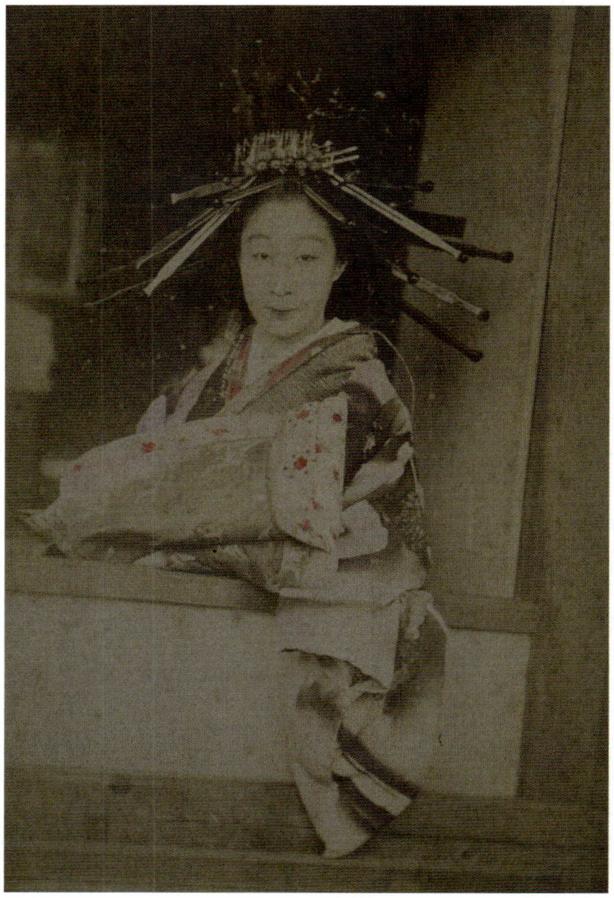

FIG. 6

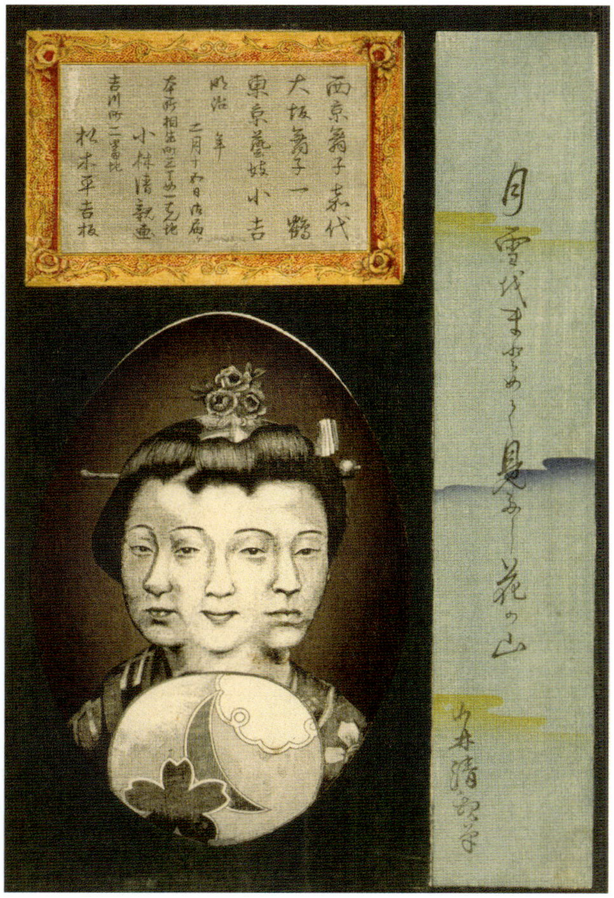

FIG. 7

und den idealisierten Merkmalen wiedergeben kann, die den üblichen *bijinga*-Konventionen entsprechen.

Die japanische Holzschnittindustrie erlebte während der Meiji-Zeit (1868–1912) drastische Veränderungen, als sich importierte Reproduktionstechniken wie Kupferstich, Gravur, Lithografie und Fotografie in Japan mehr und mehr durchsetzten. Die neuen Technologien waren auch deswegen so reizvoll, weil sie neu waren und grösseren Realismus versprachen – aus demselben Grund betrachteten die Hersteller von Holzschnitten sie jedoch als Bedrohung. Die rasante Verwestlichung Japans ist Thema eines Holzschnitts von Utagawa Yoshifuji (1828–1887), der auf die frühen 1870er-Jahre zurückgeht und den Titel *Importierte und regionale Ware: lustiges Bild, auf dem die Handlichkeit von Werkzeugen verglichen wird (Hakurai wamono tawamure dôgu chôhô kurabe zu)* trägt (FIG. 5).[12] Yoshifujis Satire zeigt die neu importierten westlichen Systeme und Technologien im Überlebenskampf mit ihren traditionellen japanischen Gegenstücken. Unter den von Yoshifuji dargestellten Wettstreiten sind der zwischen einem Regenschirm westlicher Machart und einem japanischen *kasa* aus Bambus und Ölpapier, der zwischen einem *rikisha*-Personenwagen auf Rädern und zwei Sänften aus der Edo-Zeit sowie der zwischen einem Dampfer und einem traditionellen Segelschiff.

In der linken unteren Ecke von Yoshifujis Bild findet ein weiterer Wettstreit statt, nämlich der zwischen einem

look more beautiful than they really are by means of illustrated books and sets of prints. You can't knock me down."[13] Their combat is fierce, but at least for the time being, neither side is able to gain the upper hand. While the attractiveness and utility of photography and other imported graphic media was undeniable, their popularity was not yet enough to render the traditional woodblock print industry entirely obsolete.

Still, photographic images of courtesans or geisha offered an interesting conceptual alternative, a true-to-life view of the subject rather than the idealized one offered by *ukiyo-e* prints (FIG. 6). Inspired by photography's objective approach to rendering beauty, a number of Meiji period print artists explored the hitherto untapped potential for Japan's woodblock prints to achieve graphic realism. Among them was Kobayashi Kiyochika (1847–1915), who in the late 1870s created an unusual print featuring three prominent geisha, Kayo of Kyoto, Hitotsuru of Osaka, and Kokichi of Tokyo (FIG. 7). Kiyochika clearly had photographs in mind when he produced this design, for his composition mimics the effect of a multiple photographic exposure by overlapping portraits of the three individual women, each differentiated by distinctive facial characteristics, and merging them onto a single head and torso. The result is reminiscent of a multi-headed Buddhist deity, tempting us to view the image as a secular icon to a goddess of modern beauty.

Stapel *ukiyo-e*-Holzschnitte und einem gerahmten Foto, auf denen jeweils Kurtisanen zu sehen sind. Im Kampf verhöhnen und provozieren sich die beiden Gegner. Die Fotografie prahlt: «Ich zeige nur die Wahrheit. Ich kann Fehler nicht leiden. Auch nach Jahren sehe ich noch immer interessant aus.» Woraufhin das Bündel *bijinga*-Drucke entgegnet: «Ich lasse schöne Frauen und andere Dinge mithilfe von Bildbänden und Druckserien nur noch schöner aussehen, als sie wirklich sind. Mich kann man nicht umwerfen.»[13] In dem wilden Gefecht kann einstweilen keine Partei die Oberhand gewinnen. Waren der Reiz und Nutzwert der Fotografie und anderer importierter grafischer Medien auch unbestreitbar, so reichte ihre Popularität noch nicht aus, um die traditionelle Holzschnittindustrie ganz zu verdrängen.

Dennoch stellten die fotografischen Bilder von Kurtisanen oder Geishas eine interessante konzeptionelle Alternative dar, denn sie boten statt der idealisierten Sicht der *ukiyo-e*-Drucke einen realitätsgetreuen Blick auf die Dinge (FIG. 6). Angeregt von der objektiven Wiedergabe des Schönen durch die Fotografie, erkundeten verschiedene Holzschnittkünstler der Meiji-Zeit das noch ungenutzte Potenzial japanischer Holzdrucke und versuchten, der Realität grafisch nahezukommen. Unter ihnen war Kobayashi Kiyochika (1847–1915), der Ende der 1870er-Jahre einen ungewöhnlichen Druck mit drei prominenten Geishas gestaltete: Kayo aus Kyoto, Hitotsuru aus Osaka und Kokichi aus Tokio (FIG. 7). Kiyochika hatte offensichtlich das Medium Fotografie im Hinterkopf, als er das Motiv entwarf, denn seine Komposition imitiert den Effekt einer Mehrfachbelichtung, indem es die Porträts der drei Frauen – jedes mit seinen eigenen Gesichtszügen – überlagert und sie in einem einzigen Kopf und Torso miteinander verschmelzen lässt. Das Ergebnis erinnert an eine vielköpfige buddhistische Gottheit, und man ist versucht, es als säkulare Hommage an eine Göttin der modernen Schönheit zu betrachten.

Kiyochikas Reaktion auf die aus dem Westen importierte Technik und Ästhetik war unter traditionell ausgebildeten Malern und Druckkünstlern im späten 19. und frühen 20. Jahrhundert ungewöhnlich; viele andere griffen zu subtileren Mitteln, um modernes und traditionelles Empfinden in einem Werk zusammenzubringen. Diese Strategie verfolgten die Künstler, die mit *Shin Hanga* («neue Drucke») verbunden werden, einer Kunstrichtung, die von dem Verleger Watanabe Shôzaburô (1885–1962) ausging, der den Namen 1915 prägte.[14] *Shin-Hanga*-Bilder widmen sich traditionellen Themen wie Landschaften, Vogel- und Blumenmotiven, den Porträts von *kabuki*-Darstellern und natürlich *bijin.* Selbst die Entwurfs- und Druckverfahren waren bewusst anachronistisch, denn Watanabe behielt das System gemeinschaftlicher Produktion aus der Edo-Zeit bei, an dem sowohl Verleger als auch Künstler, Bildschnitzer und Drucker beteiligt waren.

Shin-Hanga-Drucke stellen rein äusserlich jedoch eine interessante Mischung aus Edo-Zeit und moderner

Kiyochika's response to imported Western techniques and aesthetics was unusual among traditionally trained painters and print designers in the late nineteenth and early twentieth centuries, many of whom pursued more subtle ways of merging modern and traditional sensibilities in a single work of art. Such was the strategy used by artists associated with *Shin Hanga* ("New Prints"), a print movement orchestrated by publisher Watanabe Shôzaburô (1885–1962), who coined the label in 1915.[14] *Shin Hanga* images feature traditional themes such as landscapes, bird-and-flower designs, kabuki actor portraits, and of course *bijin.* Even the designing and printing processes were intentionally anachronistic, for Watanabe retained the Edo period system of collaborative production, in which publisher, designer, carver, and printer all provided valuable input.

The look of *Shin Hanga* prints, however, presented an interesting mix of Edo period and modern aesthetic values, as exemplified by a print entitled *Woman in Summer Kimono,* designed by *bijinga* specialist Hashiguchi Goyô (1880–1921) (FIG. 8). In this design, Goyô seems to express a strong nostalgia for the Edo period, beginning with his subject of a woman seated in her private quarters before a mirror, a standard *bijinga* composition dating back centuries. Furthermore, Goyô's visual description of the room follows traditional *ukiyo-e* precedents by rendering only the most necessary elements,

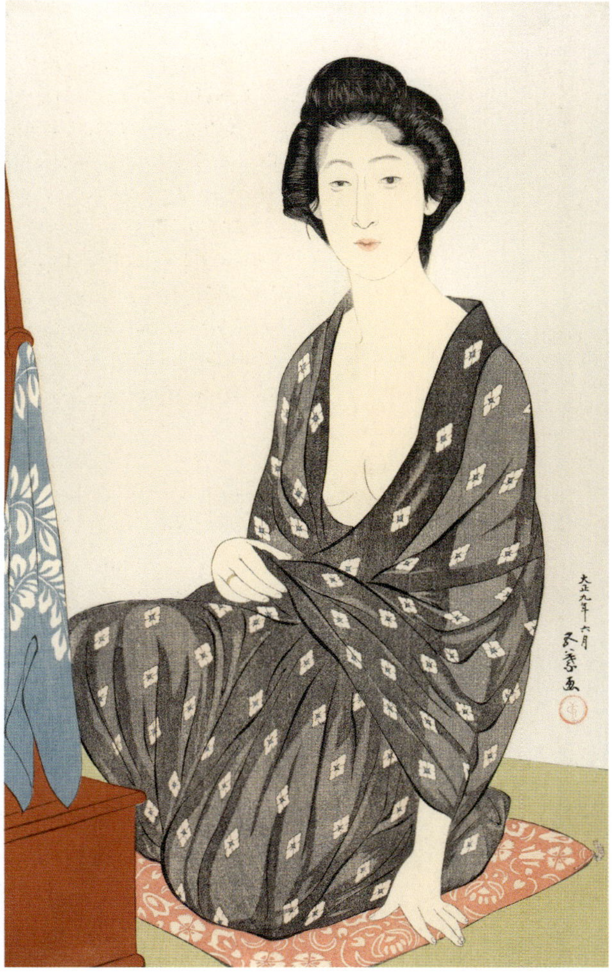

FIG. 8

Ästhetik dar, wie ein Druck mit dem Titel *Frau in einem Sommerkimono* vom *bijinga*-Spezialisten Hashiguchi Goyô (1880–1921) (FIG. 8) beispielhaft zeigt. Auf diesem Bild scheint Goyô einer starken Nostalgie nach der Edo-Zeit Ausdruck zu verleihen, angefangen mit dem Thema einer Frau, die in ihrem privaten Wohnraum vor dem Spiegel sitzt – ein typisches *bijinga*-Motiv, das Jahrhunderte zurückreicht. Ausserdem folgt Goyôs bildliche Beschreibung des Raumes den traditionellen *ukiyo-e*-Vorläufern, die sich auf das Wesentliche beschränken und den Hintergrund frei lassen. Auch die gemusterte Robe sowie die Ausstattung des Raumes könnten unmittelbar von einem Druck aus der Edo-Zeit stammen.

Ein Blick auf das Gesicht der Frau reicht jedoch aus, um den Betrachter im Nu in die Moderne zurückzuholen. Goyô war dafür bekannt, dass er sich in seinen Bildern auf gewisse Lieblingsmodelle stützte; er hielt ihre individuellen Merkmale in Bleistiftskizzen fest und sorgte dafür, dass sie im endgültigen Druck erhalten blieben.[15] Auffallend ist an *Frau in einem Sommerkimono* auch, wie selbstbewusst Goyô die Frau auftreten lässt, denn ihr Blick kreuzt sich mit unserem. In dem Moment, wo ihre und unsere Augen aufeinandertreffen, zieht die Frau am hauchdünnen Stoff ihrer Robe, um den entblössten Körper besser zu bedecken – eine Geste, die vermuten lässt, dass der Blick des Betrachters unerwartet und womöglich voyeuristisch ist, und die zugleich eine Atmosphäre voller emotionaler und erotischer Spannung schafft.

Künstlern wie Goyô, die eine zweigleisige Strategie verfolgten und mit einem Bein in der Vergangenheit, mit dem anderen in der Gegenwart standen, gelang es, ein neues prototypisches Modell für «Bilder schöner Frauen» zu schaffen. Auf der einen Seite würdigten und feierten diese Neo-*bijinga* die reine und idealisierte Vision der Edo-Zeit. Auf der anderen Seite vermittelten sie durch die Verwendung eines bildlichen und psychologischen Realismus eine modernistische Sensibilität. Durch entsprechendes Ausbreiten und Neuzusammenfügen von *bijinga* verliehen sie diesem 300 Jahre alten Genre neues Leben und neue Relevanz für das Japan des 20. Jahrhunderts.

1 Kobayashi 2005, S. 86.
2 Seigle 1993, S. 35–36.
3 Ebd., S. 76.
4 Ebd., S. 82.
5 Ebd., S. 182–183.
6 Ebd., S. 84.
7 Saikaku 1992, S. 89.
8 Ebd., S. 133.
9 Ebd., S. 89.
10 Ebd.
11 Übersetzung aus dem Englischen ins Deutsche: Claudia Kotte.
12 Der Druck ist mit «Ippôsai Yoshifuji» signiert, einem alternativen Künstlernamen des Holzschnittkünstlers.
13 Meech-Pekarik 1987, S. 101.
14 Weitere Angaben zur *Shin-Hanga*-Bewegung findet man in Brown und Goodall-Cristante 1996.
15 Goyô gab die äussere Erscheinung seiner Modelle so gewissenhaft wieder, dass sie auf unterschiedlichen Drucken wiederzuerkennen sind. Für *Frau in einem Sommerkimono* griff Goyô auf ein Modell namens Nakatani Tsuru zurück, das auf vielen seiner *bijinga* erscheint. Merritt 1990, S. 72.

and leaving the background blank. As for the subject's patterned garment and room furnishings, these could have been taken directly out of an Edo-period print.

With one look at the woman's face, however, the viewer is immediately returned to the modern age. Goyô was known for basing his compositions on a few favorite models, capturing their individualistic features in pencil sketches and carefully preserving them in the final print.[15] Another striking aspect of *Woman in Summer Kimono* is how Goyô subtly asserts his subject's character by intersecting her gaze with our own. Furthermore, at the same moment our eyes meet, the woman pulls at the gauzy fabric of her robe to better conceal her exposed body, a gesture that suggests the viewer's presence is unexpected and possibly voyeuristic, creating an atmosphere rife with emotional and erotic tension.

Using a two-fold strategy that kept one foot in the past and one in the present, artists like Goyô successfully created a new prototypical model for images of female beauties. On the one hand, these neo-*bijinga* acknowledged and celebrated the Edo period's pure and idealized vision. On the other, they brought a modernist sensibility through their use of pictorial and psychological realism. By unpacking and reassembling *bijinga* in this way, they instilled new life in the 300-year-old subject genre, giving it new relevance for Japan's twentieth century.

1 Kobayashi 2005, p. 86.
2 Seigle 1993, pp. 35–36.
3 Ibid., p. 76.
4 Ibid., p. 82.
5 Ibid., pp. 182–183.
6 Ibid., p. 84.
7 Saikaku 1992, p. 89.
8 Ibid., p. 133.
9 Ibid., p. 89.
10 Ibid.
11 Translation by John D. Szostak.
12 The print is signed "Ippôsai Yoshifuji," an alternative artist's name for this print designer.
13 Meech-Pekarik 1987, p. 101.
14 For more information on the *Shin Hanga* movement, see Brown and Goodall-Cristante 1996.
15 Goyô was so faithful in recording his models' appearances that they are recognizable from design to design. For *Woman in Summer Kimono,* Goyô used the modeling services of a woman named Nakatani Tsuru, who appears in many of his *bijinga* prints. Merritt 1990, p. 72.

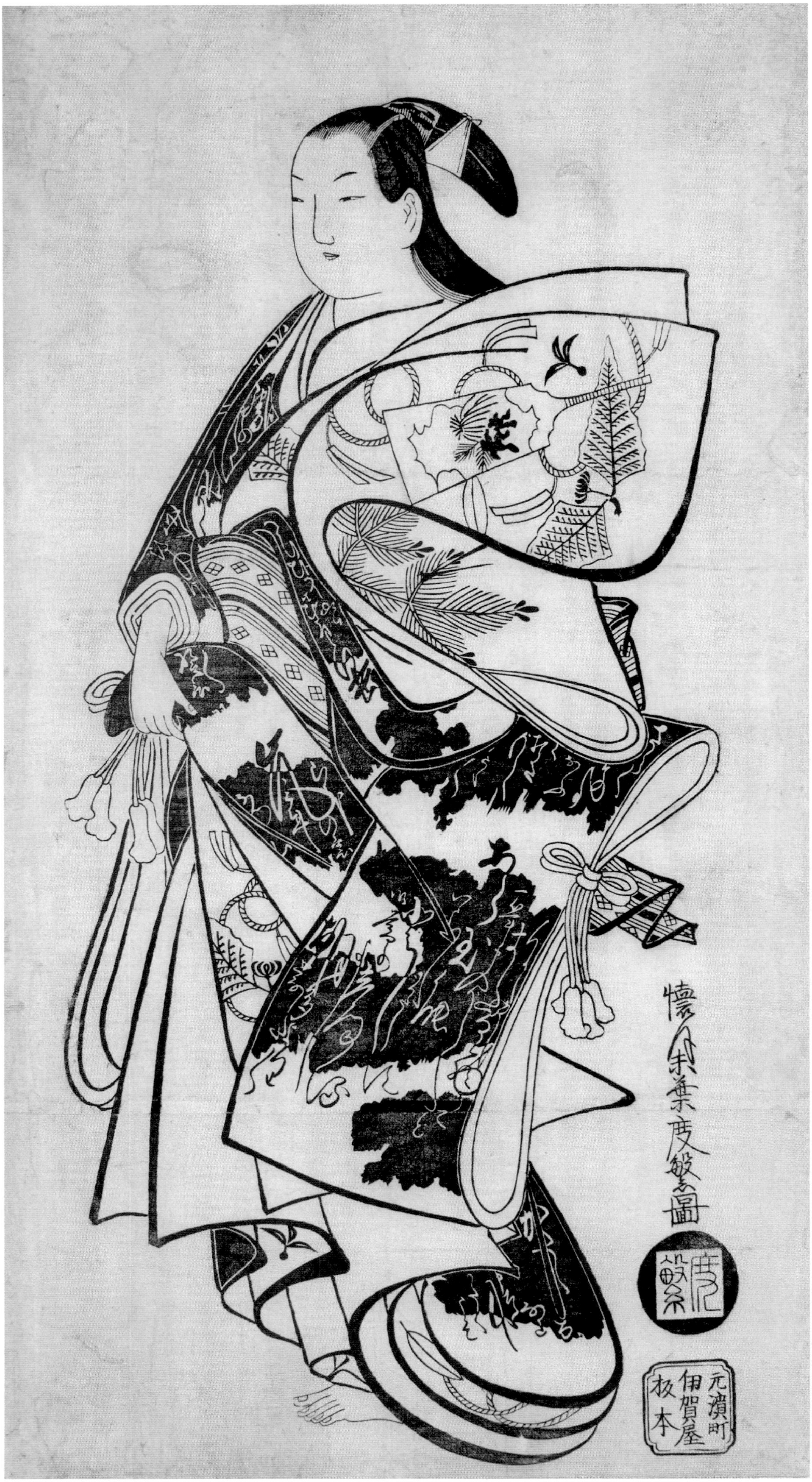
懐月末葉度繁之圖
元濱町 伊賀屋 板本

Dieser prächtige Druck ist von besonderer historischer Bedeutung, da er schon 1896 bei einer der ersten grossen öffentlichen Präsentationen japanischer Drucke in den USA gezeigt wurde. Er soll aus der Sammlung von Ernest Francisco Fenollosa stammen, dem Urvater der japanischen Kunstgeschichtsschreibung im Westen, und markiert die Anfänge des *ukiyo-e*-Einzelblattdrucks, der der Entwicklung des Farbdrucks vorausging. Während viele Drucke der Kaigetsudô-Schule handkoloriert sind, lässt hier die fehlende Farbe eine vollständige Würdigung der erlesenen technischen Qualität des Druckverfahrens zu. Die majestätische Eleganz und Förmlichkeit der Kurtisanen der Kaigetsudô-Schule, die Betonung der schwungvollen Stoffmuster durch weich fliessende Linien bestimmten den Kanon der weiblichen Schönheit im *ukiyo-e* während der gesamten ersten Hälfte des 18. Jahrhunderts.

Die Muster auf dem Unterkimono zeigen mit *hagoita*-Schläger und Kiefernzweigen an, dass die Kurtisane das neue Jahr feiert. *Hagoita* verwendete man in einem badmintonähnlichen Spiel namens *hanetsuki,* bei dem ein Federball hin und her geschlagen wurde. Als dekoratives Element symbolisierten sie das Neujahr und sind in dieser Funktion bis heute beliebt. Das Kimonomuster enthält darüber hinaus in Schreibschrift verfasste Neujahrsgedichte. Sie schlagen eine visuelle Brücke zwischen dem Bild der Kurtisane und der Signatur des Künstlers unten rechts, die gefolgt ist von einem runden Siegel mit der Inschrift «Dohan» und einem quadratischen Siegel mit dem Hinweis auf den Verleger, Igaya Kan'emon in Motohama-chô.

This superb print has an important historical significance, since it was included in one of the first major public displays of Japanese prints in the United States in 1896, and is believed to have come from the collection of the patriarch of Japanese art historical scholarship in the West, Ernest Francisco Fenollosa. It marks the beginnings of single-sheet *ukiyo-e* prints, before the development of color printing. While prints of the Kaigetsudô School often are hand-colored, the absence of color here allows the exquisite technical quality of the printing to be fully appreciated. The stately elegance and formality of the Kaigetsudô School courtesans, with an emphasis on dynamic clothing patterns accomplished by fluid lines, defined the canons of feminine beauty for *ukiyo-e* throughout the first half of the eighteenth century.

The designs on the courtesan's inner kimono, including a *hagoita* paddle and pine branches, indicate that she is celebrating the New Year. Although *hagoita* paddles were used to play a game resembling badminton called *hanetsuki,* in which a shuttlecock was batted back and forth, they were also decorated as symbols of the New Year, and they remain popular for this function to the present day. The kimono further incorporates New Year's poems in cursive script into its design, providing a bold graphic element. The poems establish a visual resonance between the image of the courtesan and the artist's signature in the lower right, followed by a round seal reading "Dohan" and a square seal indicating the publisher, Igaya Kan'emon in Motohama-chô.

SHAWN EICHMAN (SE)

懐月堂 度繁

1
Kurtisane
Courtesan
Kaigetsudô DOHAN

Auf einer Bank sitzt anmutig eine junge Frau und übt *shamisen* (japanische Laute). Das aufgeschlagene Notenbuch auf ihrem Schoss verrät, dass sie *Matsu no uchi* («Unter Kiefern») spielt, dessen Titel sich auf die Kiefernzweige bezieht, die in den ersten zwei Wochen des neuen Jahres die japanischen Strassen schmücken. Das Lied wurde erstmals 1718 im Ichimura-Theater gesungen, einem *kabuki*-Theater in Edo, und dürfte zum Zeitpunkt der Veröffentlichung des Drucks eine beliebte Melodie gewesen sein. Das Gefühl lebhafter Bewegung, das die Lagen und Falten des Gewandes vermitteln, wird verstärkt von dem verheissungsvollen Muster aus stilisierten Gebinden getrockneter Seeohren *(noshi awabi)*, einer muschelförmigen Schneckenart. Der eingesperrte Vogel oben rechts bildet einen wirkungsvollen Gegenpol zur Frauenfigur. Er trägt zur Ausgewogenheit der Komposition bei und spiegelt das musikalische Thema. Zugleich könnte der Künstler eine Übereinstimmung zwischen dem Vogel in seinem Käfig und der Frau angedeutet haben, die hier vor einem vergitterten Fenster sitzt: Analogien zwischen den Kurtisanen des Yoshiwara-Viertels und in Käfigen gehaltenen Singvögeln tauchen in Gedichten und Theaterstücken dieser Periode auf.

Das Werk repräsentiert ein frühes Stadium der Druckkunst, in dem die Umrisse und die schwarzen Bereiche gedruckt wurden, während die Kolorierung, in Schattierungen aus Orange und Rot, von Hand erfolgte. Mit beigemischten Metallpulvern liess sich, wie in diesem Fall, die Oberfläche zusätzlich verfeinern. Bis in die 1740er-Jahre hinein waren sämtliche Holzdrucke Schwarz-Weiss-Abzüge, die von einem einzigen Druckstock genommen und nachträglich ausgemalt wurden. Erst die Entwicklung des Druckens mit mehreren Druckstöcken, die in den 1760er-Jahren in vielfarbigen «Brokatbildern» *(nishiki-e)* gipfelte, machte das aufwendige Handkolorieren überflüssig. Obwohl das Werk nicht signiert ist, stehen das breite Gesicht und das runde Kinn der Figur, die kräftigen Muster ihres *kosode* (wörtlich «kleiner Ärmel») und die Andeutung einer Kulisse stilistisch in Bezug zu jenen Künstlern, die in den 1720er-Jahren aktiv waren, insbesondere zu Okumura Masanobu.

A young woman sits gracefully on a bench, practicing the *shamisen*. From the music book open on her lap, we know she is playing *Matsu no uchi* ("Among the Pines"), the title referring to the pine boughs that decorate the streets during the first two weeks of the New Year. This song was first performed in 1718 at the Ichimura Theater, a kabuki theater in Edo, and would have been popular at the time of the print's publication. There is a sense of lively movement in the layers and folds of the robe, which is enhanced by the auspicious design of stylized bundles of dried abalone *(noshi awabi)*. The caged bird in the upper right provides an effective counterpoint to the figure, helping to balance the composition and echoing the musical theme. The artist may also have been suggesting a correspondence between the woman, here sitting in front of a barred window, and the bird in its cage: analogies between the courtesans of the Yoshiwara district and caged songbirds can be found in poetry and plays of the period.

The work represents an early stage of printmaking, in which the design and areas of black were printed, while the coloring, in shades of orange and red, was applied by hand. Metallic powder could be added, as here, to embellish the surface further. Until the 1740s, all prints were black-and-white images created from a single block, with the colors added later. The development of multi-block printing, which culminated during the 1760s with full-color, "brocade" prints *(nishiki-e)* made laborious hand-coloring unnecessary. Although this work is not signed, the figure, with her broad face and rounded jaw, the bold patterns on her *kosode,* and the inclusion of a briefly rendered setting relate the style to artists active in the 1720s, particularly Okumura Masanobu.

CAROL MORLAND (CM)

2
Ein Mädchen spielt Shamisen
Girl Playing Shamisen
Anonym/Anonymous

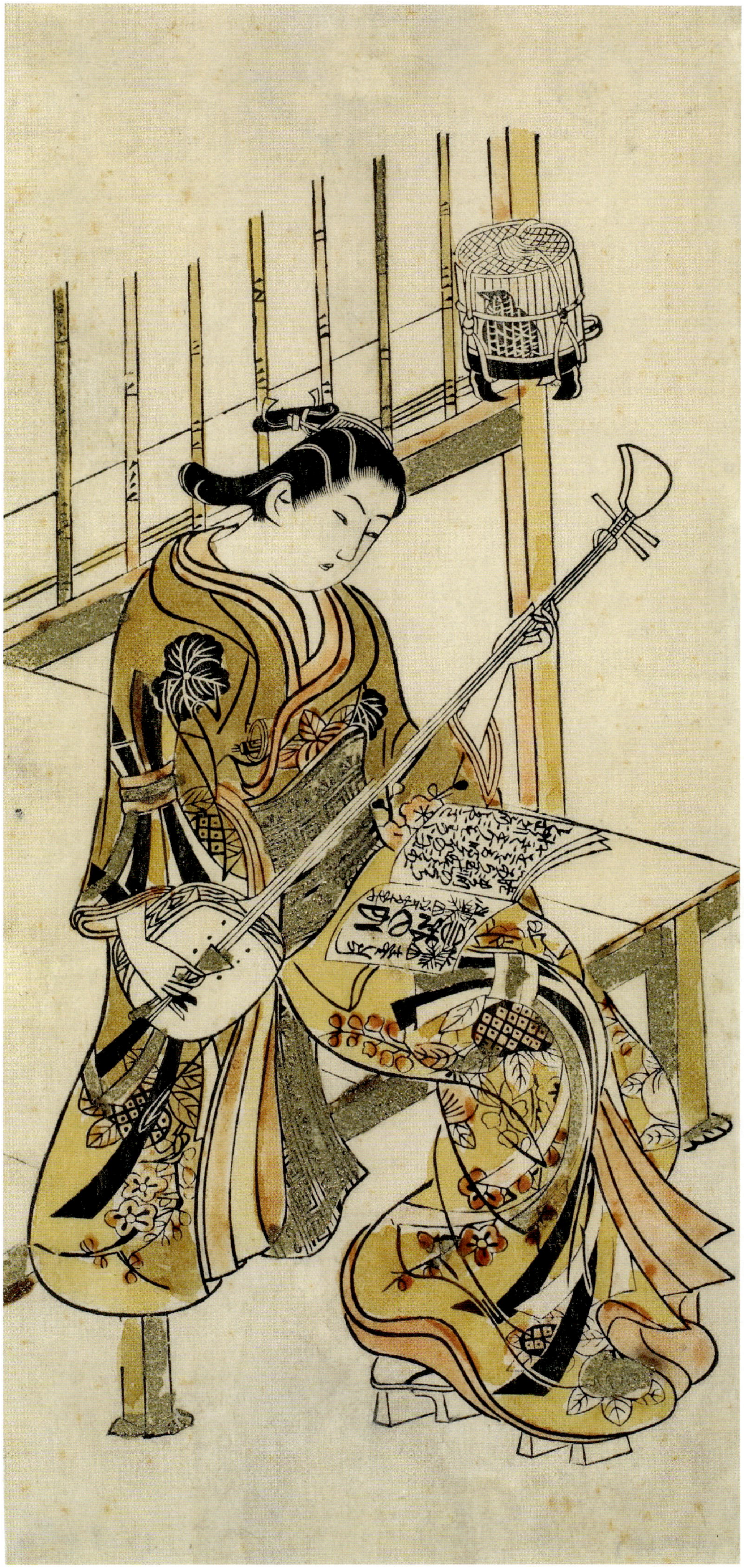

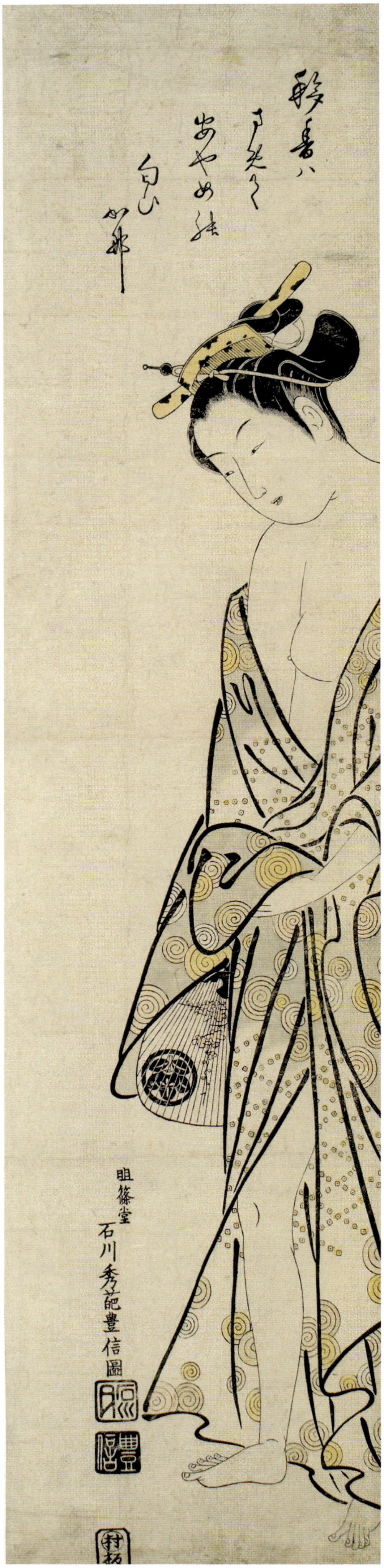

咀篠堂
石川秀葩豊信圖

Sein schwebender Duft
Geht über
*In den Wohlgeruch der Iris.**

His lingering scent
Fades into
*The fragrance of iris.**

Die privaten Momente der Kurtisanen, den Körper nicht für einen Kunden, sondern allein zur Freude des Betrachters zwanglos entblösst, sind ein verbreitetes Thema im *ukiyo-e.* Darstellungen dieser Art erzeugen ein Gefühl von Intimität, das sich von dem genussvollen Anblick einer prachtvoll gekleideten Kurtisane in der Öffentlichkeit stark abhebt. Das schmale Format des *hashira-e* («Pfostenbild») verstärkt das voyeuristische Erlebnis, indem es nur einen Ausschnitt zeigt. Weil Drucke mit offen sexuellen Motiven Anfang der 1720er-Jahre verboten wurden, fanden Werke wie dieses, *abuna-e* («gewagte Drucke») genannt, ein breites Publikum. Die erotische Wirkung wird hier von dem begleitenden Gedicht gesteigert, das die Sehnsucht der Frau nach ihrem Geliebten ausdrückt.

Der Fächer in der Hand der Kurtisane trägt das Wappen eines bekannten Schauspielers von Edo, Ichimura Kamezô I, und bezeugt die engen Bande zwischen den Bewohnerinnen Yoshiwaras und der Welt des *kabuki.*

* Nach einer Übersetzung von Robert Huey.

A courtesan caught in a private moment, her body casually revealed, not for a client, but solely for the delight of the viewer, is a theme found frequently in *ukiyo-e.* Such depictions create a sense of intimacy different from the pleasure of seeing the courtesan splendidly dressed and on public display. The narrow format of the *hashira-e* ("pillar print") heightens the voyeuristic experience by presenting only a partial view. Since overtly sexual prints were banned in the early 1720s, works such as these, called *abuna-e* ("risqué pictures"), found a wide audience. Here, the erotic nature of the image is enhanced by the accompanying poem expressing the woman's longing for her lover.

In the courtesan's hand is a fan with the crest of a popular Edo actor, Ichimura Kamezô I, testament to the close ties between the residents of the Yoshiwara and the world of kabuki.

CM

* Translation by Robert Huey.

石川豊信

3
Schwebender Duft
Lingering Scent
Ishikawa TOYONOBU

4

Beäugen eines eitlen Jünglings

Spying on a Dandy

Okumura MASANOBU

奥村 政信

Obwohl Masanobu auch mit *benizuri-e* (wörtlich «Rotdruck-Bilder») experimentierte, einer frühen Form des Zweifarbendrucks, entstand dieser Druck noch vor der Einführung des Vielfarbendrucks. Die verschiedenen Rot- und Gelbtöne wurden stattdessen sorgfältig von Hand hinzugefügt. Weil der Künstler einen eigenen Verlag betrieb, konnte er den gesamten Produktionsprozess überwachen, was zu der hohen technischen Qualität führte, die in allen Bereichen des Werks sichtbar ist – vom Schneiden des Holzstocks über den Druckvorgang bis zum Kolorieren.

Man nimmt an, dass die Hauptfigur, ein elegant gekleideter junger Mann auf einem Pferd mit aufwendig verziertem Zaum- und Sattelzeug, nach dem Vorbild des bekannten *kabuki*-Schauspielers Sanogawa Ichimatsu I gestaltet wurde. Die Vorstellung von Schönheit war im *ukiyo-e* nicht allein auf die Kurtisanen aus den Freudenvierteln beschränkt oder auf Frauen im Allgemeinen. Denn dass auch Männer wegen ihres Äusseren zu Objekten werden konnten, zeigen die beiden Bewunderinnen, die den Reiter aus einem nahen Fenster heraus beobachten.

Although Masanobu experimented with *benizuri-e* (literally "pink-printed images"), an early technique using two colors, this print was made before the advent of full-color printing, and instead has different shades of red and yellow meticulously added by hand. Since the artist established his own publishing business, he was able to supervise the entire production process, resulting in the high technical quality of all aspects of the present work, from block carving to printing and coloring.

The main subject, an elegantly dressed young man on a horse with elaborately decorated tack, is thought to have been modeled after the popular kabuki actor Sanogawa Ichimatsu I. The concept of beauty was not limited in *ukiyo-e* to courtesans from the pleasure quarters, or to women in general; the two admirers spying upon the man from a nearby window reveal that men also could be objectified for their appearance.

SE

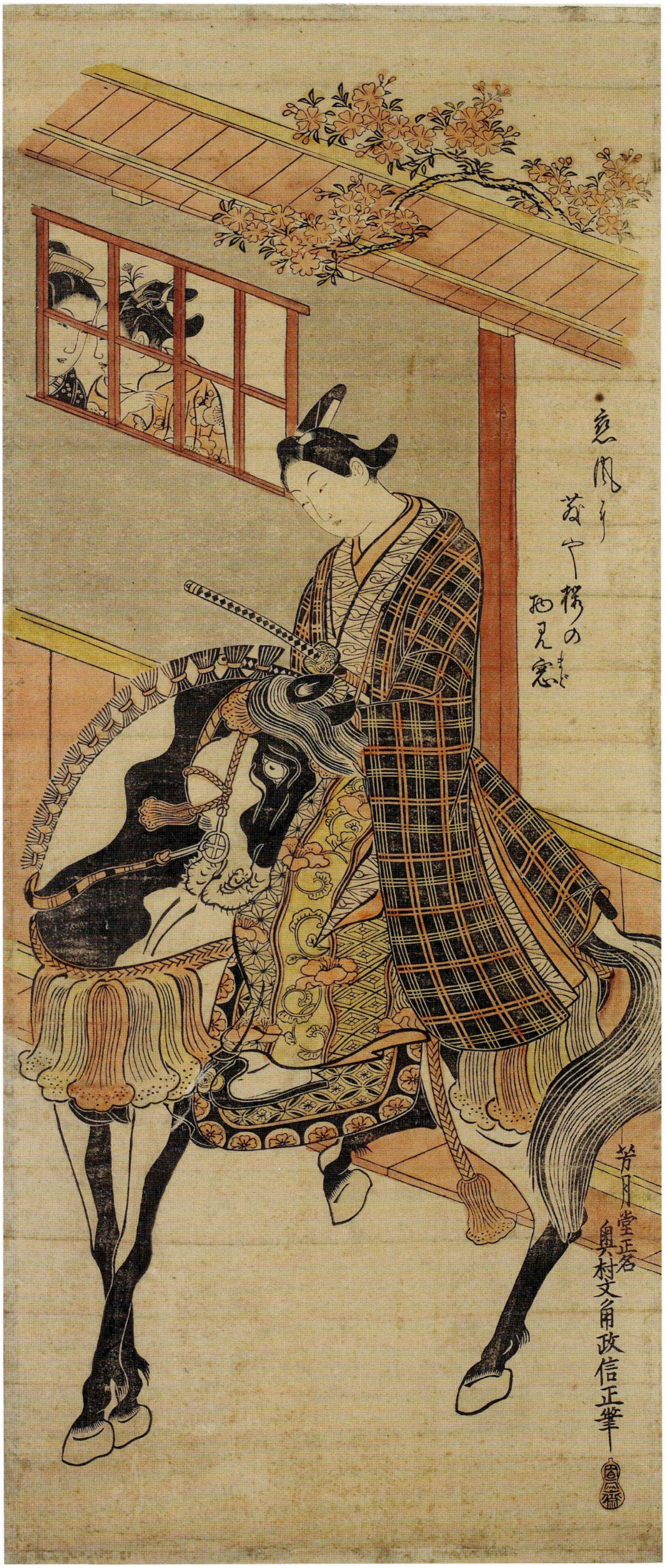
芳月堂正名
奥村文角政信正筆

Im Verlauf seiner langen Karriere stieg Masanobu nicht nur zu einem der führenden *ukiyo-e*-Künstler seiner Zeit auf, sondern experimentierte zugleich mit zahlreichen technischen Neuerungen, darunter dem vertikalen Format, das bei diesen beiden Drucken zu sehen ist (und sich schliesslich zum *hashira-e* oder «Pfostenbild» entwickelte). Sie entstanden wie der Druck *Beäugen eines eitlen Jünglings* (KAT. 4) vor der Einführung des Vielfarbendrucks und wurden daher von Hand zart koloriert.

Obwohl beide Blätter zunächst wie einfache Kurtisanendarstellungen erscheinen, könnte es sich bei *Gehende Kurtisane* um die Kurtisane Agemaki handeln, eine Frauenrolle aus dem bekannten *kabuki*-Theaterstück *Sukeroku,* die von einem männlichen Schauspieler *(onnagata)* verkörpert wurde. Verwirrung entsteht obendrein dadurch, dass von einem anderen Künstler, Toyonobu, zwei weitere Varianten desselben Motivs bekannt sind: eine Kurtisane und eine *onnagata*-Figur. Das *kabuki* wurde zwar von Frauen begründet, die unverhohlene Erotik einiger früher Aufführungen veranlasste die Regierung jedoch 1629, Frauen (und später aus demselben Grund auch junge Männer) von der Bühne zu verbannen. Das hatte zur Folge, dass einige ikonische *ukiyo-e*-Porträts schöner Frauen faktisch vermutlich Männer in weiblichen *kabuki*-Rollen darstellen.

Over the course of his long career, Masanobu not only became one of the leading *ukiyo-e* artists of his time, but also experimented with a number of technical innovations, including the vertical format seen in these two prints (eventually developing into *hashira-e,* or "pillar prints"). Like *Spying on a Dandy* (CAT. 4), they were made before the advent of full-color printing, and instead are delicately hand-colored.

Although both prints at first glance appear to be straightforward depictions of courtesans, it has been proposed that *Courtesan Walking* might in fact be the courtesan Agemaki from the popular kabuki play *Sukeroku,* a female role that would have been portrayed by a male actor *(onnagata)*. The issue is further confused by the fact that two variations on the same design exist by another artist, Toyonobu, one of which is of a courtesan, while the other portrays an *onnagata* role. Although kabuki was started by women, the overt eroticism of some early performances caused the government to ban female actors in 1629 (and later to ban young boys for the same reason). As a result, some iconic *ukiyo-e* images of beauties in fact are likely to depict men performing female kabuki roles.

SE

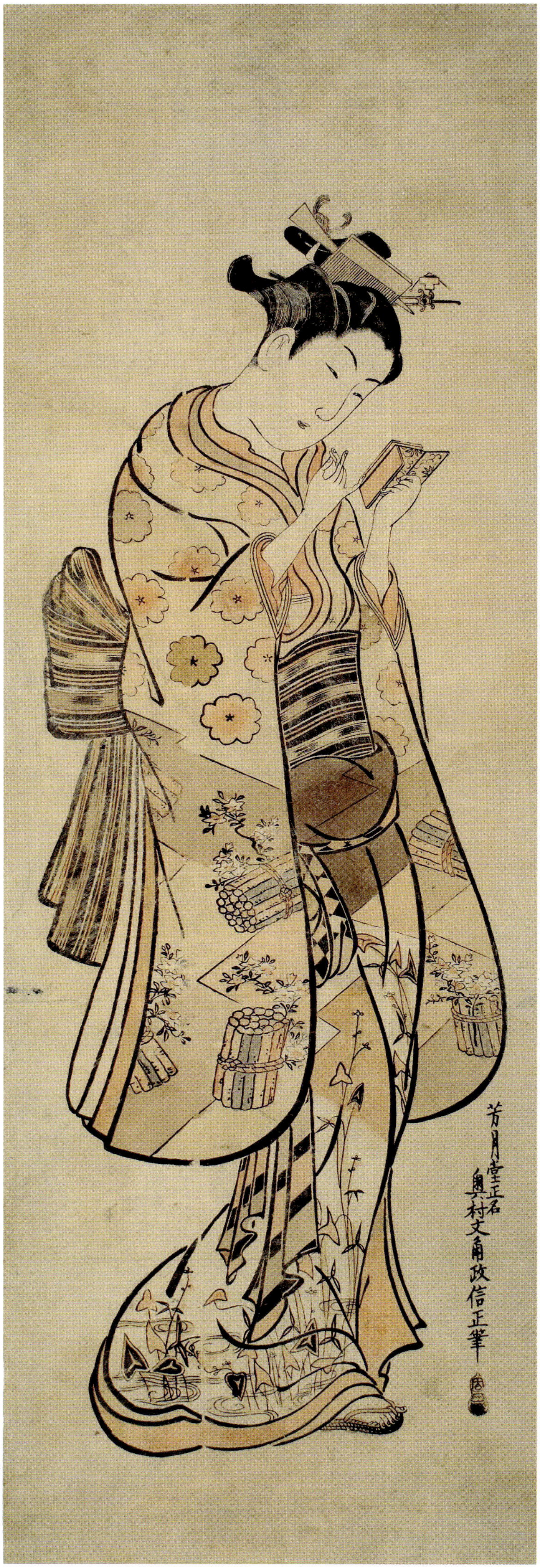

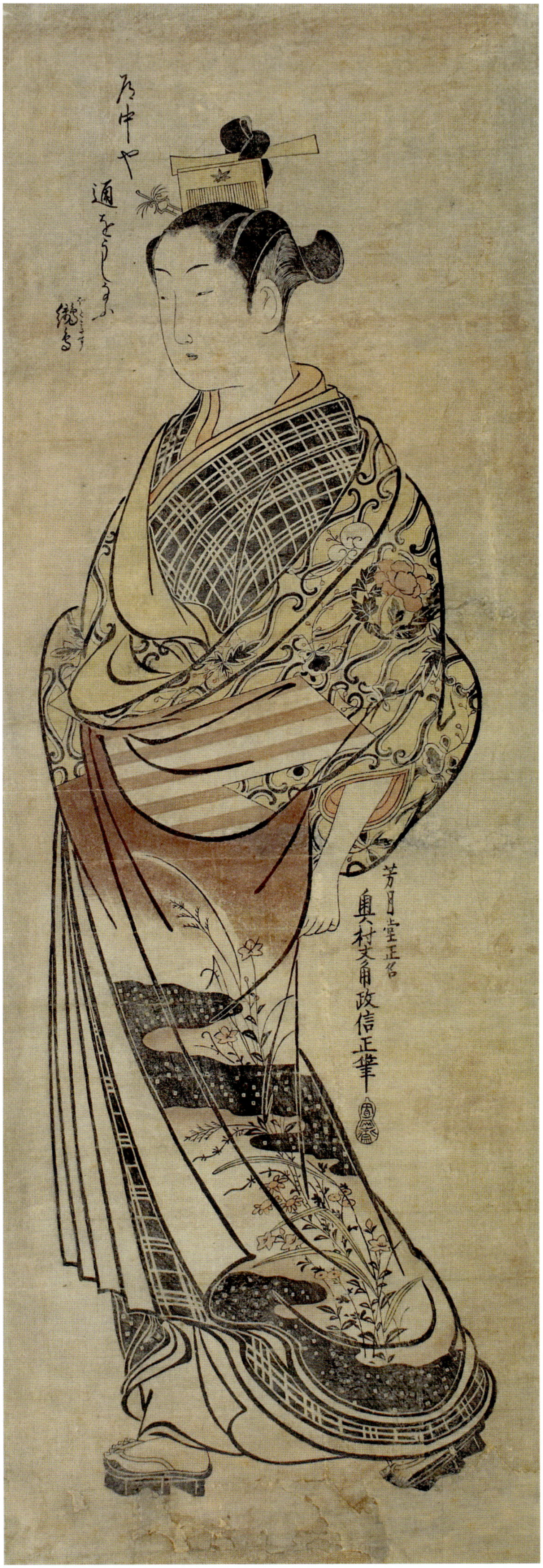

6

奥村 政信

5
Schöne Frau mit einem Spiegel
Beauty with a Mirror
Okumura MASANOBU

奥村 政信

6
Gehende Kurtisane
Courtesan Walking
Okumura MASANOBU

Sie verbarg ihre Liebe
Doch gab ihr Gesicht diese preis
Als sie den Kuckuck hörte.

She hid her love
But it showed on her face
When she heard the cuckoo.

石川豊信

7
Mädchen mit Schirm
Girl with Umbrella
Ishikawa TOYONOBU

石川豊信

8
Mädchen mit Schirm
Girl with Umbrella
Ishikawa TOYONOBU

Die beiden Frauen auf diesen *hashira-e* («Pfostenbildern») sind charakteristisch für Toyonobus Schönheitsideal: Eine eindrucksvolle körperliche Präsenz wird durch ein zartes Muster und eine dezente, vornehme Pose abgemildert. Der Regenmantel mit Kragen *(sode gappa)* ist eine Abwandlung des europäischen Mantels, den portugiesische Missionare und Kaufleute im späten 16. Jahrhundert nach Japan brachten; das Weinrankenmuster des Mantels rechts ist kontinentalen Ursprungs. Der Aussenhandel belebte auch das Schildpatt-Handwerk neu, was in den schmuckvollen Haarkämmen zu erkennen ist. Das Gedicht oberhalb der Figur mit dem aufgespannten Schirm beschreibt ihre Reaktion auf eine Nachricht von ihrem Geliebten.

Mit ihrem schmalen Hochformat animierten *hashira-e* zu grossen, auffälligen Motiven mit dramatischen Umrahmungen. Die hier gezeigten Beispiele entstanden vor der Einführung des Vielfarbendrucks: Ihre Konturlinien und die schwarzen Bereiche wurden gedruckt, die unterschiedlichen Gelbtöne sorgfältig mit der Hand aufgetragen. Obwohl nicht als Paar veröffentlicht, bilden die Blätter in der Zusammenschau ein wirkungsvolles Arrangement.

The two women in these *hashira-e,* or "pillar prints," are characteristic of Toyonobu's ideal of beauty, in which an imposing physical presence is softened by a delicate pattern and a gentle, refined pose. The collared raincoat *(sode gappa)* is a modified version of the European coat brought to Japan by Portuguese missionaries and traders in the late sixteenth century; the grapevine pattern of the coat on the right is of continental origin. Foreign trade also revived the tortoise shell craft, and we see that material used in the decorative hair combs. Above the figure with the open umbrella is a poem describing her reaction on receiving a message from her lover.

Hashira-e, with their narrow vertical format, encouraged large, bold designs that were dramatically framed. These examples were produced before the introduction of full-color printing, and while the lines and areas of black have been printed, the shades of yellow have been meticulously applied by hand. Although not published as a pair, the two form an effective composition when viewed together.

CM

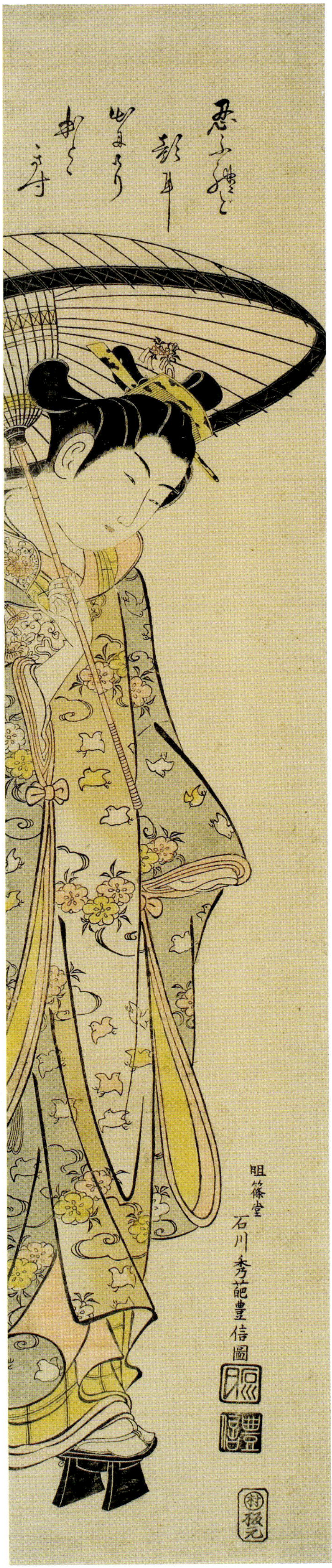

7

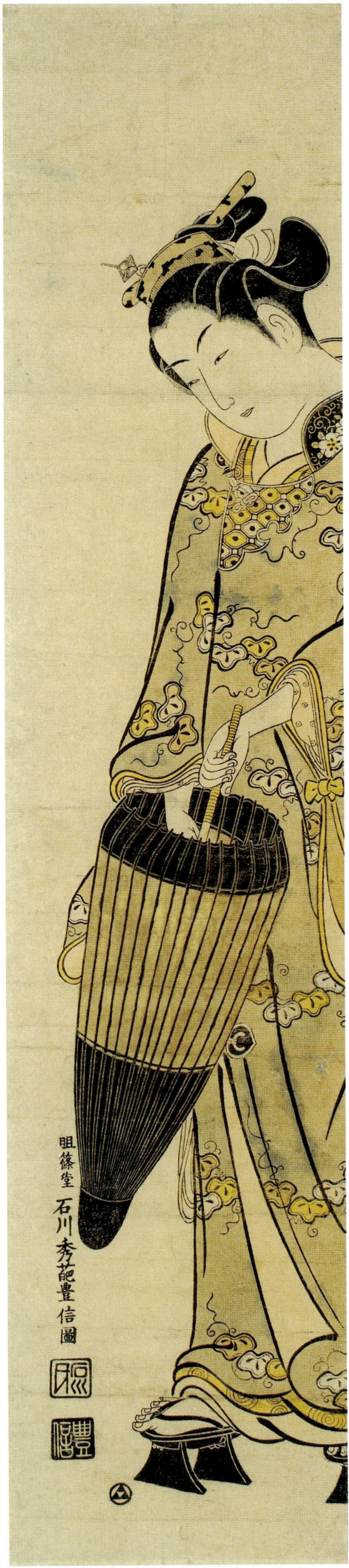

8

礒田 湖龍斎

9
Schnee am Abend
in Yamashita –
Acht Ansichten von
Edos Freudenvierteln
Evening Snow at Yamashita
– The Eight Views of
Edo's Pleasure Quarters
Isoda KORYÛSAI

鈴木 春信

10
Nakatsukasa –
Die Sechsunddreissig
Unsterblichen
der Dichtkunst
Nakatsukasa –
Thirty-six Immortal Poets
Suzuki HARUNOBU

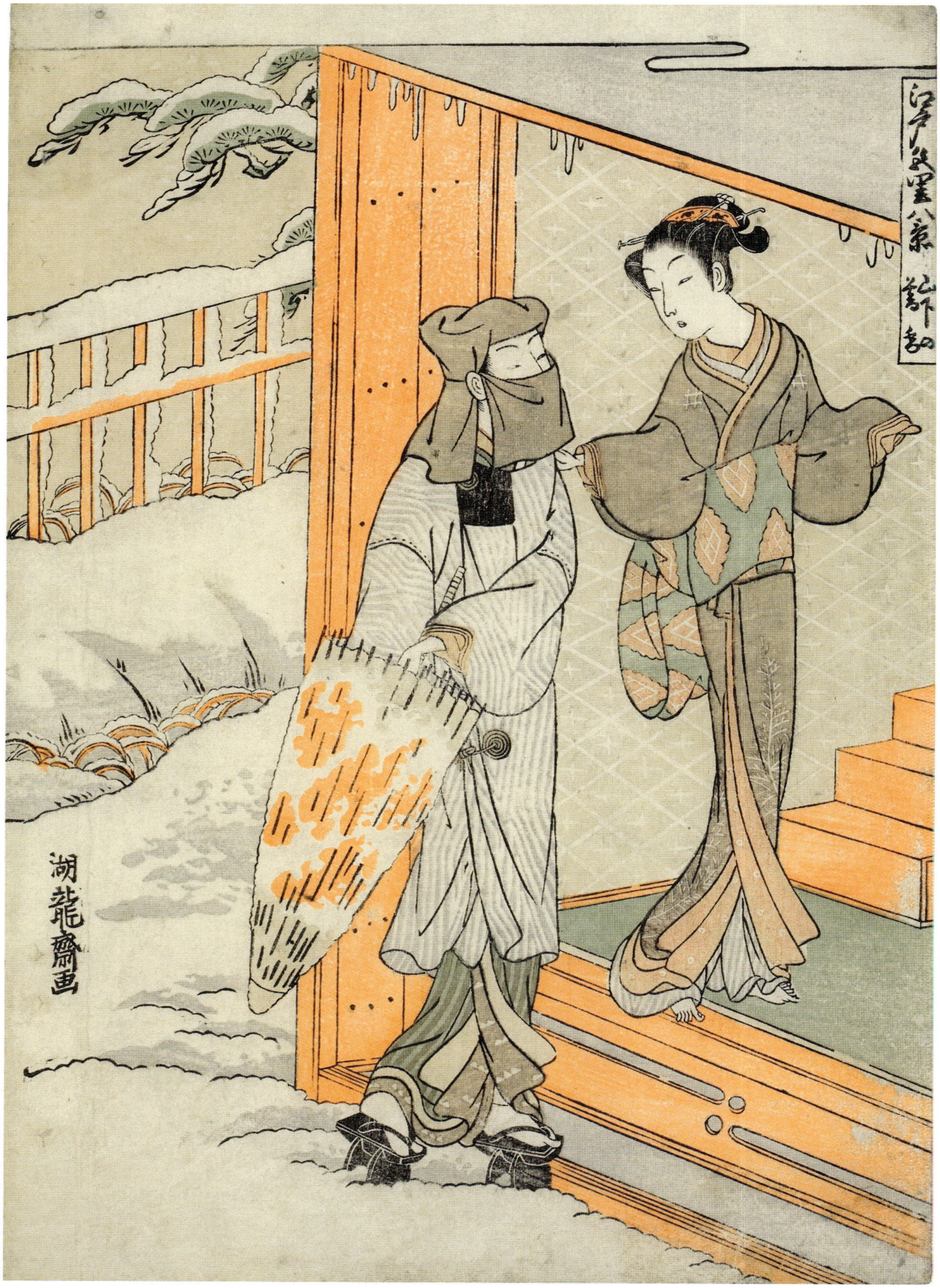

9

Der Herbstwind hat zu wehen begonnen
Und noch immer kommst du nicht.
Selbst der Buschklee klopft schon an!

The autumn wind has begun to blow
And still you do not come.
Even the bush clover is knocking!

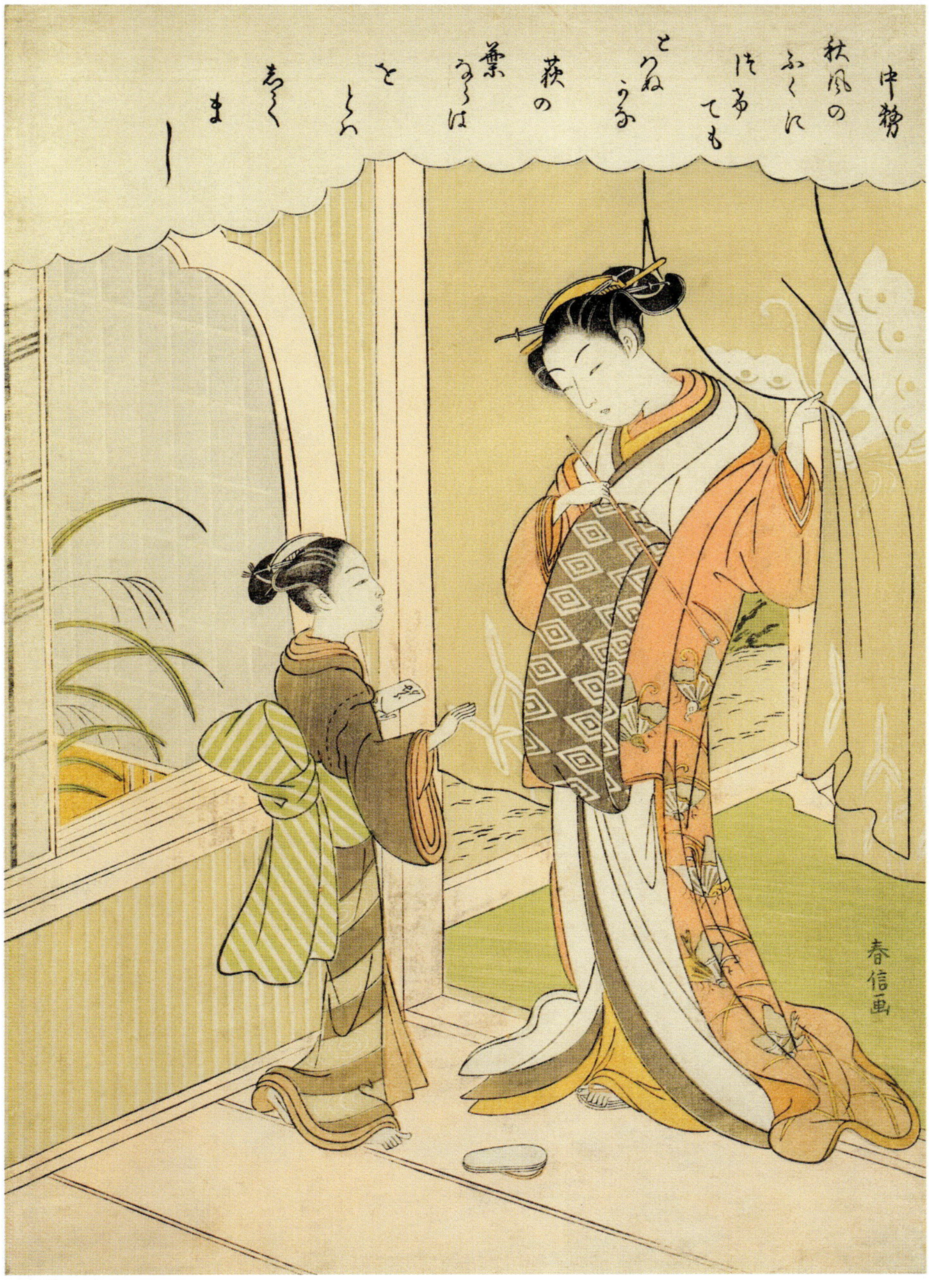

Das Spiel mit klassischen Themen, die im Umfeld der Freudenviertel nachempfunden wurden, gehörte zu den beliebtesten Sujets des *ukiyo-e.* Hier sehen wir zwei dieser *mitate-e* («Bilder mit Parodien»): die als Kurtisane wiedergeborene *waka*-Dichterin Nakatsukasa aus dem 10. Jahrhundert (KAT. 10) und die *Acht Ansichten* (KAT. 9), ursprünglich Szenen mit malerischen Landschaften in China, die respektlos in die Bordellviertel von Edo verlegt wurden. In Harunobus Entwurf ist Nakatsukasa an die Tür geeilt, um von einer *kamuro* (kindliches Lehrmädchen) den Brief eines Kunden entgegenzunehmen. Nakatsukasas Originalgedicht wurde durch leichte Abwandlungen zu einer Klage über die im Brief formulierte Absage verfremdet.

Im Druck von Koryûsai ist der Kunde beharrlicher und tritt trotz des schlechten Wetters seinen Besuch an. Eine verschneite Landschaft gehörte zu den traditionellen Bestandteilen der *Acht Ansichten* in Japan und China. Hier sehen wir eine Kurtisane, die im unlizenzierten Rotlichtviertel Yamashita (in Ueno) ihren Liebhaber herzlich empfängt. Seine hohen *geta* (Holzsandalen), der schneebedeckte Schirm und der Gesichtsschutz unterstreichen die Beschwerlichkeit seiner Reise. Koryûsai war ein enger Anhänger Harunobus. In seinen Arbeiten aus dieser Zeit kommen die zarten, mädchenhaften Schönheiten dem von Harunobu perfektionierten Ideal sehr nahe.

Playing with classical themes by recreating them in the context of the pleasure quarters was a favorite subject in *ukiyo-e.* Here we see two such *mitate-e* (parody pictures): the tenth-century *waka* poet Nakatsukasa reborn as a courtesan (CAT. 10), and the "Eight Views" (CAT. 9), originally of scenic spots in China, applied irreverently to the brothel districts of Edo. In the print by Harunobu, Nakatsukasa has rushed out to greet a *kamuro* (child trainee), who is bringing a letter from a client. Nakatsukasa's original poem has been changed slightly to render it a lament over the customer's failure to visit.

The client in the print by Koryûsai is more persistent, coming to visit despite the inclement weather. A landscape in snow was included in the traditional Chinese and Japanese versions of the Eight Views theme. Here, we see a courtesan from the unlicensed red-light district of Yamashita (in Ueno) warmly welcoming her lover, whose high *geta,* snow-covered umbrella, and face-protector emphasize the difficulty of his journey. Koryûsai was a close disciple of Harunobu, and, in the work of this time, his delicate, child-like beauties are very close to the ideal perfected by Harunobu.

CM

Beim Durchsehen des Führers
«Sie ist es!»
Ruft die Hausfrau.

Looking through the guidebook
"It's her!"
Cries the housewife.

Die Bezeichnung *bijin* («Schönheit») war nicht auf die Kurtisanen in den Freudenvierteln beschränkt, sondern wurde auch für Hausfrauen und junge Männer verwendet. Harunobus Entwurf zeigt zwei männliche Prostituierte im Kerzenschein beim Betrachten von Holzschnittbüchern (KAT. 12). Ihr schmaler Körperbau und die feinen Gesichtszüge lassen ihr Geschlecht kaum bestimmen, doch die Quasten am *obi* (Gürtel) identifizieren sie als junge Männer. Harunobu hat seine Signatur so geschickt platziert, dass sie die Inschrift eines Gemäldes auf der Schiebetür bildet, einer Flusslandschaft im Schnee.

In Kiyonagas Druck blättert eine Ehefrau in einem Bordellführer von Yoshiwara (KAT. 11). Sie sucht den Namen der Kurtisane, mit der ihr Mann ein Verhältnis hat. Das Gedicht am oberen Rand der Szene beschreibt den Moment, in dem sie fündig wird.

Die Entwicklung der verschiedenen Schönheitsideale wird hier deutlich: Die mädchenhaften Figuren in Harunobus Werk sind den grösseren und kräftigeren Frauengestalten gewichen, die Kiyonagas Drucke bevölkern. Wie alle *ukiyo-e*-Künstler seiner Generation steht jedoch auch Kiyonaga in Harunobus Schuld – wegen dessen Beiträgen zum Vielfarbendruck sowie der innovativen Kompositionen und Themenkreise.

The term *bijin* was not limited to courtesans of the pleasure quarters, but could refer to housewives and young men as well. In Harunobu's design, two male prostitutes sit looking at woodblock books by candlelight (CAT. 12). Their slight physiques and delicate features make their sex difficult to determine, but their tasseled *obi* identify them as young men. Harunobu has cleverly placed his signature as if it were the inscription on the sliding-door painting of a river scene in snow.

In Kiyonaga's print, a wife leafs through a guidebook to the Yoshiwara brothels, looking for the name of the courtesan with whom her husband is involved (CAT. 11). The poem above describes the moment of discovery.

The evolution in different ideals of beauty is evident here: the child-like figures in Harunobu's work have given way to the taller, more robust women that populate Kiyonaga's prints. Like all *ukiyo-e* artists of his generation, however, Kiyonaga is indebted to Harunobu for his contributions to full-color printing and his innovative composition and themes.

CM

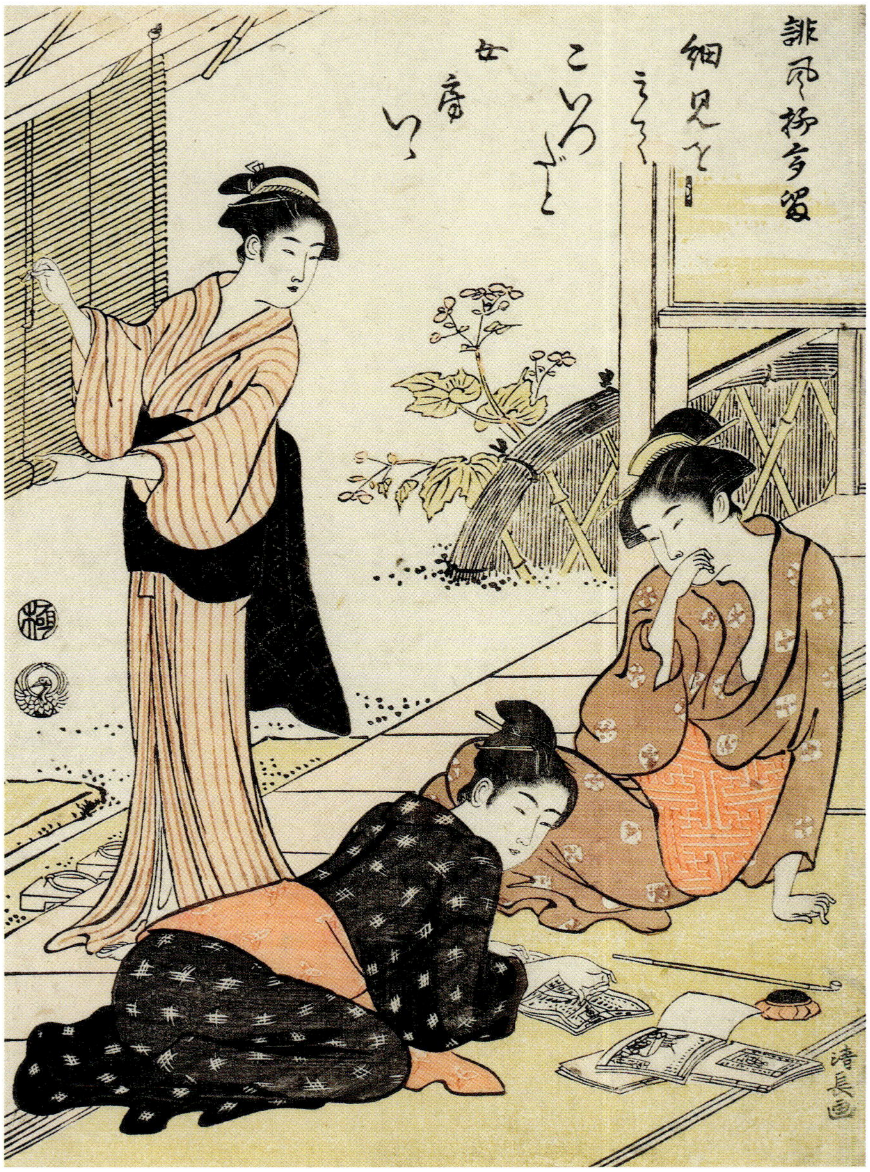

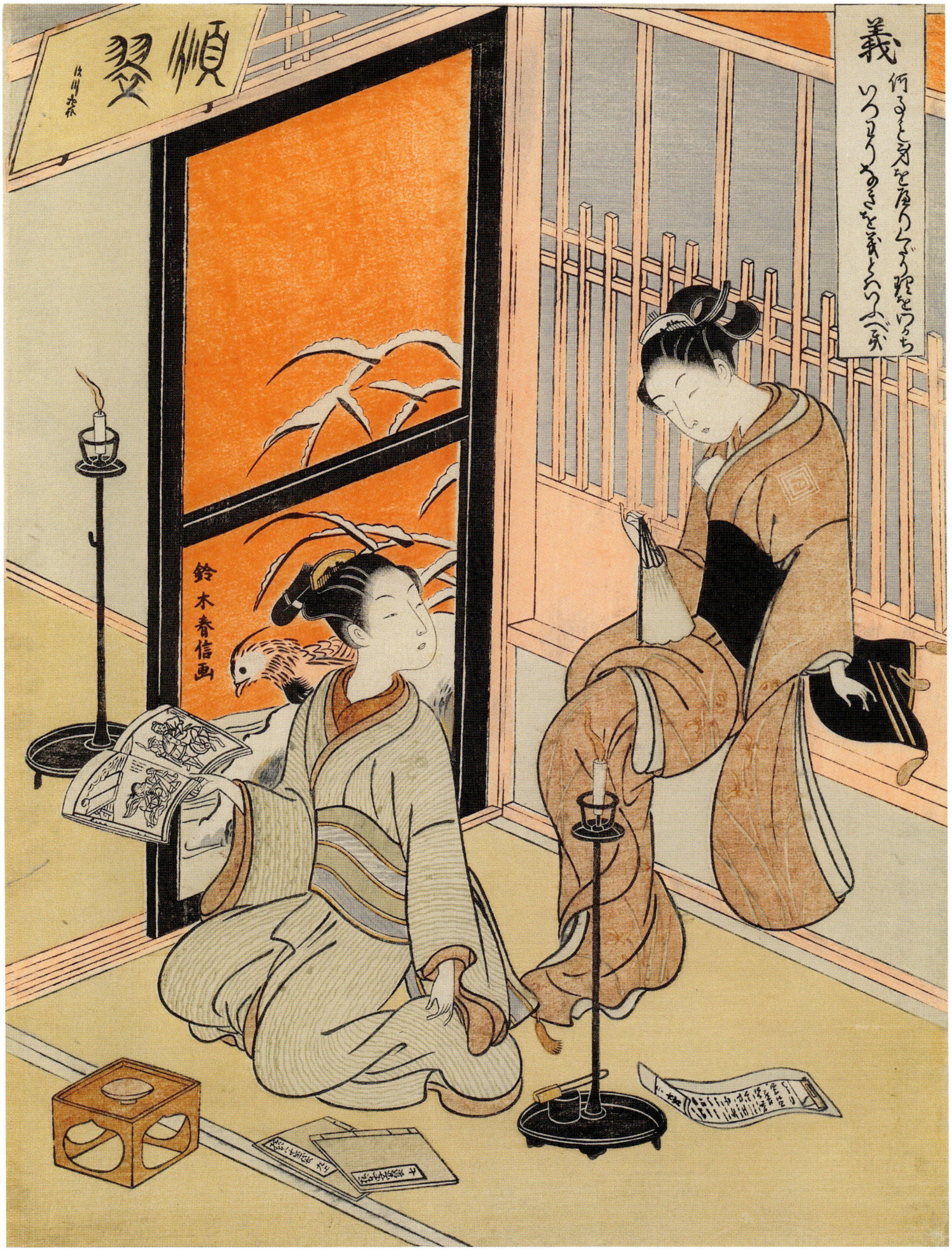

12

鳥居清長

11

Entdeckung des Namens der heimlichen Geliebten – Eine Sammlung humorvoller Gedichte

Discovering the Address of a Husband's Sweetheart – A Collection of Humorous Poems

Torii KIYONAGA

鈴木春信

12

Aufrichtigkeit und Gerechtigkeit – Die fünf Kardinaltugenden

Righteousness – The Five Cardinal Virtues

Suzuki HARUNOBU

In Kasamori lässt der Regen nach,
im Sommerschatten steht Osen.

At Kasamori the rain ceases,
Osen stands in the summer shade.

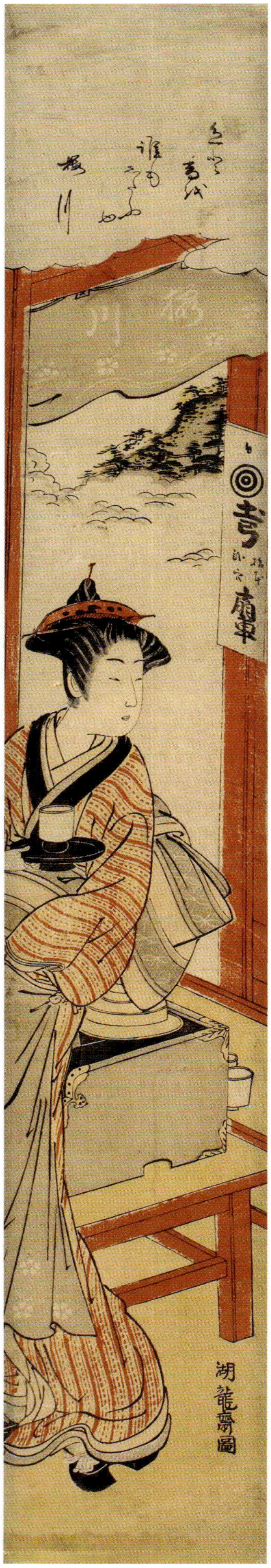

13

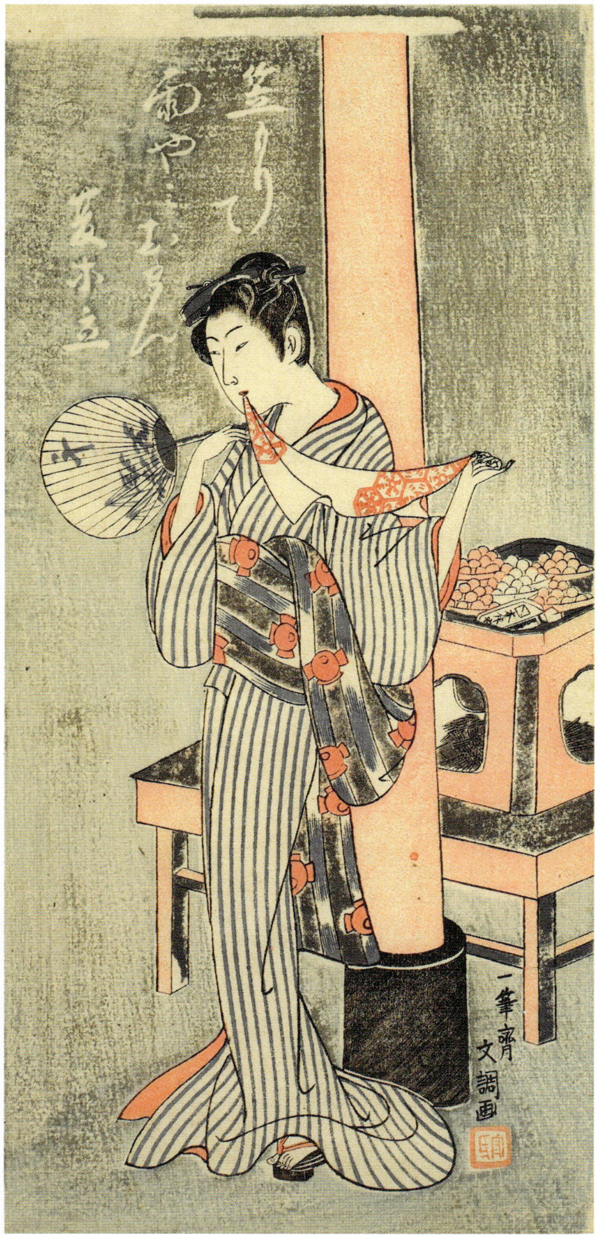

14

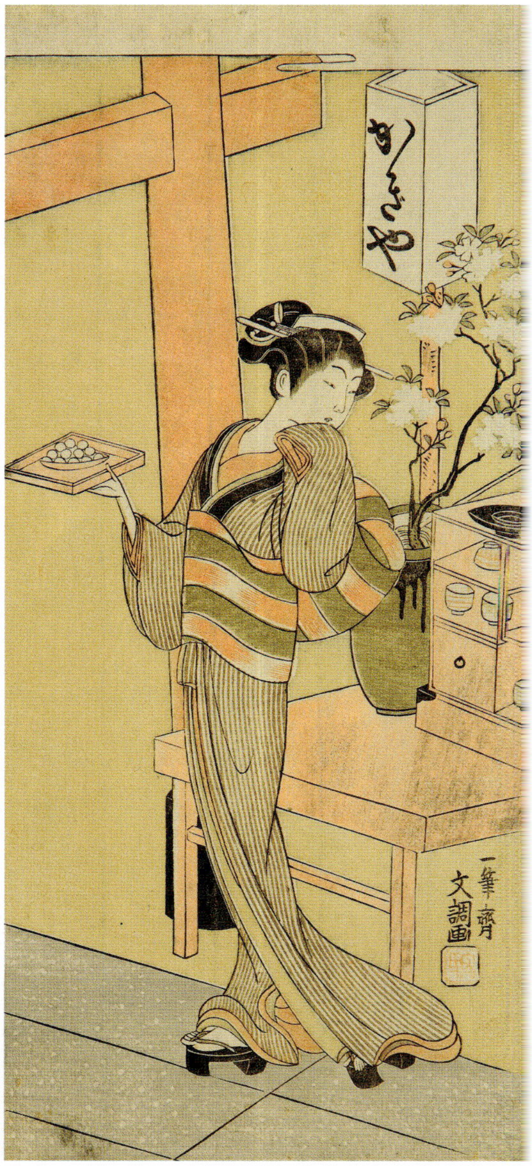

15

In den 1760er-Jahren wurde der Vielfarbendruck entwickelt. Einer der wichtigsten Wegbereiter der sogenannten «Brokatbilder» *(nishiki-e)* war Harunobu, der auch ein neues Schönheitskonzept durchsetzte. Von ihm betonte Eigenschaften wie zurückhaltende Emotionalität, zierliche Jugendlichkeit und zarte Gesichtszüge unterschieden sich dramatisch von der Dynamik eines Masanobu oder der Majestätik der Kaigetsudô-Schule im früheren 18. Jahrhundert. Sein stilistischer Einfluss reichte lange über seinen Tod hinaus, wie in Bunchôs *Osen aus dem Kagiya-Teehaus* zu erkennen ist.

Die Kurtisanen aus den Freudenvierteln waren nicht die einzigen, die von den *ukiyo-e*-Künstlern unsterblich gemacht wurden. Als Modelle für diese vier Drucke wählten Harunobu, Koryûsai und Bunchô einfache Teehausmädchen aus, die in ihren jeweiligen Etablissements die Hauptattraktion darstellten. Tatsächlich bleibt die Identität der Tee-Serviererinnen in Harunobus Werk und einem der Bunchô-Drucke unklar, während Osode und Osen mit den Teehäusern gleichzusetzen waren, in denen sie arbeiteten. In Koryûsais Druck verweist allein der Name des Teehauses auf die Identität der Bedienung; ihr Name selbst geriet in Vergessenheit, nur ihre Schönheit hat im Werk des Künstlers überlebt.

In Bunchôs zweiter Darstellung von Osen identifiziert er sie mithilfe des begleitenden Gedichts.

The 1760s saw the development of full-color, or "brocade," printing *(nishiki-e)*, of which Harunobu was one of the key innovators. Harunobu further introduced a new concept of beauty emphasizing restrained lyricism, fragile youthfulness, and delicate features, which was dramatically different from the dynamism of Masanobu or the stateliness of the Kaigetsudô School earlier in the eighteenth century. His style remained influential into the decade after his death, as can be seen in Bunchô's *Osen of the Kagiya Teahouse.*

The courtesans of the pleasure quarters were not the only women immortalized by *ukiyo-e* artists; Harunobu, Koryûsai, and Bunchô all have taken as their subjects in these prints humble waitresses, who were the main attractions for their respective establishments. Indeed, the waitresses of Harunobu's print and one of Bunchô's are not identified, but both Osode and Osen were synonymous with their teahouses. The waitress in Koryûsai's print is similarly indicated only by her teahouse, but unfortunately her name has been lost to history, and only her beauty still survives through the artist's work.

In Bunchô's other depiction of Osen, she is identified in the poem accompanying the print.

SE

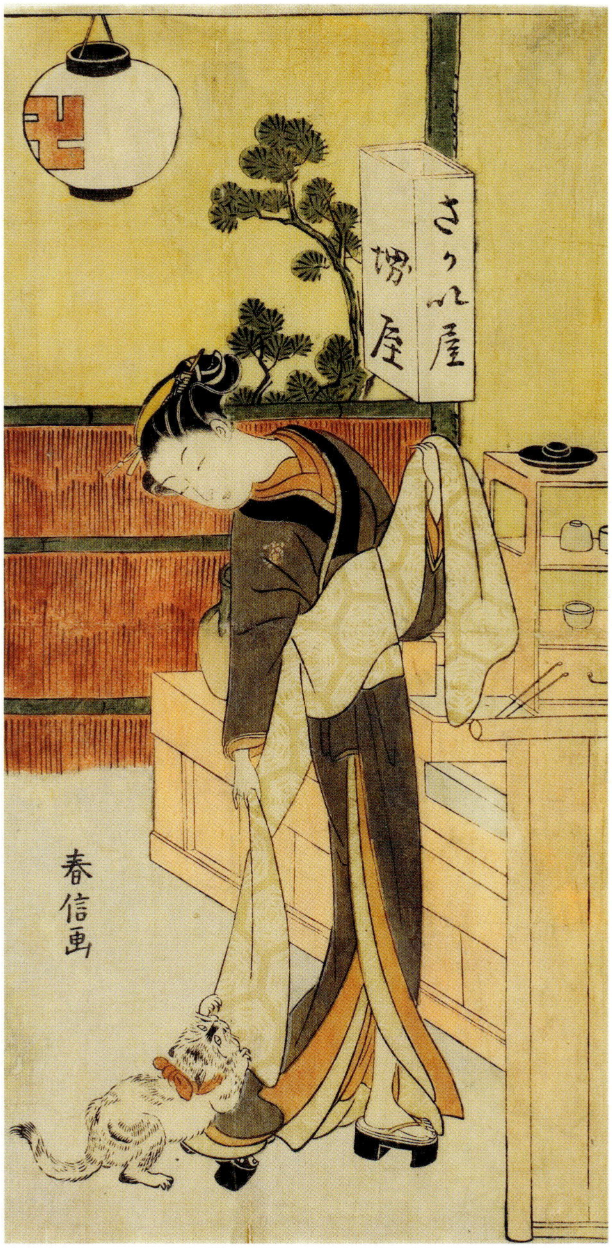

16

礒田湖龍斎
13
Das Sakuragawa-Teehaus
The Sakuragawa Teahouse
Isoda KORYÛSAI

一筆斎文調
14
Osen des Kasamori-Schreins
Osen of Kasamori Shrine
Ippitsusai BUNCHÔ

一筆斎文調
15
Osen aus dem Kagiya-Teehaus
Osen of the Kagiya Teahouse
Ippitsusai BUNCHÔ

鈴木春信
16
Osode aus dem Sakaiya-Teehaus
Osode of the Sakaiya Teahouse
Suzuki HARUNOBU

Historisch galten Holzschnitte bisweilen eher als Ausdruck der Populärkultur denn als Kunstform. Bis heute haften ihnen hartnäckige Vorurteile an. Dessen ungeachtet liessen sich viele *ukiyo-e*-Entwerfer von der klassischen Dichtkunst inspirieren, deren lyrische Empfindungen besonders gut zu Harunobus neuem Stil passten. In zweien dieser Drucke illustriert der Künstler Verse der altjapanischen Schriftsteller Minamoto no Saneakira (910–970) und Fujiwara no Toshiyuki (gest. 901 oder 907), die den «Sechsunddreissig Unsterblichen der Dichtkunst» *(Sanjû rokkasen)* angehörten.

Harunobu interpretierte beide Gedichte als Ausdruck unerwiderter Liebe. Die jungen Frauen, allein in ihren Kammern, blicken gedankenvoll in die Aussenwelt hinaus, während sie ihren Gefühlsschmerz auf die vergehende Zeit projizieren.

Historically, woodblock prints sometimes have been understood more as an expression of popular culture than as an art form, and they are still affected by lingering prejudice. However, *ukiyo-e* designers often were inspired by classical poetry, the lyrical sentiments of which were particularly suitable to Harunobu's new style. In two of these prints, the artist illustrates verses by the ancient writers Minamoto no Saneakira (910–970) and Fujiwara no Toshiyuki (d. 901 or 907), both members of the famous "Thirty-six Immortal Poets" *(Sanjû rokkasen)*.

Both poems have been interpreted by Harunobu as expressions of unrequited love, with young women isolated in their chambers, looking pensively beyond into the outside world as they project their emotional distress onto the passage of time.

SE

鈴木春信

17
Zwei Schönheiten am Flussufer
Two Beauties by the Water's Edge
Suzuki HARUNOBU

鈴木春信

18
«Herbstmond», Minister Minamoto no Saneakira
"Harvest Moon," Minister Minamoto no Saneakira
Suzuki HARUNOBU

鈴木春信

19
«Herbstwind», nach einem Gedicht von Fujiwara no Toshiyuki
"Autumn Wind," after the poem by Fujiwara no Toshiyuki
Suzuki HARUNOBU

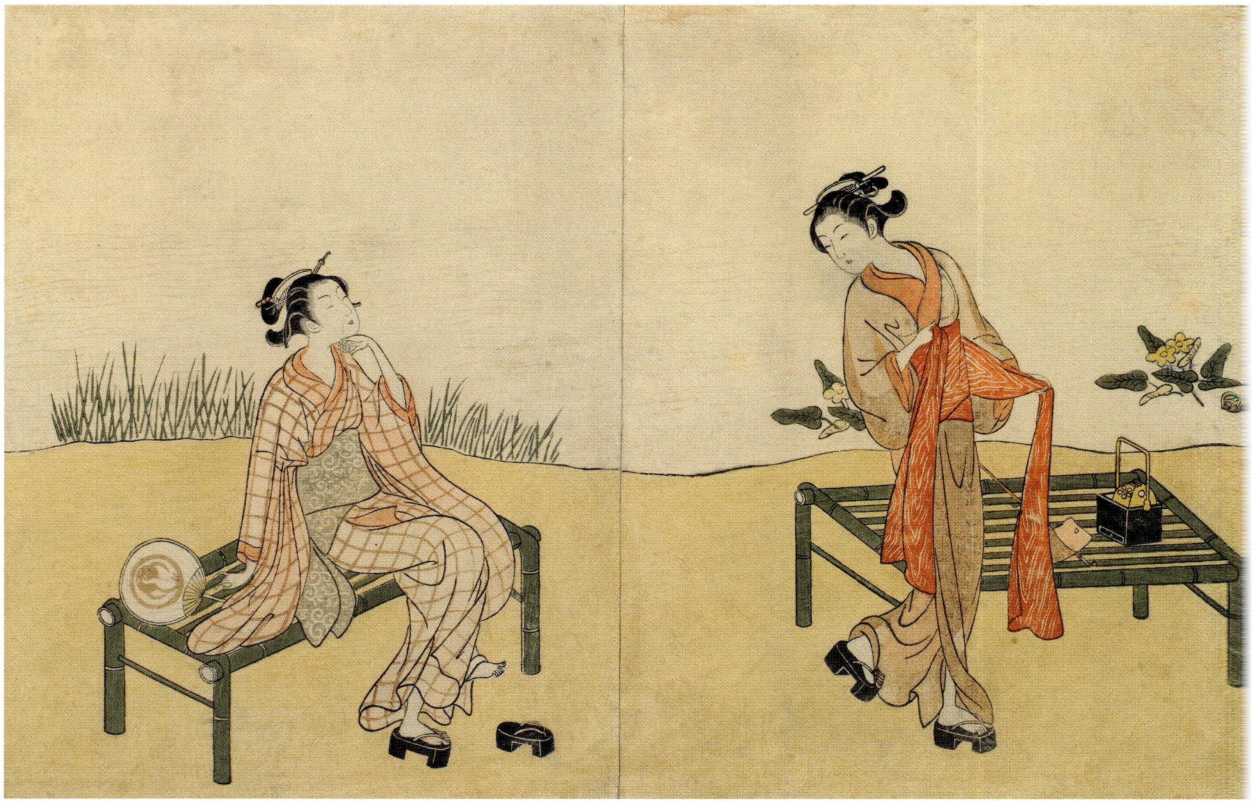

17

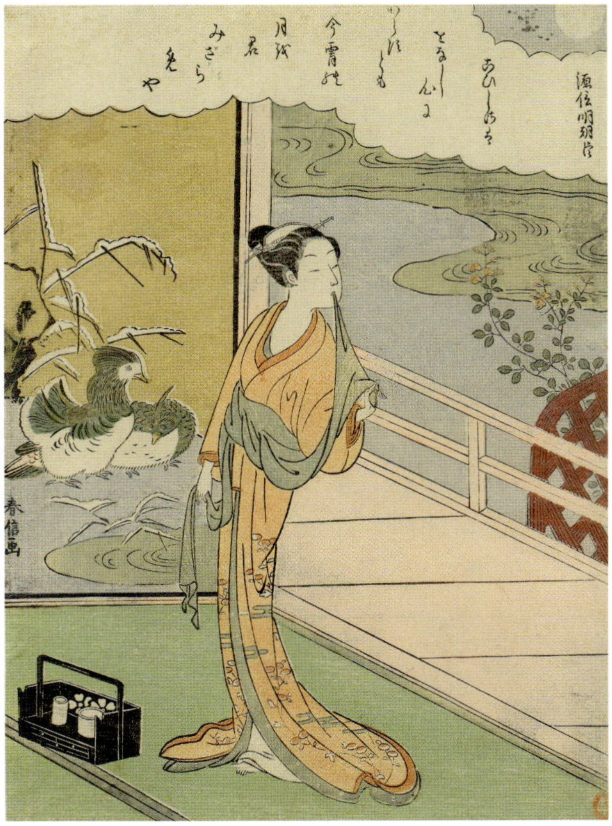

18

Was für eine Verschwendung,
dieser Mond und diese Blüten,
in solch einer Nacht;
wenn ich sie nur mit jemandem teilen könnte,
der sie so schätzt wie ich.

What a waste, this moon and these blossoms,
on such a night;
if only I could share them with one
who appreciates them as I do.

Nichts sprach allzu deutlich zu meinen Augen,
dass der Herbst gekommen war,
aber der Klang des Herbstwindes
schreckte mich auf.

Nothing said too clearly to my eyes
that fall had come,
yet I was startled by the sound of autumn's wind.

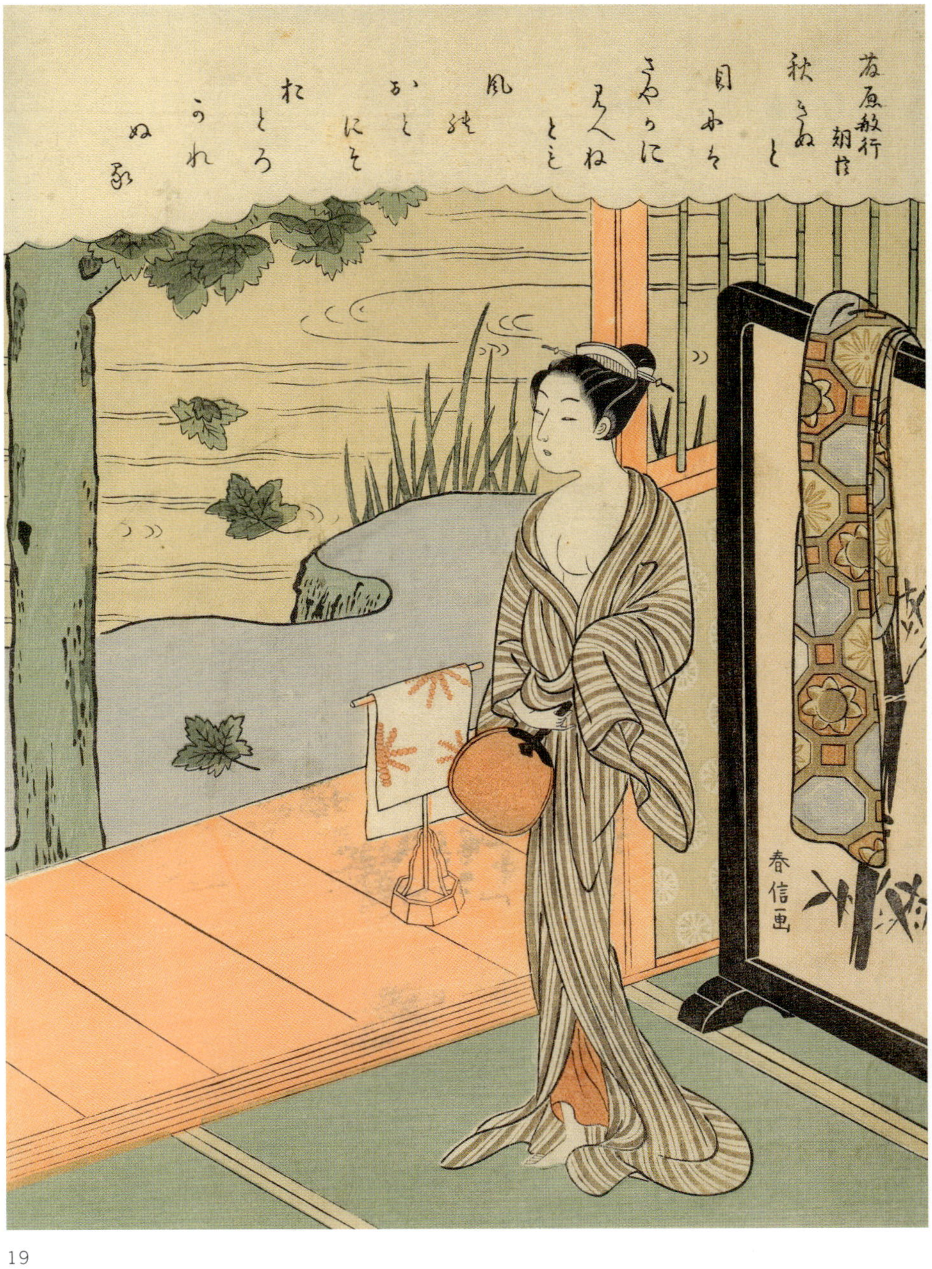

19

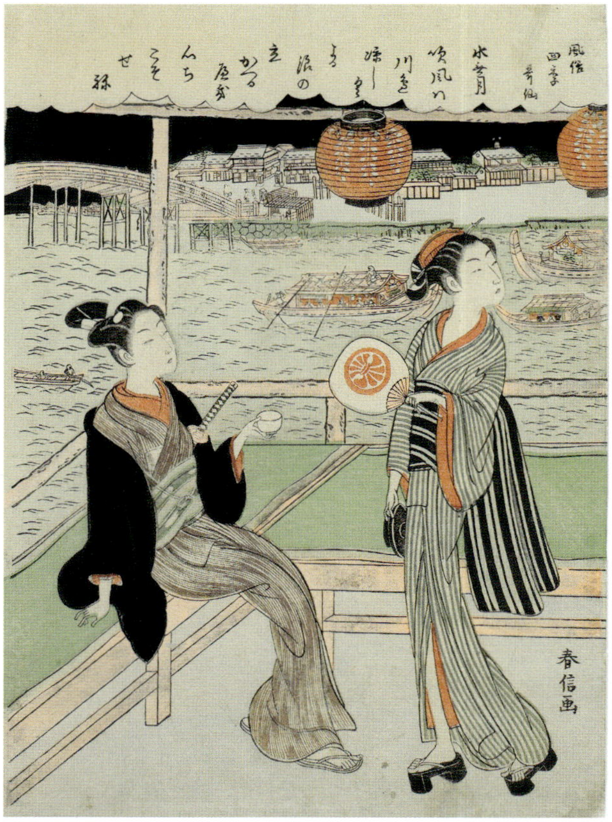

21

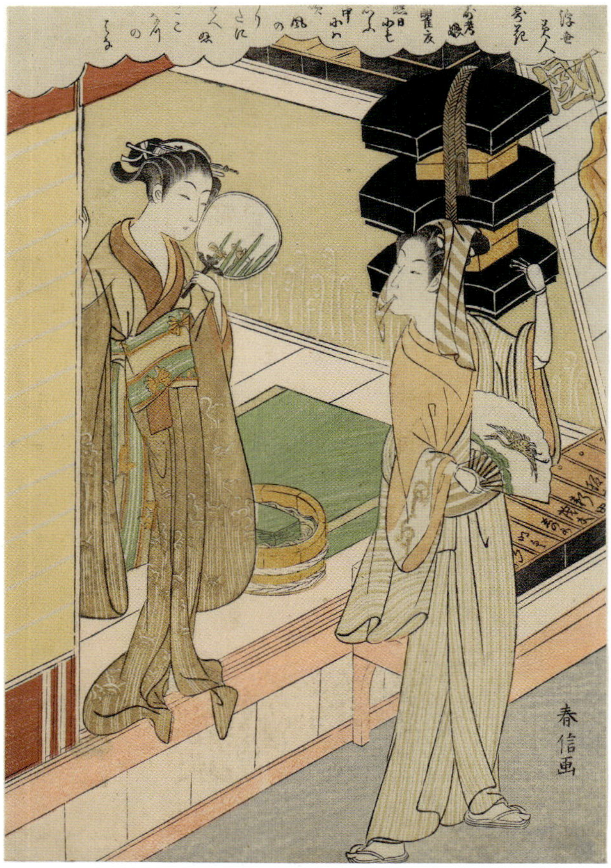

20

Der Wind bläst frisch über das Flussufer,
Auch ich sollte
Mit den dahinströmenden Wellen gehen;
Aber ach, es ist so wunderschön!

The wind blows cooling the riverside,
I too should leave with the rebounding waves;
Ah, but it is so very pleasant!

Jahreszeitliche Assoziationen haben in der japanischen Kunst von jeher eine grosse Rolle gespielt und sollten dem *ukiyo-e* zusätzliche Bedeutung verleihen. In *Zweiter Monat* symbolisiert der Frühling die junge Liebe. Vom Baum im Garten eines Schreins pflückt der Verehrer heimlich Pflaumenblüten für seine Geliebte, die mit ihrem Ärmel die Laterne verdunkelt, damit er nicht entdeckt wird. *Sechster Monat* zeigt das sommerliche Abbild eines Paares in der vollen Blüte seiner Liebe; zugleich kündet das Gedicht von bevorstehenden Veränderungen.

Die Bildsprache von *Zehnter Monat* ist subtiler. Eine Frau beobachtet den Mann auf der Veranda beim Lesen eines Briefes, in dem sie ihm vermutlich ihre Gefühle gestanden hat. Das Gedicht lässt darauf schliessen, dass der Regen ihre jugendliche Offenheit repräsentiert, der herbstliche Ahornzweig jedoch deutet eher auf ein Ende denn auf einen Anfang hin.

Die in *Lady Rokô* dargestellte Frauenfigur, eine bekannte Schönheit, ist ein interessantes Beispiel für einen Rollentausch: Ihr Name entspricht dem Pseudonym eines berühmten *onnagata*-Schauspielers, dem sie ähnlich sah. Ohne ansatzweise zum Objekt zu werden, lenkt sie mit koketter Pose die Aufmerksamkeit des vorbeigehenden Fächerverkäufers auf sich.

Seasonal associations have always been important in Japanese art, and were featured in *ukiyo-e* to provide additional nuances of meaning. *Second Month* uses spring to symbolize new love, with a suitor surreptitiously taking plum blossoms from the grounds of a shrine for his beloved, who shades the lantern with her sleeve to keep him from being seen. *Sixth Month* shows a couple in the full flowering of their relationship during the summer; at the same time, the poem suggests changes to come.

The imagery of *Tenth Month* is more subtle. A woman spies on the man on the veranda, reading a letter that presumably confesses her feelings for him; the poem indicates that the rain represents her youthful sincerity, but the branch of autumn maple leaves suggests an ending rather than a beginning.

The famous beauty Lady Rokô in the print is an interesting example of role reversal, since she takes her name from the pseudonym of a famous *onnagata* (male portraying a female role) actor she resembled. Far from being passively objectified, she poses coyly to attract the attention of the fan seller passing by her shop.

SE

鈴木春信
20
Lady Rokô, genannt Tokonatsu – Blumen der Schönheit aus der «Fliessenden Welt»
Lady Rokô – Flowers of Beauty from the "Floating World"
Suzuki HARUNOBU

鈴木春信
21
Sechster Monat – Populäre Darstellungen der Gedichte der Unsterblichen der Dichtkunst in den vier Jahreszeiten
Sixth Month – Popular Versions of Immortal Poets in the Four Seasons
Suzuki HARUNOBU

鈴木春信
22
Zehnter Monat – Populäre Darstellungen der Gedichte der Unsterblichen der Dichtkunst in den vier Jahreszeiten
Tenth Month – Popular Versions of Immortal Poets in the Four Seasons
Suzuki HARUNOBU

鈴木春信
23
Zweiter Monat, Pflaumenbaum am Flussufer – Modische Darstellungen der Gedichte der Unsterblichen der Dichtkunst in den vier Jahreszeiten
Second Month, Plum Tree at the Water's Edge – Fashionable Versions of Immortal Poets in the Four Seasons
Suzuki HARUNOBU

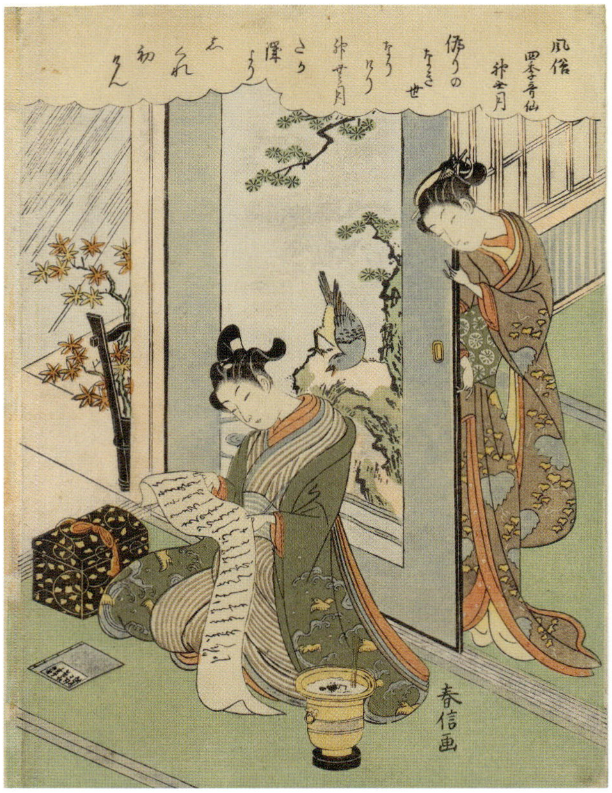

22

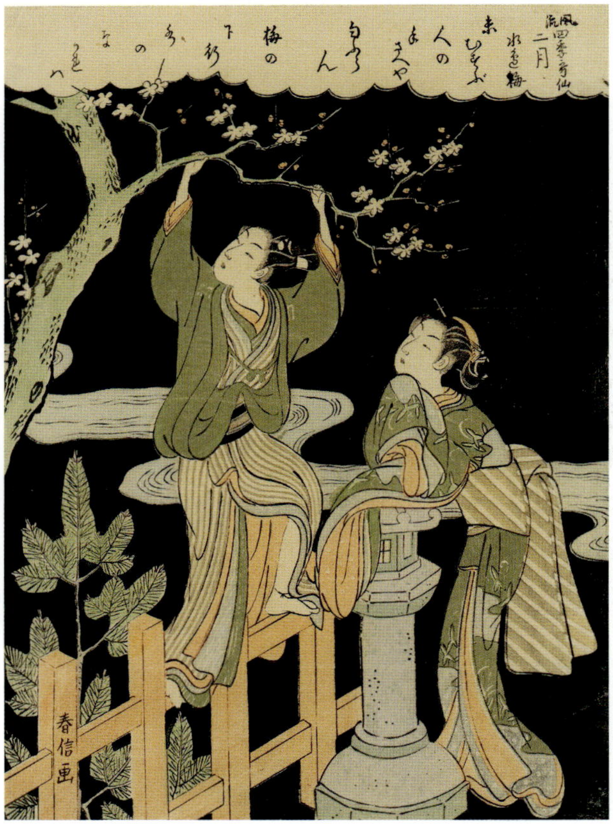

23

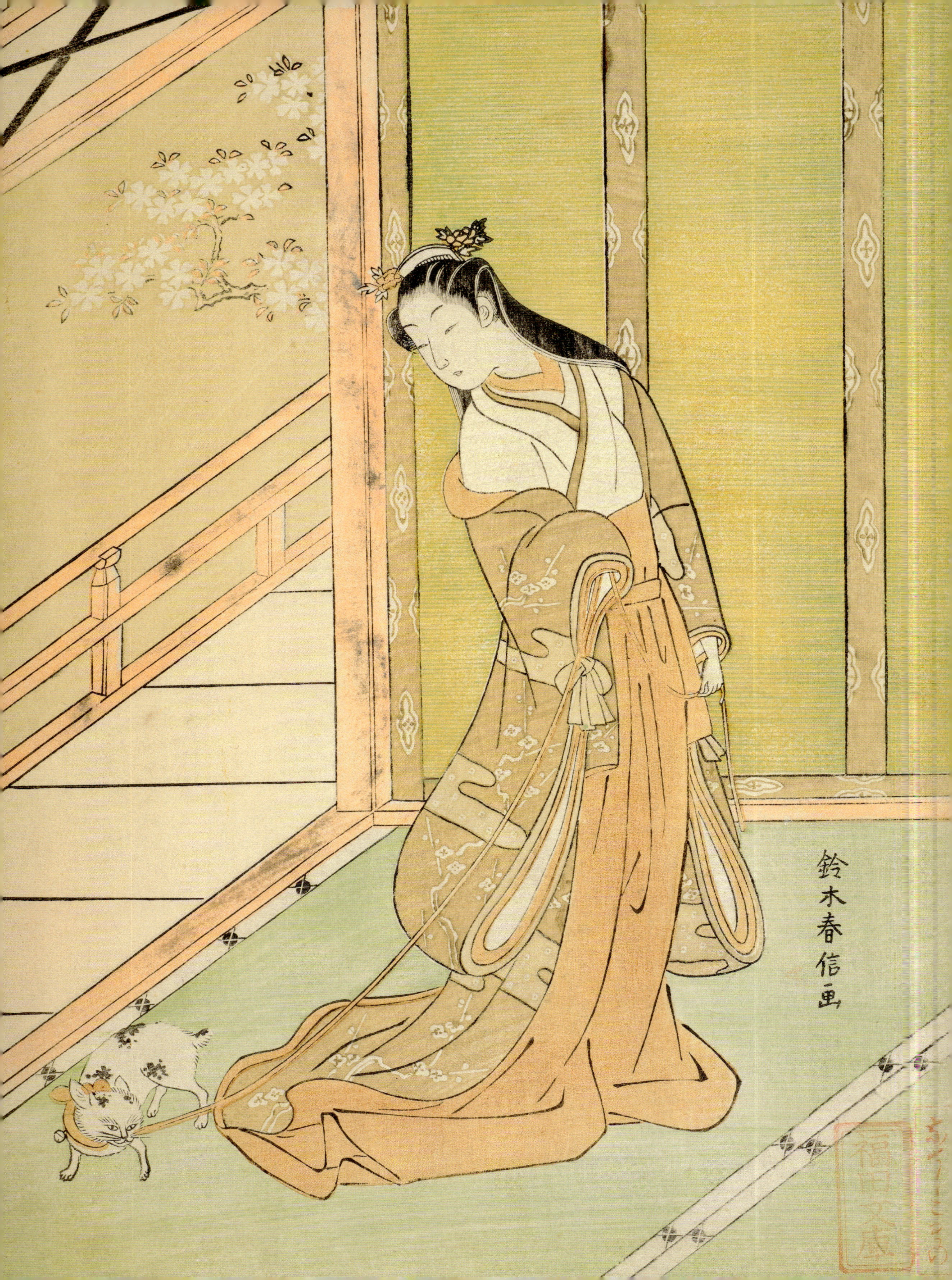
鈴木春信画

Die klassische *Geschichte vom Prinzen Genji* war in der Edo-Zeit eine beliebte Quelle für *bijinga*-Motive. Dieser Druck zeigt Prinzessin Sannomiya in einer Szene aus dem 34. Kapitel des in der Heian-Zeit entstandenen Romans, wie sie neben der Veranda in ihrem Zimmer mit einer Katze an der Leine steht. Im Ornat einer Hofdame gewandet, stellt sie eine elegante Erscheinung dar. Die Kirschblüten, deren ursprünglich zartblaue Färbung weisslich verblasst ist, zeigen den Frühling an.

Laut Roman ist Sannomiya nur flüchtig zu sehen, als ihre Katze mit dem Bambusvorhang spielt, der die Prinzessin eigentlich verbergen soll. In der weniger verborgenen Welt des *ukiyo-e* zeigt sie sich in voller Grösse. Allerdings verlangte das Fehlen eines Begleittextes vom Publikum, mit der Geschichte vertraut zu sein, um von den vorhandenen Hinweisen auf den klassischen Bezug schliessen zu können.

The classical *Tale of Genji* was a popular source for *bijinga* themes during the Edo period. This print shows Sannomiya (the Third Princess) from the 34th chapter of the Heian-period novel, standing just inside her room, holding her cat on a leash. Dressed in the costume of a court lady, she is an elegant figure. The season is spring, indicated by the cherry blossoms, originally pale blue, now faded to white.

In the novel, Sannomiya is glimpsed only briefly as the cat plays with the bamboo curtain that is meant to conceal her. In the less subtle world of *ukiyo-e,* the princess presents herself in full view. Still, the lack of an explanatory text meant that the audience had to be familiar enough with the story to recognize the classical reference from the clues provided.

CM

鈴木春信

24
Prinzessin Sannomiya, die dritte Prinzessin aus der «Geschichte vom Prinzen Genji»
Princess Sannomiya, the Third Princess from the "Tale of Genji"
Suzuki HARUNOBU

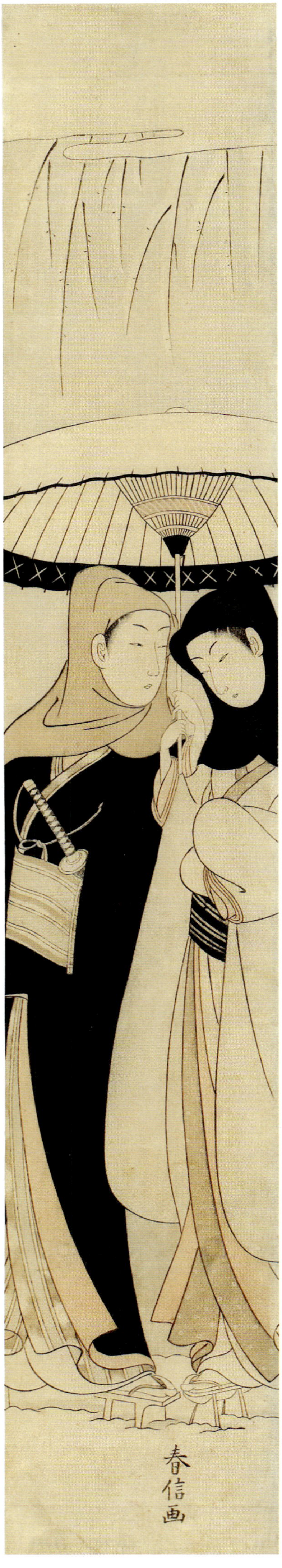
春信画

Harunobu ist berühmt für seine Beiträge zur Entwicklung des *nishiki-e* (Vielfarbendruck oder «Brokatbild»), doch hier ist es der Kontrast zwischen Tiefschwarz und Weiss, der am meisten ins Auge sticht. Das grössere Bild enthielt ursprünglich Prägungen, die im schwarzen Kimono des jungen Mannes noch sichtbar sind. Das Motiv der zwei Figuren unter einem Schirm, im *ukiyo-e* der Edo-Zeit ein Symbol für die Liebe, besteht in modernen Graffiti unverändert fort. In diesen Drucken wiederholen sich die geschwungenen Posen und Konturen der einen Figur in der jeweils anderen und betonen so die Intimität einer privaten Sphäre, die von der verschneiten Welt jenseits des Schirms abgegrenzt ist. Die unterschiedlichen Formate der ikonografisch identischen Drucke haben zu unterschiedlichen Entscheidungen aufseiten des Künstlers geführt. Der verengte Bildraum des *hashira-e* («Pfostenbild») hatte zur Folge, dass der Hintergrund und weitere Details reduziert wurden und die Bildränder sehr stark beschnitten sind, wodurch die Figuren in extremer Nahsicht erscheinen. Im grösseren Bild heben die kalte Luft, die die Liebenden umgibt, und der mit Eis überzogene Baum hinter ihnen die Wärme des gemeinsamen Raums unter dem Schirm eindrucksvoll hervor.

Suzuki Harunobu is known for his contributions to the development of *nishiki-e* (full color, or "brocade" prints), but here it is the contrast between deep black and white that is most striking. The larger print originally contained embossing; one can see that technique remaining on the black kimono of the young man. The motif of two figures under an umbrella is a standard symbol for love in Edo-period *ukiyo-e,* one that continues in graffiti even today. In these prints, the curved poses and lines of the robe of one figure echo that of the other, emphasizing the sense of an intimate space separate from the snowy world beyond the umbrella. While the iconography is the same in both prints—a young man and woman, dressed in hooded garments, standing in a snowy landscape—the different formats have led to different choices on the part of the artist. The constricted space of the *hashira-e,* or "pillar print," has resulted in an abbreviation of the background and other details and in dramatically cropped borders that bring the figures very close to the viewer. In the larger print, the cold air surrounding the lovers and the ice-covered tree behind them effectively accentuate the warmth of their shared space.

CM

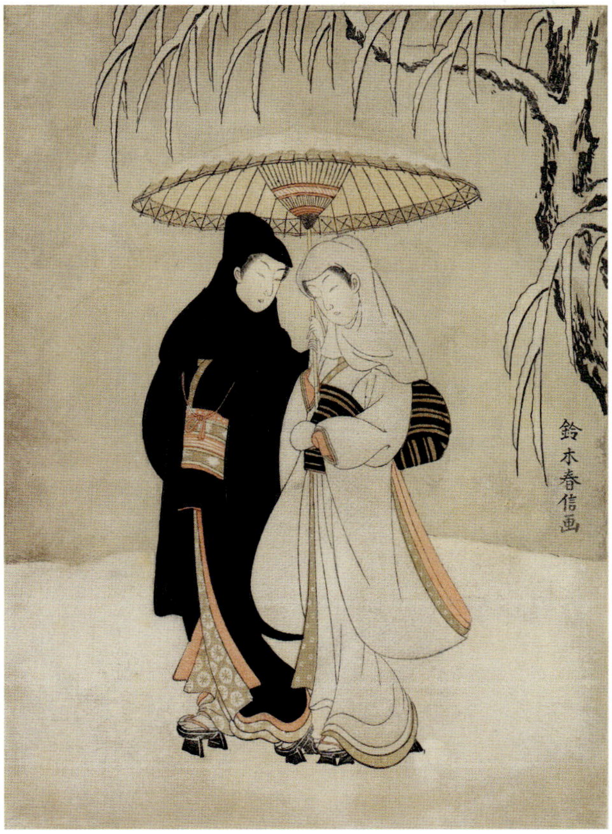

26

鈴木春信

25
Liebespaar unter einem Schirm
Lovers Sharing an Umbrella
Suzuki HARUNOBU

鈴木春信

26
Liebespaar unter einem Schirm
Lovers Sharing an Umbrella
Suzuki HARUNOBU

In dieser heiteren Szene greift eine junge Frau über sich, um die Papierblätter wieder einzufangen, die aus ihrer *kamiire* (ähnlich einer Brieftasche) gerutscht sind und im Wind tanzen. Die *kamiire* selbst liegt am Boden, anstatt wie üblich im *obi* (Bauchschärpe) zu stecken. Über dem Kopf der Figur erblicken wir die Ursache des Durcheinanders: den bösartigen Windgott Fûjin, der mit offensichtlichem Vergnügen auf das Chaos hinabsieht, das er angerichtet hat. Die Kraft des Sturms setzt auch der Frau selbst zu. Obwohl sie sich redlich bemüht, ihren Kimono geschlossen zu halten, legen die im Sturm auffliegenden Säume bereits ihre nackten Beine frei. Die unmissverständliche Andeutung, dass es dem Windgott Freude bereitet, auf diese Weise mit der Frauengestalt zu spielen, macht aus dem Bild ein frühes Beispiel eines *abuna-e* oder «gewagten Drucks».

In this humorous scene, a young woman reaches up to catch pieces of paper that have slipped out of her *kamiire* (akin to a billfold) and are being blown about by the wind. The *kamiire* itself is lying on the ground, having been dislodged from its usual place tucked inside her *obi.* Looking above the figure, the viewer encounters the force behind this chaos: the mischievous wind god Fûjin, who stands peering down with obvious delight at the scene he has created. The force of the wind has also played havoc with the woman herself. Although she modestly tries to keep her kimono from flying open, the force of the wind parts the edges to reveal her bare legs. The clear implication that the god enjoys toying with her in this way makes the print an early example of *abuna-e,* or suggestive art.

CM

鈴木 春信

27
Der Windgott schickt eine überraschende Sturmböe
The Wind God's Sudden Squall
Suzuki HARUNOBU

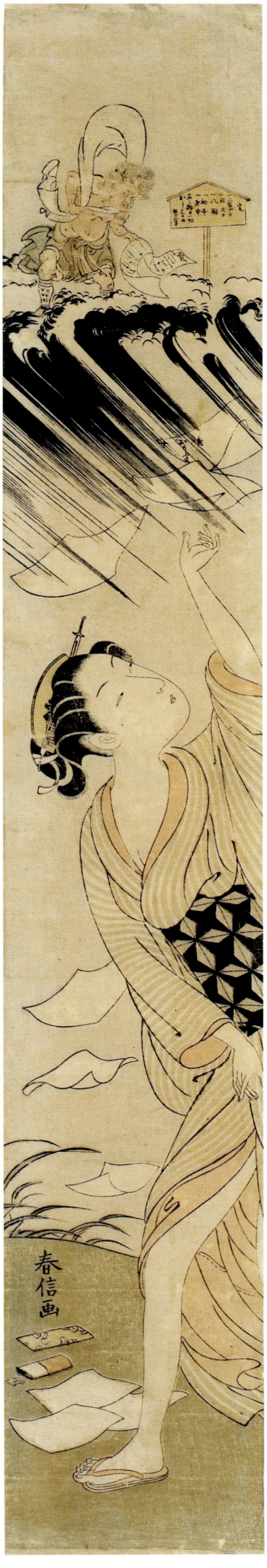
春信画

Dieser seltene Druck stellt vermutlich die Parodie einer Szene aus dem 7. Akt des *Chûshingura* dar, einer Erzählung von 47 Kriegern, die den vom Hofbeamten Kira Kôzuke-no-suke Yoshinaka verursachten Tod ihres Herrn rächen. Um keinen Verdacht zu wecken, täuscht der Anführer der Krieger, Yuranosuke, in der Szene das Leben eines Trunksüchtigen vor und geht sogar so weit, beim Essen mit Kiras Spionen Krakenfleisch zu verspeisen (was am Todestag seines Herrn verboten ist). Während des Mahls erhält Yuranosuke einen Brief, den einer der Spione heimlich mitzulesen versucht, weil er vermutet, dass darin ein Racheplan gegen Kira enthüllt wird. In Bunchôs Druck hat Yuranosuke die Gestalt einer jungen Schönheit angenommen, die intime Briefe liest, während ihr Liebhaber ihr über die Schulter sieht und ein Krake das Ende der Schriftrolle ergreift.

Die Bedeutung des Hummers in dieser Szene ist noch unerforscht. Da Hummer jedoch symbolisch mit dem neuen Jahr in Verbindung stehen, könnte der Druck als *egoyomi* (Bildkalender) gedient haben, eine nicht amtliche Übersicht über die langen und kurzen Monate des kommenden Jahres.

This rare print is likely to be a parody of a scene from Act 7 of the *Chûshingura,* a tale of revenge by forty-seven warriors for the death of their lord, caused by the official Kira Kôzuke-no-suke Yoshinaka. In the scene, the leader of the warriors, Yuranosuke, adopts the life of a drunkard in order to avoid suspicion, going so far as to dine with Kira's spies and eat octopus (forbidden on the anniversary of his lord's death). During the meal, Yuranosuke receives a letter, and one of the spies, suspecting that it might reveal a plot for revenge against Kira, tries to see the contents in secret as Yuranosuke reads it. In Bunchô's print, Yuranosuke has been transformed into a young beauty who reads intimate correspondence as her love looks over her shoulder, while an octopus catches the end of the scroll.

The significance of the lobster remains to be determined, but lobsters have symbolic associations with the New Year, and the print might have been intended as an *egoyomi,* or "calendar print," an unofficial indication of the long and short months for the coming year.

SE

28
Parodie des 7. Aktes des «Chûshingura»
Parody of Act 7 of the "Chûshingura"
Ippitsusai BUNCHÔ
一筆斎文調

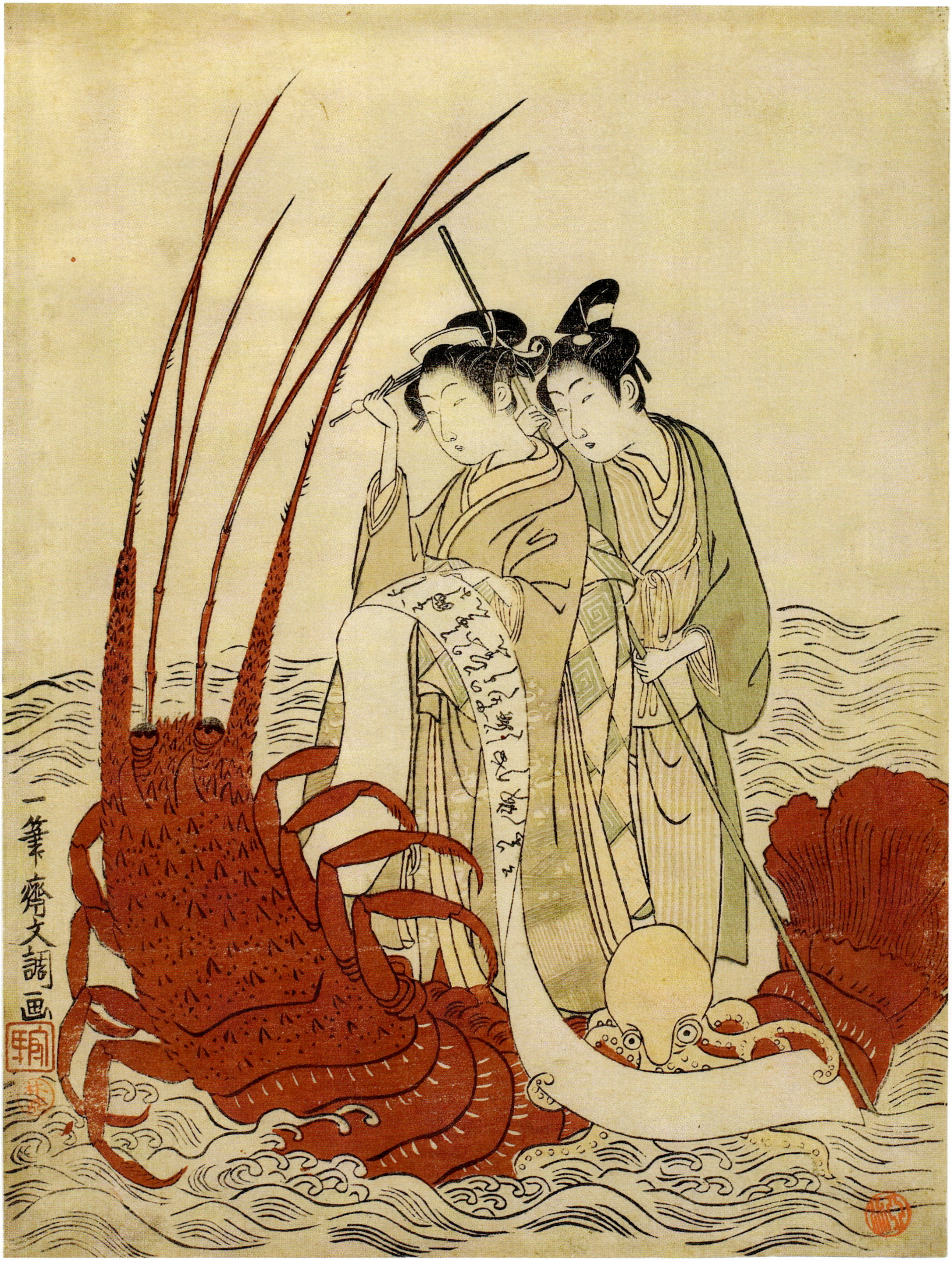
一筆齋文調画

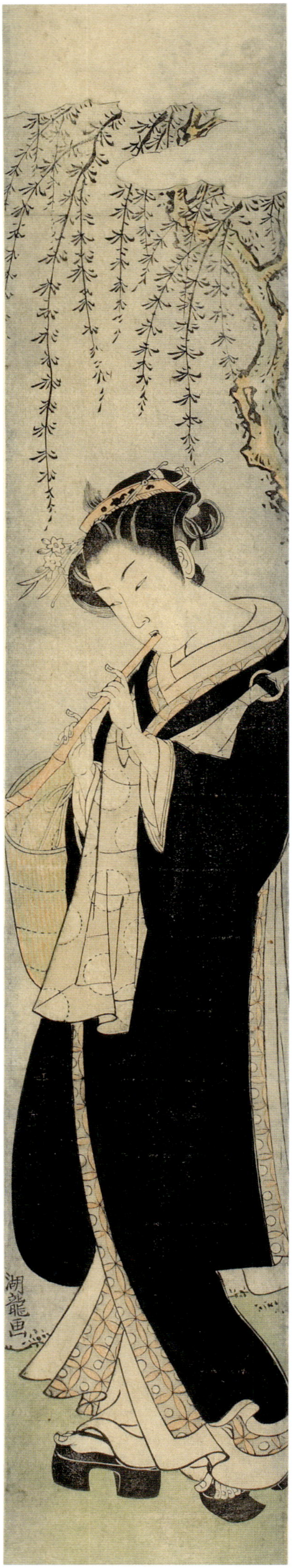

Das charakteristische Format dieser drei Drucke ist als *hashira-e* («Pfostenbild») bekannt. Die Bezeichnung leitet sich von den in der japanischen Holzrahmenbauweise üblichen Stützpfosten ab. Zuweilen wurden *hashira-e* direkt an die Pfosten geklebt und trugen so zum Schmuck eines Hauses bei. Sowohl Harunobu als auch Koryûsai in *Dame füttert ihre zahme Ratte* haben das schmale Hochformat effektiv genutzt, um den Szenen einen Hauch von Voyeurismus zu verleihen, so als sähen wir die jungen Frauen mit den gelösten Gewändern in ihren Kammern aus einem verborgenen Blickwinkel. Die Ratte suggeriert, dass Koryûsais Druck aus dem Jahr 1768, dem Jahr der Ratte, stammen könnte. Er wäre damit das älteste Werk des Künstlers in der Sammlung des Honolulu Museum of Art.

Dame als Bettelmönch verkleidet erzielt mit dem *hashira-e*-Format eine abweichende, aber nicht weniger interessante Wirkung. Die Kleidung der jungen Frau parodiert das Gewand eines buddhistischen Bettelmönchs (*komusô* oder «Mönch der Leere»). Ihr Kimono ähnelt der Ritualtracht eines Priesters, und die Bambusflöte *(shakuhachi)*, auf der sie spielt, ist ein typisches Kennzeichen der *komusô*. Die Mönche waren berühmt für die geflochtenen Körbe, die sie als Zeichen ihrer Selbstlosigkeit über dem Kopf trugen. Hier aber hängt der Korb am Arm der Frau herab, sodass er ihre Schönheit nicht verstecken kann.

These three prints are in a distinctive format known as *hashira-e,* or "pillar prints." The term takes its name from the supporting posts common to traditional Japanese wood-frame architecture, and in some cases *hashira-e* actually were pasted to these posts to decorate the home. Both Harunobu, and Koryûsai in *Woman Feeding Her Pet Rat,* have made effective use of the narrow vertical format to provide a sense of voyeurism to the scene, as if the young women in their chambers, with their robes loosened, were being seen from an obstructed vantage point. The rat suggests that Koryûsai's print might have been made in the year of the rat, 1768, making this the earliest work by Koryûsai in the Honolulu Museum of Art's collection.

Woman Disguised as a Komusô uses the *hashira-e* to different effect, but is no less interesting. The young woman is dressed in parody of an itinerant Buddhist monk (*komusô,* or "monk of emptiness"), her kimono resembling the ritual robes of a priest, while she plays on the bamboo flute, or *shakuhachi,* associated with the *komusô.* These monks were famous for the woven baskets they wore over their heads as a sign of their freedom from sense of self; however, the basket here has been hung from her arm, so that it does not hide her beauty.

SE

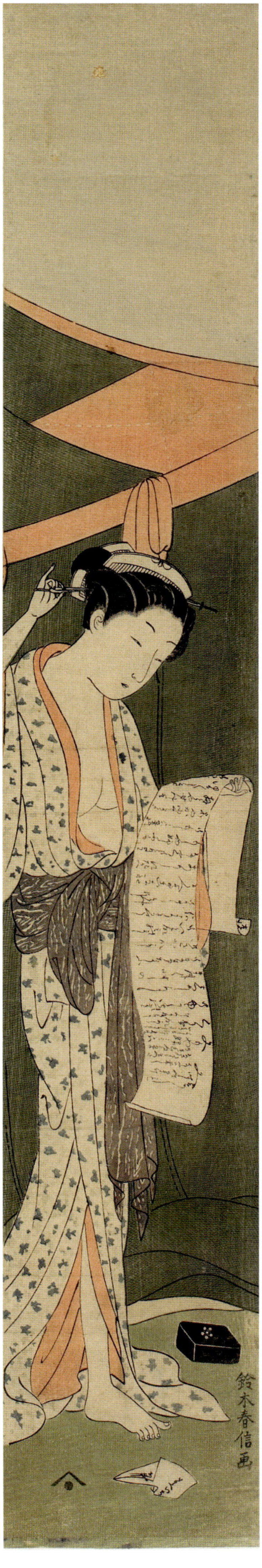

30

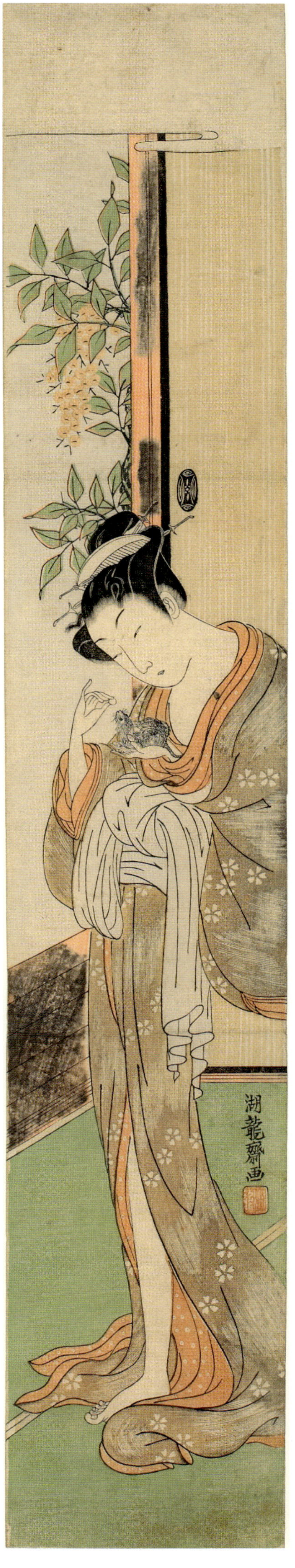

31

礒田 湖龍斎

29
Dame als Bettelmönch verkleidet
Woman Disguised as a Komusô
Isoda KORYÛSAI

鈴木 春信

30
Schönheit ausserhalb des Moskitonetzes, einen Brief lesend
Beauty Reading a Letter Outside Mosquito Netting
Suzuki HARUNOBU

礒田 湖龍斎

31
Dame füttert ihre zahme Ratte
Woman Feeding Her Pet Rat
Isoda KORYÛSAI

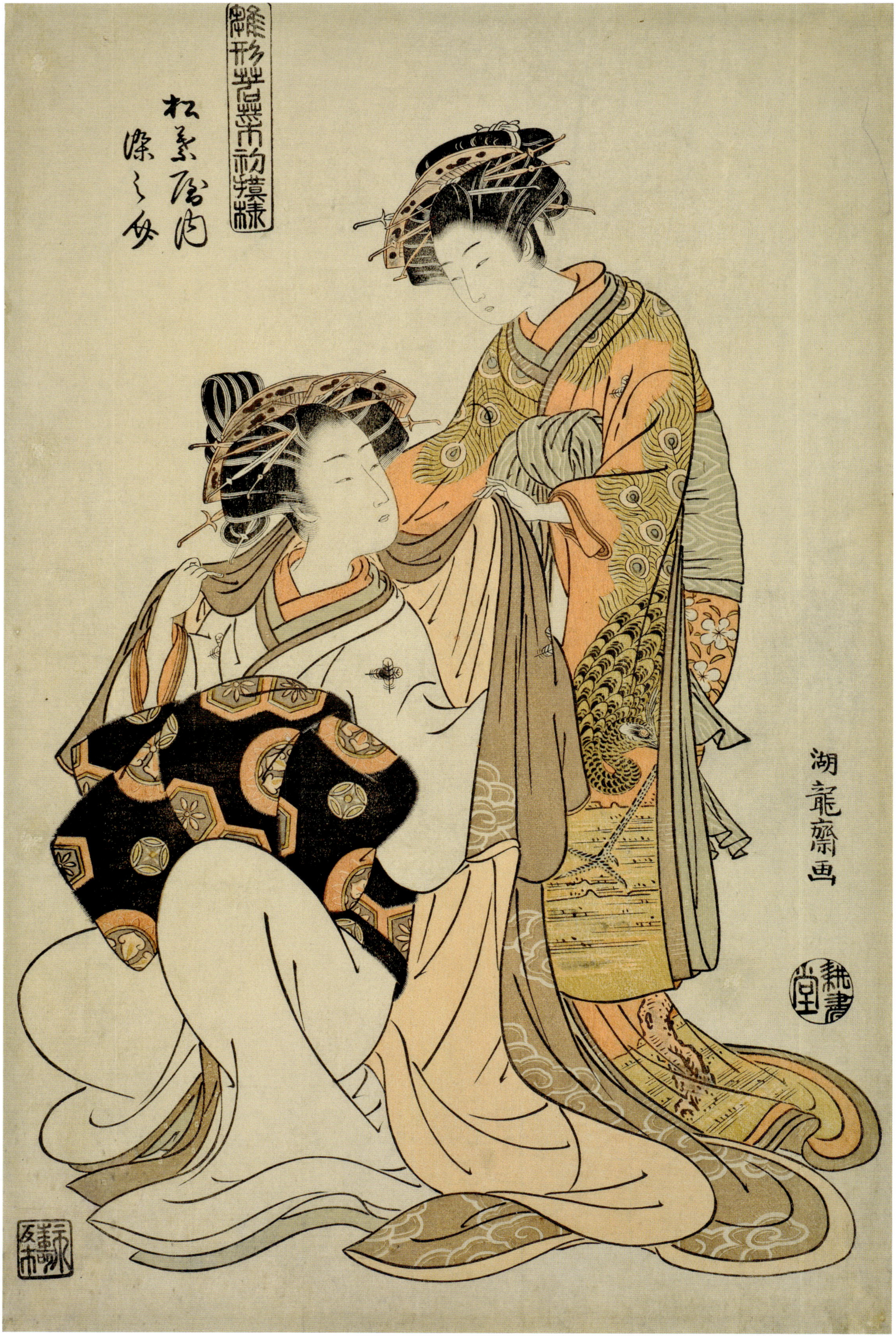
雛形若菜初模様
松葉屋内
湖龍斎画

Die Bewohnerinnen der Freudenviertel gaben in der Modewelt von Edo den Ton an, was zum grossen Teil die Popularität von Drucken erklärt, auf denen Kurtisanen in den neuesten Kimonos und Haartrachten abgebildet waren. Die Serie, aus der dieses Werk stammt, war besonders erfolgreich. Vermutlich um 1775 begonnen, umfasste sie am Ende rund 140 Entwürfe von Koryûsai, bevor sie von Kiyonaga bis in die 1780er-Jahre hinein fortgesetzt wurde.

Dieses Blatt zeigt Somenosuke, eine hochrangige *yûjo* (Kurtisane), beim Anlegen ihres Übergewandes mit der Hilfe ihrer *shinzô* (jugendliche Begleiterin). Beide Frauen tragen Frisuren im *tôrôbin*-Stil (wörtlich «Seitenhaar-Lampion»). Prächtige Stoffdessins wie das Pfauenmuster auf dem Gewand der Begleiterin, das auch in anderen Bildern der Serie auftaucht, waren sehr beliebt. Koryûsais frühe Schönheiten orientierten sich noch eng am Stil seines Lehrmeisters Harunobu, doch bis zum Ende der 1770er-Jahre hatten seine Frauenfiguren einen kräftigeren Körperbau angenommen, waren dem Äusseren nach älter geworden und zeigten geziertere Posen und Gesten. Die anmutige Haltung der hier abgebildeten Kurtisane, die sich umwendet, um das Gewand entgegenzunehmen, die fliessenden Linien der Stoffe und das feine Stoffmuster ergeben zusammen hohe modische Eleganz.

Women of the pleasure quarters were leaders in the Edo fashion world, a phenomenon that accounts in large part for the popularity of prints featuring famous courtesans wearing the latest kimono designs and hairstyles. The series from which this work comes was especially successful. Begun probably around 1775, it eventually ran to some 140 prints by Koryûsai, before being continued into the 1780s by Kiyonaga.

This print shows Somenosuke, a high-ranking *yûjo,* being helped on with her outer robe by her *shinzô* (adolescent assistant). Both women wear their hair in the *tôrôbin* manner. The peacock design on the attendant's robe is featured in other prints in the series, and indeed such showy patterns were very popular. Koryûsai's early beauties closely followed the style of his teacher Harunobu, but by the late 1770s, his figures had become more substantial in physique, older in appearance, and more mannered in pose and gesture. Here, the graceful posture of the courtesan as she turns to accept the robe, the fluid lines of the drapery, and the finely rendered textile pattern combine to create an elegant fashion statement.

CM

礒田湖龍斎

32

Somenosuke aus dem Freudenhaus Matsubaya – Modelle für die Mode: Neue Muster, so frisch wie junge Blätter

Somenosuke of the Matsubaya Brothel House – Models for Fashion: New Designs as Fresh as Young Leaves

Isoda KORYÛSAI

Dieser Druck stammt aus einer Serie von Abbildern berühmter Kurtisanen, die nach den neuesten Modetrends gewandet und frisiert sind. Als eines der repräsentativsten Sammelwerke Koryûsais in der Gattung der *bijinga* markiert die Serie eine wichtige Entwicklungsstufe des Vielfarbendrucks für die Herstellung von «Brokatbildern» *(nishiki-e)*. Das Fundament war ein Jahrzehnt zuvor von Harunobu gelegt worden, an den die Figuren teilweise noch erinnern. Ihre hervorgehobene Stellung in der Komposition jedoch, die auf eine Hintergrundgestaltung nahezu vollständig verzichtet, und die umfassende Verwendung von Rot, das hier wirkungsvoll mit verschiedenen Grau- und Schwarztönen kontrastiert, sind kennzeichnend für Koryûsai. Michinoku liest in dem Sammelband *100 Gedichte von 100 Dichtern (Hyakunin isshu)*, ihre Begleiterinnen sind in ein Kartenspiel vertieft, bei dem sie die Gedichte paarweise zusammenstellen müssen. Passend zur Jahreszeit trägt Michinoku einen schwarzen Überkimono mit einem Muster aus Kiefernzweigen, der die Schultern nicht bedeckt und so den Blick auf die kontrastreich gemusterten Untergewänder freigibt. In den Kimonos ihrer Begleiterinnen wiederholen sich das Rot des Futterstoffs und das Kiefernzweigmuster von Michinokus Überkimono.

This print is from a series depicting famous courtesans wearing the most recent fashions. One of the most representative of Koryûsai's works in the *bijinga* genre, the series marks an important stage in the development of full-color, or "brocade," prints *(nishiki-e)*, consolidating upon the foundation established by Harunobu a decade earlier. Although the figures are in some ways reminiscent of Harunobu, their more prominent role in the composition, with background elements virtually eliminated, is characteristic of Koryûsai, as is the extensive use of red, here effectively contrasted against different shades of gray and black. Michinoku reads from the compilation *One Hundred Poems by One Hundred Poets (Hyakunin isshu)*, while her attendants play a card game in which the poems have to be matched. Appropriate to the season, Michinoku has a black outer kimono with a design of pine boughs, worn off the shoulder to reveal the contrasting design of her inner robes. Her attendants' kimonos match the red lining of her own, with the same pattern.

SE

磯田 湖龍斎

33
Michinoku mit Begleiterinnen – Modelle für die Mode: Neue Muster, so frisch wie junge Blätter
Michinoku with Attendants – Models for Fashion: New Designs as Fresh as Young Leaves
Isoda KORYÛSAI

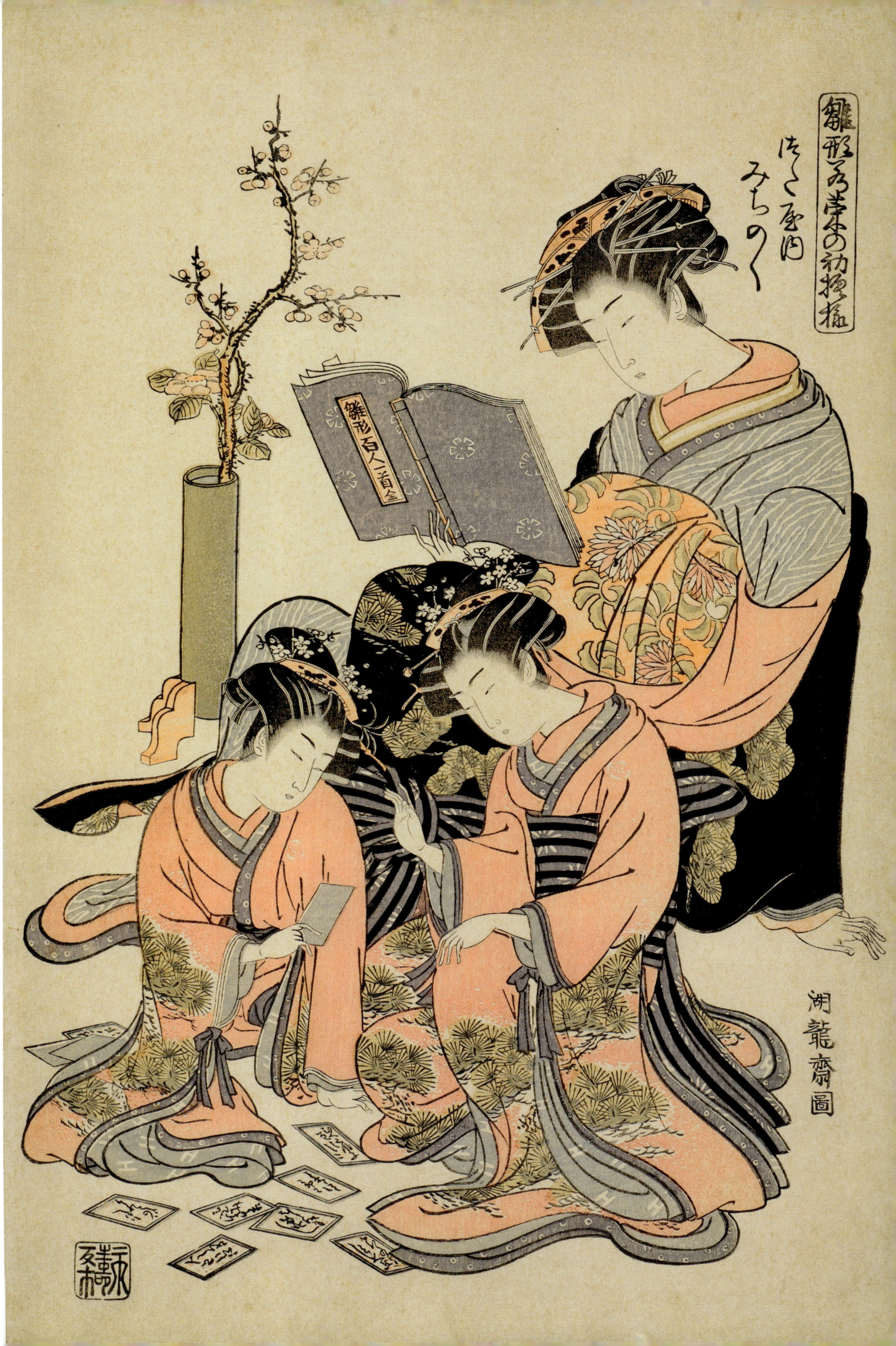
雛形若菜の初模様
はく屋内
みちのく
雛形百人一首全
湖龍齋圖

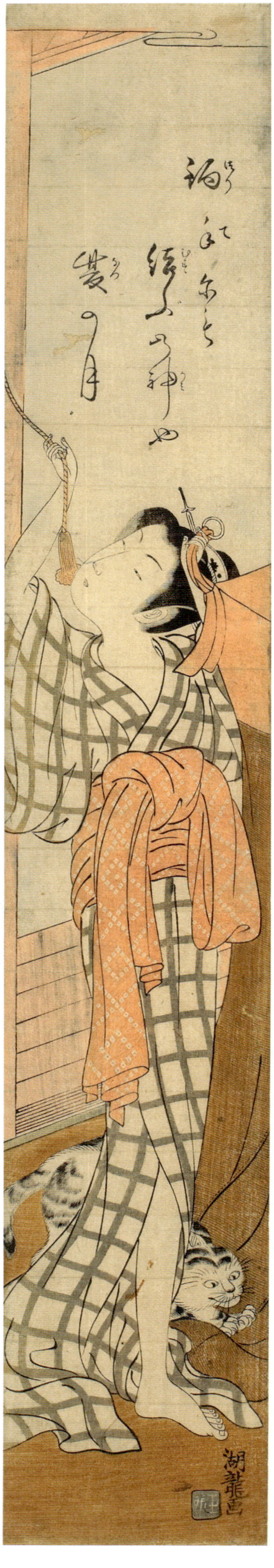

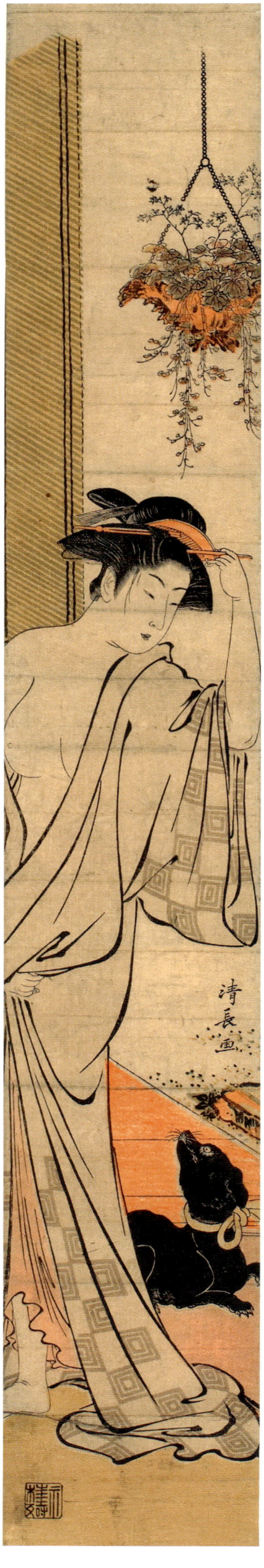

Auch er knüpft die Fäden des Moskitonetzes,
Der Gott der Ehe,
Unter einem Sommermond.

He also ties the cords of mosquito netting,
The God of Marriage,
Under a summer moon.

Sowohl Koryûsai als auch Kiyonaga nutzten das schmale Format des *hashira-e* («Pfostenbilder») für die voyeuristische Darstellung ihrer Figuren, hier einer Frau beim Aufhängen eines Moskitonetzes, dort einer Frau nach dem Bad. In beiden Fällen lässt sich der Sommer als Jahreszeit ausmachen. Koryûsais Entwurf wird im oberen Bereich von einem Gedicht begleitet.

Das Gedicht verleiht der Szene zusätzliche Bedeutung, indem es das Befestigen des Netzes mit der Sehnsucht der Frau verknüpft, mit ihrem Geliebten in der Ehe verbunden zu sein. Die grosse kompositionelle Ähnlichkeit der beiden Drucke lässt auf den ersten Blick erkennen, dass Kiyonaga von Koryûsai beeinflusst wurde. Während jedoch Koryûsais Frauengestalt (mit ihrer überschlanken Figur und den feinen Zügen) gleichzeitig noch den von Harunobu eingeführten Idealen folgt, verweisen der stabilere Körperbau und die deutlich artikulierteren Gesichtszüge in Kiyonagas Darstellung bereits auf den neuen Schönheitskanon, den der Künstler in den 1780er-Jahren einführen sollte.

Both Koryûsai and Kiyonaga take advantage of the *hashira-e,* or "pillar print," format to create voyeuristic depictions of their subjects, in one case a woman hanging mosquito netting, and in the other a woman after her bath. In each case, the season can be identified as summer. Koryûsai's print is accompanied by a poem in the upper register. The poem adds nuance to the significance of the scene, associating the woman's tying of the netting with her desire to be bound to her love in marriage.

Kiyonaga was influenced by Koryûsai, as is immediately evident from the close similarity of composition in these two prints. At the same time, while Koryûsai's subject follows the ideals established by Harunobu (in her slender figure and delicate features), the more substantial physique and clearly articulated features of Kiyonaga's portrayal already suggest the new canons of beauty that he would introduce during the 1780s.

SE

34
Schöne Frau beim Aufhängen eines Moskitonetzes
Beauty Hanging a Mosquito Net
Isoda KORYÛSAI
礒田 湖龍斎

35
Nach dem Bad
After the Bath
Torii KIYONAGA
鳥居 清長

Der üblicherweise männliche Blick auf eine weibliche Schönheit ist in diesem Werk umgekehrt: Hier beugt sich eine junge Frau aus ihrem Fenster, um einen vorbeigehenden *wakashû,* einen eitlen Jüngling, anzuschauen. Da die *wakashû* jedoch in erster Linie Objekt männlicher Begierde waren, kann der elegante Jüngling als Blickfang sowohl für die Kurtisane als auch für den (männlichen) Betrachter des Bildes angesehen werden. Im gestreiften Kimono mit rotem *obi* (Gürtel), einer Tracht, die als *iki* bekannt war und als Inbegriff des Understatements galt, gibt der junge Mann mit dem Schwert an der Seite eine ansehnliche Figur ab.

Hashira-e («Pfostenbilder») konnten an die Stützpfeiler eines Wohnhauses geklebt oder aufgezogen und wie Gemälde in die *tokonoma* (Bildnische) gehängt werden. Das Format stellte für manchen Holzschnittkünstler eine Herausforderung dar. Nicht so für Kiyonaga, der die Grenzen des Formats besonders geschickt nutzte, um neuartige und interessante Entwürfe hervorzubringen. In diesem Fall hat er sich des schmalen Hochformats bedient, um die lebhafte junge Frau und den eher passiv verharrenden Jüngling, der sich bewundern lässt, effektvoll nebeneinanderzustellen.

The usual male gaze directed at a female beauty is subverted in this work, as a girl leans out of her window to watch a *wakashû,* or young dandy, walk by. Since *wakashû* were primarily objects of male desire, however, the elegant youth can be seen as the focus of attention on the part of both the courtesan and the (male) viewer of the print. The young man, a sword at his side, cuts a dashing figure in his striped kimono and red *obi,* the epitome of the understated style known as *iki.*

Hashira-e, or "pillar prints," could be pasted onto the supporting posts of a residence or mounted and hung in the *tokonoma,* or alcove, like a painting. The format could pose a challenge to print designers, but Kiyonaga was particularly adept at using its limitations to create novel and interesting designs. Here he has used the narrow vertical shape to effectively juxtapose the lively young woman and the more passive youth, who appears to pause for everyone's admiration.

CM

鳥居清長

36
Eine junge Frau beobachtet einen Jüngling
A Young Woman Watching a Youth
Torii KIYONAGA

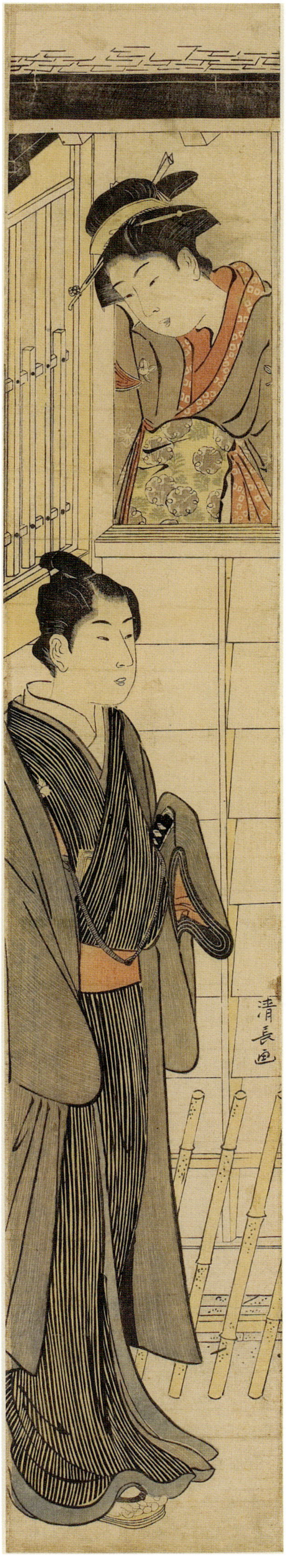
清長画

鳥居 清長

37
Sommerliche Morgen-dämmerung am Ufer des Sumida-Flusses
Summer Twilight on the Banks of the Sumida River
Torii KIYONAGA

鳥居 清長

38
Frauen vor dem Tor eines Schreins
A Group of Women at a Shrine Gate
Torii KIYONAGA

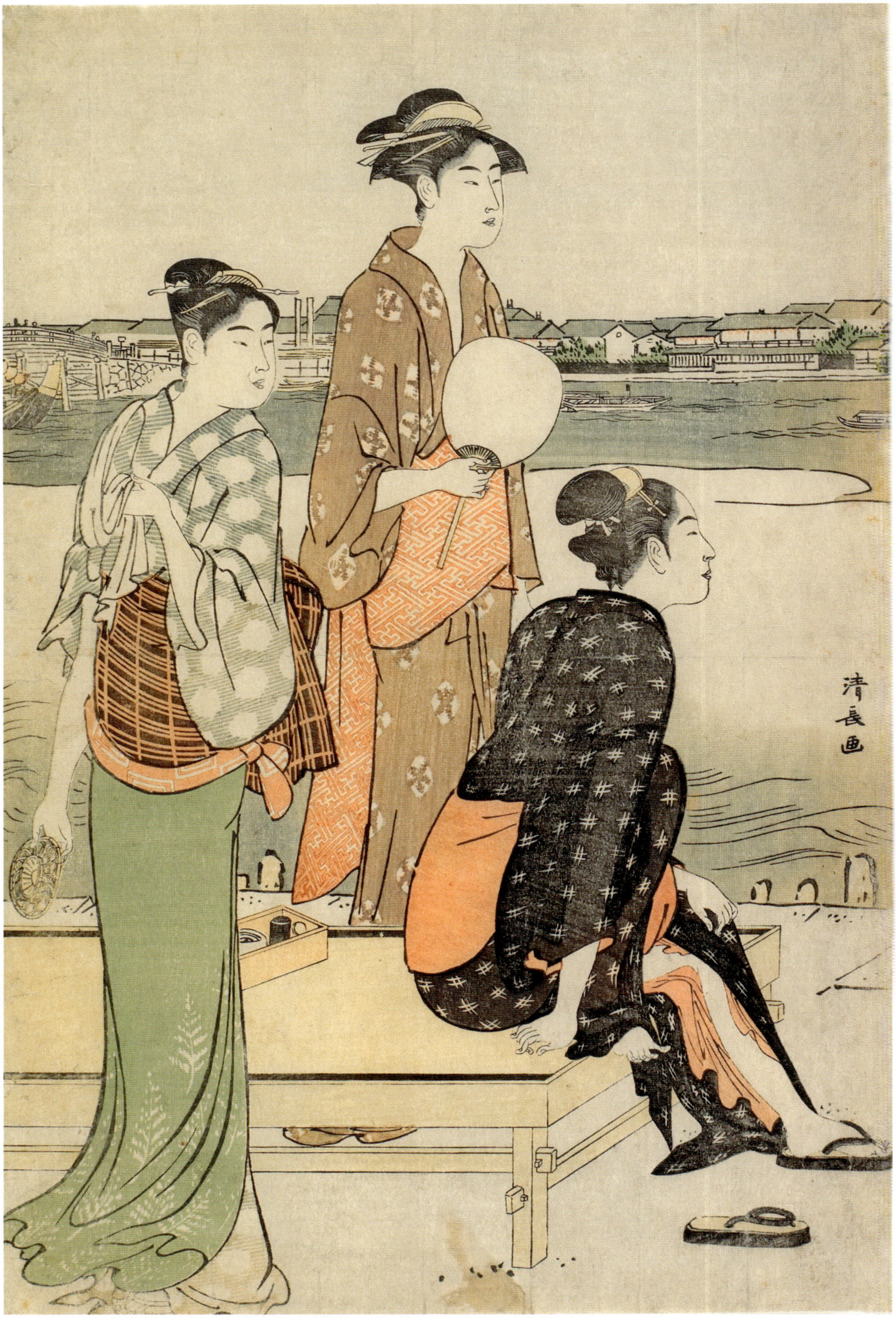

37

Kiyonagas hochgewachsene, würdevolle Frauenfiguren führten in den 1780er-Jahren neue Schönheitsmassstäbe ein, die von der zarten Emotionalität eines Harunobu abwichen. Elegante, typischerweise in schlichten, ausgewogenen Arrangements angeordnete Frauen beherrschten die Kompositionen. Der geometrische Aufbau von *Sommerliche Morgendämmerung* ist charakteristisch für Kiyonagas Werk: Die drei Frauen bilden ein Dreieck, das vom horizontalen Band des Flusses und der Häuserreihe in der Ferne im Gleichgewicht gehalten wird. Die tiefe Horizontlinie und die Einführung einer Perspektive als bildnerische Mittel westlicher Prägung tauchen in zahlreichen *ukiyo-e* der Periode auf.

Auf dem zweiten Blatt durchschreiten vier Frauen das *torii* (Tor) eines Shinto-Schreins. Sie machen einen Neujahrsbesuch, wie die Kiefern- und Pflaumenzweige und der Bambus, allesamt Symbole dieser Jahreszeit, verraten. Die Hüte *(agebôshi)* der Frauen kennzeichnen ihren Samurai-Status. Die Figur im schwarzen Kimono, wahrscheinlich die Mutter der jungen Dame in Hellgrün, lenkt die Aufmerksamkeit ihrer Tochter auf irgendetwas knapp ausserhalb der Bildfläche, während die Tochter am Ärmel der Mutter zupft. Beide tragen Kimonos, deren Stil in den 1780er-Jahren populär war: Der modisch breite *obi* (Gürtel) erforderte Kimonomuster, die sich hauptsächlich auf die untere Hälfte der Rumpfteile und auf die Säume konzentrierten.

Kiyonaga's tall, stately figures initiated a new standard of beauty in the 1780s, one that departed from the delicate lyricism of Harunobu. These sophisticated women, typically arranged in simple, well-balanced configurations, dominate his compositions. *Summer Twilight* is characteristic of the artist's work in its geometric organization: the three women form a triangle, balanced by the horizontal line of the river and distant buildings. The low horizon and introduction of perspective are Western-style pictorial devices seen in many *ukiyo-e* of the period.

In the second print, four women pass through the *torii* (gate) of a Shinto shrine. They are making a New Year's visit, as indicated by the presence of pine, bamboo, and plum, symbols of that season. Their hats *(agebôshi)* denote their samurai status. The figure in the black kimono, likely the mother of the young lady in light green, directs her daughter's attention to something just beyond the border of the print, while the daughter tugs at her mother's sleeve. Both figures wear a style of kimono popular during the 1780s, in which the fashionably wide *obi* demanded patterns that were concentrated primarily at the bottom and along the edges of the garment.

CM

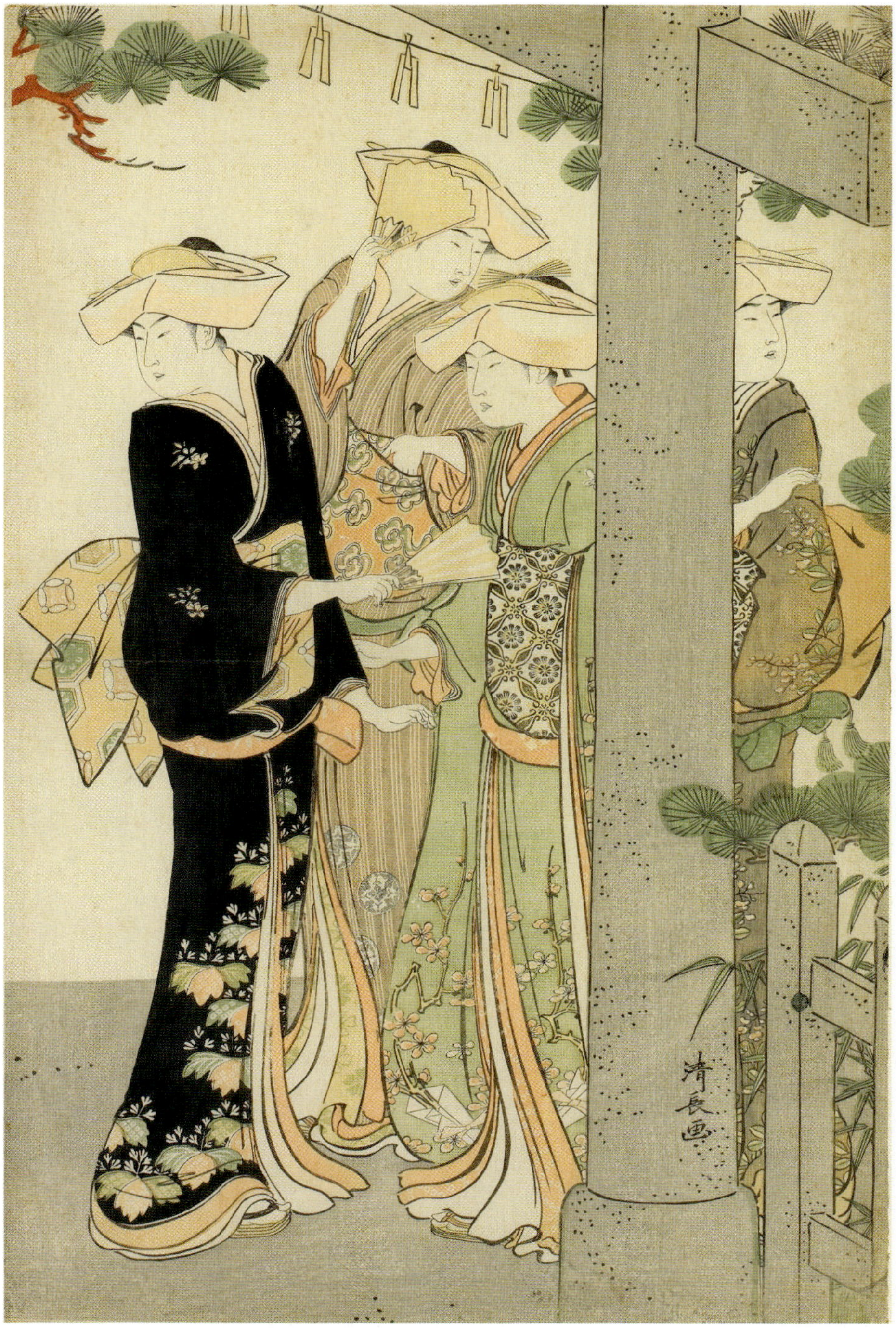

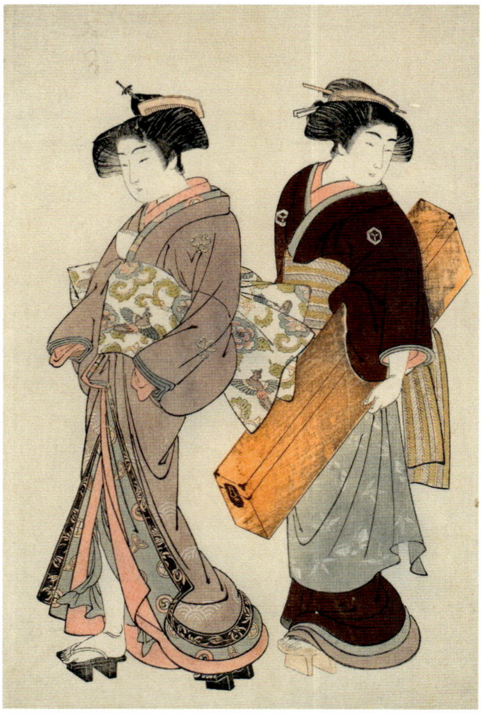
40

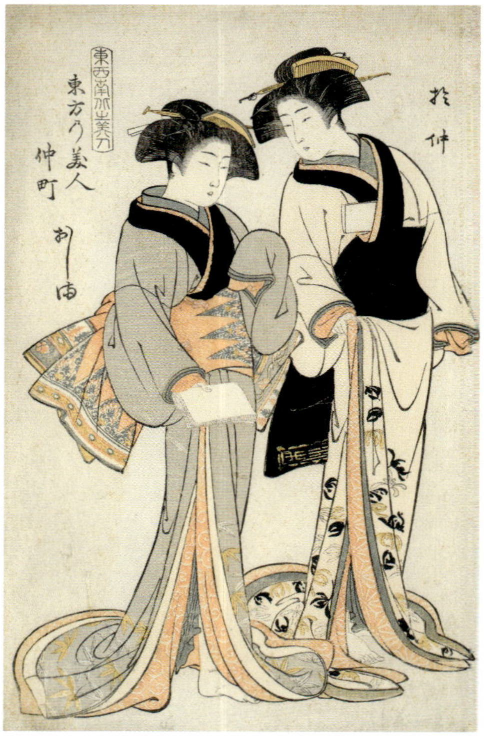

41

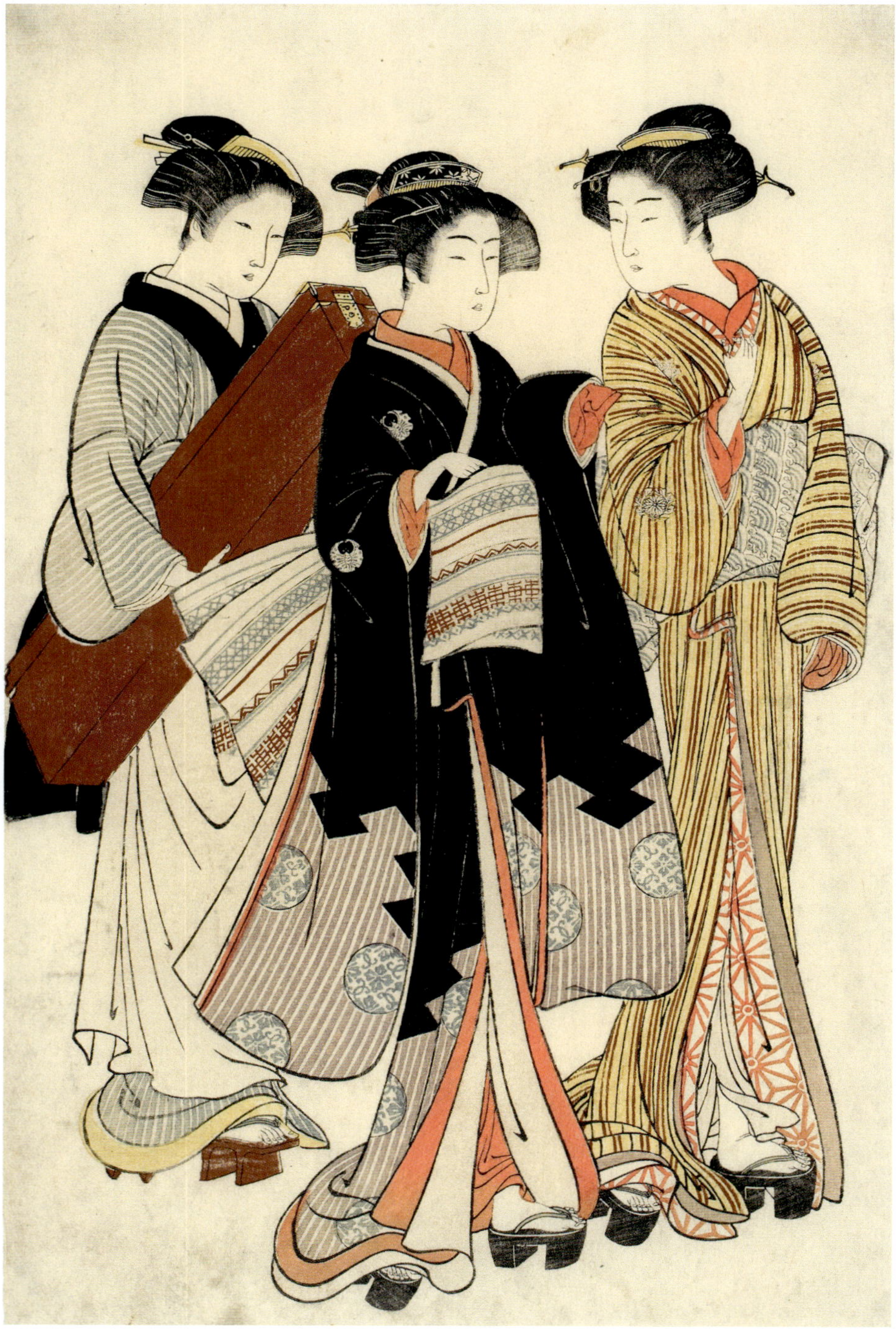
39

Kurtisanen lebten in der abgeschlossenen Welt der Freudenviertel und waren für Aussenstehende so gut wie unerreichbar. Gleichzeitig konnten die einfachen Leute flüchtige Blicke auf Kurtisanen werfen, wenn diese, in kunstvollen Gewändern aufwendig zurechtgemacht, vor oder nach einem Termin durch die Strassen gingen. Der Markt für *ukiyo-e* war weit grösser als der Kreis derjenigen, die sich die Gunst der Damen leisten konnten. Für die meisten Käufer von Holzschnitten wie diesen stellten die abgebildeten Szenen die grösstmögliche Annäherung an eine ranghohe Kurtisane dar. Von den in zahlreichen gesellschaftlichen Umgangsformen ausgesprochen bewanderten Kurtisanen erwartete man, dass sie ihre Gäste auch musikalisch unterhielten; oft wurden sie von einer Dienerin begleitet, die eine *shamisen* (japanische Laute) in einem schützenden Lackkoffer mit sich führte.

Ein Vergleich der Drucke von Shigemasa mit den zehn Jahre älteren Werken von Harunobu zeigt deutliche Unterschiede. Die vollständig fehlende Kulisse lenkt alle Aufmerksamkeit auf die Figuren, die, was noch wichtiger ist, sorgfältig zu Gruppen arrangiert sind. Sie bilden die Vorläufer der unverkennbaren Kompositionstechniken eines Kiyonaga ein Jahrzehnt später. Gleichzeitig kam die als *tôrôbin* bezeichnete Haartracht in Shigemasas Bildern, eine beliebte Frisur der 1770er-Jahre, bereits wieder aus der Mode, als Kiyonaga 1781 *Heimgehende Geisha* schuf.

Courtesans lived in the closed world of the pleasure quarters, and largely were inaccessible to those outside. At the same time, it was possible for ordinary people to catch glimpses of them, fully made-up in their elaborate costumes, going to and from their appointments. The market for *ukiyo-e* extended beyond those who could afford their attentions, and for the majority of people who would have bought prints such as these, the scenes depicted were as close as they would ever get to an actual encounter with an elite courtesan. Highly skilled in a variety of social graces, courtesans were expected to entertain their guests with music, and they often were accompanied by an attendant carrying a *shamisen* (lute, protected by a lacquered case).

A comparison of the prints by Shigemasa with Harunobu from a decade earlier reveals significant differences. Background elements have been eliminated, placing the viewer's full attention on the figures. Most importantly, the subjects are arranged into carefully composed groupings, establishing a precedent for Kiyonaga's distinctive compositional techniques in the following decade. At the same time, the *tôrôbin* hairstyle evident in Shigemasa's prints, popular in the 1770s, had already started to fall out of fashion by the time Kiyonaga made *Departing Geisha* in 1781.

SE

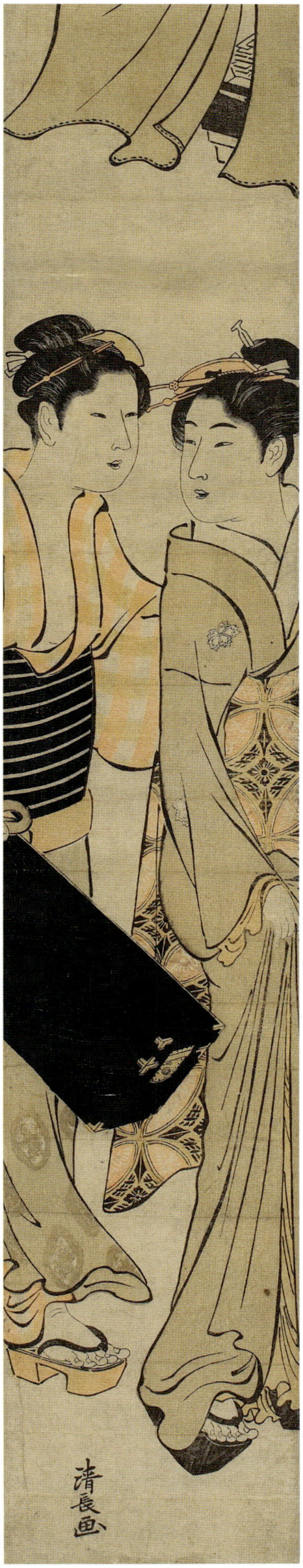

42

北尾重政

39
Eine Geisha auf dem Weg zur Arbeit
A Geisha on Her Way to Work
Kitao SHIGEMASA

北尾重政

40
Eine Geisha und ihre Dienerin
A Geisha and Her Servant
Kitao SHIGEMASA

北尾重政

41
Schönheiten des Ostens im Stadtviertel Nakachô. Onaka und Oshima – Schönheiten des Ostens, Westens, Nordens und Südens
Beauties of the East in Nakachô. Onaka and Oshima – Beauties of the East, West, North, and South
Kitao SHIGEMASA

鳥居清長

42
Heimgehende Geisha
Departing Geisha
Torii KIYONAGA

鳥居 清長

43
Mehr an sich selbst denken als an den Ehemann – Lehrbuch für junge Mädchen
Thinking More of Yourself Than of Your Husband – A Textbook for Young Girls
Torii KIYONAGA

栄松斎 長喜

44
Das Takashimaya-Teehaus
The Takashimaya Teahouse
Eishôsai CHÔKI

鳥居 清長

45
Im Stadtbezirk Asakusa – Zehn Sommerszenen in der Östlichen Hauptstadt
Asakusa – Ten Summer Scenes in the Eastern Capital
Torii KIYONAGA

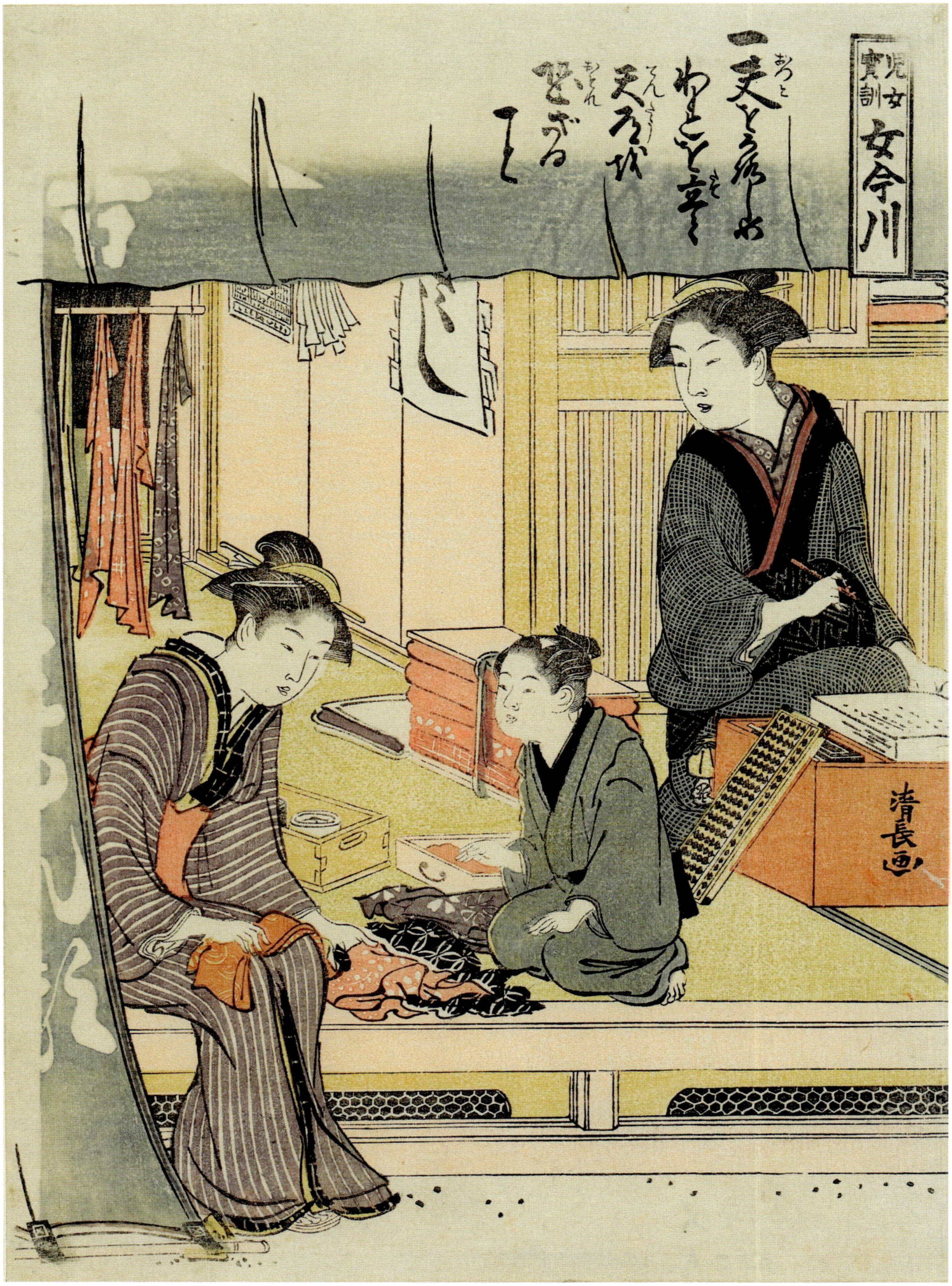

43

Frauendarstellungen im *ukiyo-e* beschränkten sich nicht auf formale Kurtisanenporträts, und sowohl Kiyonaga als auch Chôki haben sich hier für Alltagsszenen als Kulisse für ihre Schönheiten entschieden. Chôki beobachtet das Zusammenspiel eines Teehausmädchens mit ihrer Kundin (KAT. 44). Die Körpersprache zwischen ihnen, die Kundin wendet sich ab, als sei das Mädchen Luft, wird nur umso interessanter vor dem Hintergrund, dass es sich bei der Bedienung im Takashimaya tatsächlich um Ohisa handelte, eine der namhaftesten Schönheiten ihrer Zeit. Die Kundin aber ist gegen ihre Reize eindeutig immun!

In *Asakusa* (KAT. 45) zeigt Kiyonaga auf ähnliche Weise, wie eine Teequirlverkäuferin am Sensôji-Tempel, einem der Wahrzeichen der dicht besiedelten «Unterstadt» *(shitamachi)* von Edo, eine Kundin zu ködern versucht. Deren Verachtung wird vom sie begleitenden Dienstmädchen geteilt. Das Blatt wurde zwar vom Originaldruckstock gedruckt, entpuppt sich beim Vergleich seiner Farben mit denen der beiden anderen Blätter jedoch als späterer Nachdruck.

Der zweite Kiyonaga-Entwurf kehrt die Dynamik zwischen Kundin und Verkäuferin um (KAT. 43). Die Frau zur Linken hadert mit dem Kauf eines Tuches, was dem Titel zufolge gegen den Willen ihres Mannes verstossen könnte. Die Ladenbesitzerin unterbricht ihre Buchhaltung mit einem Ausdruck stiller Zuversicht, wohl wissend, dass sie das Geschäft machen wird.

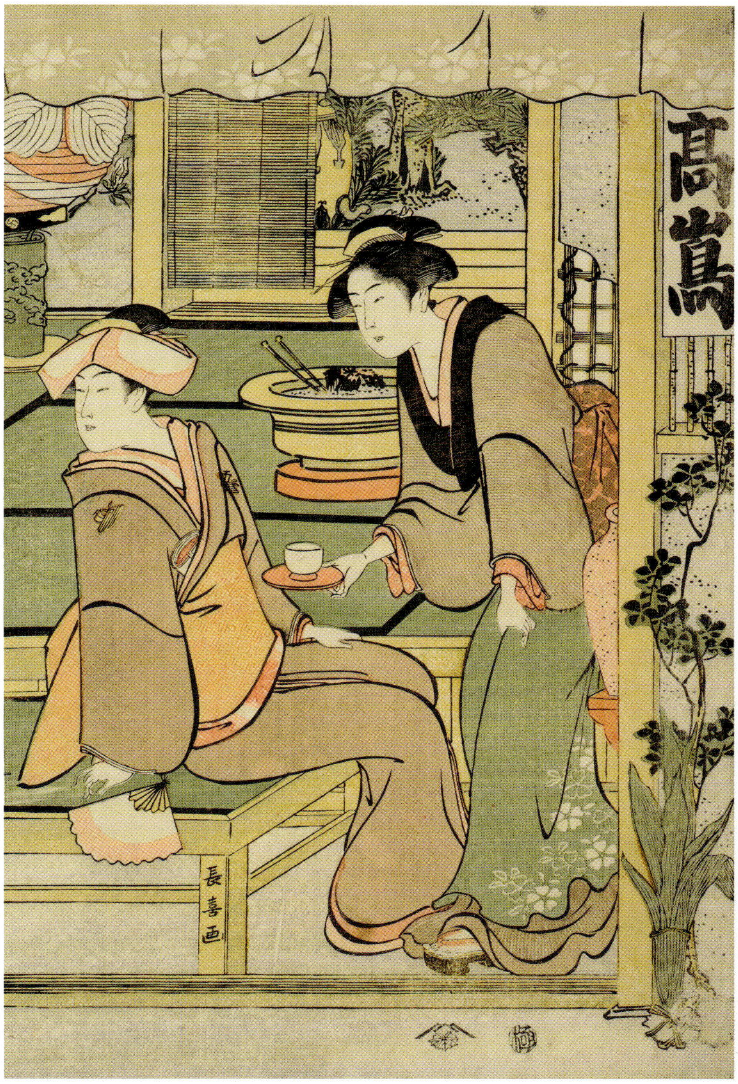

44

Depictions of women in *ukiyo-e* were not limited to formal portraits of courtesans, and both Kiyonaga and Chôki have chosen here to use everyday scenes as the settings for their beauties. Chôki observes the interaction between a teahouse waitress and her customer (CAT. 44). The body language between them, with the customer turning away as if the waitress did not exist, becomes even more interesting when we realize that the waitress of the Takashimaya was in fact Ohisa, one of the most renowned beauties of her time. However, her customer is clearly immune to her charms!

Similarly, in *Asakusa* (CAT. 45), Kiyonaga shows a seller of tea whisks at Sensôji Temple, one of the landmarks of the "low town" *(shitamachi)* in which many Edo urbanites made their homes, trying to attract a customer, whose disdain is shared by her maid. Although this impression was printed from the original blocks, a comparison of the colors with those of the other two prints reveals it to be a later printing.

The remaining print by Kiyonaga reverses the dynamic between seller and client (CAT. 43). The woman on the left struggles over a purchase that the inscription indicates she suspects would go against her husband's wishes; the shop's matron pauses in her bookkeeping to watch, the quiet confidence of her expression suggesting she knows she will make the sale.

SE

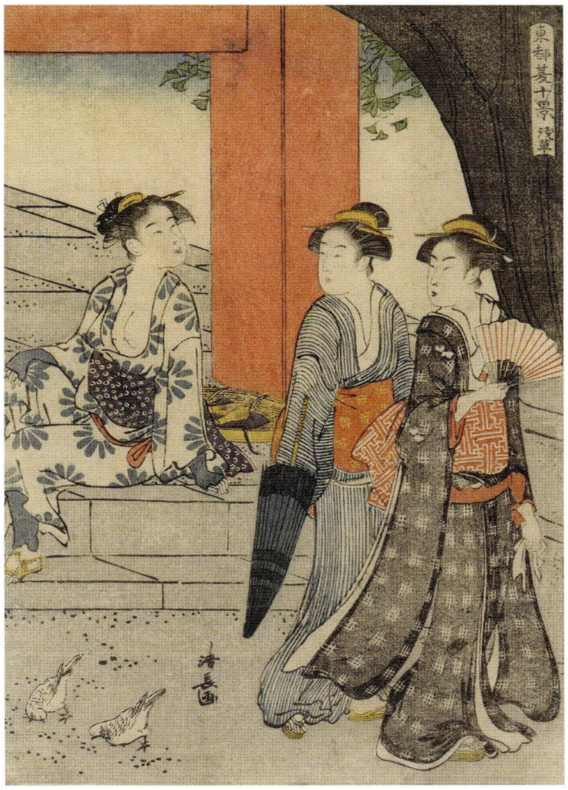

45

Kiyonaga erweiterte die Möglichkeiten des Einzelblattdrucks von Holzschnitten mit zahlreichen ausladenden Motiven, die sich über Diptychen und Triptychen erstreckten. Darüber hinaus liess er das zarte, jugendliche Körperideal Harunobus hinter sich und begründete mit seinen würdevoll gelängten Frauenfiguren einen neuen Schönheitskanon, der die 1780er-Jahre beherrschte. Entscheidend für den Erfolg seines neuen Kompositionsstils war der Einsatz geometrischer Arrangements von sorgfältig geordneten Figuren, häufig in pyramidenförmigen Dreiergruppen. Der Detailreichtum von *Menschen auf der Strasse in Nihonbashi,* einer Szene im Lagerhausviertel von Edo während des Neujahrsfestes, erstreckt sich vom Berg Fuji im Hintergrund bis zu der jungen Pilgerin im grünen Kimono, die gerade vom Schrein auf Enoshima zurückgekehrt ist (wie die Aufschrift auf ihrem Hut verrät).

In der humorvollen Szene *Schnee am Morgen vor dem Freudenhaus* werden die Kurtisanen von der Hausmutter aufgeschreckt, die wie inszeniert mit zwei lebenden Karpfen in der Hand von rechts ins Bild tritt. Der Kunde der Damen hält beim Schreiben seines Briefes inne, um den Tumult mit einem Schmunzeln zu beobachten. Das Lager, an das er sich lehnt, ist ein subtiler Hinweis auf die Freuden der vorangegangenen Nacht, während draussen der Schnee die Landschaft sanft bedeckt.

Kiyonaga extended the possibilities of single-sheet woodblock prints through his many expansive subjects spreading over diptychs and triptychs. In addition, he left behind the delicately youthful physical ideal developed by Harunobu, and his stately, elongated women introduced new canons of beauty that dominated the 1780s. Key to the success of his new compositional style was the use of geometric arrangements of carefully organized figures, often in groups of three forming a pyramid. *Street Traffic at Nihonbashi,* depicting a scene in Edo's commercial warehouse district during the New Year, is rich in detail, from the presence of Mount Fuji in the background to the young pilgrim in a green kimono returning from the shrine at Enoshima (indicated on her hat).

Morning Snow at the Brothel House depicts a humorous scene of courtesans startled by the entrance of the house matron from the right, as if staged, carrying two live carp. Their male patron pauses from writing a letter to chuckle at the pandemonium, the bedding upon which he leans subtly suggesting the pleasures of the night before, as snow gently covers the landscape outside.

SE

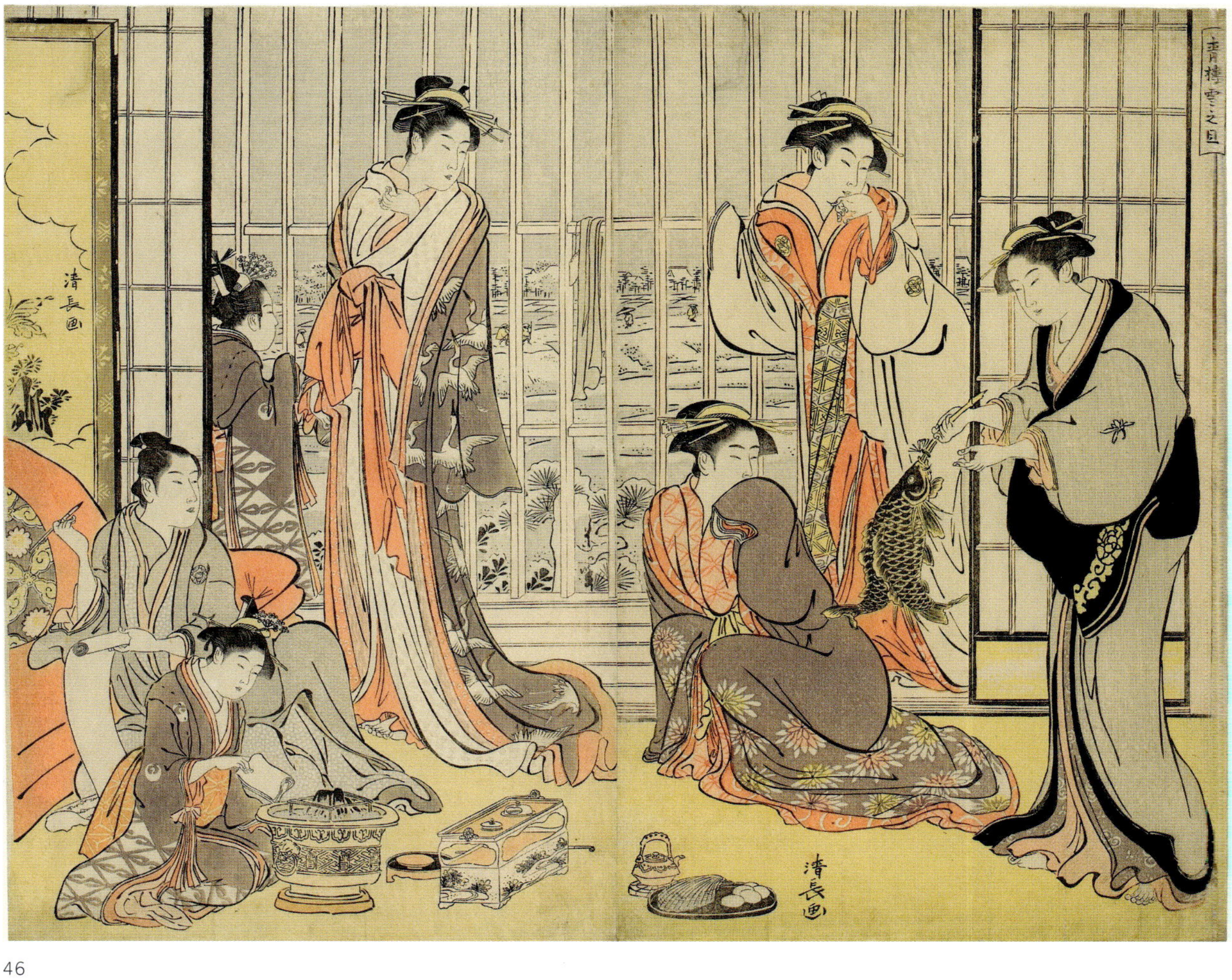

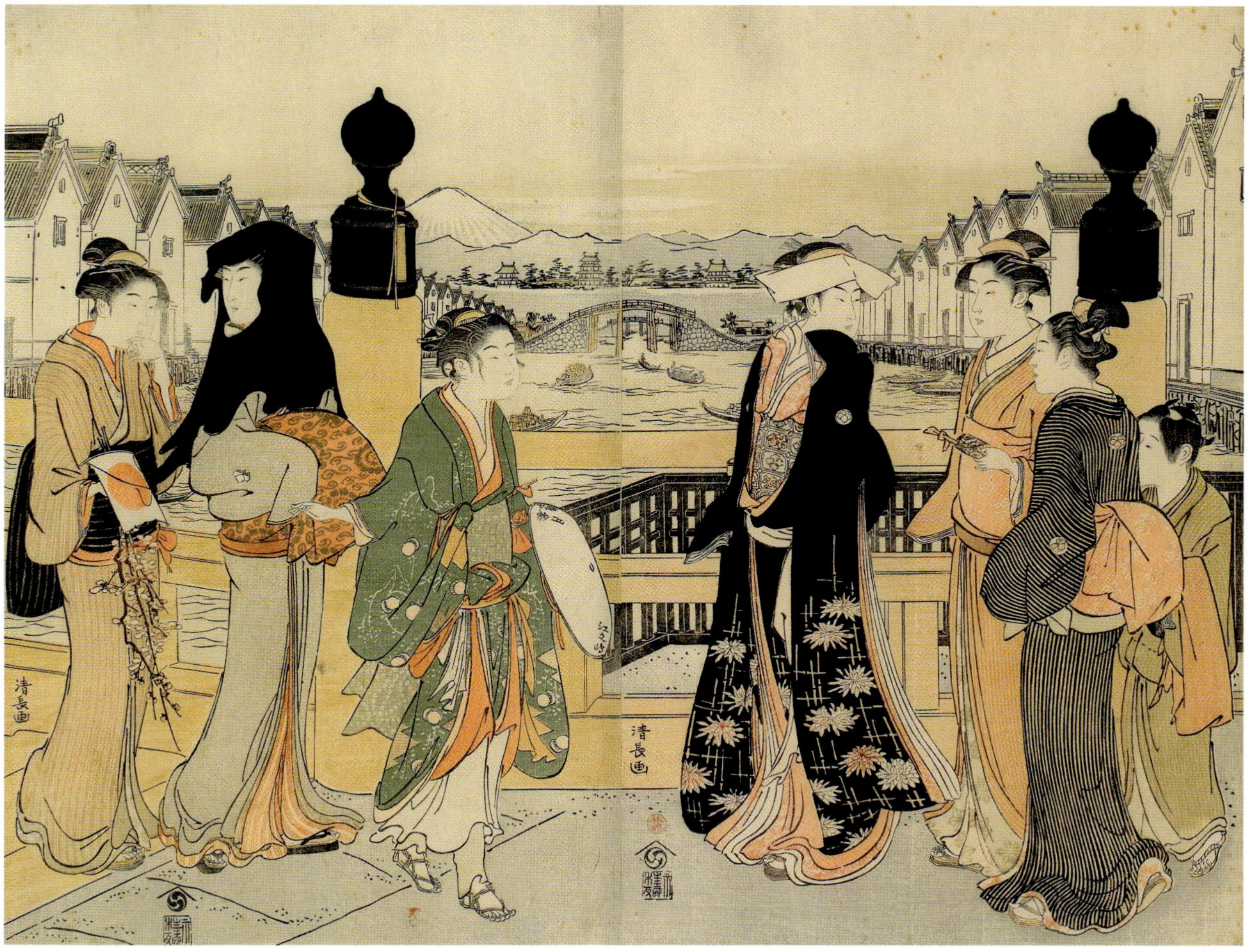

47

鳥居 清長

46

Schnee am Morgen vor dem Freudenhaus

Morning Snow at the Brothel House

Torii KIYONAGA

鳥居 清長

47

Menschen auf der Strasse in Nihonbashi

Street Traffic at Nihonbashi

Torii KIYONAGA

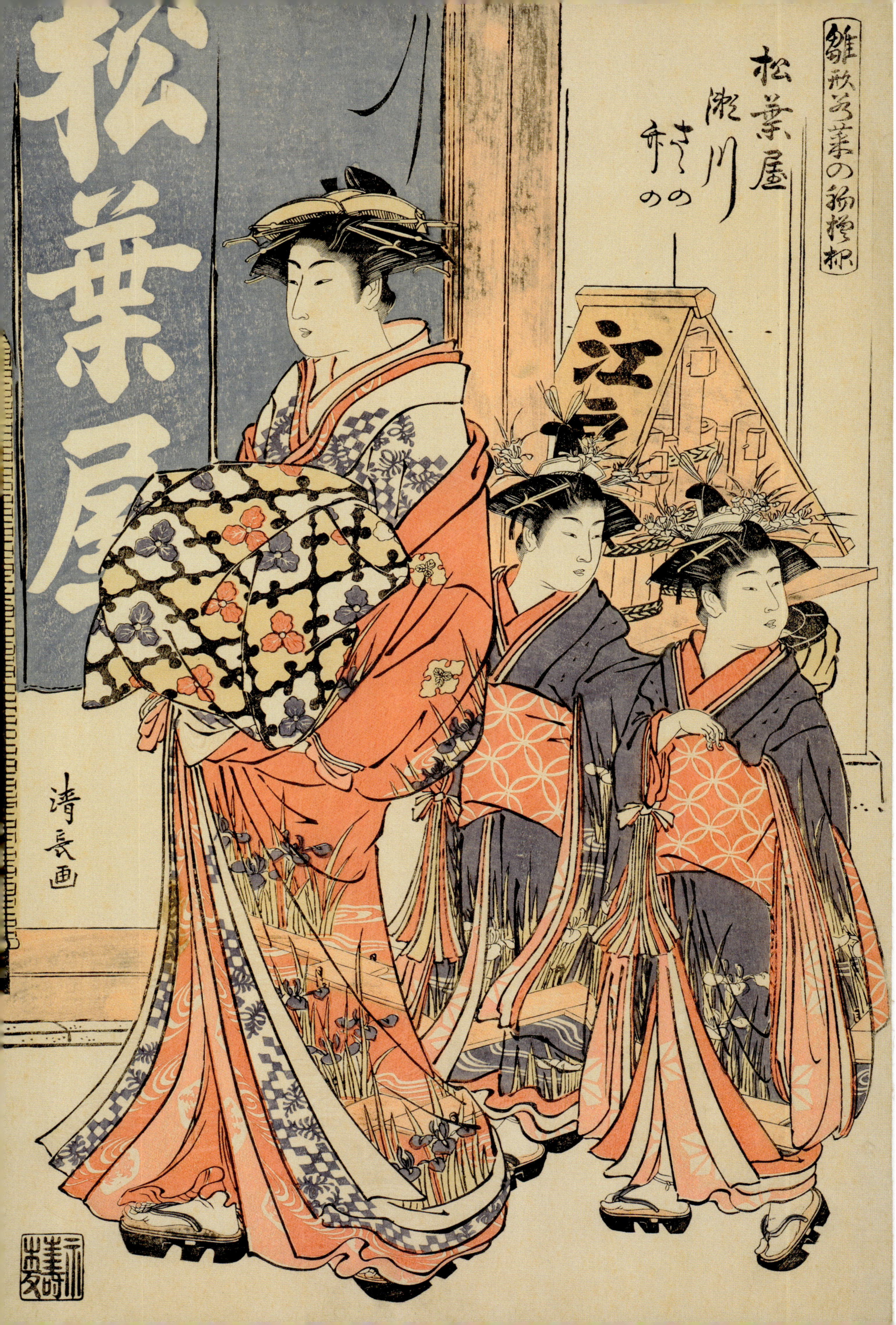

雛形若菜の初模様
松葉屋
瀬川
さゝの
たけの
松葉屋
江戸
清長画

Unter der Regie des Verlegers Nishimuraya setzte Kiyonaga die von Koryûsai begonnene Serie fort und ergänzte das höchst erfolgreiche Projekt um zehn Entwürfe. Jeder von ihnen stellt eine ranghohe, nach der neuesten Mode gekleidete Kurtisane mit ihren Begleiterinnen dar. Dieser Druck, in der Reihe vermutlich der erste, zeigt Segawa auf ihrem Spaziergang durch das Yoshiwara-Viertel vor dem Teehaus Matsubaya (nicht zu verwechseln mit dem gleichnamigen Bordell). Ihre beiden *kamuro* (kindliche Lehrmädchen), Sasano und Takeno, begleiten sie. Die Namen der Kurtisane, der *kamuro* und des Hauses, dem sie angehörten, erscheinen oben rechts im Bild. Darunter ist ein Brunnen zu erkennen, dessen Holzeimer kaum zu sehen ist. Die drei Figuren tragen aufeinander abgestimmte Stoffmuster aus Iris, einem Fluss und einer achtplankigen Brücke. Das Publikum von Edo erkannte darin augenblicklich Motive aus den *Erzählungen von Ise* aus dem 10. Jahrhundert, die so für zusätzliche Bedeutungsebenen sorgten.

Under the direction of the publisher Nishimuraya, Kiyonaga continued the series begun by Koryûsai, contributing ten designs to this highly successful project. Each work features a high-ranking courtesan with her attendants, dressed in the latest fashion. This print is believed to be the earliest. It depicts Segawa walking in front of the Matsubaya teahouse (different from the brothel) on her promenade through the Yoshiwara district. Her two *kamuro* (child trainees), Sasano and Takeno, accompany her. The names of the courtesan and the *kamuro,* as well as the house with which they were associated, appear in the upper right. Below is a well, the wooden bucket just visible. The three figures wear coordinated designs of irises, a stream, and an eight-plank bridge. For an Edo audience, these motifs would have immediately evoked the tenth-century *Tales of Ise,* adding additional layers of meaning.

CM

鳥居清長

48

Segawa mit den Schülerinnen Sasano und Takeno aus dem Freudenhaus Matsubaya – Modelle für die Mode: Neue Muster, so frisch wie junge Blätter

Segawa with Sasano and Takeno of the Matsubaya Brothel House – Models for Fashion: New Designs as Fresh as Young Leaves

Torii KIYONAGA

Abbilder ranghoher Kurtisanen beim Spaziergang mit ihren Begleiterinnen sind ein häufiges Thema in der Gattung der *bijinga.* Wie bei Holzschnitten der Zeit üblich, wurden die Namen der Kurtisane, ihres Hauses und der begleitenden *kamuro* mit abgedruckt. Der Stil der hier dargestellten Schönheiten macht deutlich, wie sehr die Künstler sich dem Ideal der hochgewachsenen, schlanken Frauenfiguren verpflichtet fühlten, das Kiyonaga und Utamaro durchgesetzt hatten. Shunchôs Arbeiten waren besonders in den späten 1780er-Jahren gefragt, als Kiyonaga die Leitung der Torii-Schule übernahm. In den 1790er-Jahren erreichte Eishi den Gipfel seiner Schöpfungskraft und nahm es an Beliebtheit mit Utamaro auf.

Eishis Druck zeigt Utaura, wie sie gemeinsam mit Hanaki und Chidori, ihren zauberhaften kindlichen *kamuro,* und ihrer jugendlichen *shinzô* im Gefolge vor dem grossen Tor von Yoshiwara haltmacht. Im Hintergrund sehen wir die Sakehandlung Okuda, den grössten Spirituosenlieferanten des Freudenviertels. Shunchôs Entwurf gehört zu einer Serie mit dem Titel *Die fünf Feste* und stellt das Knabenfest dar, das am fünften Tag des fünften Monats gefeiert wurde. Der eingekreiste Turm oben rechts im Bild symbolisiert das Fest und liefert so den Titel für den Druck. Das Karpfenmuster auf Seyamas Robe und die Helme auf den Kimonos der *kamuro* führen das Thema des Knabenfestes fort.

A high-ranking courtesan walking with her attendants is a frequent theme in *bijinga.* As was customary in prints of the time, the names of the courtesan, her house, and those of the two *kamuro* (child trainees) are included. The style of *bijin* depicted by the two artists demonstrates their debt to the tall, slender ideal made popular by Kiyonaga and Utamaro. Shunchô's work was particularly in demand in the late 1780s, when Kiyonaga's attention turned to management of the Torii School. In the 1790s, Eishi was at the height of his powers, rivaling Utamaro in popularity.

Eishi's work shows Utaura pausing in front of the great gate of the Yoshiwara, her charming *kamuro,* Hanaki and Chidori, at her side and her *shinzô* (adolescent attendant) standing behind her. In the background is the Okuda sake store, the major liquor supplier to the pleasure quarters. Shunchô's design is part of a series titled *The Five Festivals.* Depicted here is Boy's Day, celebrated on the fifth day of the fifth month. The castle keep in the circle at upper right, symbolic of the festival, acts as the title for the print, and the picture of carp on Seyama's robe and the helmets on the kimono of the *kamuro* continue the Boy's Day theme.

CM

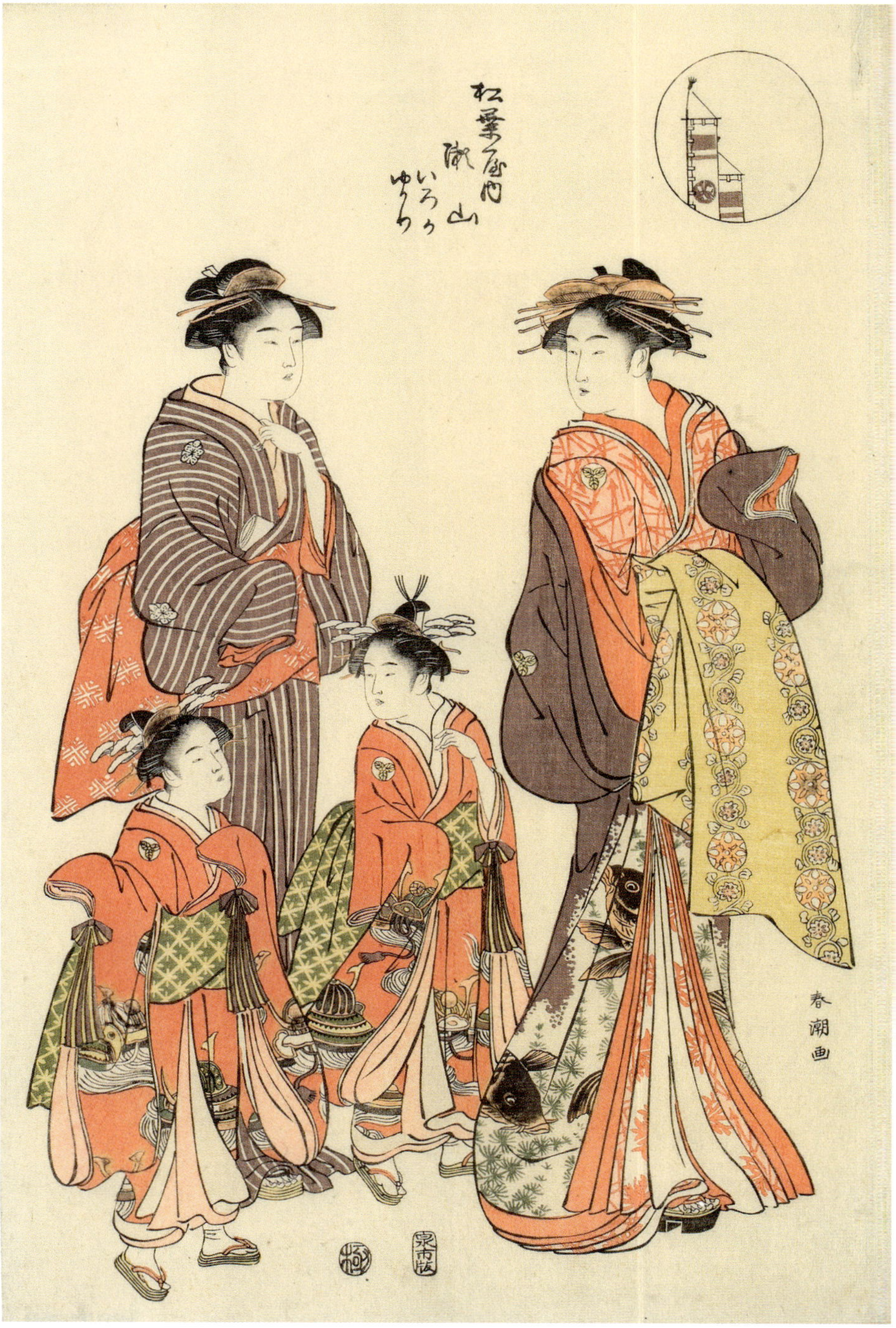

49

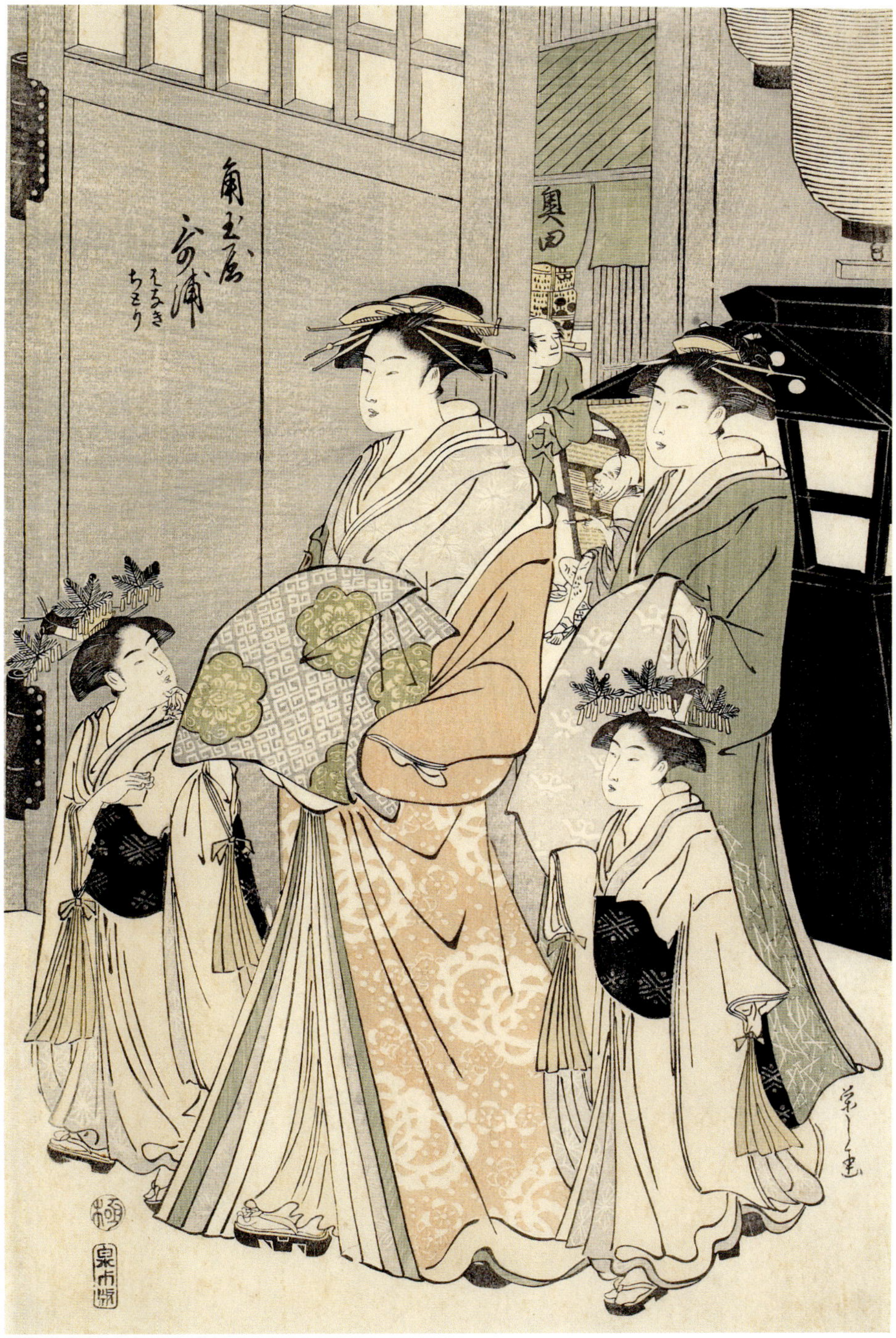

50

勝川 春潮

49

Seyama aus dem Freudenhaus Matsubaya

Seyama of the Matsubaya Brothel House

Katsukawa SHUNCHÔ

鳥文斎 栄之

50

Utaura aus dem Freudenhaus Kadotamaya

Utaura of the Kadotamaya Brothel House

Chôbunsai EISHI

Beim Verlassen des Freudenviertels wurden wichtige Gäste bis an das Tor geleitet, das den Stadtteil von Edo trennte. Der «Süden» im Bildtitel bezieht sich auf das am südlichen Stadtrand gelegene, unlizenzierte Bordellviertel in Shinagawa. In diesem Druck wird ein eleganter junger Mann, zu erkennen am Schwert, das er bei sich trägt, von einer Gruppe Kurtisanen eskortiert. Seine Aufmerksamkeit gilt jedoch einer anderen, unbeteiligten Kurtisane, die seinen Blick über die Köpfe der Begleiterinnen hinweg erwidert. Diesen bleibt die gegenseitige Anziehung der beiden nicht verborgen, und ihre unterschiedlichen Reaktionen verleihen der narrativen Darstellung zusätzliche Würze. Mit dem Diptychon-Format gelingt es Kiyonaga, der Interaktion zwischen Besucher und Kurtisane einen breiten Raum zu geben, der die Spannung erhöht und die Komposition zu einem wirkungsvollen Ganzen verbindet. Die Szene spielt vor einem dunklen Nachthimmel, der in Abstufungen von Schwarz wunderschön wiedergegeben ist.

Für James A. Michener stellte dieser Druck die Inkarnation des *ukiyo-e* dar. Über Kiyonaga selbst schrieb Michener: «Manchmal betritt ein vollkommener Künstler die Bühne, der die meisten vorangegangenen Traditionen in sich vereint und alle erforderlichen Fertigkeiten in perfekter Ausgewogenheit beherrscht. [...] Sein verblüffendes Urteilsvermögen beim Austarieren einer Masse gegen eine andere befähigte ihn, prächtige Meisterwerke zu produzieren» (MICHENER 1954, S. 125).

On leaving the pleasure quarters, important guests were escorted to the gate that separated the district from Edo. The "south" of the title refers to the unlicensed brothel district in Shinagawa, on the southern edge of the city. In this print, a fashionable young man, distinguished by the sword tucked into his *obi,* is being guided by a group of courtesans. The man's attention, however, has been captured by a different courtesan, who returns his gaze over the heads of his companions. Their mutual attraction has been noticed by the others, and the various reactions of these figures add interest to the narrative. Kiyonaga has used the diptych format to draw out the interaction between the guest and courtesan, heightening the tension and effectively unifying the composition. The scene plays out against a night sky beautifully realized in gradations of black.

For James A. Michener, this print represented the very best of *ukiyo-e.* About Kiyonaga himself, Michener wrote: "Occasionally, a complete artist appears who unites in himself most previous traditions and who commands each requisite skill in perfect proportions. ... His uncanny judgment in balancing one mass against another enabled him to produce stately masterpieces" (MICHENER 1954, P. 125).

CM

鳥居清長

51
Siebter Monat, abendlicher Abschied – Zwölf Monate im Süden
Seventh Month, Evening Send-Off – Twelve Months in the South
Torii KIYONAGA

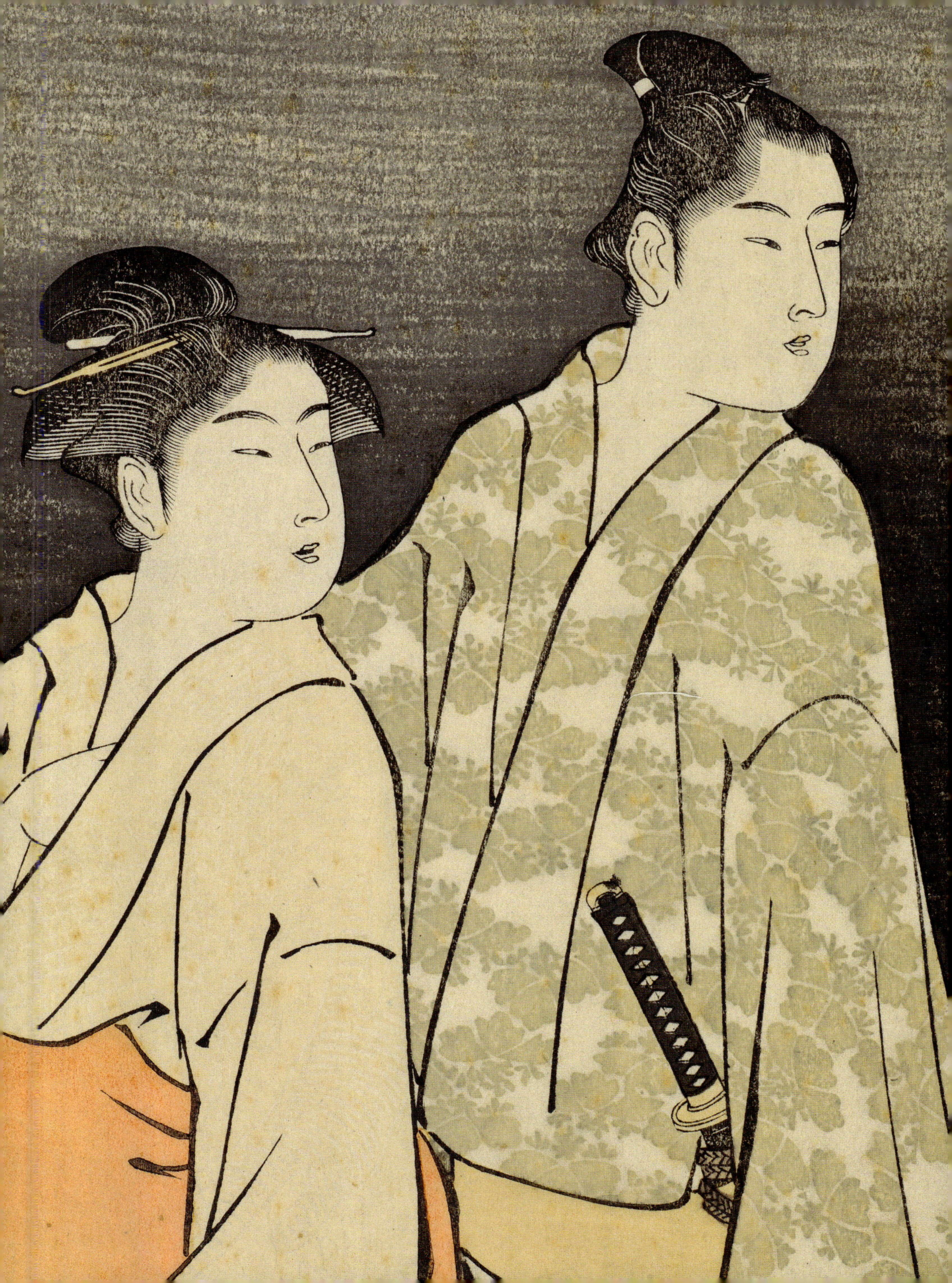

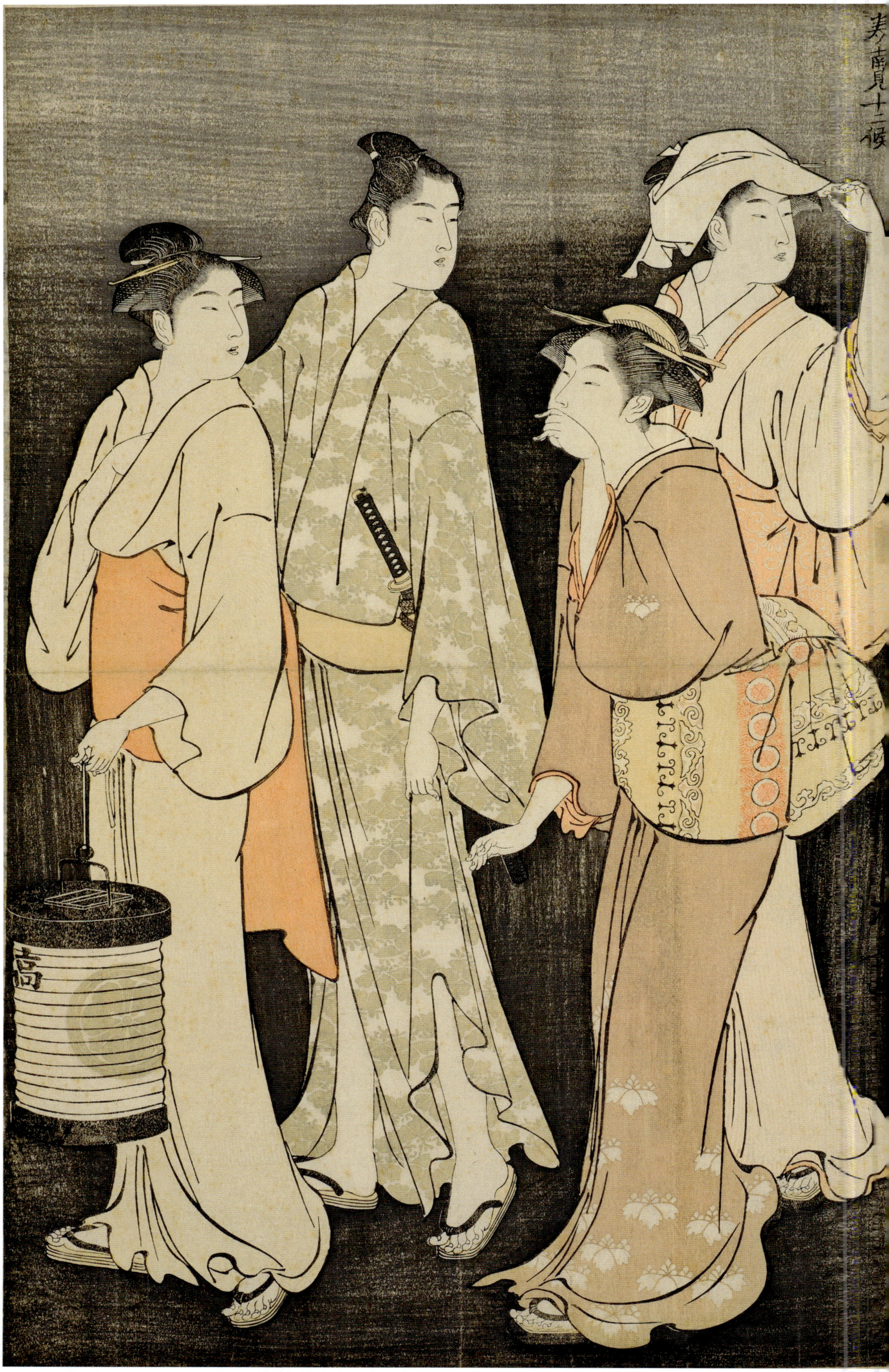
美ノ南見十二候
高

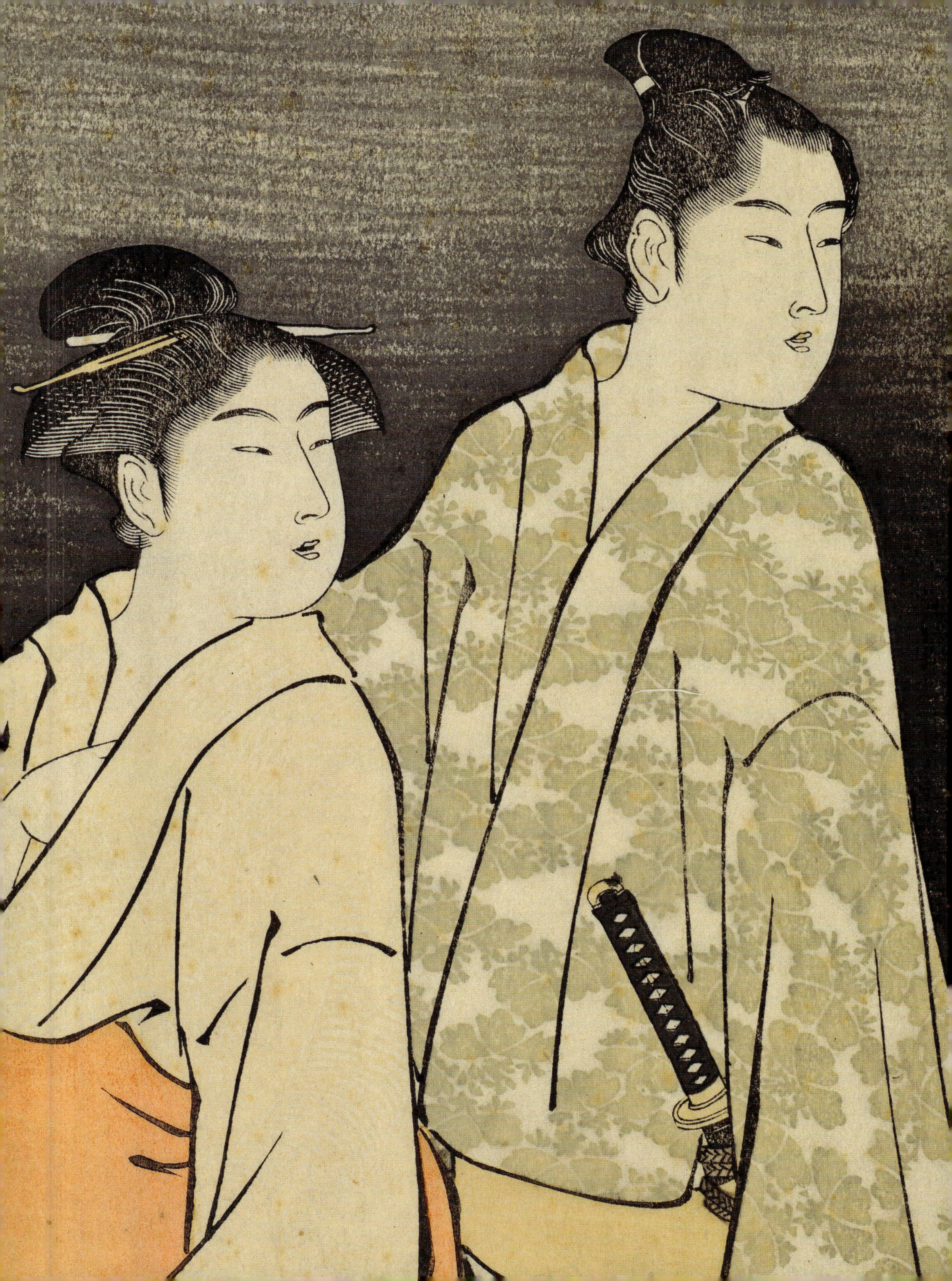

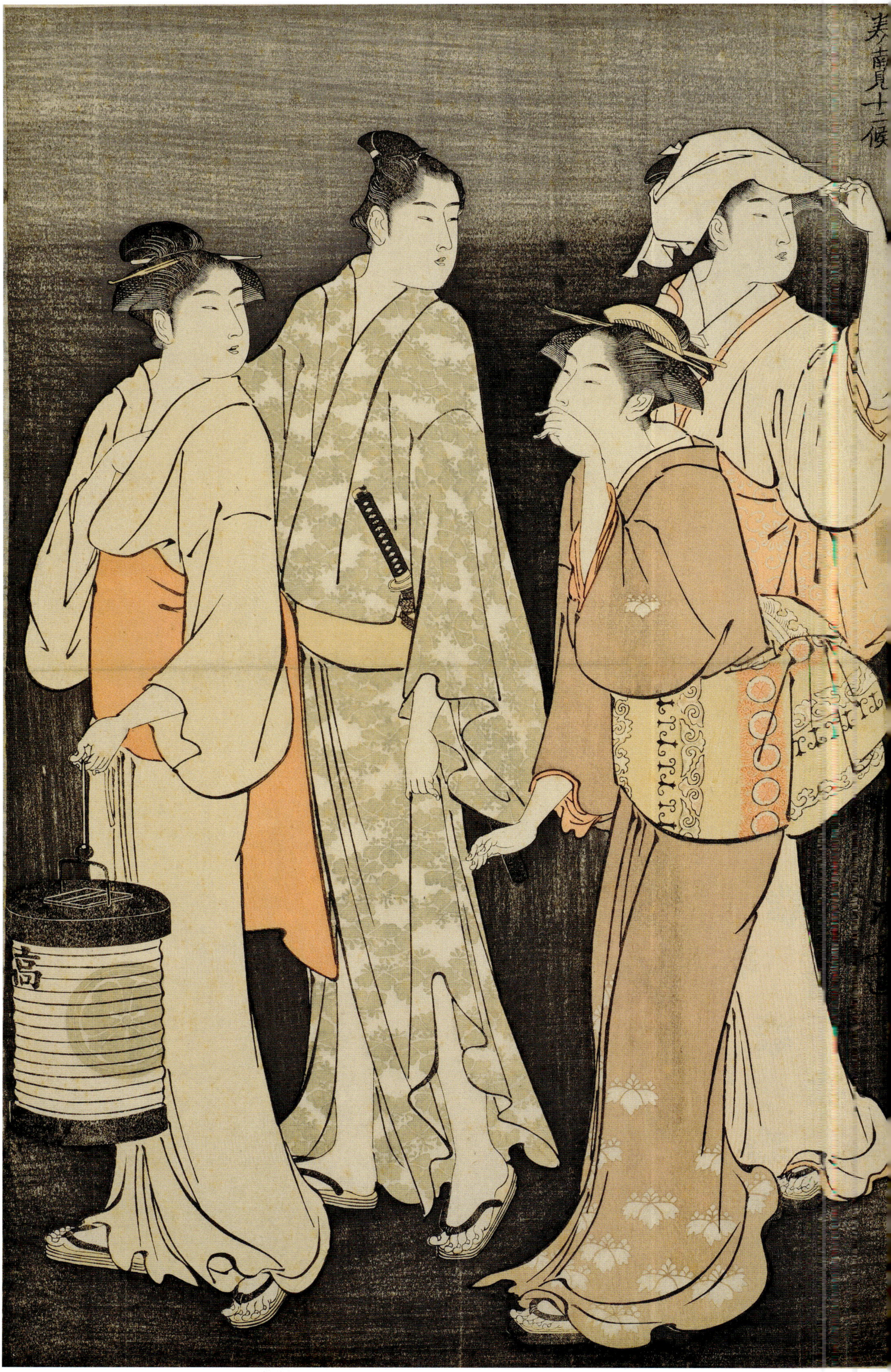

美南見十二候
高

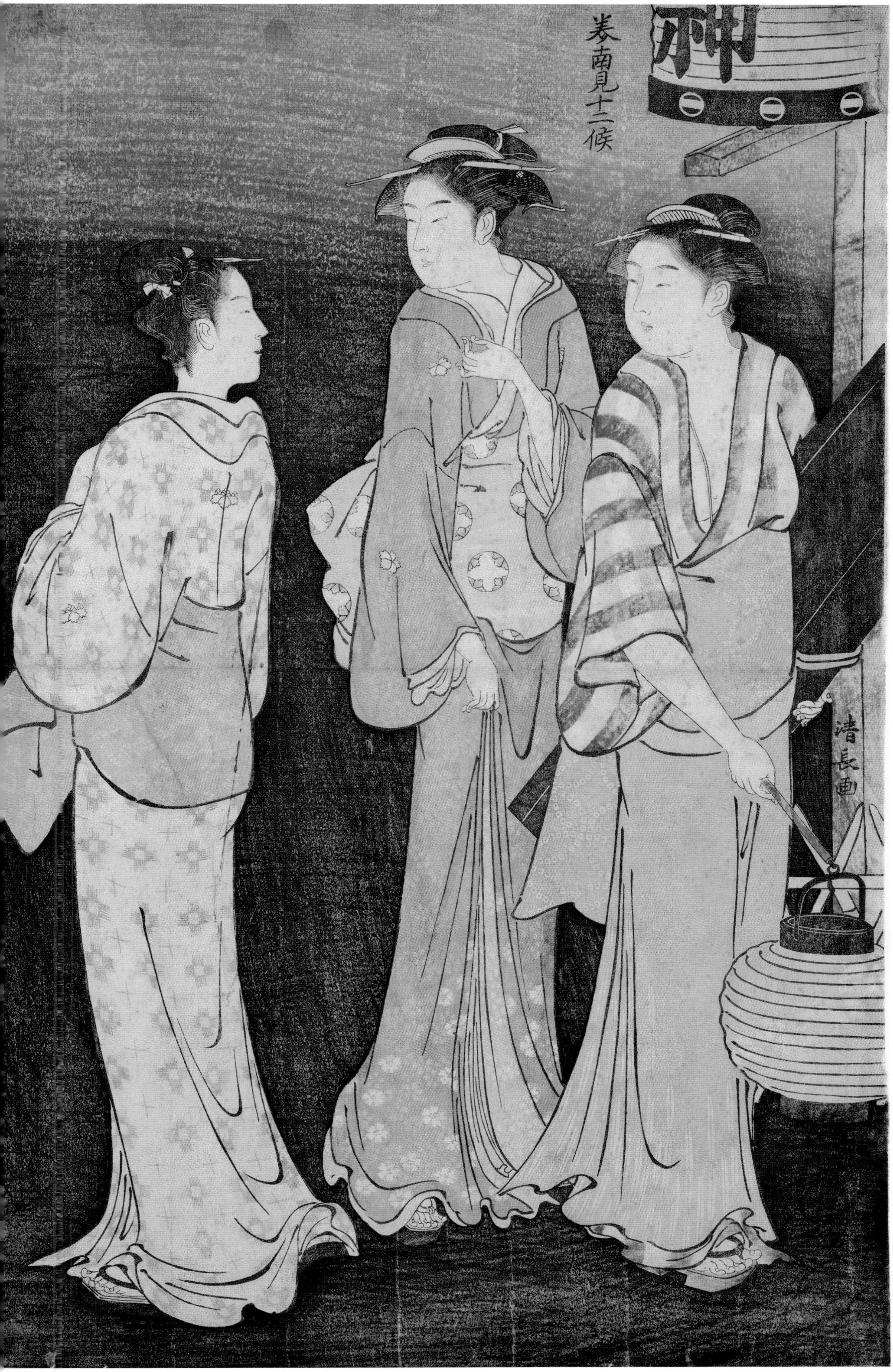
美南見十二候
清長画
神

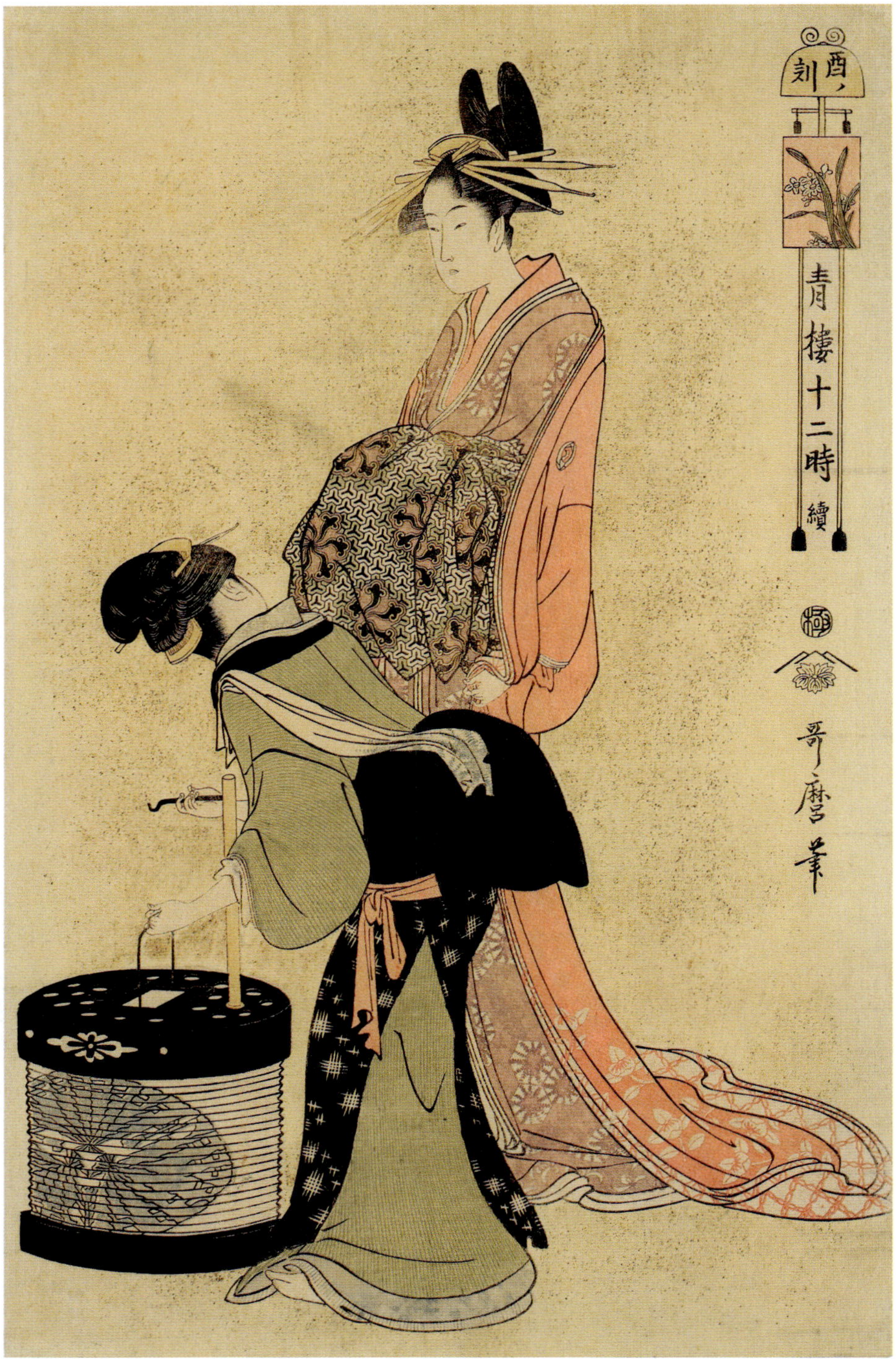

Die 24 Stunden des Tages wurden in Japan traditionell in zwölf Abschnitte unterteilt, die nach den Sternzeichen benannt waren. Diese Art der Zeitmessung lieferte Utamaro ein cleveres Gerüst für eine Serie von Darstellungen aus dem Leben der Kurtisanen in Yoshiwara. Allein oder mit ihren Begleiterinnen in Szene gesetzt, scheinen die Frauen sich unbeobachtet zu fühlen. Eine Kartusche in Form einer Pfeileruhr enthält den Titel der Serie und zeigt auf der Uhrglocke die jeweilige Stunde an. Trotz der Luxusverbote der Kansei-Reformen (1787–1793) wurden diese Blätter mit sieben Farben gedruckt und mit Metallpulver bestreut.

Die Stunde der Schlange (9–11 Uhr) ist im Tagesablauf einer Kurtisane früher Morgen. Sie hat soeben das morgendliche Bad beendet, trägt einen baumwollenen Morgenrock mit Batikmuster und lässt sich von ihrer *kamuro* den Tee servieren. Erst zur Stunde des Hahnes (18–20 Uhr), wenn die Nacht beginnt, bricht eine Kurtisane zu ihrer ersten Verabredung auf. Das Wappen auf der Laterne weist sie als Hanaôgi aus dem Freudenhaus Ôgiya aus.

Die zuvor bereits bei Kiyonaga beobachtete Längung der weiblichen Figur findet bei Utamaro nicht nur in den Körpern, sondern auch in den Frisuren ihre Fortsetzung. In diesen beiden Drucken betont er die statuarische Gestalt der ranghohen Kurtisanen, indem er die Proportionen ihrer Begleiterinnen naturgetreuer erscheinen lässt.

Traditionally in Japan, the 24-hour day was divided into twelve intervals, each named after a zodiacal sign. This way of telling time provided Utamaro with a clever schema for a series of images depicting the life of the Yoshiwara courtesan. Shown in scenes by themselves or with their attendants, the women appear to have been caught unawares. A cartouche in the shape of a pillar clock contains the title of the series, and the individual hours are announced on the bell portion. Despite the prohibitions against luxury announced in the Kansei reforms (1787–1793), these works are printed in seven colors and sprinkled with metallic powder.

The hour of the snake (9–11 a.m.) is early in the courtesan's day. Wearing a tie-dyed cotton robe, she has just come from her morning bath and is being served tea by her *kamuro* (child trainee). By the hour of the cock (6–8 p.m.), the evening has begun, and a courtesan is leaving for her first assignation. The crest on the lantern suggests that she is Hanaôgi of the Ôgiya.

The elongation of the female figure seen earlier in the work of Kiyonaga is carried further in Utamaro's series, not only in the body, but in the hairstyle as well. In these two prints, the statuesque proportions are emphasized by the juxtaposition of the high-ranking courtesan with her more realistically proportioned attendant.

CM

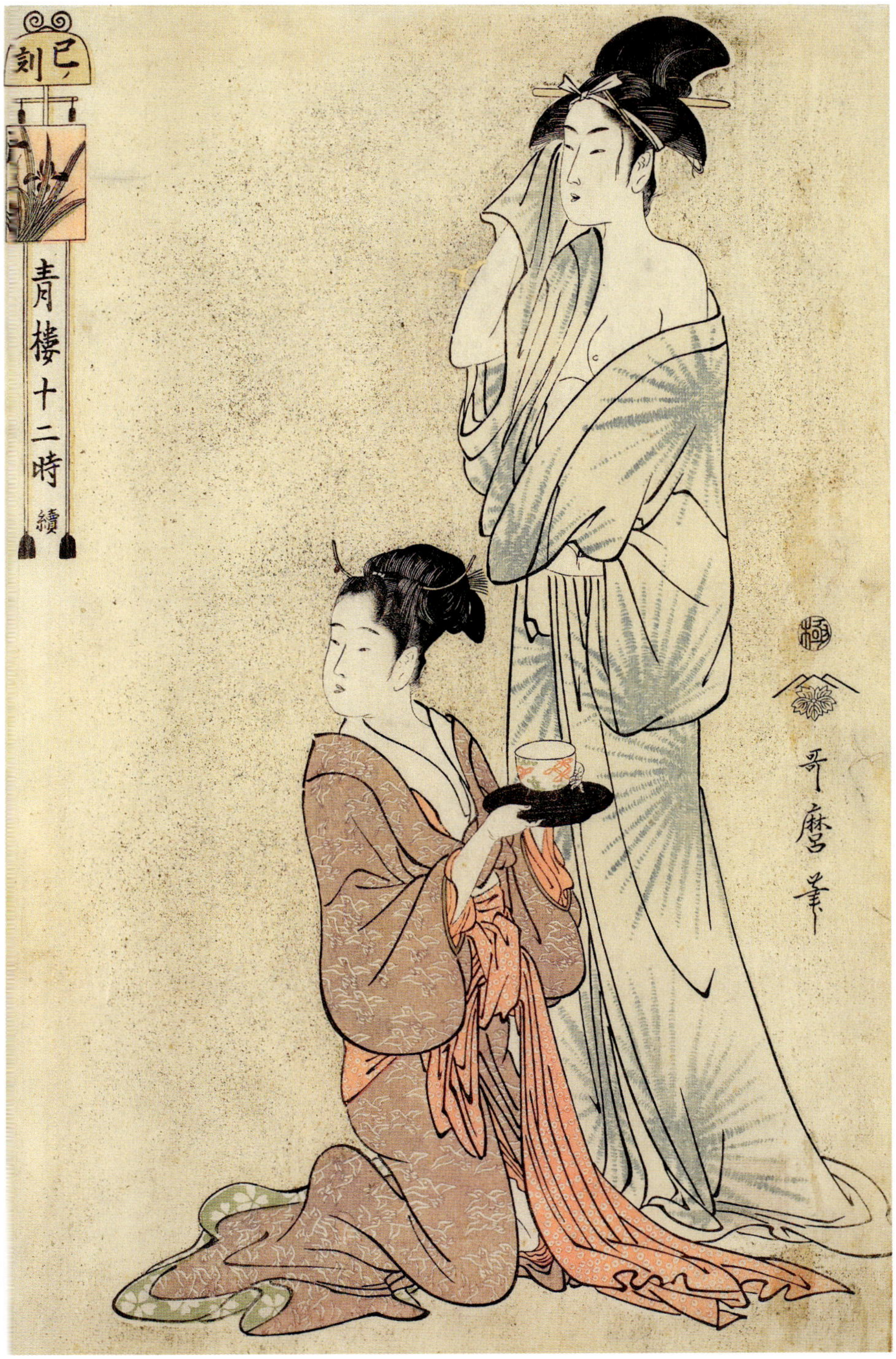

53

喜多川 歌麿

52
Die Stunde des Hahnes – Zwölf Stunden im Freudenviertel Yoshiwara
The Hour of the Cock – Twelve Hours in the Yoshiwara
Kitagawa UTAMARO

喜多川 歌麿

53
Die Stunde der Schlange – Zwölf Stunden im Freudenviertel Yoshiwara
The Hour of the Snake – Twelve Hours in the Yoshiwara
Kitagawa UTAMARO

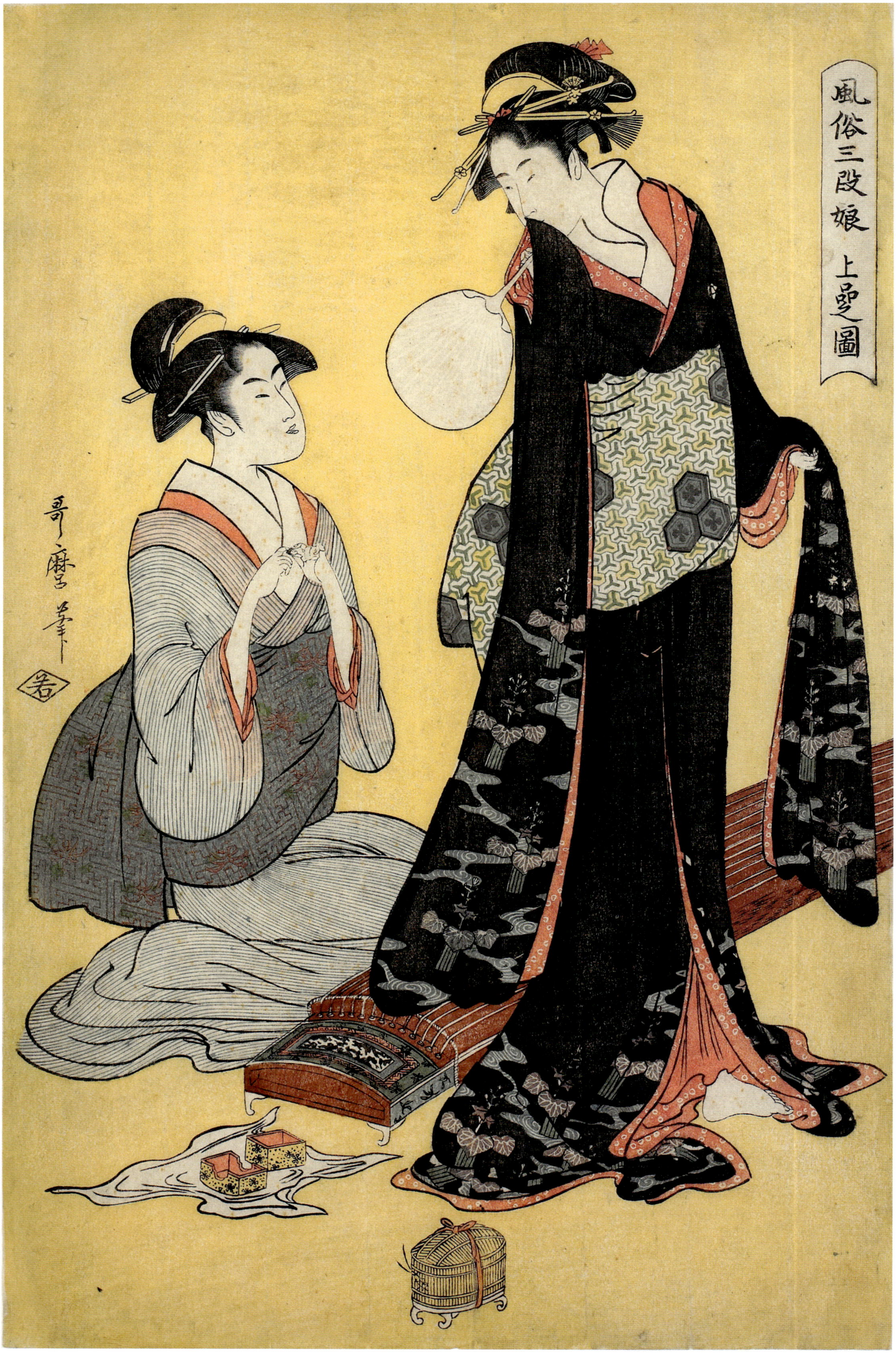
風俗三段娘
上之圖
哥麿筆

Musikalische Begabung wurde nicht nur von Kurtisanen erwartet, sondern war auch ein wesentlicher Bestandteil der kulturellen Ausbildung von Töchtern aus wohlhabenden Familien. Gleichzeitig sind an den verschiedenen Musikinstrumenten in diesen beiden Drucken die sozialen Unterschiede zwischen den Frauen abzulesen. Im Schoss der von Kunimasa abgebildeten Kurtisane liegt eine in Stoff gewickelte *shamisen* (japanische Laute). In der erhobenen Hand erkennen wir das Plektrum zum Anschlagen der Saiten. *Shamisen* wurden zwar nicht ausschliesslich, aber doch sehr eng mit Kurtisanen assoziiert, und Kurtisanendarstellungen, die die Frauen in Begleitung einer Dienerin mit *shamisen* auf dem Weg zu einem Kundentermin zeigen, sind im *ukiyo-e* omnipräsent. Im Gegensatz dazu erlernt die junge Frau aus der Oberschichtsfamilie in Utamaros Druck das Spiel der angeseheneren *koto* (Zither). Nicht zu übersehen ist jedoch, dass sie alles andere als konzentriert übt und sich vom Zirpen ihrer zahmen Grille im Käfig am unteren Bildrand nur allzu leicht ablenken lässt.

Musical talent was not limited to courtesans, but also was an essential part of the cultural training for daughters of well-to-do families. At the same time, a social distinction can be seen in the different instruments with which the women in these two prints are identified. Kunimasa's courtesan has a *shamisen* (lute) wrapped in fabric on her lap, and holds the tool used to pluck its strings in her exposed hands. While not limited to them, *shamisen* were closely associated with courtesans, and depictions of these women on their way to an appointment with a client while accompanied by a servant carrying a *shamisen* were ubiquitous in *ukiyo-e*. On the other hand, the young woman from an upper-class family in Utamaro's print learns the more respectable *koto* (zither) from her teacher. However, one cannot help but notice that she is less than diligent in her studies, and easily distracted by the chirping of her pet cricket, in a cage occupying the foreground.

SE

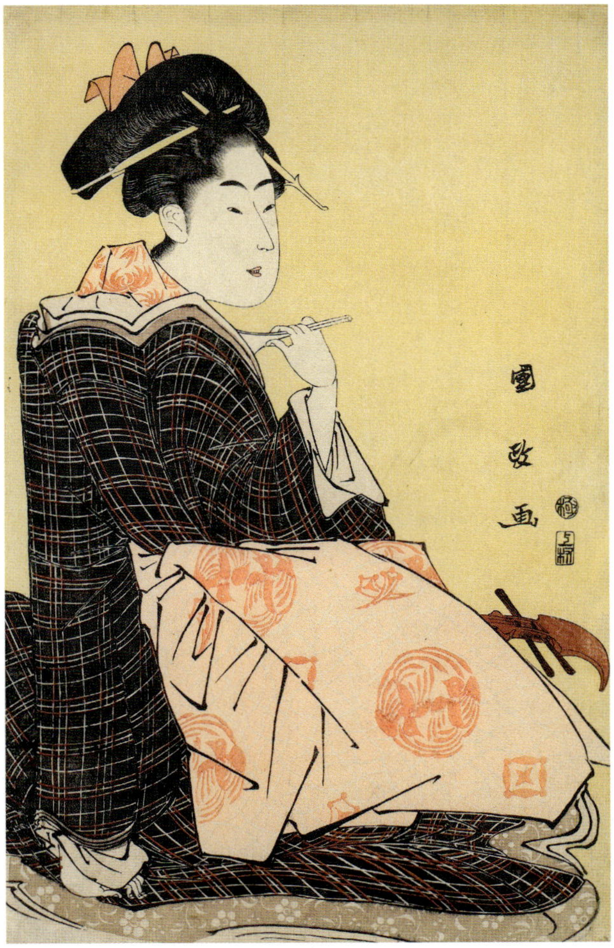

55

喜多川歌麿

54
Darstellung der Oberschicht – Junge Frauen aus drei gesellschaftlichen Schichten, erkennbar an ihrer Kleidung
Picture of the Upper Class – Three Ranks of Young Women According to Their Fashions
Kitagawa UTAMARO

歌川国政

55
Eine Geisha mit Shamisen
Geisha with Shamisen
Utagawa KUNIMASA I

Die aus der berühmten Musikerfamilie Tomimoto stammende Toyohina war, zusammen mit den Teehausmädchen Okita und Ohisa, die ebenfalls zu Utamaros Lieblingsmotiven zählten, eine der drei berühmtesten Schönheiten ihrer Zeit. Die Regierung begann 1790 damit, Holzschnitte zu zensieren, indem sie die Vorlage sämtlicher Entwürfe zur amtlichen Abnahme vorschrieb, hier zu erkennen an dem *kiwame*-Siegel (wörtlich «geprüft») unten links. Zusätzliche Anti-Luxus-Gesetze, die seit Ende 1794 die Verwendung edler Materialien wie Glimmerpulver untersagten, grenzen die Entstehungszeit dieses Drucks weiter ein. Der weisse Glimmerdruck des Hintergrunds, der raffinierte Farbeinsatz und das elegante Motiv der Toyohina beim Betrachten eines *surimono* (privat in Auftrag gegebenes Gedichtblatt) machen diesen Holzschnitt zu einer besonders erlesenen Arbeit in Utamaros Gesamtwerk.

Das einige Jahre später entstandene Bildnis von Karagoto gehört zu derselben Serie wie Utamaros eindrucksvolle Darstellung von Hanaôgi (KAT. 72) und zeigt dieselbe aussergewöhnliche Reife und Neuartigkeit in der Ausführung. Wie die übrigen Drucke der Serie bezeichnet die Kartusche nicht nur die Kurtisane, sondern gibt auch den Namen und die Anschrift ihres Geschäftssitzes an. Als *tayû* oder Kurtisane höchsten Ranges war Karagoto eine Berühmtheit der 1790er-Jahre. Sie hält ein Landschaftsgemälde in den Händen, dessen Signatur «Morinobu» vom offiziellen Hofmaler Kanô Tanyû (1602–1674) verwendet worden war. Es verweist auf den herausragenden Kunstverstand, der für Karagotos Berufsstand unerlässlich war.

From the famous Tomimoto family of musicians, Toyohina was one of the three most renowned beauties of her time, together with the teahouse waitresses Okita and Ohisa, who were also among Utamaro's favored subjects. The government began to censor prints in 1790 by requiring designs to be submitted for official approval, as is evidenced by the *kiwame* seal in the lower left. Further sumptuary laws prohibiting the use of luxurious materials such as mica were enforced starting late in 1794, providing a time frame for this print. The white mica background, refined use of color, and elegant subject of Toyohina examining a *surimono* (privately commissioned prints) make this a work of special distinction within Utamaro's corpus.

From several years later, Karagoto is in the same series as Utamaro's striking depiction of Hanaôgi (CAT. 72), and shows the same exceptional maturity and innovation in its design. Like the other prints from the series, the cartouche not only identifies the courtesan, but also provides the name and address of her place of business. Karagoto was a famous high-ranking courtesan, or *tayû,* of the 1790s. She holds a landscape painting with the signature "Morinobu," used by the official artist Kanô Tanyû (1602–1674), suggesting the mastery of connoisseurship essential to training in her profession.

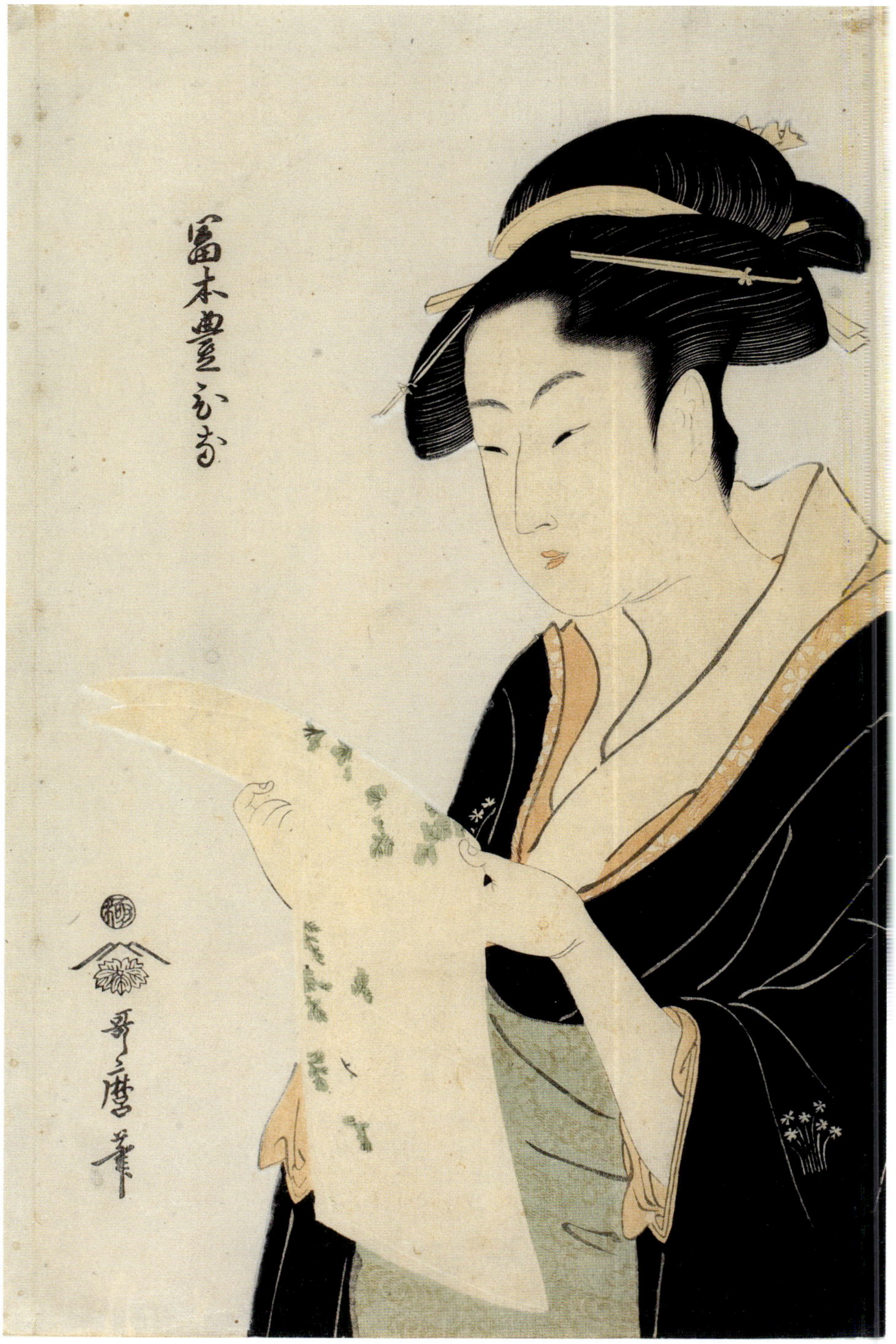

56

SE

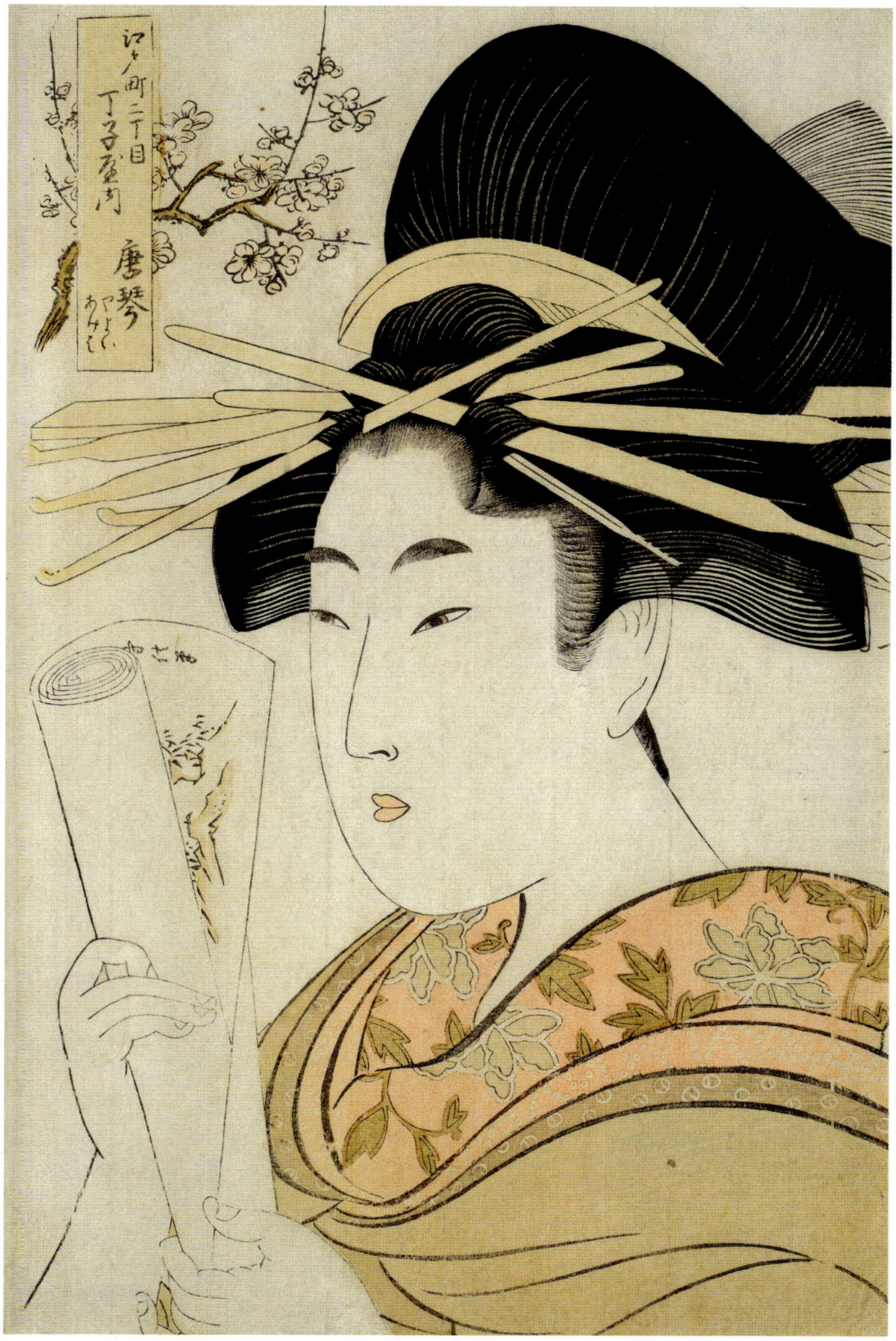

57

喜多川 歌麿

56
Tomimoto Toyohina
Tomimoto Toyohina
Kitagawa UTAMARO

喜多川 歌麿

57
Karagoto aus dem Freudenhaus Chôjiya in Edochô Nichôme – Kurtisanen verglichen mit Blumen
Karagoto of the Brothel House Chôjiya in Edochô Nichôme – A Comparison of Courtesan Flowers
Kitagawa UTAMARO

In diesem Druck, einem aparten Beispiel für eine komplexe wie überzeugende Komposition Utamaros, hängen drei junge Frauen Lampions für die abendlichen Lustbarkeiten auf. Den unterschiedlichen Posen der Figuren entsprechend, sind auch die Lampions in drei Phasen dargestellt, vom Entzünden der Kerze bis zum Festbinden des entfalteten Papierballons am Glyzinienspalier. Teehäuser wie dieses wurden für Verabredungen genutzt. Der gemusterte Stoff auf der Bank, eine Laube aus Blauregen und die brennenden Lampions bildeten dabei den passenden Rahmen für die Kurtisane, die ihre Reize zur Schau stellte, während sie auf ihren Kunden wartete. Die für den Künstler typische Auffassung von Schönheit zeigt sich in ganzer Pracht in den hochgewachsenen, schlanken und anmutigen Frauengestalten, die den Entwurf dominieren. Ihre Vitalität zeigt sich deutlich in der zentralen Figur, die mit einer brennenden Laterne in den Händen selbstbewusst auf die Bank steigt. Vollkommen vertieft in ihre Aufgabe, scheint allen dreien der betrachtende Blick von aussen gleichgültig zu sein.

Three young women hang lanterns for the evening's festivities in this striking example of a strong and complex composition by Utamaro. Each figure is differently posed, and the lanterns are depicted in three separate stages of being prepared and tied to the wisteria trellis. Teahouses such as this one were used for assignations, and the bench covered with a patterned cloth, the wisteria arbor, and the lighted lanterns would have provided an appropriate setting for the courtesan to display her charms as she waited for her client. The artist's characteristic depiction of beauty is fully evident in the tall, slim, and graceful women that dominate the design. Their vitality is encapsulated by the central figure stepping confidently onto the bench, a lit lantern in her hands. Completely absorbed in the task at hand, they appear indifferent to the viewer's gaze.

CM

喜多川 歌麿

58
Teehausmädchen unter einem Glyzinienspalier
Teahouse Maidens under a Wisteria Trellis
Kitagawa UTAMARO

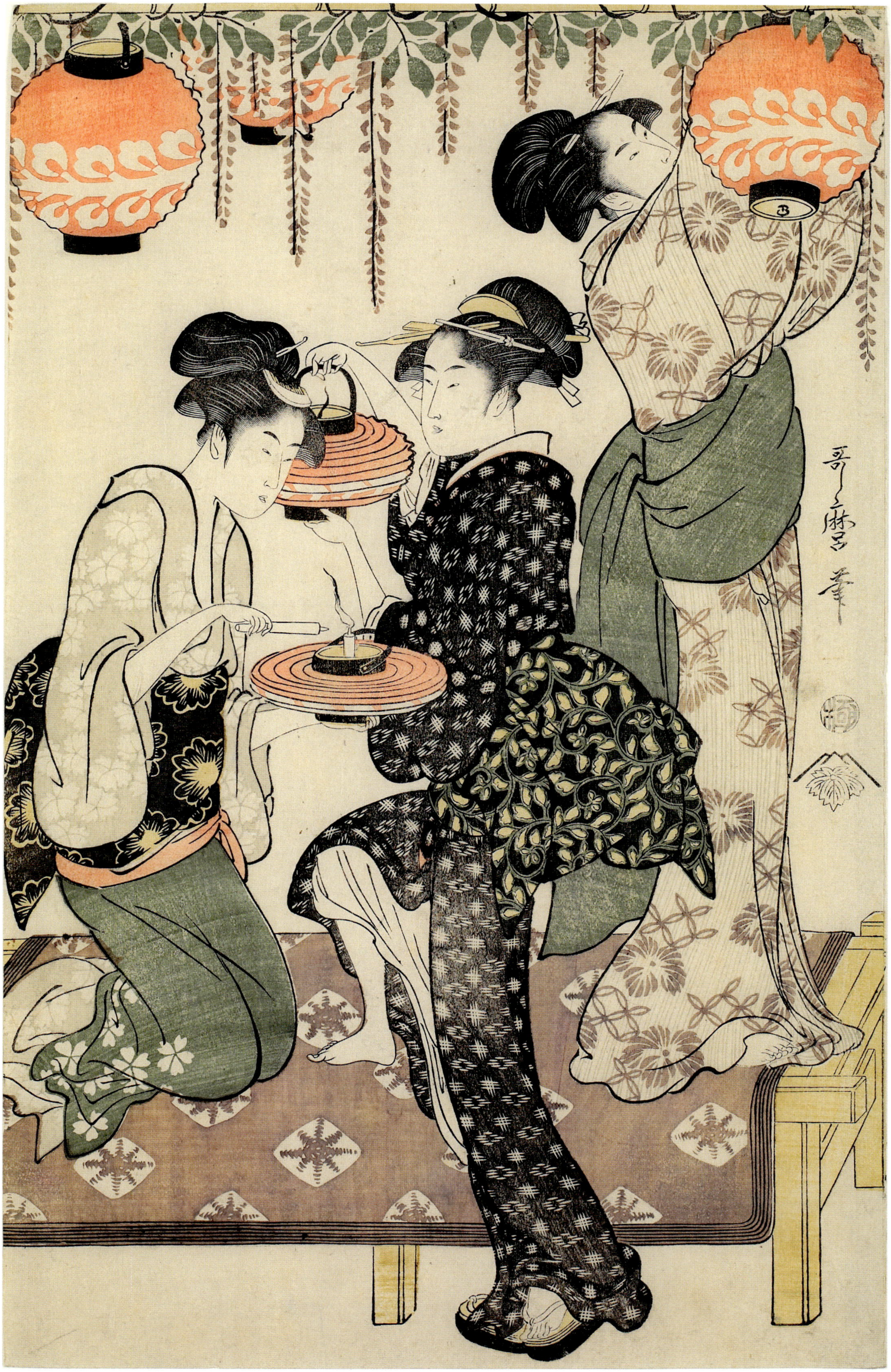
哥麿筆

Das Besondere an diesem Druck sind die Brille oben rechts, die als Kartusche den Titel der Serie enthält, und das Glas, aus dem die Frau ihren Sake trinkt – zwei exotische Importgegenstände, die über niederländische Handelsmissionen nach Japan gelangten. Trotz der Nähe des Bildes zum ausschweifenden Lebensstil in den Freudenvierteln dienten explizite und manchmal ironische Darstellungen von Zügellosigkeit im *ukiyo-e* dazu, ungebührliches Verhalten zu verhindern. Utamaros Serie *Durch die moralisierende Brille der Eltern gesehen* verfolgt diese Absicht in zehn bekannten Motiven, die den Betrachter dazu animieren, sich selbst zu fragen, wie wohl andere das eigene Handeln wahrnehmen. Die Eleganz des Entwurfs und der aufwendige Druck täuschen über das Motiv hinweg: eine nachlässig gekleidete Figur, deren lose über die Schulter hängendes Gewand ihre Brust enthüllt, während sie sich dem übermässigen Genuss von Essen und Trinken hingibt. Die zentrale Aufschrift in der oberen Bildhälfte beschreibt sie als Person ohne jeden Anstand und stellt genussvoll ihre mangelnde Selbstbeherrschung zur Schau.

Of special interest in this print are the eyeglasses of the cartouche series title in the upper right, and the glass from which the woman drinks sake, both exotic imports brought to Japan through Dutch trade missions. Despite its intimate association with the dissolute lifestyle of the pleasure quarters, depictions of debauchery in *ukiyo-e* sometimes ironically were intended to dissuade inappropriate behavior, as in Utamaro's series *A Parent's Moralizing Spectacles,* with ten known prints encouraging viewers to consider how their actions might be perceived by others. The elegance of the design and sophisticated printing belie the subject, a slovenly figure with her robe hanging loosely about her shoulders, revealing her breast as she indulges in excessive food and drink. The inscription in the upper center describes her as someone who is completely without propriety, and takes delight in flaunting her lack of self-restraint.

SE

喜多川歌麿

59
Gewöhnlich als leichtes Mädchen bezeichnet – Durch die moralisierende Brille der Eltern gesehen
Vulgarly Called the Wanton – A Parent's Moralizing Spectacles
Kitagawa UTAMARO

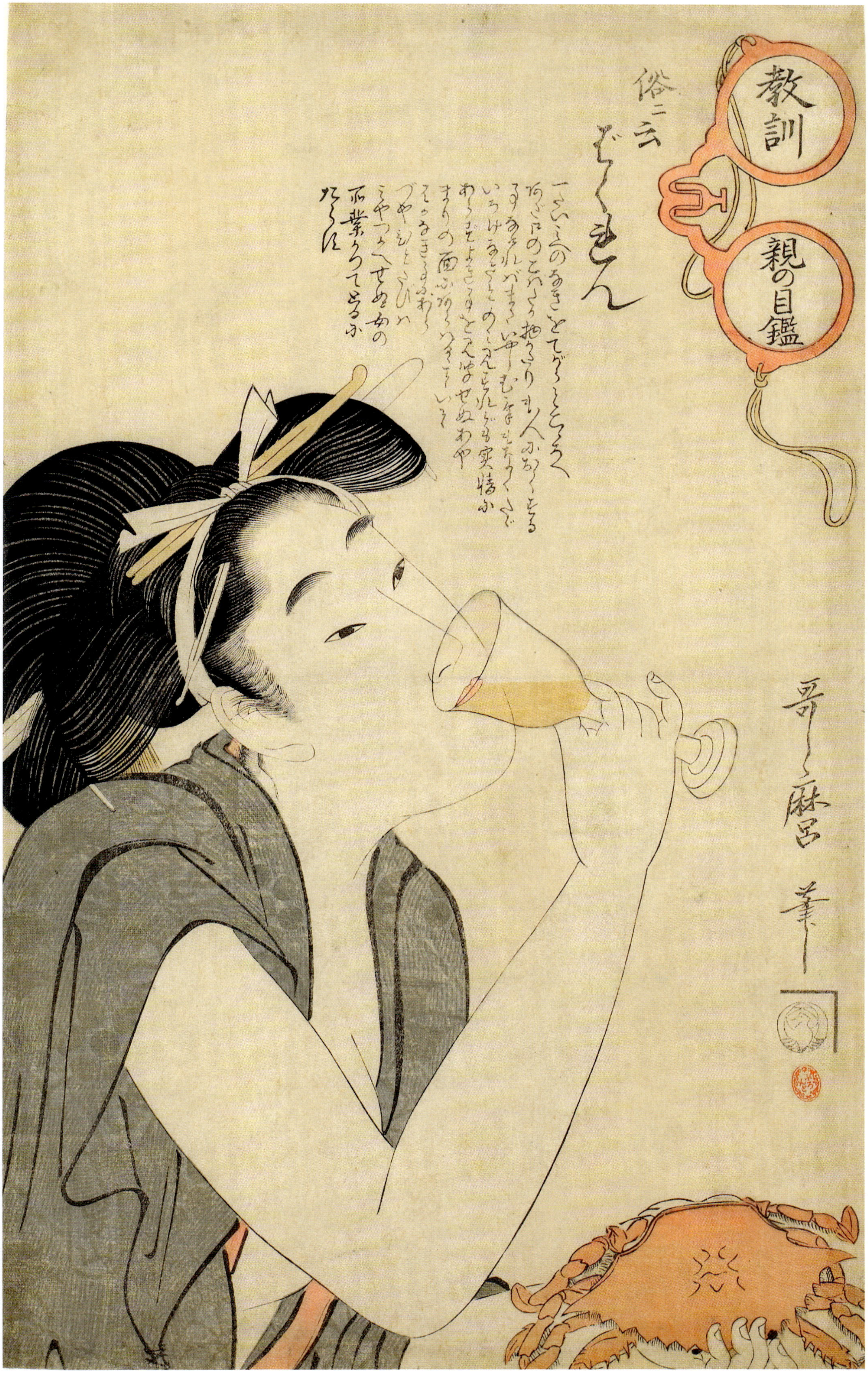

教訓
親の目鑑
俗ニ云 ばくれん
哥麿筆

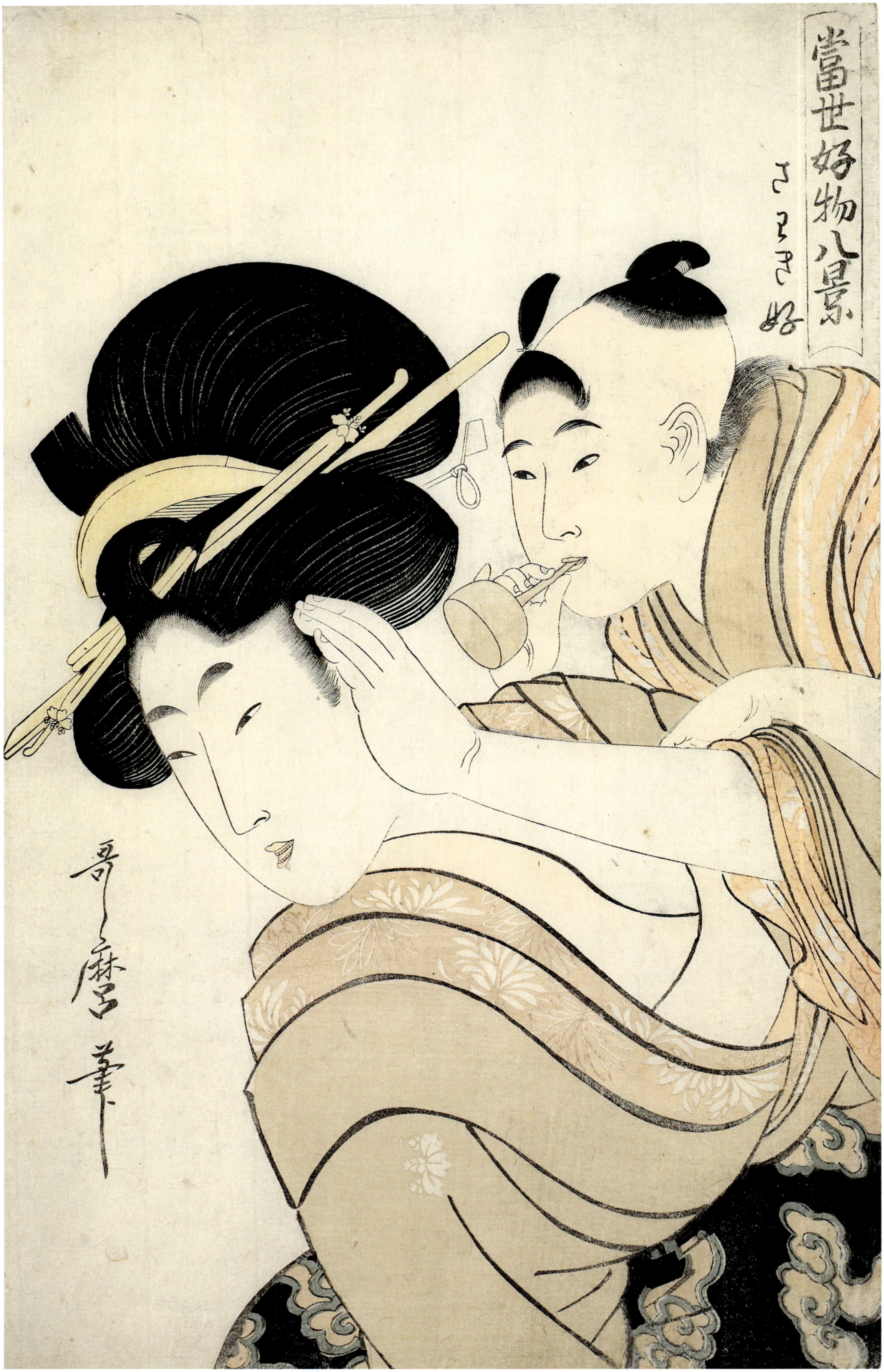
當世好物八景
哥麿筆

Dieser Druck zeigt ein Kind, das mit einem damals als «Knallflöte» bekannten Spielzeug die Geduld seiner Mutter auf die Probe stellt. Das über niederländische Handelsmissionen aus Europa importierte Spielzeug bestand aus einem Glasrohr mit erweitertem Schalltrichter und produzierte beim Hineinblasen ein lautes, knallendes Geräusch. Zu Lebzeiten des Künstlers scheint diese Glasflöte sehr beliebt gewesen zu sein, denn er hat sie mehr als einmal im Bild festgehalten. Obwohl Utamaro durch seinen Hauptverleger Tsutaya Jûzaburô, der aus Yoshiwara stammte und sich auf Bilder aus dem Freudenviertel spezialisiert hatte, enge Verbindungen in das Viertel unterhielt, thematisierte er die Schönheit nicht nur in Kurtisanenporträts, sondern auch in einer breiten Palette anderer Frauentypen, vom Teehausmädchen bis zum Mutterschaftssymbol wie im hier gezeigten Werk. Für Utamaros reife Periode charakteristisch, zeigt der Druck grosse technische Finesse: Der ausgeprägte Sinn des Künstlers für die Linie spiegelt sich effektvoll im Schnitt der Holzstöcke, die streng kontrollierte Komposition ist im Interesse der Klarheit auf das Wesentliche reduziert, und die Farben wurden dezent aufeinander abgestimmt.

This print depicts a child testing the limits of his mother's patience with a toy commonly known as a "poppin." Imported from Europe through Dutch trade missions, the poppin consisted of a glass pipe flaring to a bell that would produce a loud popping noise when air was blown through it. The toy seems to have been popular during the artist's time, and he depicted it more than once. Although Utamaro was intimately connected with the Yoshiwara pleasure quarter through his main publisher Tsutaya Jûzaburô, who was born in the Yoshiwara and specialized in images of it, his depictions of beauty were not limited to courtesans, and included a wide range of feminine types, from teahouse waitresses to icons of motherhood, as in the present work. Typical of Utamaro's mature period, the print shows a high level of technical refinement, with the artist's exquisite sense of line effectively captured in the carving of the blocks, a tightly controlled composition reduced to its essential elements for clarity, and a subtle harmonization of color.

SE

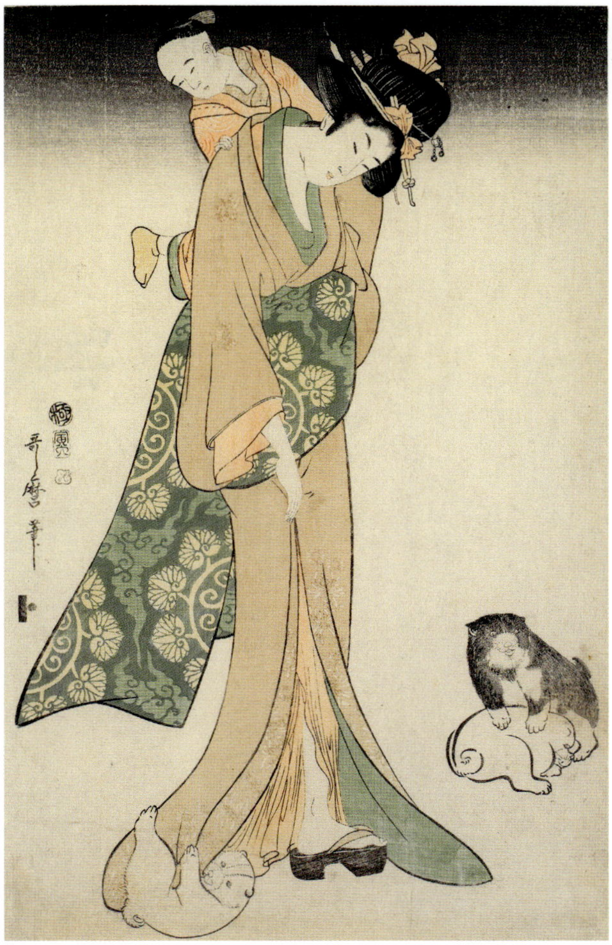

61

喜多川歌麿

60

Kind findet Gefallen an lauten Geräuschen – Die acht Darstellungen von beliebten Dingen

Lover of Loud Noises – The Eight Views of Popular Things

Kitagawa UTAMARO

喜多川歌麿

61

Mutter und Kind mit Welpen

Mother and Child with Puppies

Kitagawa UTAMARO

喜多川 歌麿

62
Zwei Schönheiten.
Die eine hält eine Pfeife,
die andere
einen Rundfächer
Two Beauties.
One Holding a Pipe,
the Other a Round Fan
Kitagawa UTAMARO

喜多川 歌麿

63
Eine Schwäche für Liebe –
Jeder hat seine Fehler
A Weakness for Love –
Everyone Has Faults
Kitagawa UTAMARO

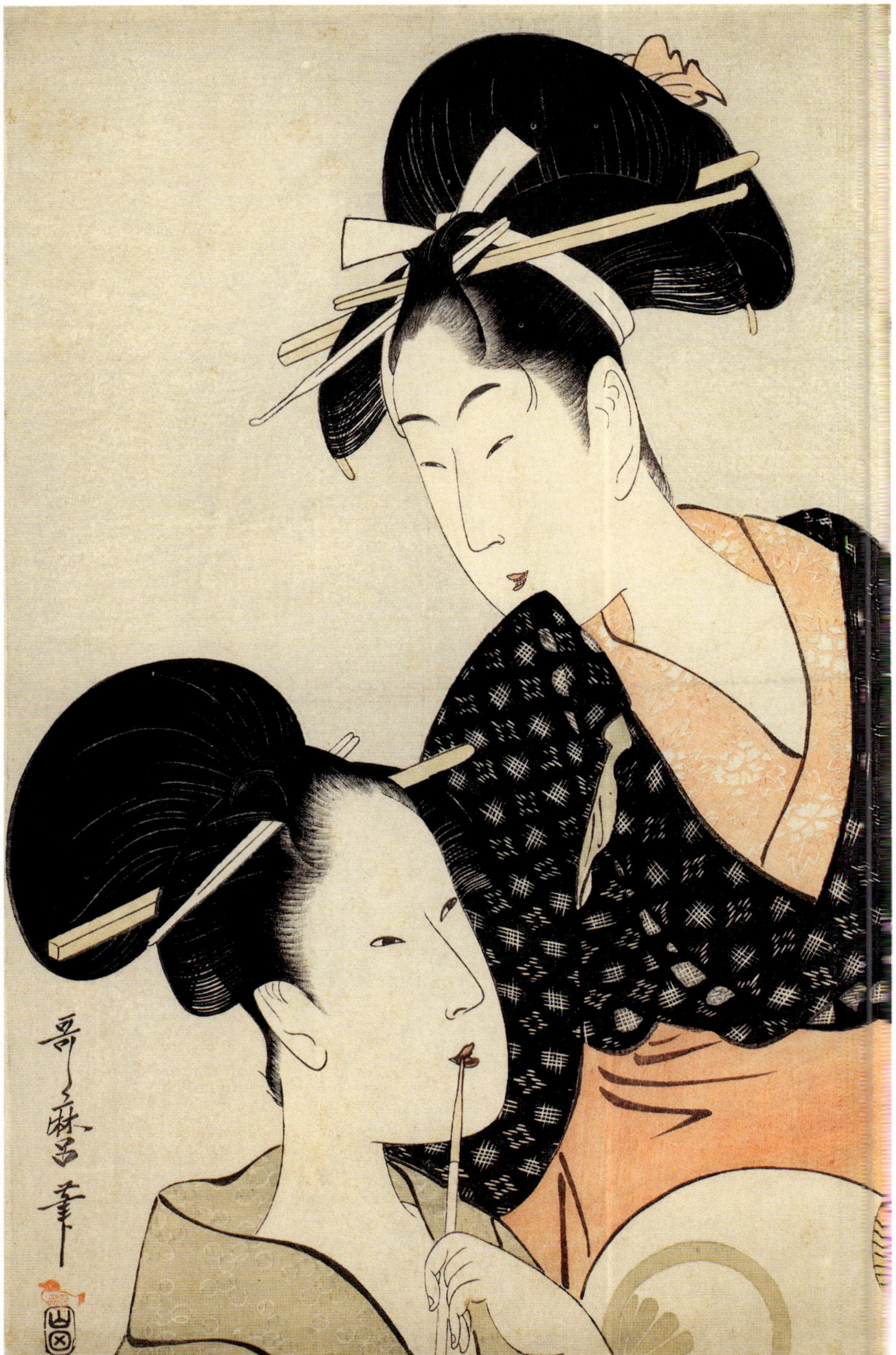

62

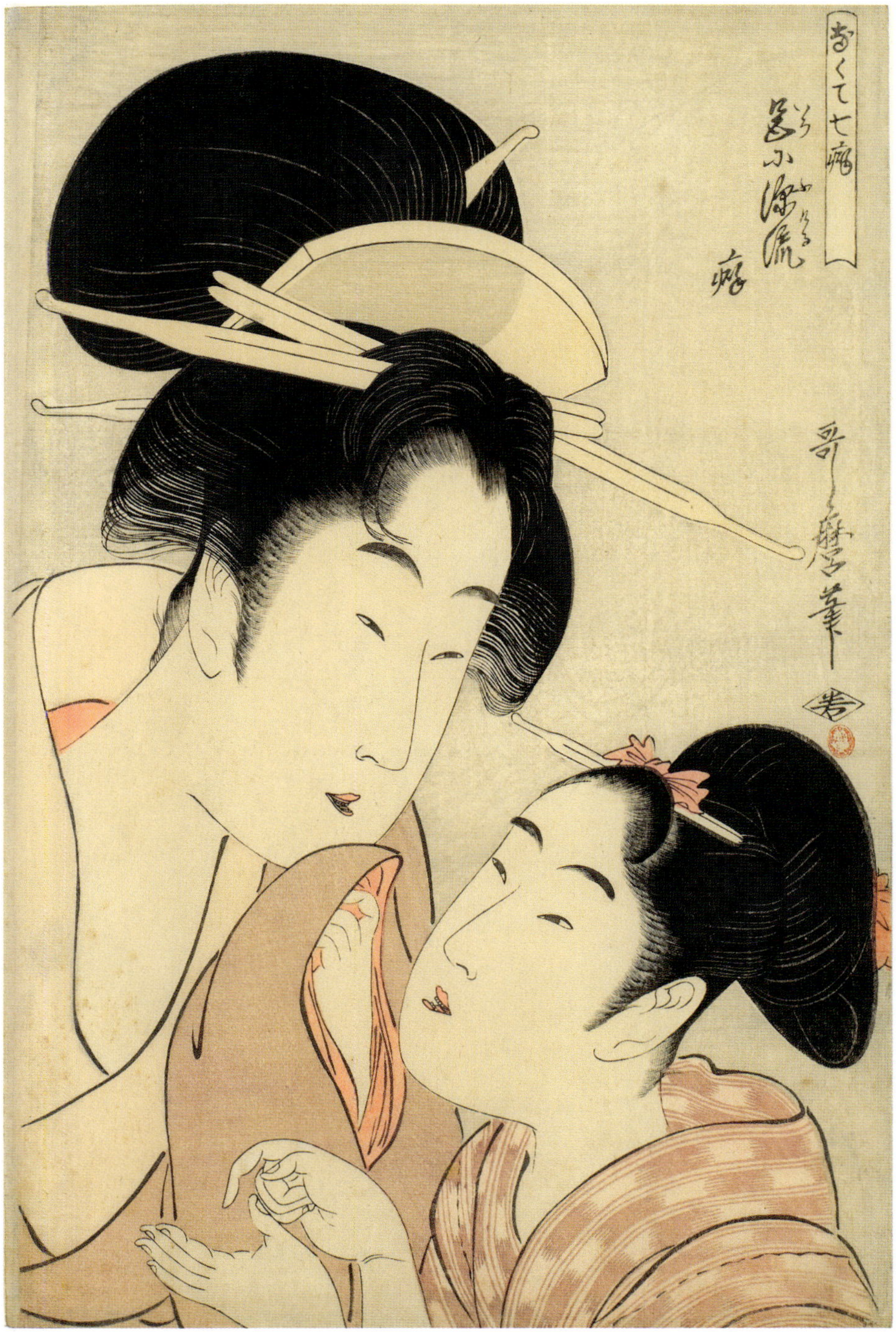

63

Utamaro interessierte sich für die Darstellung familiärer Beziehungen im *ukiyo-e* – wie hier gleich drei Drucke belegen. *Zwei Schönheiten* zeigt keineswegs zwei Kurtisanen, wie der Titel vermuten lässt, sondern zwei miteinander verwandte Frauen unterschiedlichen Alters (vielleicht Mutter und Tochter). Feine Details wie die gezupften Augenbrauen und geschwärzten Zähne der älteren Frau oder das Ikatmuster des bunteren, mit gefärbten Schussfäden nach der *kasuri*-Technik gewebten Kimonos der jüngeren entsprachen den Modestandards der verschiedenen Altersgruppen. Die charmante Szene *Eine Schwäche für Liebe* zeigt ein Mädchen, das seine ältere Schwester in Herzensdingen befragt. Das Anliegen des Künstlers, das Innenleben seiner Figuren abzubilden, kommt im naiv-unsicheren Eifer des Mädchens und dem vergnügten Selbstvertrauen seiner Beraterin hervorragend zum Ausdruck.

Während diese beiden Bilder auf Brusthöhe enden, um die Aufmerksamkeit auf die Details in Gesichtszügen und Ausdruck zu konzentrieren, stellt das dritte Motiv, *Mutter und Kind mit Welpen* (KAT. 61), eine Ganzkörperansicht dar: eine Mutter mit einem Kind auf den Schultern sowie zwei spielende Hundewelpen, die zu ihren Füssen die Szene beleben. Das Kleid der Frau verrät modische Veränderungen im ausgehenden 18. Jahrhundert, als aufwendige *obi* immer stärker mit den dezenter gemusterten Kimonos kontrastiert wurden.

Utamaro had an interest in depicting familial relationships unusual in *ukiyo-e,* evident in three variations in these prints. *Two Beauties* shows not the pair of courtesans that one might expect from such a title, but rather related older and younger women (perhaps mother and daughter). Subtle details, such as the older woman's shaved eyebrows and blackened teeth, and the younger woman's more colorful kimono with a design woven into the fabric in weft ikat using the *kasuri* technique, set standards of beauty for different age groups. *A Weakness for Love* portrays a charming scene of a girl querying her older sister on matters of the heart; the artist's interest in capturing the inner psychology of his subjects is superbly represented by the girl's naively insecure eagerness, juxtaposed with her advisor's amused confidence.

While both of these prints crop their subjects at the bust to draw attention to details of facial features and expression, *Mother and Child with Puppies* (CAT. 61) instead expands the view to include not only a mother with a child on her shoulders, but also puppies playing at her feet that enliven the scene. Her dress reveals changing fashions at the end of the eighteenth century that increasingly emphasized elaborate *obi* (sashes) against more subtly patterned kimono in contrasting colors.

SE

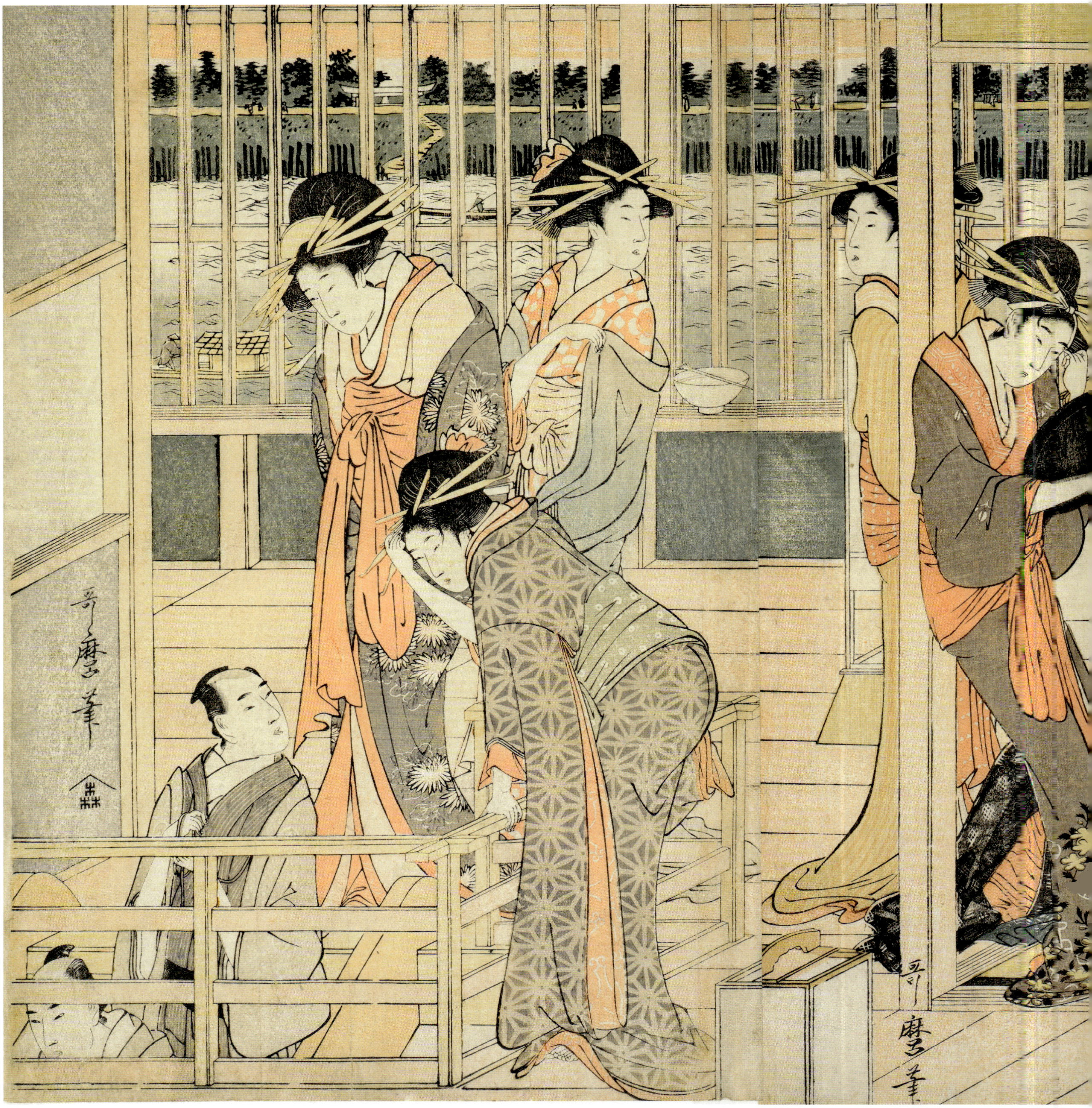
哥麿筆
哥麿筆

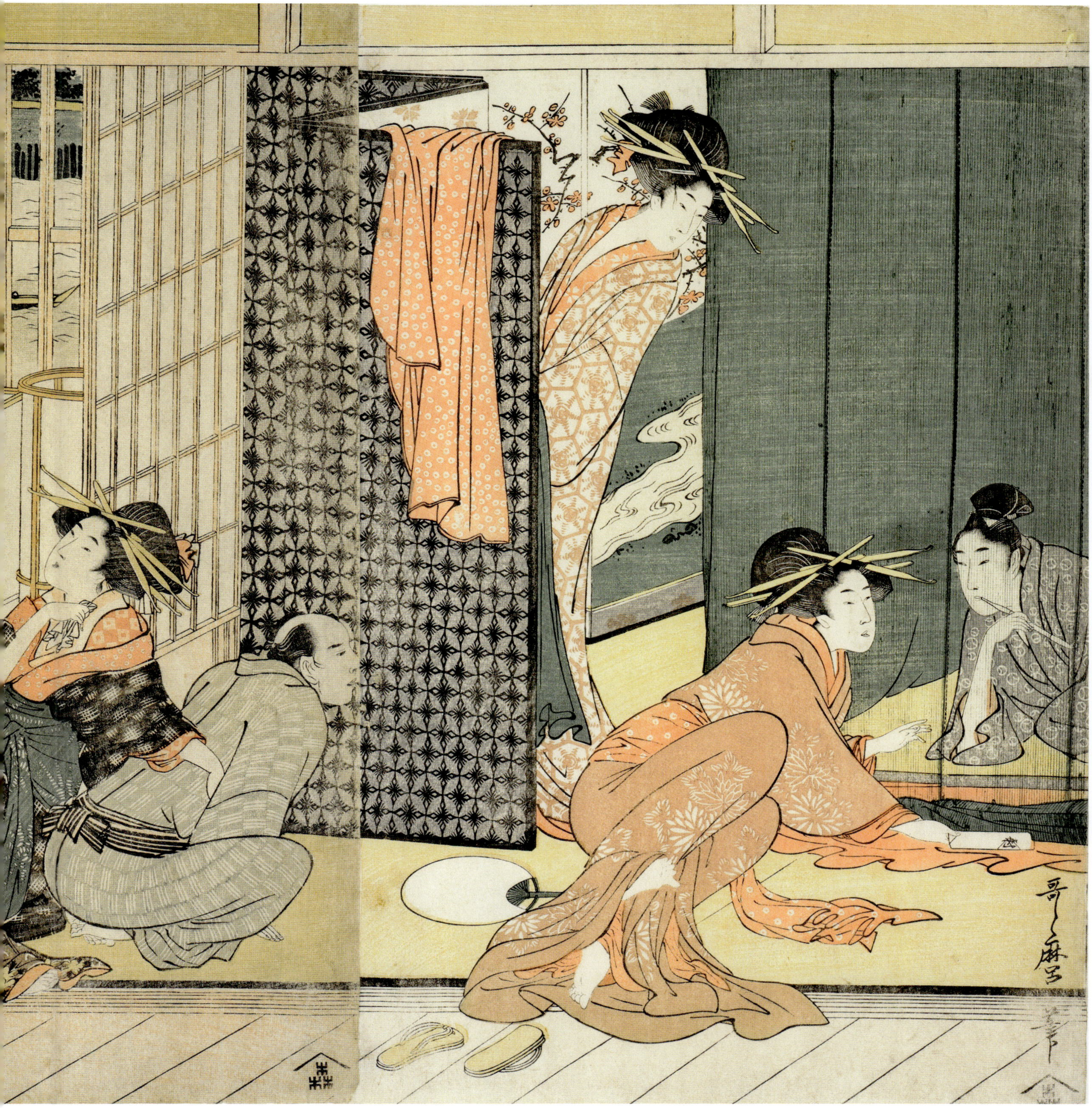
哥ゝ麿筆

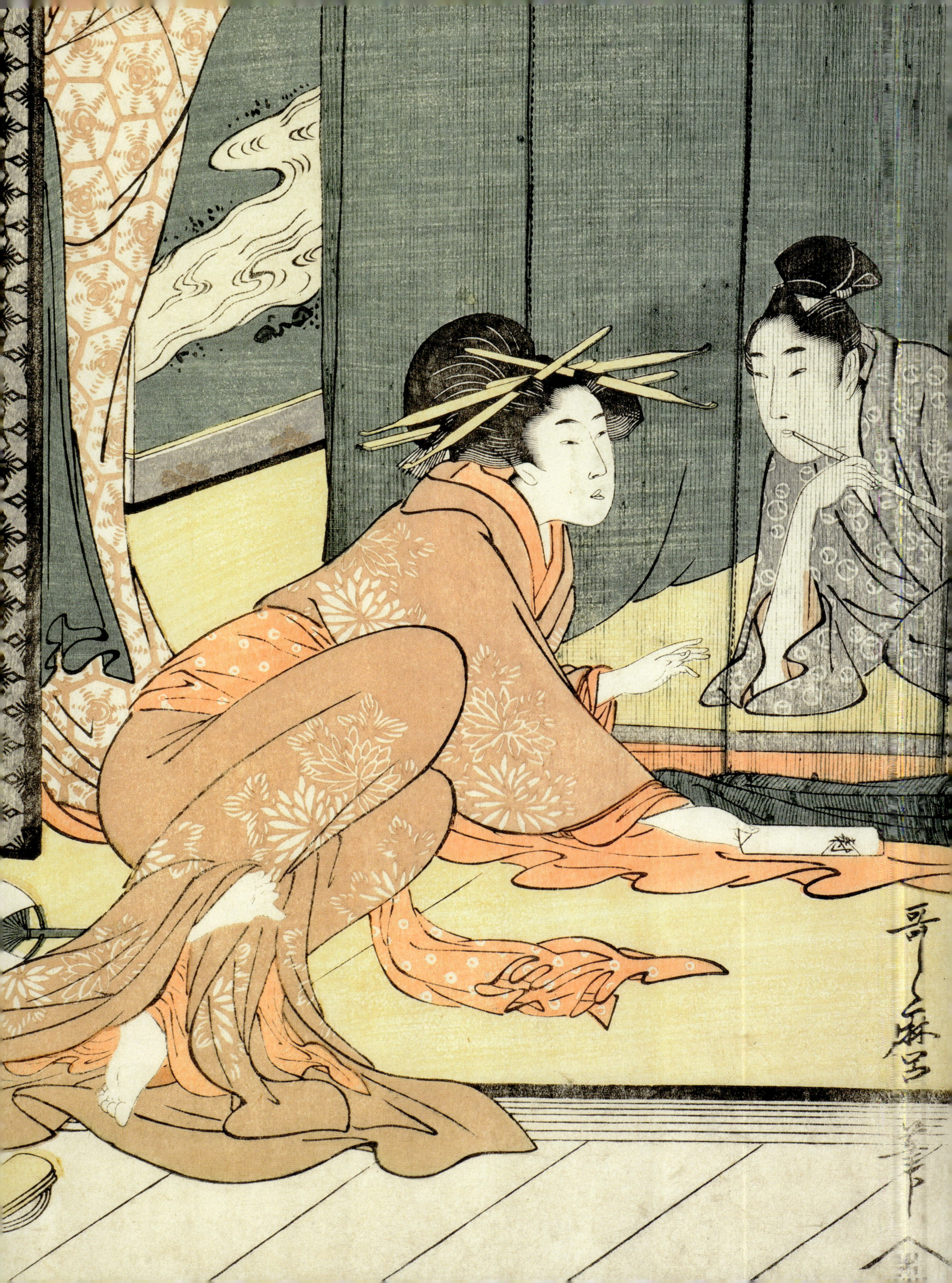

Verheerende Brände waren in der Stadt Edo keine Seltenheit. Immer, wenn Yoshiwara betroffen war, gestattete man den Freudenhäusern, sich bis zu ihrer Wiedererrichtung ausserhalb des Viertels niederzulassen. Dieses Triptychon zeigt einen Morgen in einem solchen «Behelfsquartier». In entspannter und informeller Atmosphäre beginnen sich die Kurtisanen auf den Tag vorzubereiten. Auf der Fensterbank stehen eine Zahnbürste und eine Schale für die Mundspülung. Hinter einem Paravent bekleidet sich eine Kurtisane, eine andere hält einen Spiegel, während sie ihre Augenbrauen nachzieht. Ganz rechts aussen, hinter dem Moskitonetz, räkelt sich plaudernd ein wartender Kunde und raucht, während ganz links im Bild zwei andere Kunden den Raum verlassen. In einer Geste, die die Freuden der letzten Nacht wachruft, vergräbt eine Kurtisane die Hand im Kimono ihres Kunden. Das blanke Holz des Interieurs und die Lage des Hauses am Fluss Sumida verleihen der Szene etwas Rustikales, das sich von den eigentlichen Freudenhäusern in Yoshiwara unterscheidet. Am anderen Flussufer ist das markante Tor des Mimeguri-Schreins erkennbar, was darauf schliessen lässt, dass dieses vorübergehende Quartier sich im Ostteil der Stadt befand.

An Utamaros Schönheiten fallen besonders das Selbstvertrauen und die Selbstgenügsamkeit auf, die sie ausstrahlen. Mit Leichtigkeit beherrschen seine Frauengestalten sowohl die Szenerie, in der sie abgebildet werden, als auch die Kunden, mit denen sie umgehen. Anders als bei vielen anderen im *ukiyo-e* dargestellten Kurtisanen ist ihr Zauber nicht abhängig von feinen Gewändern oder aufwendigen Frisuren: Selbst in ihrer zwanglosen Aufmachung sind sie noch elegant.

Devastating fires were a frequent occurrence in the city of Edo. When the Yoshiwara was affected, the brothel houses were given permission to relocate outside the district until they could be rebuilt. This triptych portrays a morning in one such "temporary lodging." The atmosphere is relaxed and informal, as the courtesans start to ready themselves for the day. A toothbrush and mouth-rinsing bowl sit on the windowsill; a courtesan is dressing behind a screen, and another holds a mirror as she paints her eyebrows. On the far right, a client lingers, smoking and chatting through the mosquito netting, while, on the far left, two customers are departing. In a gesture that evokes the pleasures of the night before, a courtesan places a hand inside her client's kimono. The bare wood of the interior and the proximity of the house to the Sumida River lend the setting a rustic touch that is different from the brothel in the Yoshiwara proper. Across the river the distinctive gate of the Mimeguri Shrine is visible, indicating that these temporary lodgings were in a district in the eastern part of the city.

Utamaro's *bijin* are remarkable for the confidence and sense of self-sufficiency they project. His women easily dominate both the settings in which they are placed and the clients with whom they interact. Unlike many of the courtesans depicted in *ukiyo-e,* their attraction is not dependent on fine robes or elaborately dressed hair: even in dishabille, they are elegant women.

CM

喜多川 歌麿

64
Morgenstimmung in einem Freudenhaus am Fluss
Morning at the Temporary Lodgings
Kitagawa UTAMARO

65 文浪
Falkner und Mädchen
Falconer and Maid
BUNRÔ

66 喜多川 歌麿
Agemaki und Sukeroku
Agemaki and Sukeroku
Kitagawa UTAMARO

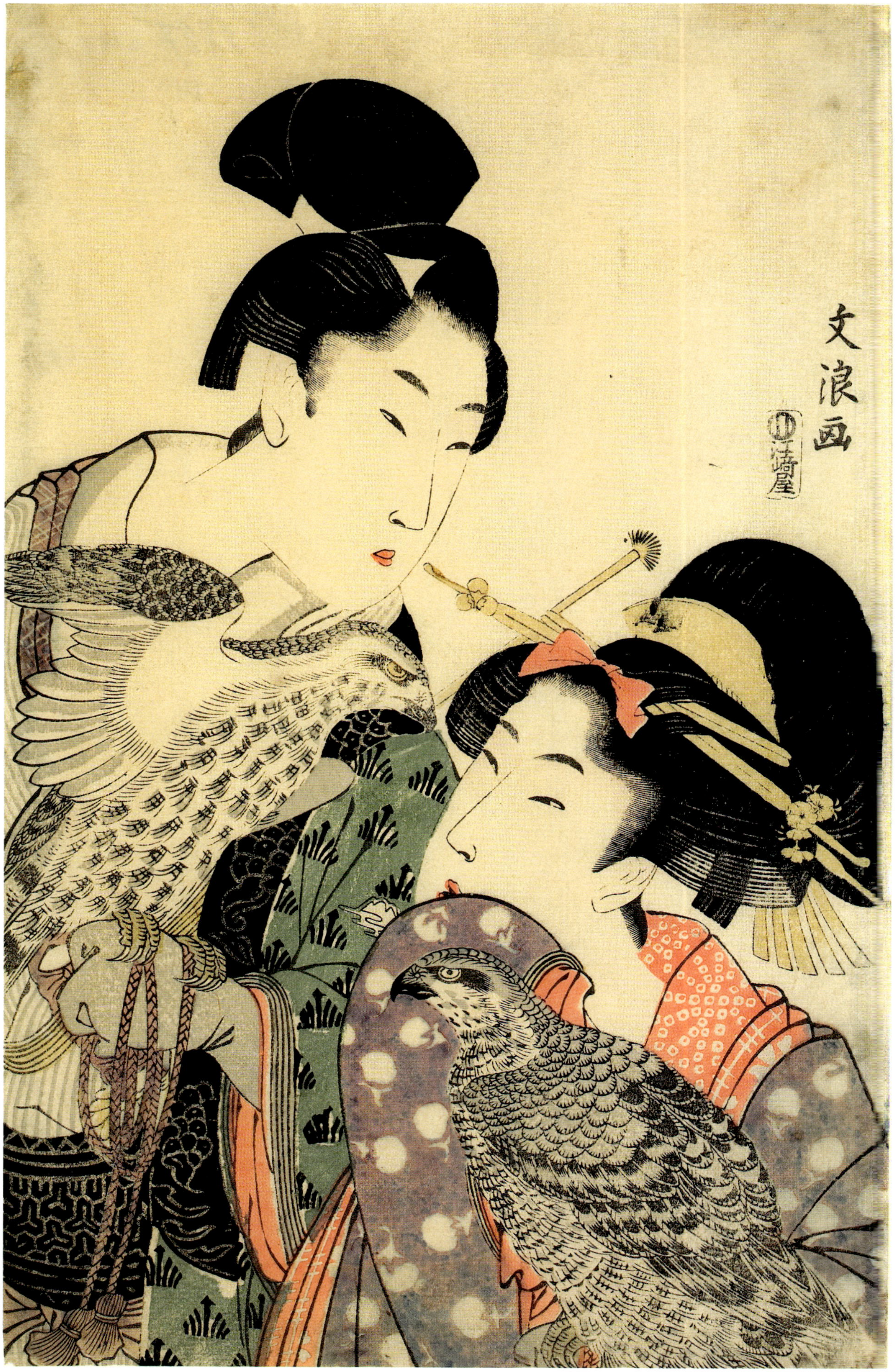

65

Obwohl Utamaro Darstellungen von *kabuki*-Schauspielern üblicherweise vermied, machte er zwei der berühmtesten *kabuki*-Charaktere, Sukeroku und seine Geliebte, die Kurtisane Agemaki, zum Thema dieses Drucks. Auf ihre Namenszüge oben links hätte er dabei im Grunde verzichten können, da Sukeroku an seinem unverwechselbaren Stirnband zu erkennen ist. Angelehnt an die Blutrachegeschichte der Soga-Brüder, die sich im 12. Jahrhundert ereignete und ein geläufiger Stoff für das *kabuki* war, täuscht Sukeroku auf der Suche nach dem Mörder seines Vaters ein lasterhaftes Leben im Freudenviertel vor, als Agemaki sich dort unsterblich in ihn verliebt. Die Pfeife, die sie ihm gibt, ist daher nicht nur Teil der rituellen sozialen Etikette zwischen einer Kurtisane und ihrem Kunden, sondern auch Ausdruck von Zuneigung. Sie spielt ausserdem auf eine andere Szene des Stücks an, in der ein auf Sukeroku eifersüchtiger Kunde von Agemaki verlangt, ihm eine Pfeife anzubieten, was diese verweigert. Die ungewöhnliche, durch das schmale «Pfostenbild»-Format zusätzlich betonte Positionierung Agemakis, die den sitzenden Sukeroku weit überragt, könnte zudem auf eine spätere Szene hinweisen, in der sich Sukeroku vor demselben Kunden unter den Gewändern seiner Geliebten versteckt.

Nur wenig ist über den Künstler Bunrô bekannt, doch die Komposition von *Falkner und Mädchen,* zwischen Brustbild und Halbfigur in einem geschlossenen Kreis angeordnet, lässt deutlich den Einfluss von Utamaros reifem Stil erkennen.

Although Utamaro avoided depictions of kabuki actors, this print takes as its subject two of the most famous kabuki characters, Sukeroku and his lover, the courtesan Agemaki. While they are mentioned in the upper left, this is hardly necessary as Sukeroku can be identified by his distinctive headband. Paralleling an earlier story of revenge by the Soga brothers that took place in the twelfth century (a common artifice in kabuki), Sukeroku feigns a life of dissolution in the pleasure quarters as he searches for his father's killer. Agemaki falls passionately in love with him; the pipe that he receives from her is not only part of the etiquette of social rituals between courtesans and their clients, but also an expression of affection. It further references a scene in the play, where another of Agemaki's clients, jealous of Sukeroku, demands that she offer him a pipe, but she refuses. The unusual placement of Agemaki towering over Sukeroku, emphasized by the vertical *hashira-e* format, might indicate a later scene in the play, in which he hides from the same client under Agemaki's robes.

Little is known about the artist Bunrô, but the composition of this print, with two figures cropped at the bust and arranged in a closed circle, clearly reveals the influence of Utamaro's mature style.

SE

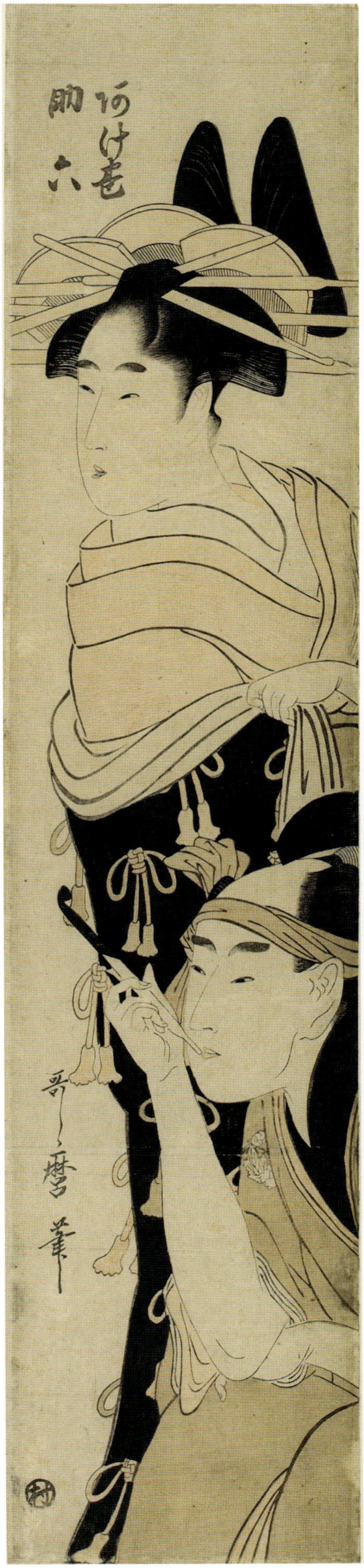

Das Niwaka-Fest fand jedes Jahr während des achten Mondmonats im Yoshiwara-Freudenviertel statt. Im Verlauf des Fests improvisierten die Kurtisanen öffentliche Theateraufführungen. Der Druck zeigt drei kostümierte Kurtisanen, die in der Kartusche oben rechts beschrieben werden. Die Komposition kann in vielerlei Hinsicht als Schlusspunkt des vorherrschenden Stils der 1780er-Jahre betrachtet werden, den Kiyonaga (ein Zeitgenosse Utamaros) geprägt hatte. Die Geometrie, die der Anordnung jedes einzelnen Bildelementes zugrunde liegt, wird beherrscht von der stabilen Pyramide der drei Frauenfiguren – die auch in Utamaros einige Jahre später entstandenem Holzschnitt *Drei Schönheiten aus dem Freudenviertel Yoshiwara* (KAT. 70) zu erkennen ist. Andererseits wurden die Figuren an der Büste beschnitten, gegen den ungestalteten Hintergrund freigestellt und mit Kleidung und anderen Details ausgestattet, die ihren Gesichtern einen Rahmen geben. Im Verlauf der 1790er-Jahre entwickelten sich diese Techniken zum reifen Stil des Künstlers, der in Werken wie *Hanaôgi vom Freudenhaus Ôgiya* (KAT. 72) zum Ausdruck kommt.

The Niwaka Festival was an annual event in the Yoshiwara pleasure quarter outside Edo, held during the eighth lunar month. As part of the festival, courtesans would improvise theatrical performances in public. The print depicts three courtesans dressed in costume, described in a cartouche in the upper right. In many ways, the composition can be understood to mark a transition from the dominant style of the 1780s, characterized by Kiyonaga (who was Utamaro's contemporary). There is an underlying geometry to the arrangement of each individual element, dominated by the stable pyramid formed by the three figures (this can also be seen in Utamaro's *Three Beauties of the Yoshiwara* from a few years later). On the other hand, the figures are cropped at the bust, with background elements removed, and clothing and other details transformed into framing devices for the women's faces. Over the course of the 1790s, these techniques would develop into the artist's mature style, seen in such prints as *Hanaôgi of the Ôgiya Brothel House at Edochô Itchôme* (CAT. 72).

SE

喜多川 歌麿

67
Fächertänzerin, Landmädchen als Herbsttänzerin und Tänzerin als Vollmond – Geisha-Tänzerinnen vom Niwaka-Fest
Fan Dancer, Country Maiden Autumn Dancer, and Full Moon Blossom – Geisha Dancers from the Niwaka Festival
Kitagawa UTAMARO

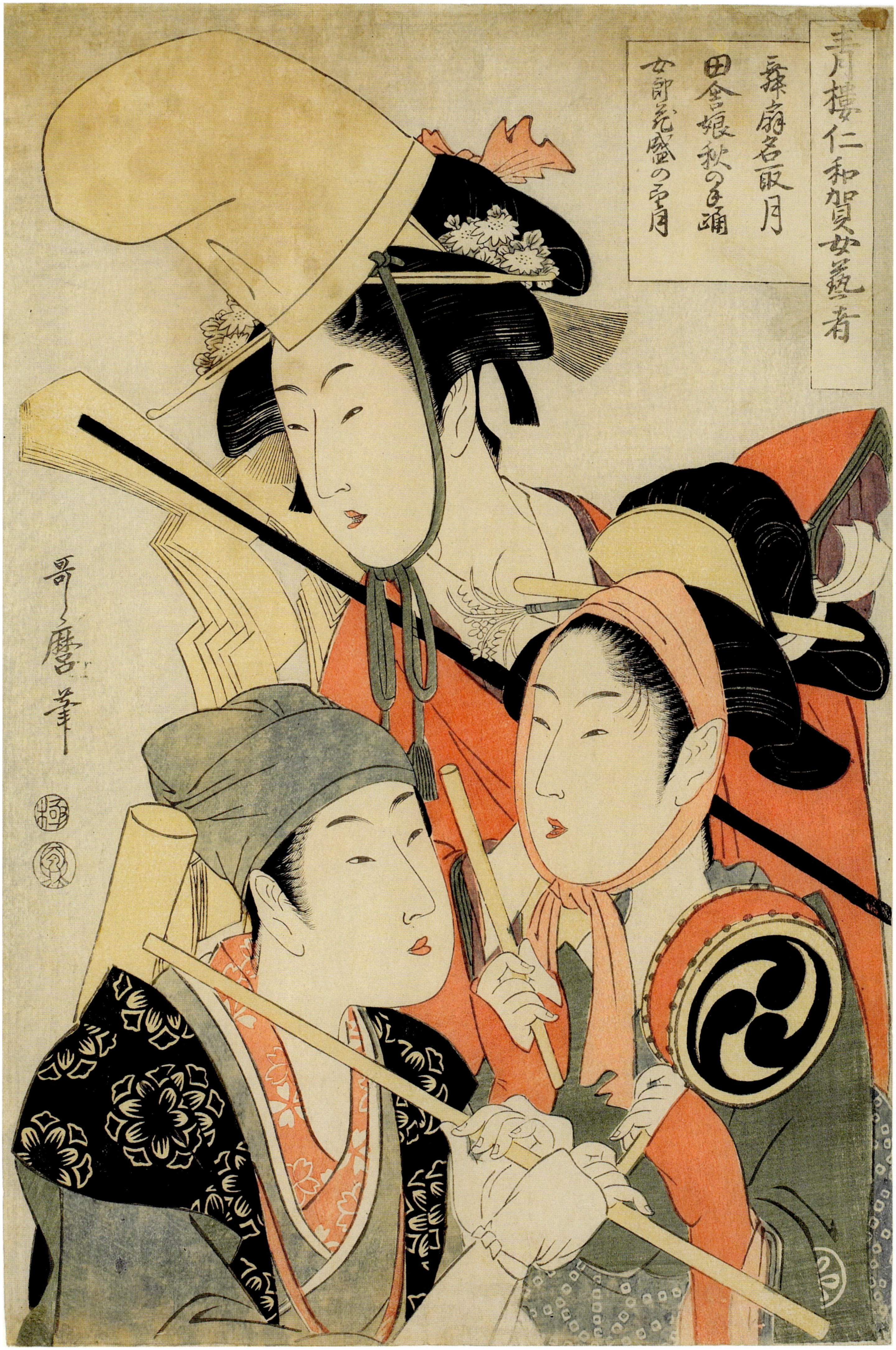
青樓仁和賀女藝者
舞扇名取月
田舎娘秋の手踊
女郎花盛の月
哥麿筆
極

Diese humorvollen Drucke setzen die Rivalität zwischen Okita und Ohisa, zwei der bekanntesten Schönheiten der Zeit, buchstäblich ins Bild. Die beiden Frauen waren weder Kurtisanen noch von nennenswertem gesellschaftlichem Rang, sondern einfache Teehausmädchen. Okita bediente im Naniwaya-, Ohisa im Takashimaya-Teehaus (eine gänzlich andere Darstellung von Ohisa findet sich in Chôkis *Das Takashimaya-Teehaus,* KAT. 44). Auf einem der beiden Bilder sehen wir Okita und Ohisa beim Kräftemessen mit einer Schärpe um den Hals; für den Fall, dass jemand die Szene zu wörtlich nimmt, stehen auf den Fächern ihrer Kampfrichterinnen die Worte *zetsu* («allergrösste») und *bi* («Schönheit»). Ein interessantes Detail ist der für die Gewänder beider Wettstreiterinnen verwendete *kasuri*-Stoff, der bei jungen Frauen damals modern war und auch in Utamaros *Zwei Schönheiten* (KAT. 62) zu finden ist.

Im zweiten Druck messen sich die Frauen in der Kunst des *ikebana* (Blumenstecken). Okita macht eine Pause und füllt ihre Pfeife mit Tabak vom vor ihr stehenden Tablett, während Ohisa sich mit einer Schere in der Hand zurücklehnt, um ihr Werk zu betrachten. Einen Hauch von Voyeurismus vermittelt der zur Seite gerutschte Überkimono, der Okitas Untergewand freilegt, wie es sich um ihr rechtes, dem Betrachter zugewandtes Bein schmiegt. Als der Druck entstand, war Ohisa etwa 15 Jahre alt und arbeitete seit rund einem Jahr im Takashimaya-Teehaus.

These prints give humorously literal interpretations to the rivalry between two leading beauties of the time, Okita and Ohisa. Neither was a courtesan, or of noteworthy social rank; Okita was a waitress at the Naniwaya teahouse, while Ohisa was a waitress at the Takashimaya teahouse (a very different depiction of Ohisa can be found in Chôki's *The Takashimaya Teahouse,* CAT. 44). In one, Okita and Ohisa are shown in a test of strength with a sash tied around their necks; the fans carried by their judges read *zetsu* ("utmost") and *bi* ("beauty"), lest the viewer understand the scene too literally. An interesting detail is the same *kasuri* fabric used in both of their outfits, fashionable for young women at the time and also found in Utamaro's *Two Beauties* (CAT. 62).

In the other print, they are engaged in an *ikebana* (flower-arranging) contest; Okita pauses to fill her pipe from the tray in front of her, while Ohisa holds scissors as she leans back to examine her work. A sense of voyeurism is imparted by the fact that Okita's outer kimono has fallen aside to reveal her under-robe around her leg closest to the viewer. At the time the print was made, Ohisa was about fifteen years old, and had been working at the Takashimaya for about a year.

SE

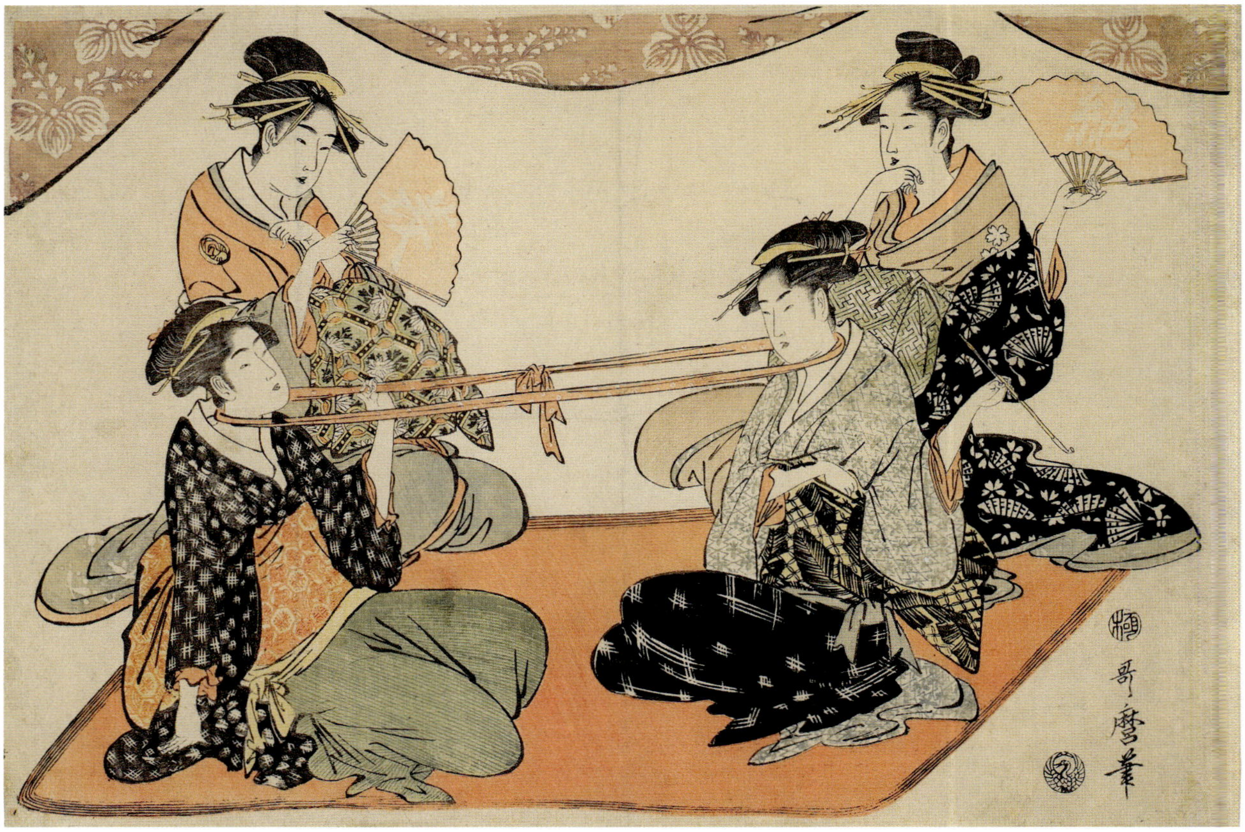

68

68
喜多川歌麿
Okita und Ohisa beim Kräftemessen mit einer Schärpe um den Hals
Okita and Ohisa in a Tug-of-War with a Sash Looped Around Their Necks
Kitagawa UTAMARO

69
喜多川歌麿
Wettstreit im Blumenstecken zwischen Okita und Ohisa
Flower Arrangement Contest between Okita and Ohisa
Kitagawa UTAMARO

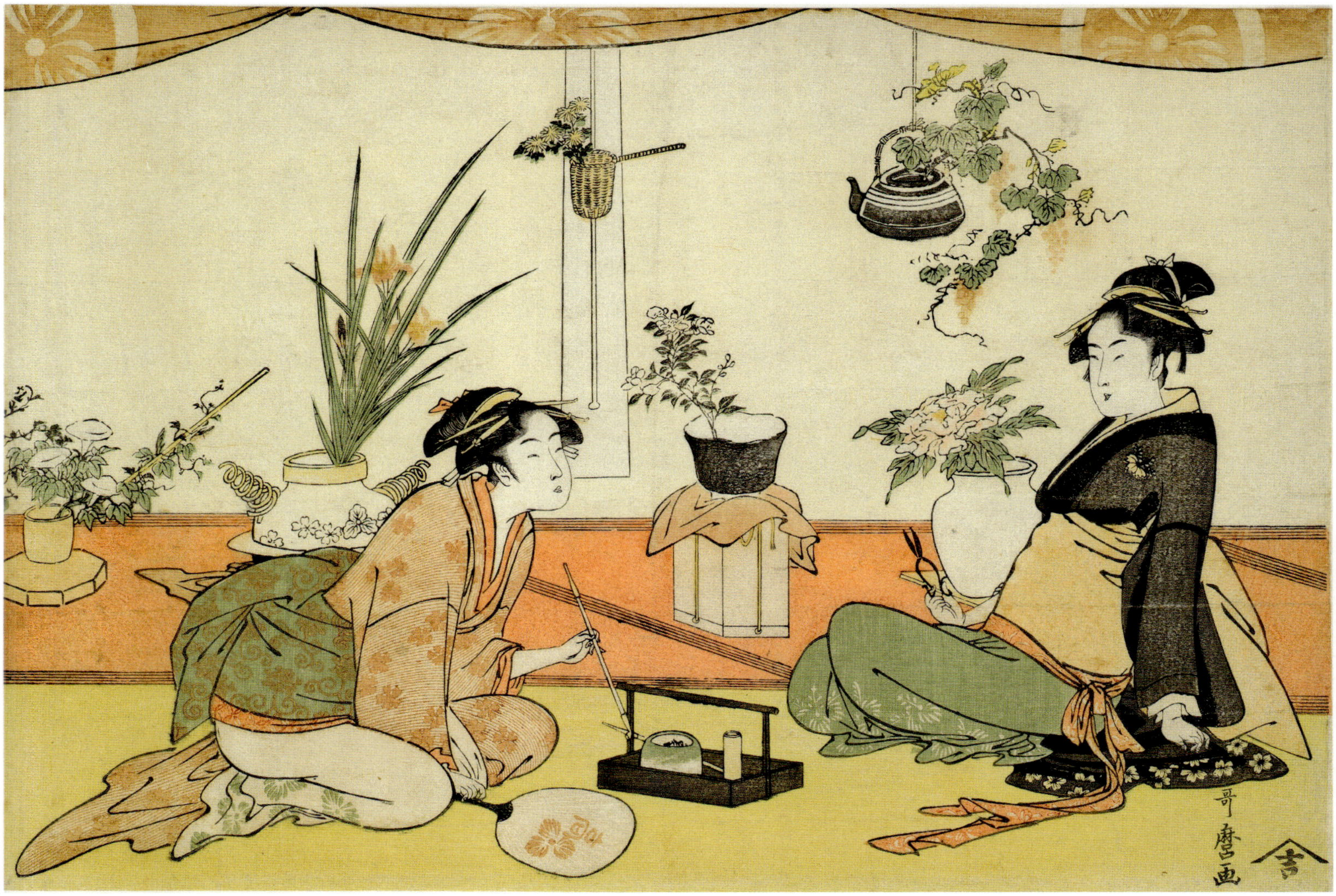

69

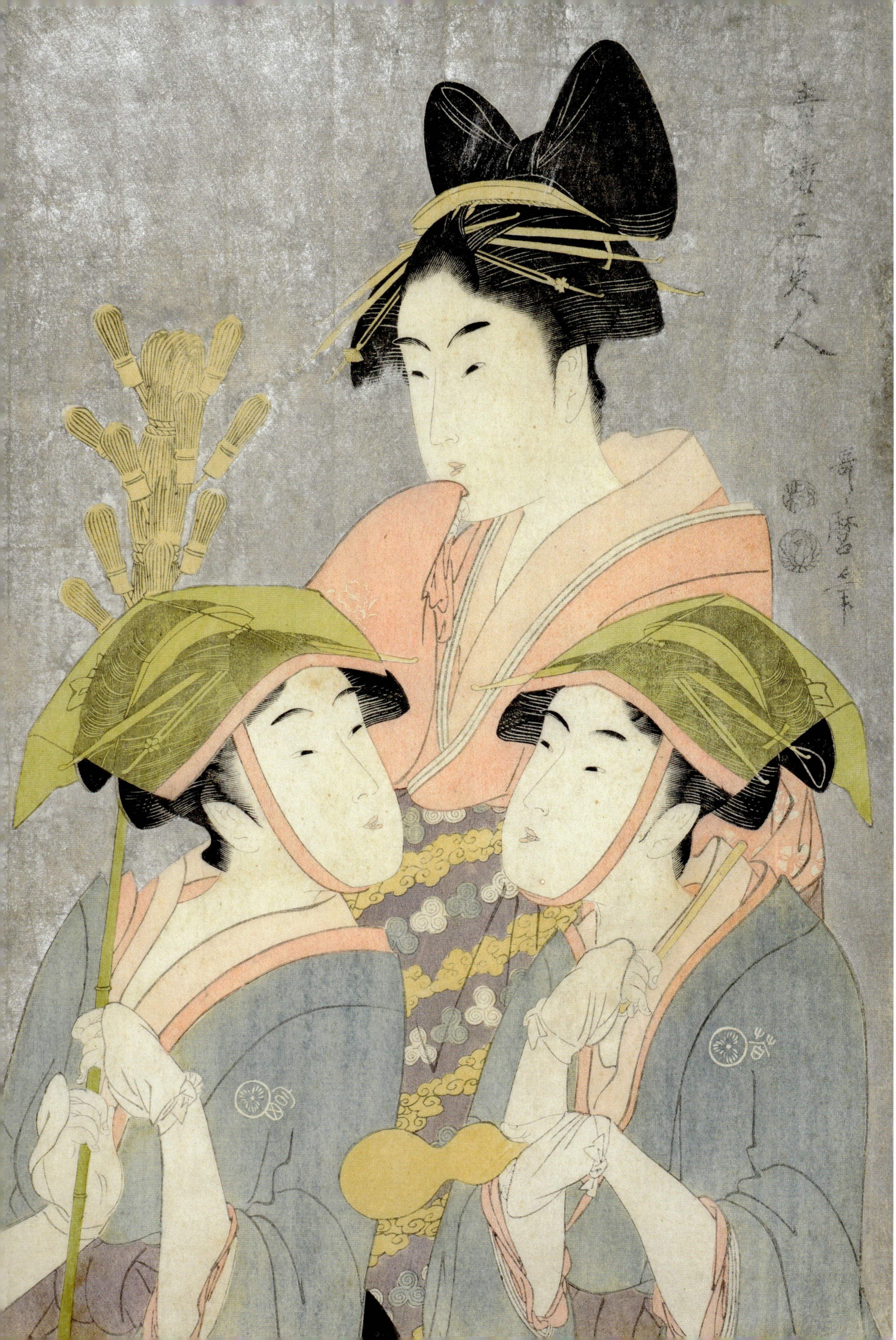
青楼三美人
歌麿筆

Utamaro vertraute häufig auf Kompositionen, in denen Halbfigurenporträts schöner Frauen in Gruppierungen angeordnet waren, die einer buddhistischen Trias ähnelten. Auf diese Weise konnte der Künstler sich ganz auf die Gesichter und Frisuren der Frauen konzentrieren und unter Verwendung grosser farbiger und gemusterter Bereiche überzeugende Entwürfe schaffen. Der Glimmerdruck im Hintergrund verleiht dem Bild eine luxuriöse Note und bietet den kostümierten Schönheiten eine ausgezeichnete Kulisse.

In der Mitte sehen wir eine hochrangige Kurtisane aus der Klasse der *oiran,* eingerahmt von zwei Geishas in Kostümen für ihre Tanzvorführung beim Niwaka-Fest. Die Figur links hält ein Sortiment von Teebesen in der Hand, die sie zum Verkauf anbietet, die Frau rechts einen hohlen Flaschenkürbis, den sie anschlägt, um Kunden anzulocken. Während des Fests führten aufwendig kostümierte Kurtisanen Tänze, Lieder und Parodien zu unterschiedlichsten Themen entlang der Hauptstrasse in Yoshiwara auf. Das Niwaka-Fest fand im achten Monat des Jahres statt und gehörte zu einem Reigen jährlicher Feierlichkeiten, mit denen die Eigentümer von Yoshiwara die herausragende Stellung ihres Viertels aus früheren Tagen wiederherzustellen versuchten. Die mit grossem Aufwand inszenierten Darbietungen wurden zu beliebten Motiven des *ukiyo-e.* Utamaro produzierte eine Reihe von *bijin*-Bildern und Koryûsai mehrere Holzschnittserien zu diesem Thema.

Utamaro often employed compositions in which half-length portraits of beauties were arranged in a configuration similar to a Buddhist triad. This device allowed the artist to concentrate on the faces and hairstyles of the women and to create strong designs composed of large areas of color and pattern. The mica background in this print adds a note of luxury and provides a glittering backdrop to the costumed beauties.

In the center is a high-ranking courtesan known as an *oiran,* and beside her are two geisha dressed for their dance performance at the Niwaka Festival. The figure on the left holds a display of tea whisks for sale, and the woman on the right, a hollow gourd, which she beats to attract customers. During the festival, dances, songs, and skits, on a wide range of subjects, were performed along the main boulevard of the Yoshiwara by elaborately costumed courtesans. The event was held during the eighth month, one of several annual celebrations promoted by the Yoshiwara proprietors in an effort to restore their district to its former preeminent position. The elaborately staged performances became a popular subject in *ukiyo-e:* Utamaro produced a number of *bijinga* and Koryûsai did several print series on the theme.

CM

喜多川歌麿

70
Drei Schönheiten aus dem Freudenviertel Yoshiwara
Three Beauties of the Yoshiwara
Kitagawa UTAMARO

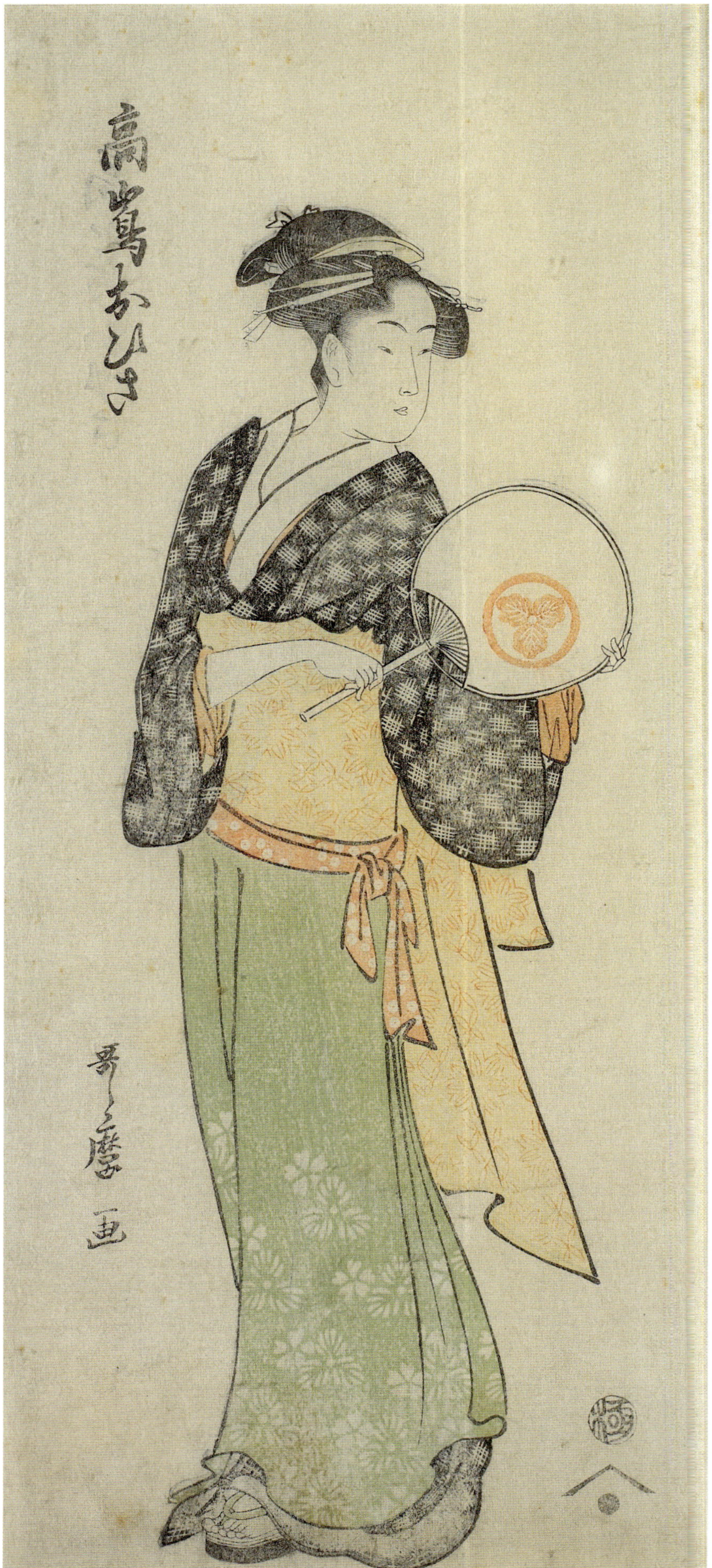

喜多川 歌麿

71
Takashima Ohisa
Takashima Ohisa
Kitagawa UTAMARO

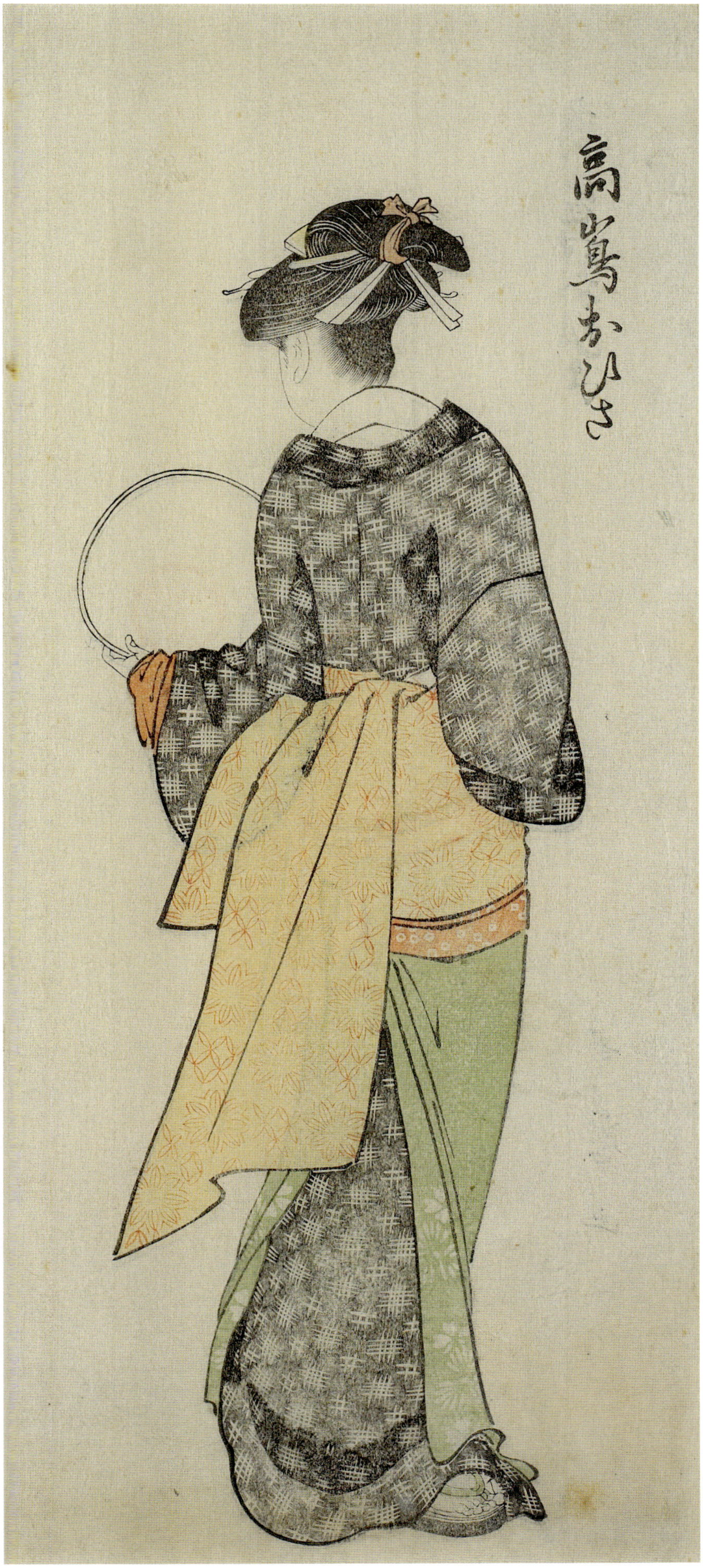

Dieses Werk zeigt die berühmte Schönheit Ohisa gleichzeitig von vorne und von hinten in der seltenen *ryômen-zuri*-Technik, in diesem Fall auf der Vorder- und Rückseite desselben Papierbogens gedruckt. Wenn man das Blatt gegen das Licht hält, liegen die Umrisslinien der Bilder nahezu perfekt übereinander. Ein ähnlicher Druck existiert auch von Okita aus dem Naniwaya-Teehaus, die gemeinsam mit Ohisa die Liste der Schönheiten in der Kansei-Zeit (1789–1801) anführte.

Ohisa zählte zu Utamaros Lieblingsmodellen. Sie war keine Kurtisane, sondern die Tochter eines reichen Kaufmanns, und arbeitete als Bedienung im Takashimaya, dem Teehaus ihres Vaters in der Nähe der Ryôgoku-Brücke in Edo. Oft wird sie, wie hier, mit einer Schürze über ihrem Kimono dargestellt. Ihr Fächer unterstreicht ihre Identifikation mit dem väterlichen Etablissement. Als dieser Druck entstand, muss sie etwas über 15 Jahre alt gewesen sein.

Berühmte Teehaus-Schönheiten waren ein häufiges Motiv im Holzdruck. Ihre unverbrauchte Schönheit und ihr unschuldiger Reiz unterschieden sie von den weltgewandten und unnahbaren Kurtisanen. Wie bei den Geishas bestand ihr Wert jedoch hauptsächlich in ihrer Fähigkeit, Kunden anzuziehen, und auch sie dienten in der öffentlichen Vorstellung und im *ukiyo-e* als Weiblichkeitsideale.

In this rare example of a *bijinga* done in the *ryômen-zuri* technique, the renowned beauty Ohisa is shown simultaneously from the front and the back, the two designs having been applied to opposite sides of one sheet of paper. When the sheet is held to the light, the outlines of the two views match almost perfectly. A similar print exists of Okita of the Naniwaya, who ranked with Ohisa as a leading beauty of the Kansei era (1789–1801).

One of Utamaro's favorite subjects, Ohisa was not a courtesan, but the daughter of a prosperous merchant. She worked as a waitress at the Takashimaya, her father's shop near Ryôgoku Bridge in Edo, and she is often depicted, as here, wearing an apron over her kimono. The fan she holds further strengthens her identification with the teahouse. At the time the print was made, Ohisa would have been about fifteen years old.

Famous teahouse *bijin* were often depicted in *ukiyo-e,* their fresh beauty and uncalculated allure distinguishing them from the more worldly and aloof Yoshiwara courtesans. Like the geisha, however, their value lay mainly in their ability to attract customers, and they, too, served as ideals of femininity in prints and popular imagination.

CM

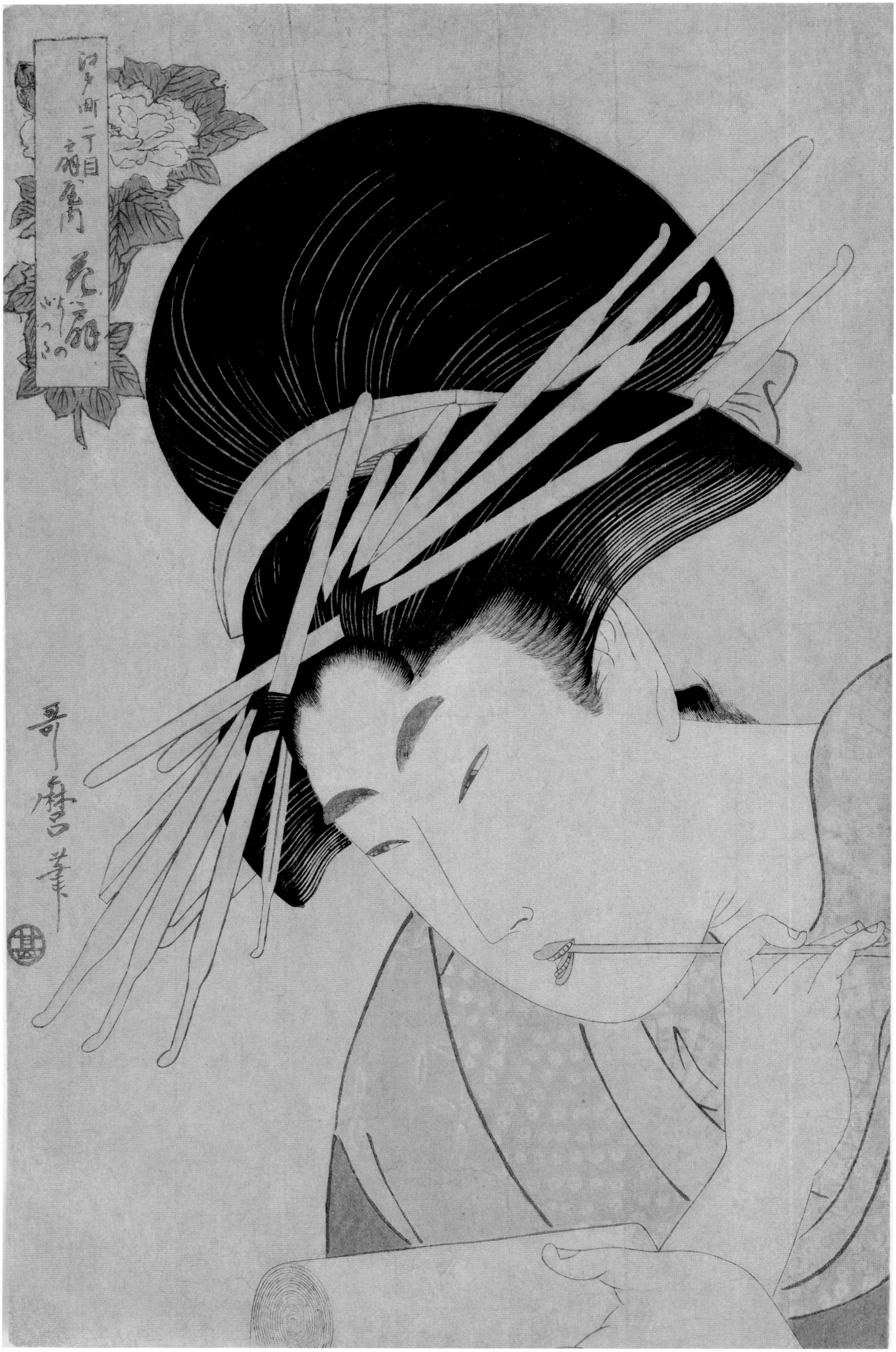

江戸町一丁目 扇屋内 花扇
よしの
たつた
哥麿筆

Für diesen Druck stand Hanaôgi Modell, eine der zu Utamaros Lebzeiten berühmtesten Kurtisanen. Obwohl sie in vielen Drucken abgebildet wurde, handelt es sich bei diesem Entwurf um ein besonders seltenes Exemplar. Die Darstellung wirkt selbst für Utamaro überaus intim und offenbart, wie sehr dieser das *ukiyo-e* von den Idealen Kiyonagas entfernt hat, der zwar nur ein Jahr älter war, dessen Werk jedoch aus einer anderen Generation zu stammen scheint. Die Komposition ist absolut ausgewogen, und obwohl Utamaro die Haarnadeln aus Schildpatt und die Stoffmuster voll Freude an der Innovation als starke Designelemente eingesetzt hat, lenkt er damit nicht von ihrer Funktion als Rahmenwerk für Hanaôgis Gesicht ab. Dieses besteht zwar nur aus wenigen dünnen Linien, die schwungvoll grosse Flächen umreissen, bildet damit aber einen starken Kontrast zu der komplizierten Haartracht und Garderobe und füllt zudem die Bildmitte aus. Auf diese Weise gelingt es dem Künstler, unsere Aufmerksamkeit wirkungsvoll auf Hanaôgis Gesichtsausdruck zu lenken, den eigentlichen Mittelpunkt des Bildes.

This print takes as its subject Hanaôgi, one of the most celebrated courtesans of Utamaro's time. Although she was depicted in many prints, this is a particularly rare example. The portrayal is especially intimate, even for Utamaro, and it reveals the extent to which he transformed *ukiyo-e* from the ideals of Kiyonaga, who was only one year older, but whose work seems from an entirely different generation. There is a perfect balance to the composition, and while Utamaro has innovatively used the tortoise shell hairpins and textile patterns as bold design elements, this does not detract from their function as framing devices for Hanaôgi's face. Although the face is accomplished through minimal use of thin, tensile lines delineating broad planes, the contrast between this and the complexity of her coiffure and dress, as well as its placement in the center, effectively draw attention to her expression as the main focal point.

SE

喜多川歌麿

72

Hanaôgi vom Freudenhaus Ôgiya in Edochô Itchôme – Kurtisanen verglichen mit Blumen

Hanaôgi of the Ôgiya Brothel House at Edochô Itchôme – A Comparison of Courtesan Flowers

Kitagawa UTAMARO

Edo war nicht der einzige Entstehungsort von *ukiyo-e*-Bildnissen schöner Frauen: Auch in den Freudenvierteln von Kyoto und Osaka suchten die Künstler nach Modellen. Dieses exquisite *ôkubi-e,* oder Brustbildporträt, zeigt die berühmte Kurtisane Tsukasa aus Osaka just in dem Moment, als etwas in ihrem Rücken ihre Aufmerksamkeit erregt und sie mit erhobenem linkem Arm den Blick über die Schulter wendet. Ihre Tracht besteht aus fünf Lagen unterschiedlicher Stoffe, darunter ein helloranges Gewand mit Mustern im *shibori*-Stil, einer speziellen Batiktechnik. Die Figur der Tsukasa veranschaulicht hier auf perfekte Weise Chôkis Weiblichkeitsideal. Michener schrieb dazu in *Japanese Prints* (1959): «Chôkis Zeichnungen sind elfenhaft und die Schultern seiner Figuren so schmal wie bei Modigliani [...]» Diese Verformung der weiblichen Figur könnte ein ähnliches Gefühl von Sinnlichkeit erzeugt haben wie Modiglianis weibliche Formen.

Edo was not the only source for *ukiyo-e* portrayals of *bijin:* artists also looked to the pleasure quarters of Kyoto and Osaka for their subjects. This exquisite *ôkubi-e,* or bust portrait, shows the famous Osaka courtesan Tsukasa. She has been depicted just at the moment her attention is caught by something behind her and she turns to look back over her shoulder, her left sleeve raised to her face. Her dress consists of five layers of different materials, including a light orange robe decorated with tie-dyed patterns using the *shibori* technique. The figure of Tsukasa here perfectly illustrates Chôki's ideal of femininity. As Michener states: "Chôki's drawing is elfin, and his figures are pinched together at the shoulder, in Modigliani style." This deformation of the female figure might have created a feeling of sensuality much like Modigliani's female forms.

CM

栄松斎 長喜

73
Tsukasa Dayû aus dem Freudenhaus Higashi Ôgiya in Osakas Shinmachi-Viertel
Tsukasa Dayû of Higashi Ôgiya in Osaka's Shinmachi District
Eishôsai CHÔKI

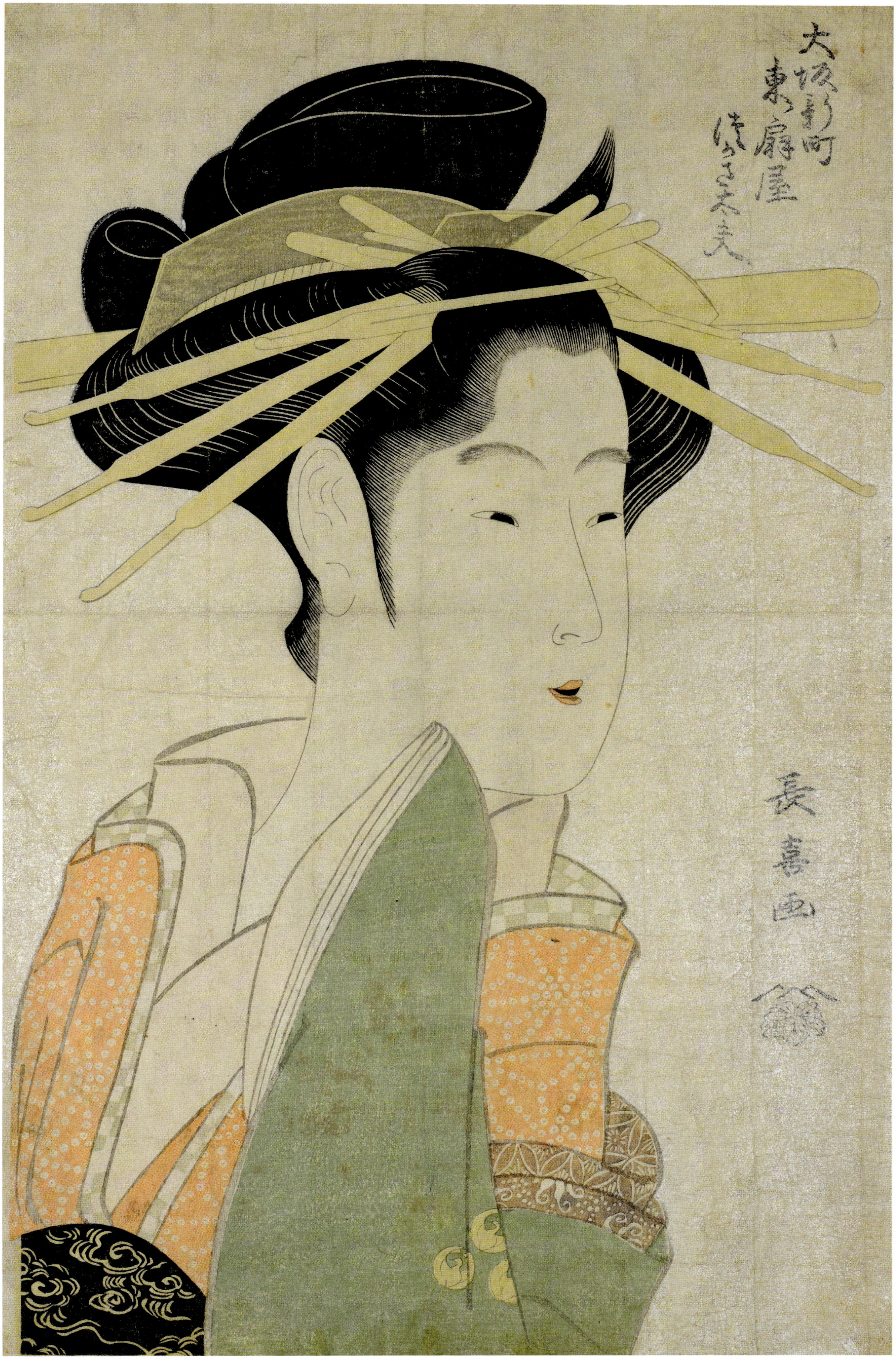
大坂新町
東扇屋
長喜画

Im Sommer und Frühherbst von Edo waren Flussfahrten auf dem Sumida ein beliebtes Freizeitvergnügen. Man genoss die kühle Brise und sah von Bord des Ausflugsbootes den Festlichkeiten am Ufer zu. In dieser lebendigen Szene haben drei solcher Boote an den Holzpfählen der Ryôgoku-Brücke angelegt. Die Kurtisanen unter den Fahrgästen lassen auf eine abendliche Bootstour schliessen, bei der die Kunden unterhalten und die Boote mit Staken flussauf und flussab gesteuert wurden. Das grösste Boot mit dem kunstvoll bemalten Bug bildete den Mittelpunkt der Lustbarkeiten. In Chôkis meisterhaft arrangierter Komposition kontrastieren die vielfältigen Posen und Gesten der bunt gewandeten Kurtisanen mit der Geometrie und dezenten Farbgebung der Brücke und der Boote.

Die Ryôgoku-Brücke wurde im *ukiyo-e* häufig als Ort dargestellt, an dem unterschiedlichste Menschen aller Klassen für einen kurzen Moment aufeinandertrafen, bevor sich ihre Wege wieder trennten. Sie stand als Sinnbild für die Energie, die Dynamik und die Spontaneität der Grossstadt – Assoziationen, die zweifellos bei der anerkennenden Betrachtung der berühmten Brücke durch das Publikum von Edo mitschwangen.

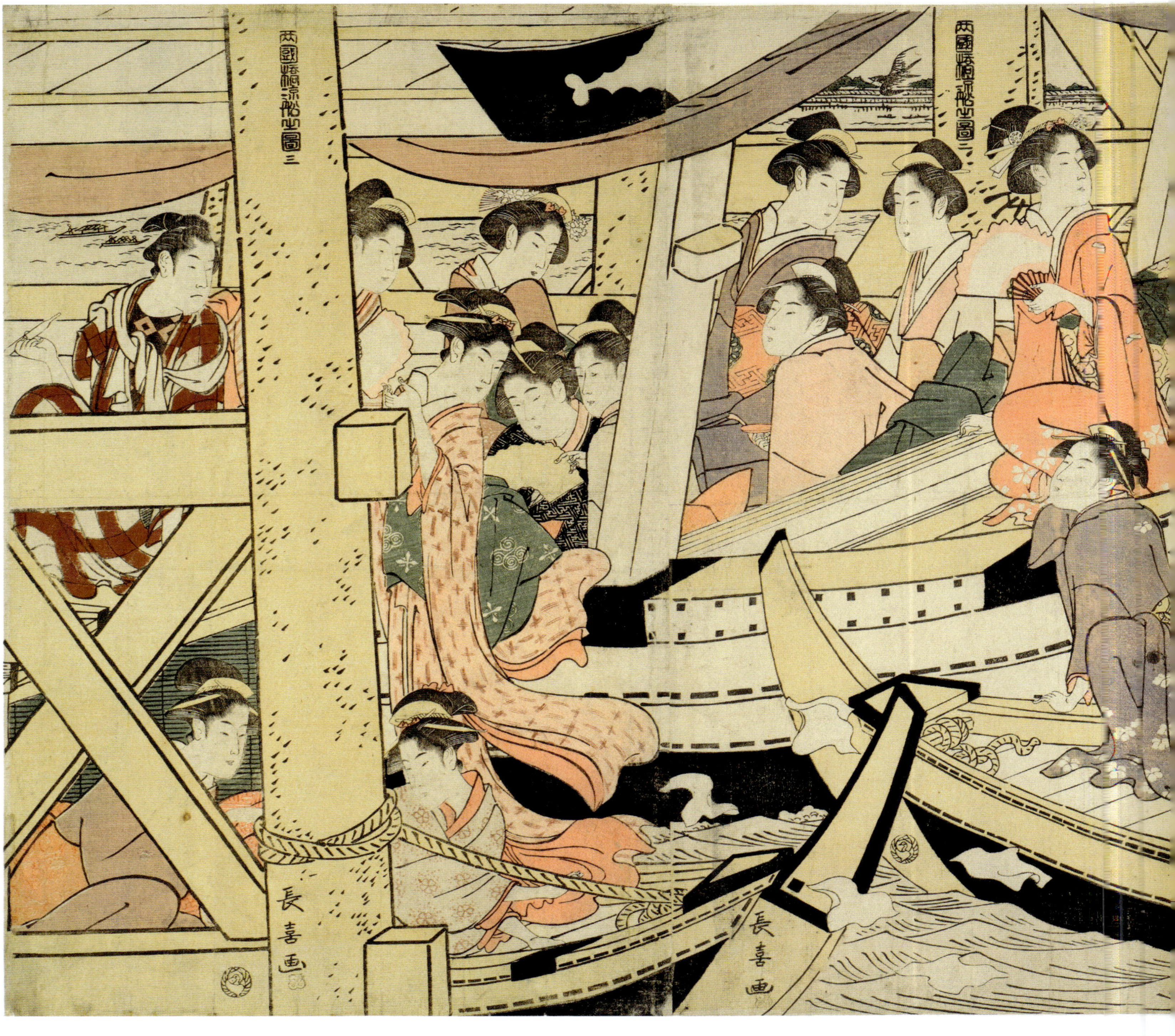

A popular activity in Edo during the summer and early autumn was a trip in a pleasure boat down the Sumida River to enjoy the cool breezes and watch the festivities held on shore. In this lively scene, three such boats are tied to the wooden pilings of Ryôgoku Bridge. The presence of the courtesans suggests an evening boating party, where clients will be entertained as the boats are poled up and down the river. The largest vessel, with its elaborately painted bow, would have been central to the festivities. Chôki has created a masterful composition, in which the color and varied pose and gesture of the courtesans are juxtaposed with the geometry and subdued color of the bridge and boats.

Ryôgoku Bridge was depicted often in *ukiyo-e* as a space in which all types and classes of people were brought together for a few moments before each went their separate way: the epitome of the energy, dynamism, and spontaneous nature of the city. These associations would have doubtless informed the Edo audience's appreciation of this view of the famous bridge.

CM

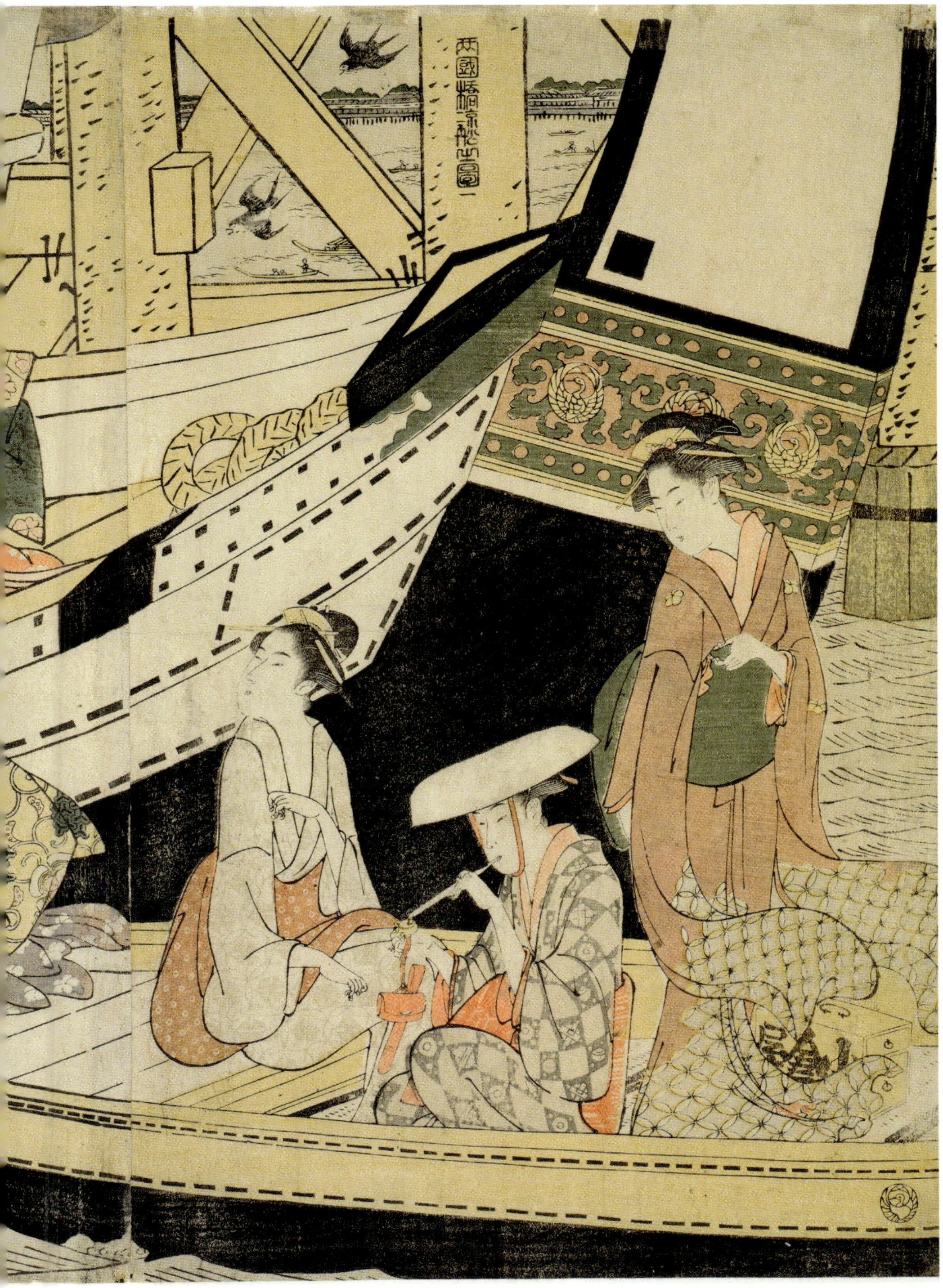

栄松斎 長喜

74
Abkühlung unter der Ryôgoku-Brücke
Cooling off under Ryôgoku Bridge
Eishôsai CHÔKI

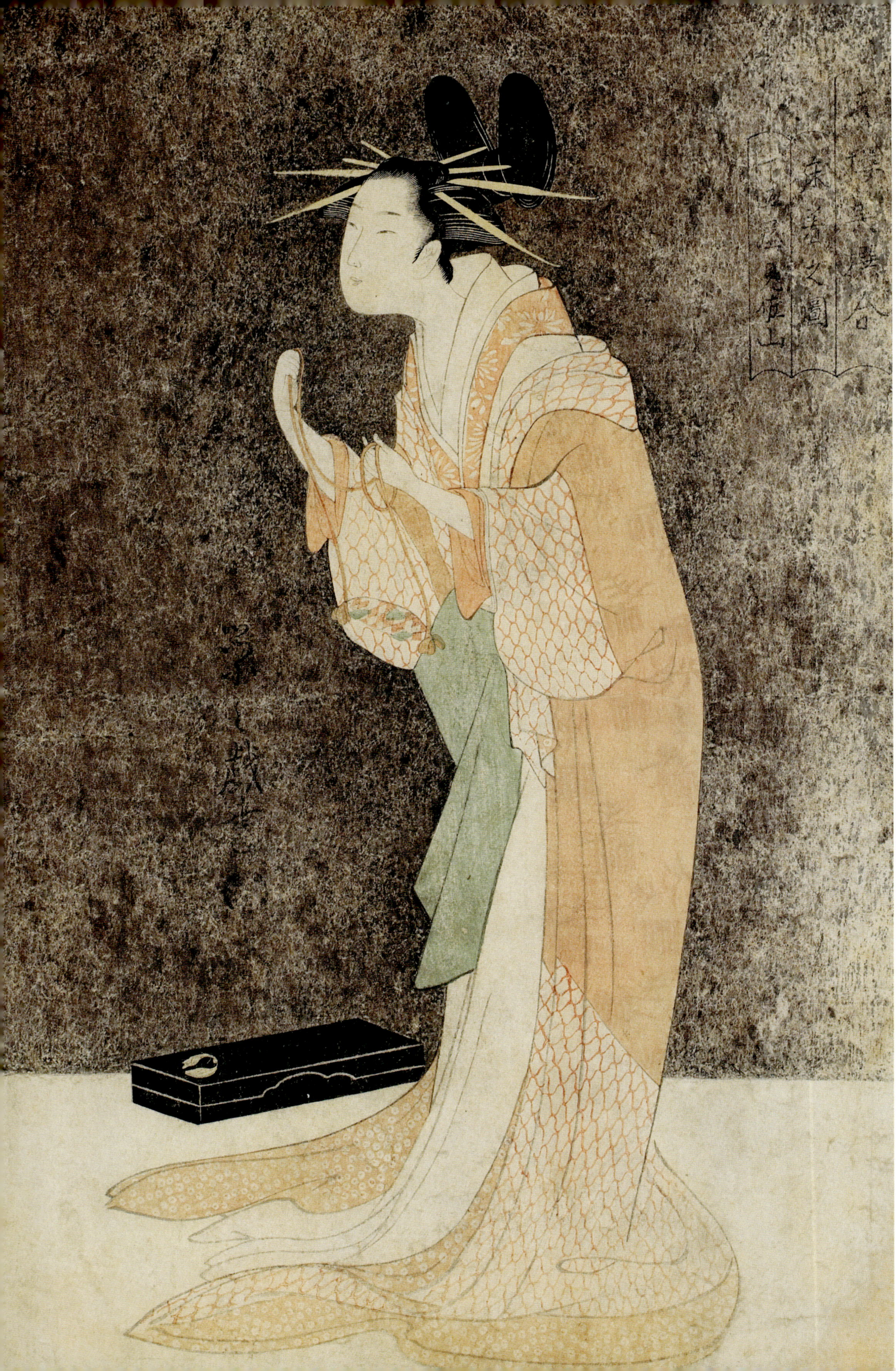

In den 1790er-Jahren trat Chôbunsai Eishi als führender Entwerfer von «Bildern schöner Frauen» und Konkurrent von Utamaro in Erscheinung. Seine gelängten Figuren erinnern an jene von Kiyonaga und Utamaro, doch ihre Zartheit, ihre anmutigen, wie getanzt wirkenden Gesten und ihre fliessenden Gewänder unterscheiden sie vom Stil seiner Zeitgenossen. In dieser Abendszene bereitet sich die ranghohe Kurtisane Misayama auf ihre Nachtruhe vor; sie hat gerade ihr Duftamulett abgenommen, hält es noch an der Halskette fest und wird es gleich in das Kästchen auf dem Boden legen. Der vor dem dunklen Hintergrund leuchtende Körper der stehenden Kurtisane beschreibt einen leichten Bogen, während ihr Gewand ihre Füsse zu umfliessen scheint. Kaum sichtbar sind in der oberen rechten Ecke des Bildes der Titel der Serie und des Einzelblatts abgedruckt. Links von Misayama erkennen wir auf halber Höhe die Signatur des Künstlers.

Chôbunsai Eishi emerged in the 1790s as a premier designer of *bijinga* and a rival to Utamaro. His elongated figures recall those of Kiyonaga and Utamaro, but their delicacy, their graceful, dance-like gestures, and their flowing garments distinguish them from the style of his contemporaries. In this night scene, the high-ranking courtesan Misayama is taking off her perfumed amulet in preparation for retiring. The box in which it will be placed is on the floor. Misayama stands holding the necklace; her body, bright against the dark background, describes a slender curve, while her robes seem to pool at her feet. Just visible in the top right-hand corner of the print are the titles of the series and the individual print; to the left of Misayama is the signature of the artist.

CM

鳥文斎 栄之

75
Misayama aus dem Freudenhaus Chôjiya in ihrem Ankleidezimmer – Schönheiten in den Freudenvierteln
Misayama of the Chôjiya Brothel House in Her Dressing Room – Beauties in the Pleasure Quarters
Chôbunsai EISHI

Das «Puppenfest», oder *hinamatsuri,* wurde traditionell am dritten Tag des dritten Mondmonats gefeiert. Es geht zurück auf alte chinesische Reinigungszeremonien und war in der Edo-Zeit am besten als Gelegenheit für Mädchen bekannt, kunstvolle Puppenensembles mit Figuren vom Kaiserhof der Heian-Zeit (794–1185) aufzustellen. Oft waren diese Sets Familienerbstücke, die sich über Generationen angesammelt hatten. Die Puppen symbolisierten ursprünglich negative Energien (wie Leid und Krankheit) – um die Gemeinde jedes Frühjahr aufs Neue zu reinigen, wurden sie in Bäche und Flüsse gesetzt, damit das Wasser sie davontragen konnte. Diese Bedeutung war jedoch, als der hier gezeigte Druck entstand, weitgehend in Vergessenheit geraten. Eishi enthüllt, dass nicht nur kleine Mädchen Puppen sammelten: Er zeigt eine festlich gewandete junge Frau beim Aufstellen einer Musikerpuppe, die in Diensten des Kaisers und der Kaiserin, der Hauptfiguren ihres Puppensets, stand.

Eishis Drucke lassen einerseits den durchdringenden Einfluss Utamaros in den 1790er-Jahren erkennen, andererseits war Eishi selbst ein wichtiger Lehrer. Kompositorische Parallelen zu diesem Druck, etwa der Einsatz ovaler Formen zur Strukturierung der Figur (besonders auffällig bei den Beinen), sind in den Arbeiten seiner Schüler zu finden, so in Eishôs *Minister Narihira wird volljährig* (KAT. 80) und in Eisuis *Somenosuke aus dem Freudenhaus Matsubaya* (KAT. 83).

The "Doll Festival," or *hinamatsuri,* was traditionally celebrated on the third day of the third lunar month. The festival traces back to ancient spring lustration ceremonies in China, but by the Edo period it had become best known as an opportunity for girls to display elaborate sets of dolls depicting the Heian-period (794–1185) royal court. These sets often were family heirlooms, sometimes assembled over generations. The dolls originally symbolized negative energies (such as disease), and were placed in flowing water to carry them away and purify the community each spring. However, this significance largely was lost by the time this print was made. Eishi reveals that the collecting of dolls was not limited to girls, as a young woman dressed in her finest for the festival prepares to place one of the musician dolls that would have been in attendance to the central figures of the emperor and empress in her set.

While Eishi's prints reveal the pervasive influence of Utamaro in the 1790s, he was an important teacher in his own right, and parallels for the compositional techniques found in this print, for example the use of ovals to provide structure to the figure (especially noticeable in the legs), can be seen in the works of his students, such as Eishô's *Minister Narihira's Coming of Age* (CAT. 80) and Eisui's *Somenosuke of the Matsubaya Brothel House* (CAT. 83).

SE

鳥文斎 栄之

76
Das Mädchenfest –
Die fünf eleganten
jahreszeitlichen Feste
The Doll Festival –
The Elegant Five Festivals
Chôbunsai EISHI

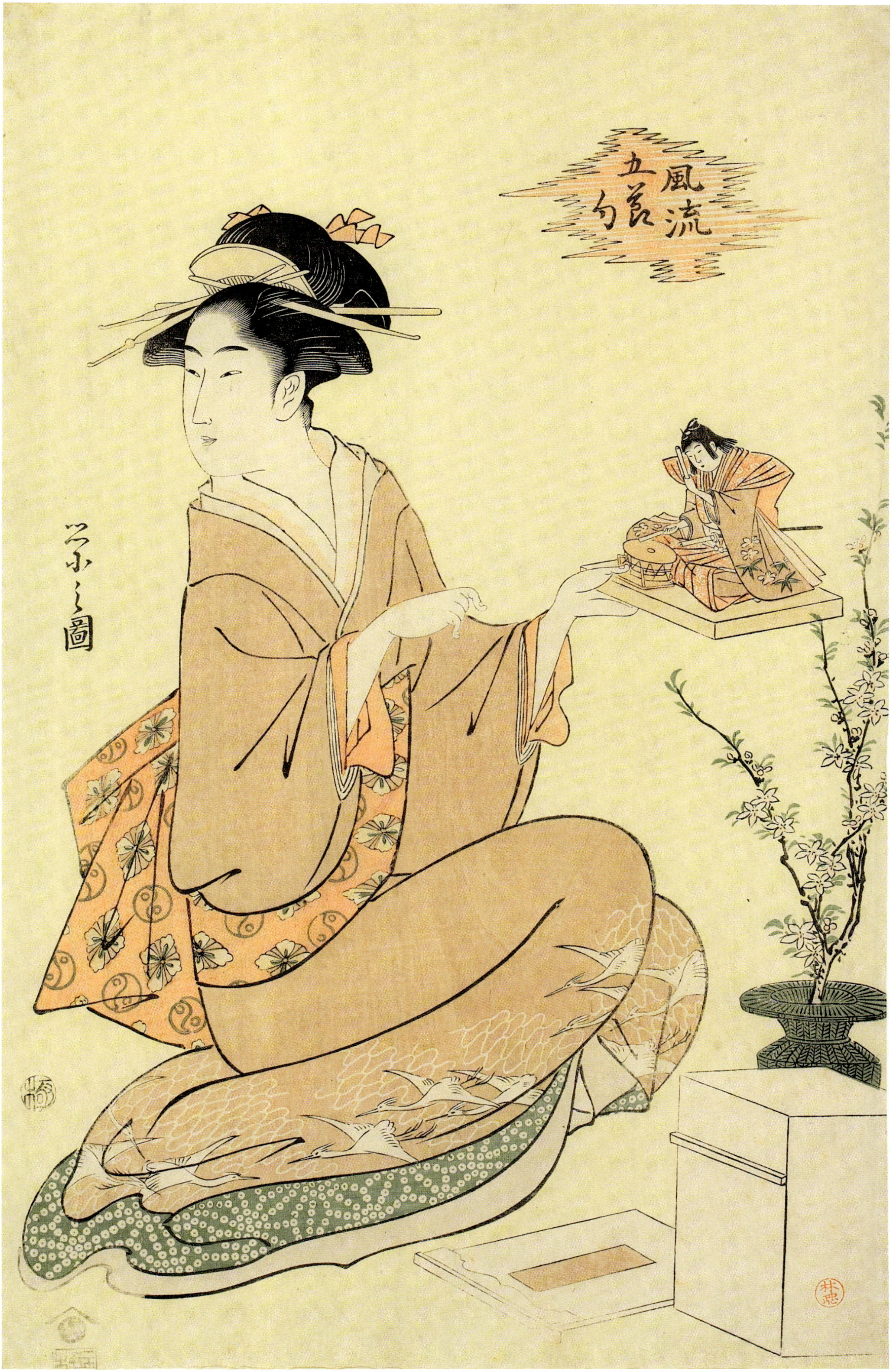
風流五節句
栄之圖

Die zwei ranghohen Kurtisanen aus dem Freudenhaus Matsubaya in Edo entsprechen – hochgewachsen, schlank und in anmutiger Pose – dem Schönheitsideal von Eishi. Die eine der beiden, Kisegawa, betrachtet eine Querrolle mit Gemälden nach den *Erzählungen von Ise*, einer Sammlung von Gedichten und Geschichten aus dem 10. Jahrhundert. Kenntnisse der japanischen Klassiker wurden auf allen gesellschaftlichen Ebenen hoch geschätzt, und die Einbindung der berühmten Schriften in dieses Porträt unterstreicht die umfassende Bildung der Kurtisane. In gewissem Sinne gehört das Bild zur Gruppe der *mitate-e* («Bilder mit Parodien»): Das Wort *rokkasen* im japanischen Titel bedeutet «sechs Blumen» und bezieht sich auf Schönheiten aus dem Freudenviertel; in der Literatur dagegen bezeichnet *rokkasen* die sechs klassischen Dichter Japans. Die mit dem Wortspiel beabsichtigte Gleichsetzung ist aber durchaus angemessen: Kurtisanen waren in einer Reihe schöner Künste bewandert, so auch in der Dichtkunst, und die Serie, zu der dieser Druck gehört, umfasst sechs Abbildungen von Kurtisanen, die zudem versierte Schriftstellerinnen waren.

Somenosuke ist hier in einem speziellen Kimono für den Neujahrstag zu sehen, einem Geschenk eines wohlhabenden Kunden und Zeichen ihres hohen Standes. Das eingetopfte Adonisröschen, auf das ihr Blick fällt, symbolisiert die Jahreszeit, der Phönix auf ihrem Kimono und der Habicht auf ihrem Übergewand sind adäquate Glückssymbole für eine Neujahrsszene.

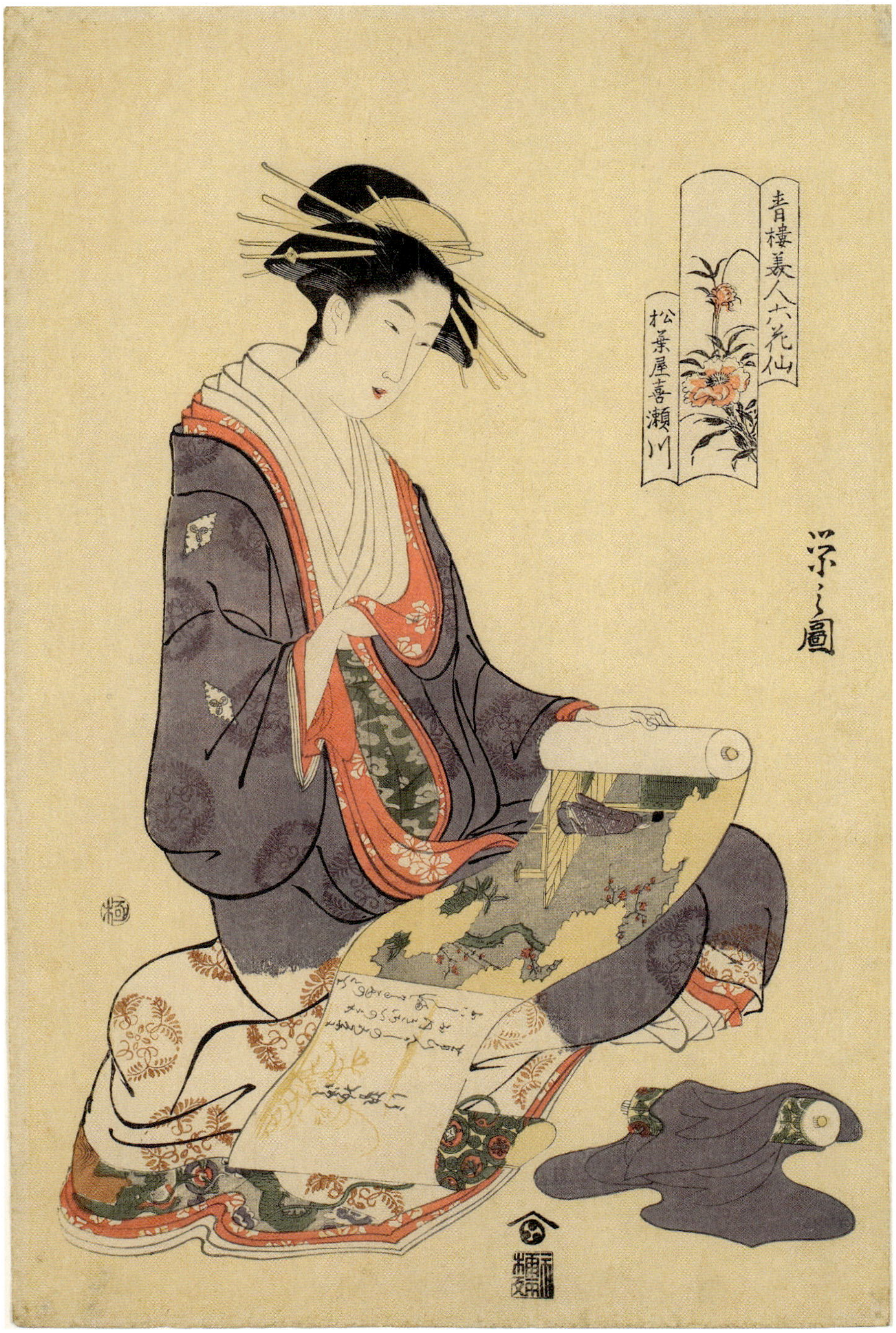

Depicted here are two high-ranking courtesans from the Matsubaya brothel in Edo. Tall, slender, and gracefully posed, they conform to Eishi's ideal of beauty. Kisegawa is shown looking at a handscroll painting of the *Tales of Ise,* a collection of poems and stories dating from the tenth century. Knowledge of the Japanese classics was highly valued by all levels of society, and the inclusion here of the famous tale emphasizes the courtesan's refinement. In a sense, the scene is a *mitate-e* (parody picture). The *rokkasen* of the Japanese title means "six flowers" and refers to beauties of the pleasure quarters; in literature, *rokkasen* denotes the six classic poets of Japan. At the same time, the identification implied in the pun is appropriate. Courtesans were skilled in a number of arts, including poetry, and the series to which this print belongs features six courtesans who were accomplished writers.

Somenosuke is shown here wearing a special kimono for New Year's Day, a present from a wealthy patron and a sign of her high rank. The potted Adonis plant on which she gazes is a symbol of the season, and the phoenix on her kimono and hawk on her outer robe are auspicious designs, appropriate for a New Year's scene.

CM

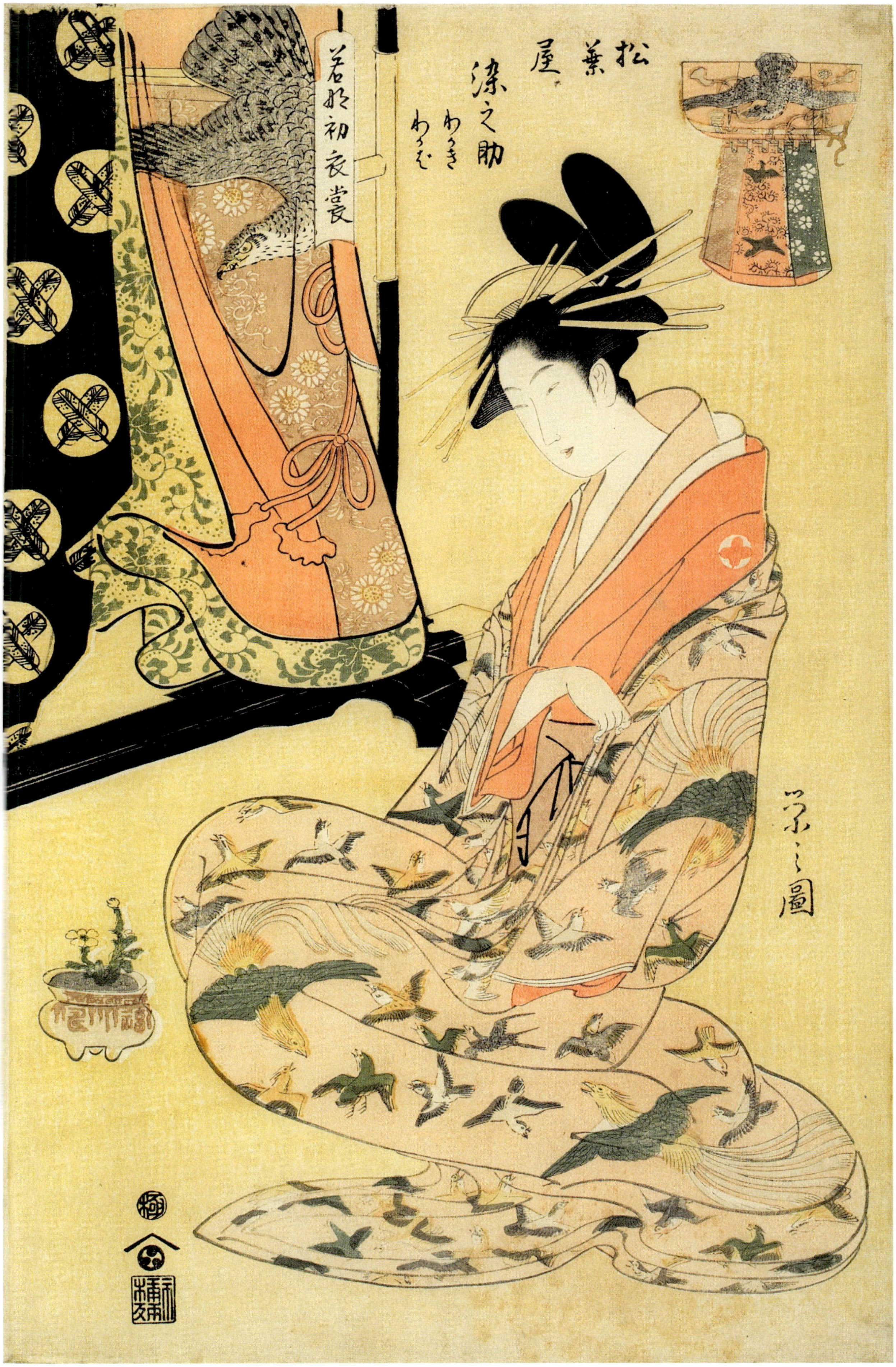

78

鳥文斎 栄之

77
Kisegawa aus dem Freudenhaus Matsubaya – Sechs schöne Blumen aus den Freudenvierteln
Kisegawa of the Matsubaya – Six Beautiful Flowers of the Pleasure Quarters
Chôbunsai EISHI

鳥文斎 栄之

78
Somenosuke aus dem Freudenhaus Matsubaya – Kurtisanen führen die Neujahrsmode vor
Somenosuke of the Matsubaya – Courtesans Modeling the New Year's Fashions
Chôbunsai EISHI

122 / 123

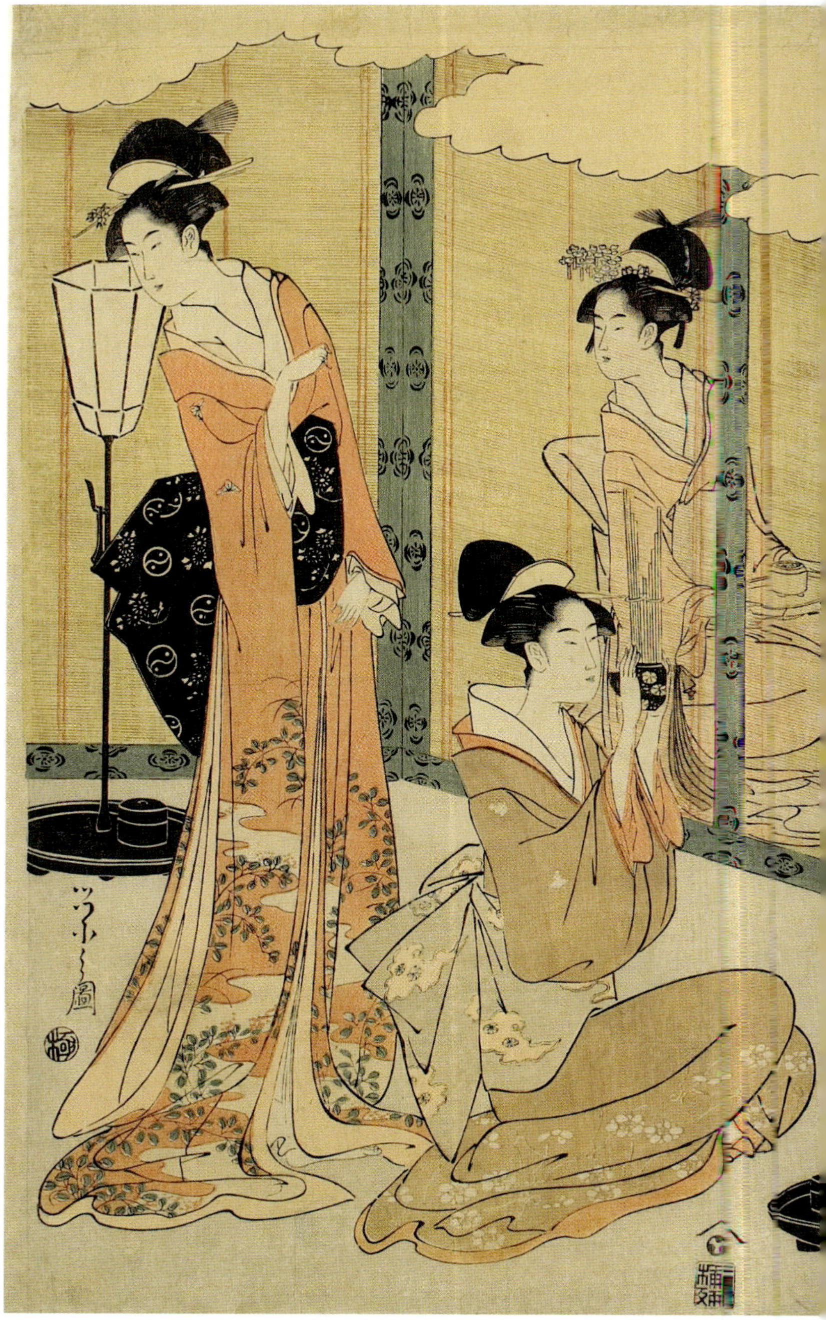

79

Eine Parodie des Ushiwakamaru und der Prinzessin Jôruri

A Visual Parody of Ushiwakamaru and Princess Jôruri

Chôbunsai EISHI

鳥文斎 栄之

Die Erzählung, auf der diese Parodie basiert, ist eine Liebesgeschichte aus dem Mittelalter. Auf einer Reise hört Ushiwakamaru, der spätere grosse Krieger Minamoto Yoshitsune, die Prinzessin Jôruri auf ihrer *koto* (Zither) spielen. Wie verzaubert erwidert er ihr Spiel auf der Flöte. Dem musikalischen Duett folgen der Austausch von Gedichten und eine Liebesnacht. Als Ushiwakamarus Pflichten es ihm jedoch unmöglich machen, bei ihr zu bleiben, nimmt Jôruri sich das Leben. In der unterhaltenden *ukiyo-e*-Version der Geschichte werden alle Rollen von Kurtisanen gespielt. Die ursprüngliche Komposition bestand aus fünf Blättern und zeigte neben Jôruri auch Ushiwakamaru, das Ziel ihres Blicks. Mit ihrer *koto* sitzt die Prinzessin hinter einem Bambusparavent in der Mitte des Bildes. Ihre Begleiterinnen stimmen in ihr Spiel ein: Die Figur links von Jôruri spielt auf einer chinesischen Mundorgel, weiter rechts sitzt eine Figur bereit, um eine grosse Trommel zu schlagen.

The tale on which this parody is based is a love story dating from the medieval period. While on a journey, Ushiwakamaru, the future great warrior Minamoto Yoshitsune, hears Princess Jôruri playing the *koto.* Entranced, he takes out his flute and joins in. Their musical duet leads to exchanges of poetry and then to their spending the night together as lovers. When Ushiwakamaru's duties make it impossible for him to remain with her, however, Jôruri commits suicide. In this light-hearted version, all the roles are performed by courtesans. The original composition comprised five prints and depicted both Jôruri and Ushiwakamaru, the object of Jôruri's gaze. Here, Jôruri sits with her *koto* behind a bamboo screen in the center of the composition. She is accompanied on her instrument by her attendants on the left, a figure plays a Chinese mouth-organ, and on the right, another sits ready to strike a large drum.

CM

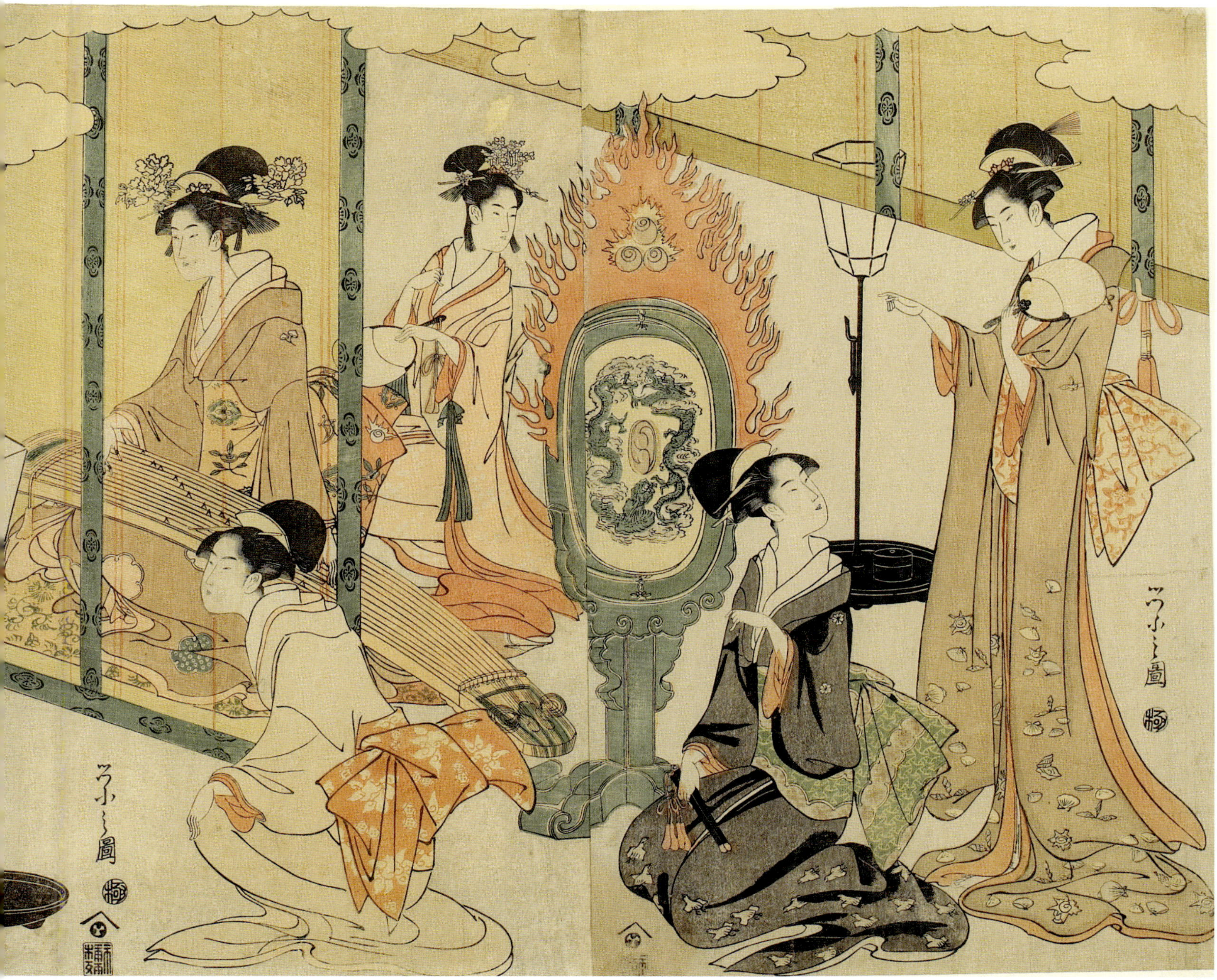

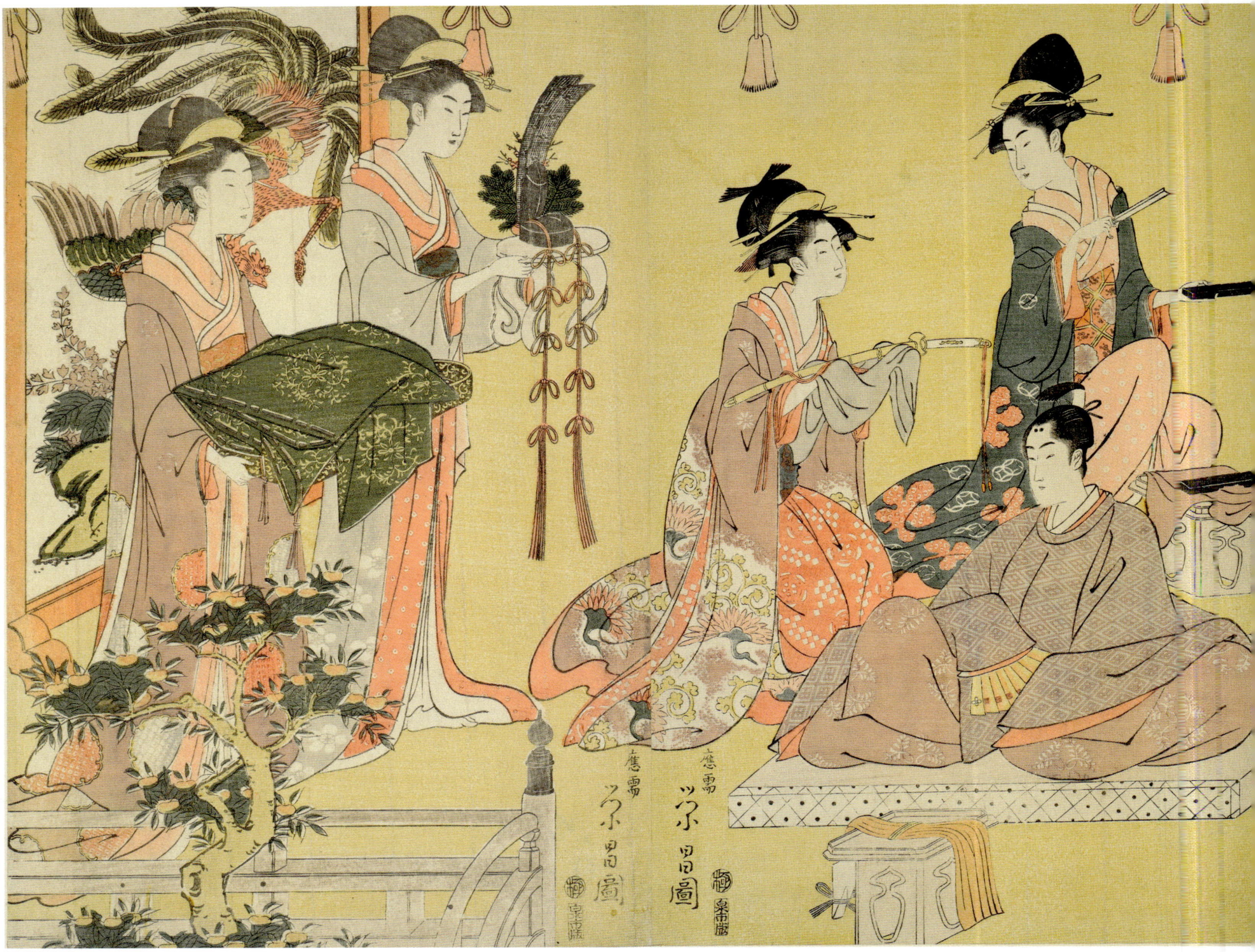

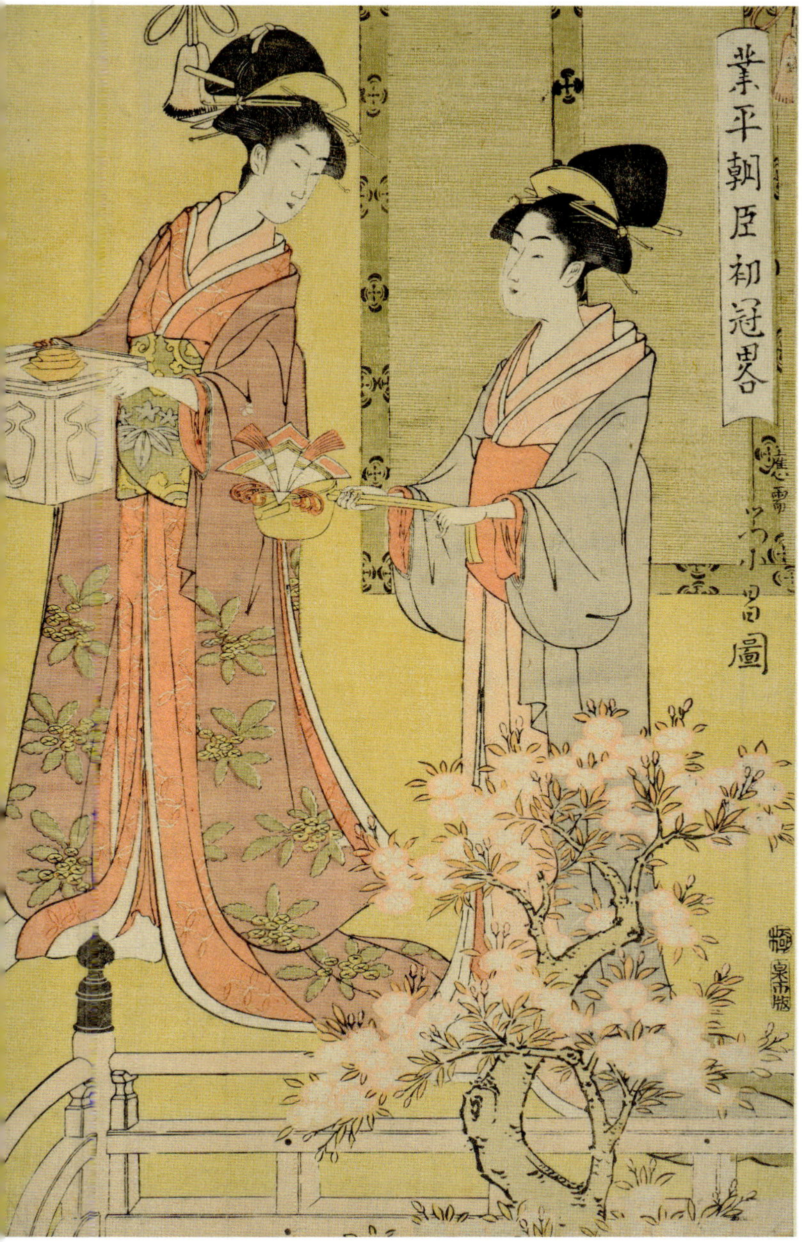

Bei der Hauptfigur dieses eindrucksvollen Triptychons handelt es sich um Ariwara no Narihira (825–880). Er gehörte der kaiserlichen Familie und den «Sechsunddreissig Unsterblichen der Dichtkunst» *(Sanjû rokkasen)* an und war als ultimative Ikone männlicher Schönheit berühmt für seine skandalträchtigen Liebesaffären. Er soll für die Hauptpersonen der *Erzählungen von Ise* und der *Geschichte vom Prinzen Genji* als Inspirationsquelle gedient haben. Thema des Drucks ist die Erhebung Narihiras in das Erwachsenenalter, die von allerlei ihn umgebenden Symbolen begleitet wird, darunter ein Zeremonialhut, ein Gewand und ein Schwert. Gleichzeitig parodiert Eishô das Ereignis, indem er sämtliche Diener in schöne Frauen verwandelt, gekleidet nach der neuesten Mode von Edo. Dabei nutzte er die stilistischen Einflüsse der beiden vorherrschenden Strömungen des *bijinga* im späten 18. Jahrhundert: Kiyonagas sorgfältig arrangierte Figurengruppen und Utamaros Gespür für die Linie – zugleich behauptete er aber einen ganz eigenen Stil, der eher an einige andere in dieser Ausstellung vertretene Künstler erinnert, etwa an Ichirakutei Eisui und dessen *Somenosuke aus dem Freudenhaus Matsubaya* (KAT. 83). Dies ist nicht verwunderlich, da sowohl Eishô als auch Eisui unter Chôbunsai Eishi studierten.

The central figure of this impressive triptych is Ariwara no Narihira (825–880). A member of the imperial family and one of the "Thirty-six Immortal Poets" *(Sanjû rokkasen)*, Narihira was famous both for his scandalous love affairs, and as the ultimate icon of masculine beauty. He is believed to have been a source of inspiration for the protagonists of both the *Tales of Ise* and *Tale of Genji*. The subject is Narihira's investiture as an adult, and various symbols of this surround him, including a ceremonial hat, robe, and sword. At the same time, Eishô parodies the event by making all of the attendants beautiful women dressed in the latest Edo fashions. Although Eishô drew stylistic influences from the two dominant forces in *bijinga* during the late eighteenth century, with carefully arranged groupings of figures deriving from Kiyonaga, and a sense of line indebted to Utamaro, he nevertheless maintained a distinctive style that is more reminiscent of other artists in this exhibition such as Ichirakutei Eisui (see *Somenosuke of the Matsubaya Brothel House*, CAT. 83), not surprising since both Eishô and Eisui studied under Chôbunsai Eishi.

SE

鳥高斎 栄昌

80
Minister Narihira wird volljährig
Minister Narihira's Coming of Age
Chôkôsai EISHÔ

Glühwürmchen tauchen in der japanischen Kunst und Dichtung verbreitet auf. Ihr flackerndes Licht symbolisiert die Flüchtigkeit des Lebens. Sie zu fangen, war ein beliebter Zeitvertreib an Sommerabenden und ist es noch heute. Die Glühwürmchen können zur Beleuchtung kleiner Papierlaternen eingesetzt werden, hier hält die knieende Figur eine solche Lampe in den Händen. Eishis Entwurf setzt die lyrische Qualität des Themas auf vollkommene Weise um. Der Künstler platzierte seine drei Figuren auf einem Floss in der Strömung eines Flusses. Die Linien des fliessenden Wassers wiederholen sich in den Falten des vom Wind aufgeblähten Kimonos der mittleren Kurtisane. Die eleganten Posen und das gelassene Auftreten der Frauen sind typisch für Eishi und charakteristisch für die idealisierte Darstellung vertrauter Aktivitäten im *ukiyo-e.* Die Felsen, Bambusgräser und Wasserpflanzen spiegeln Eishis frühe Ausbildung in der Malerei der Kanô-Schule wider.

Fireflies appear frequently in Japanese art and poetry, their flickering light a symbol of the ephemeral nature of life. Catching them was a popular activity during the summer evenings and remains so even today. They can be made to illuminate a small paper lantern, such as the one held by the kneeling figure here. Eishi's design perfectly realizes the lyricism inherent in the theme. He has placed his three figures on a raft floating in a stream, the folds of the central courtesan's billowing kimono echoing the lines of the flowing water. The elegant poses and unruffled manner of the figures are characteristic of Eishi and typical of the idealized portrayal of familiar activities in *ukiyo-e.* The rocks, bamboo grasses, and water plants reflect Eishi's early training in Kanô School painting.

CM

鳥文斎 栄之

81
Glühwürmchenjagd auf dem Floss
Catching Fireflies on a Raft
Chôbunsai EISHI

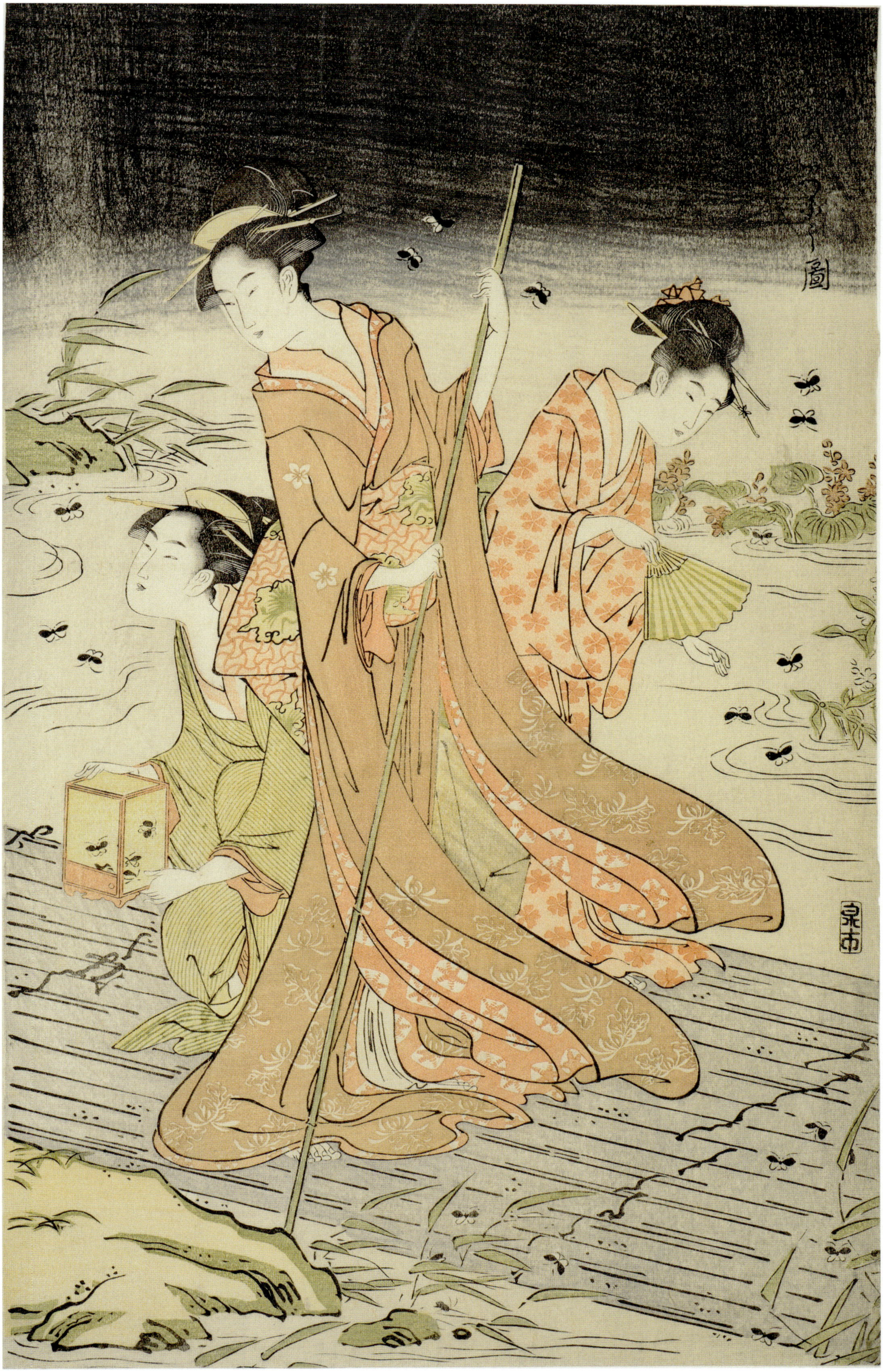
圖
泉市

Fächerdrucke wie dieses Werk von Kunimasa wurden auf dünnem Papier gedruckt, auf Bambusrahmen gespannt und häufig als Fächer benutzt. Erhaltene Exemplare sind daher rar und befinden sich oft in schlechtem Zustand. Wie bei den älteren «Pfostenbildern» von Harunobu, Koryûsai und Kiyonaga macht sich Kunimasa das ungewöhnliche Format für die voyeuristische Darstellung einer Frau zunutze, deren loses Gewand den Blick auf eine Brust freigibt, während sie an einem Sommerabend in ihrer Wohnung ein Mückenlicht entzündet. Das Netz, durch das der Betrachter sie sieht, verstärkt das Gefühl von Heimlichkeit und stellt eine bemerkenswerte technische Meisterleistung der Holzschneider dar.

In Eisuis Druck erkennen wir, wie die Fächer aufgebaut waren. Interessanter ist allerdings, dass der Künstler die Transparenz des Fächers hier auf ähnliche Weise nutzt wie Kunimasa das Netz: Er erzeugt eine (in diesem Fall bewusst verführerische) voyeuristische Stimmung, indem er Somenosukes entblösste Schulter hinter dem Fächer verbirgt. Während die Komposition eindeutig auf Utamaro zurückgeht, unterscheiden die überwiegend ovalen Formen, die zu einer dynamischen Instabilität führen, das Blatt von Utamaros Werk und erinnern vielmehr an Eisuis Lehrmeister Eishi.

Fan prints such as Kunimasa's were printed on thin paper, and intended to be mounted on bamboo frames for use; consequently, surviving examples are rare, and often in poor condition. In a similar fashion to the earlier *hashira-e* prints by Harunobu, Koryûsai, and Kiyonaga Kunimasa here takes advantage of the unusual format to create a voyeuristic depiction of a woman in her chambers on a summer evening, with her robes loosened to reveal her breast as she lights a mosquito coil. The netting behind which she is seen heightens the sense of spying, and is a remarkable technical feat on the part of the block carvers.

In Eisui's print, we can see how fans were mounted. More interesting, though, is the artist's use of the fan's transparency in a similar manner to the netting in Kunimasa's print, to impart a sense of (in this case intentionally seductive) voyeurism by hiding Somenosuke's exposed shoulder behind the fan. While the composition clearly derives from Utamaro, the predominance of ovals that introduce a dynamic instability differs from Utamaro's work, and is more reminiscent of Eisui's teacher, Eishi.

SE

歌川国政

82
Rauch gegen Mücken
Mosquito Smudge
Utagawa KUNIMASA I

一楽亭栄水

83
Somenosuke aus dem Freudenhaus Matsubaya, deren Begleiterinnen Wakahi und Wakaha hiessen – Schönheiten der fünf jahreszeitlichen Feste
Somenosuke of the Matsubaya Brothel House, Who has the Kamuro Wakahi and Wakaha – Beauties of the Five Festivals
Ichirakutei EISUI

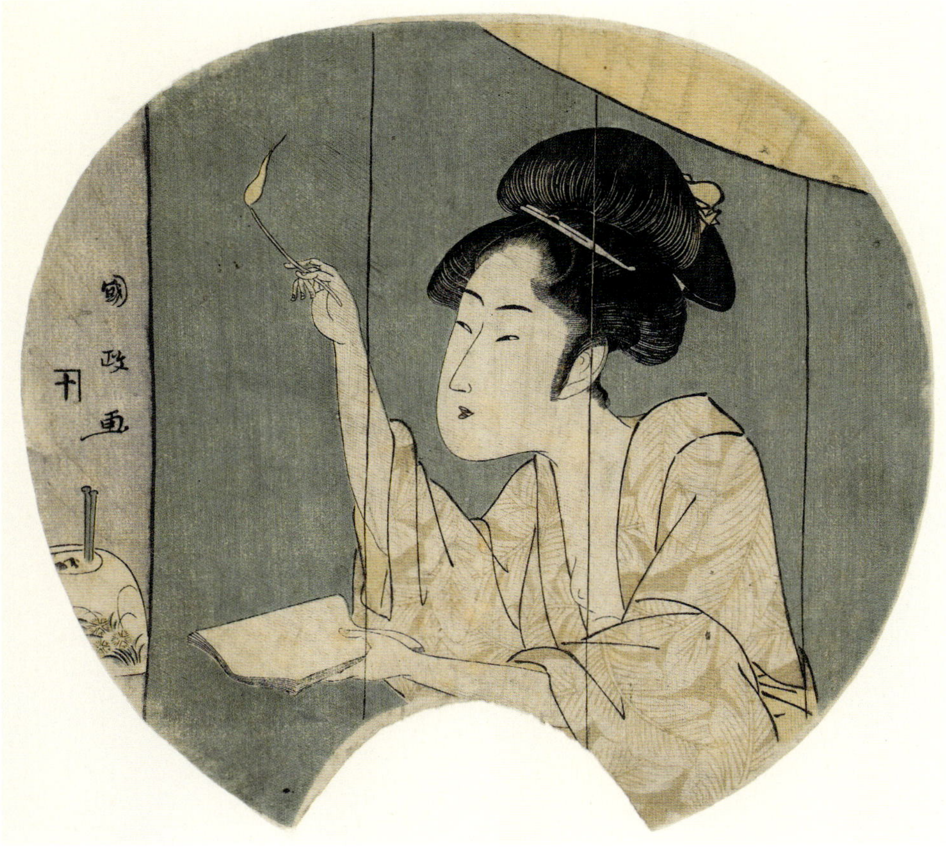

82

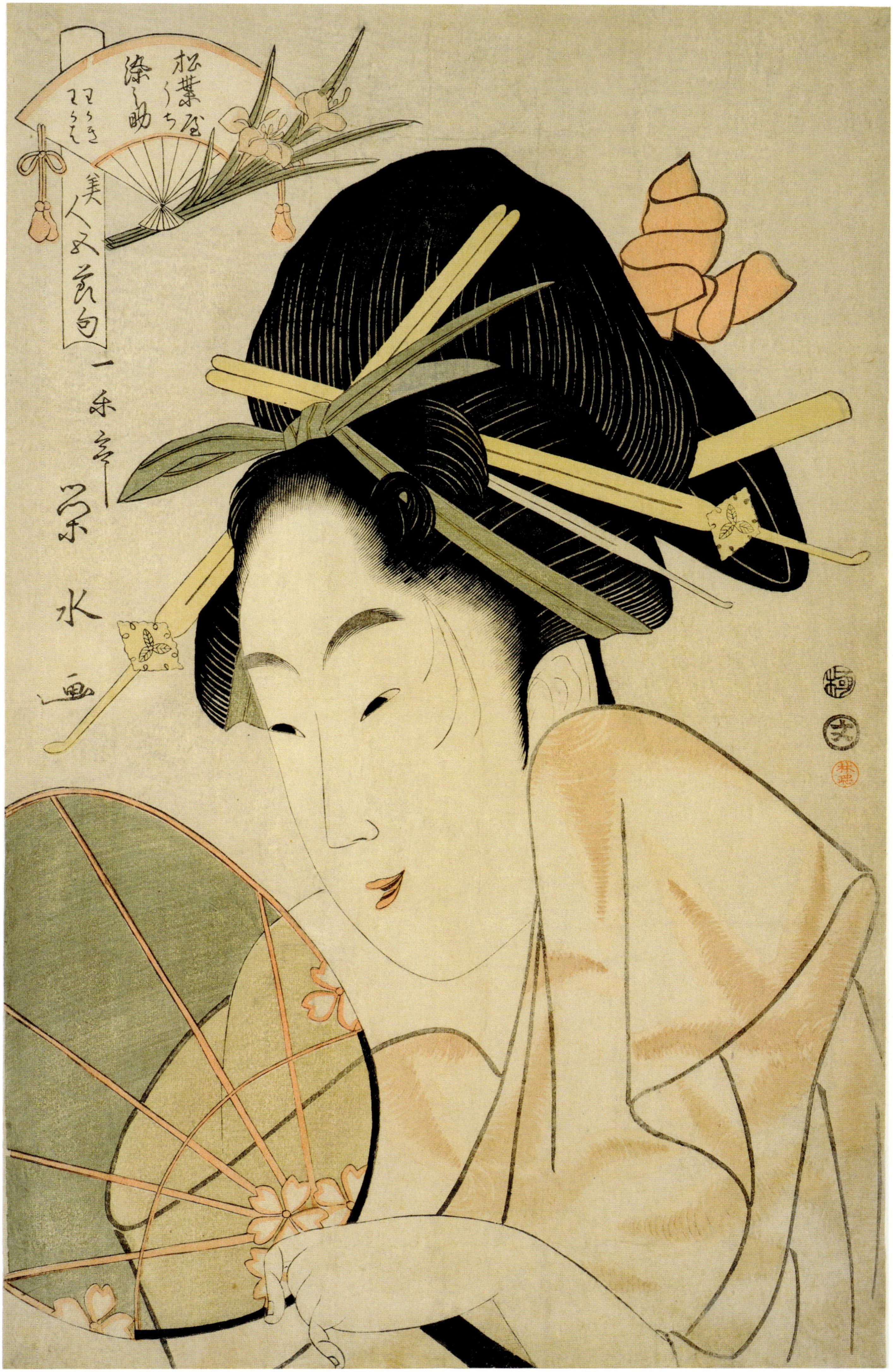
松葉屋うち
染之助
美人五節句
一楽亭栄水画

Eine Laterne mit dem Schriftzug «Eijudô: Fächer und andere Waren» steht am Eingang zu einem Ladengeschäft, in dem elegant gekleidete Kundinnen und ein Kunde sich Faltfächer und Fächerbilder ansehen. Nishimuraya Yohachi, der Verleger dieses Holzdrucks, war weder auf Fächer spezialisiert noch, soweit bekannt, Betreiber eines Geschäftes wie des hier gezeigten. Die Aufschrift des grossen, nur teilweise sichtbaren Schmuckfächers an der Rückwand verrät den tatsächlichen Namen des Geschäftes: Das Mieidô war eine bekannte Fächerhandlung in Kyoto. Das prominent platzierte «Eijudô»-Schild und die beabsichtigte Verbindung mit einer vornehmen Kundschaft machen den Druck jedoch zu einer wirksamen Werbung für das Verlagshaus.

Das Werk enthält interessante Gattungsdetails: Ein kleiner Junge spielt mit einigen jungen Hunden, und direkt im Laden liegen ein Schwert, eine Pfeife und ein Tabakbeutel, die dem gut gekleideten jungen Mann gehören, der gerade einen Fächer begutachtet. Ein weiterer Fächer, bewundert von der Frau vorne rechts, trägt das Bild eines Schauspielers aus der Ichikawa-Danjûrô-Linie in einer Aufführung des Stücks *Shibaraku* und erinnert so daran, dass Toyokuni auch ein angesehener Entwerfer von Theaterdrucken war.

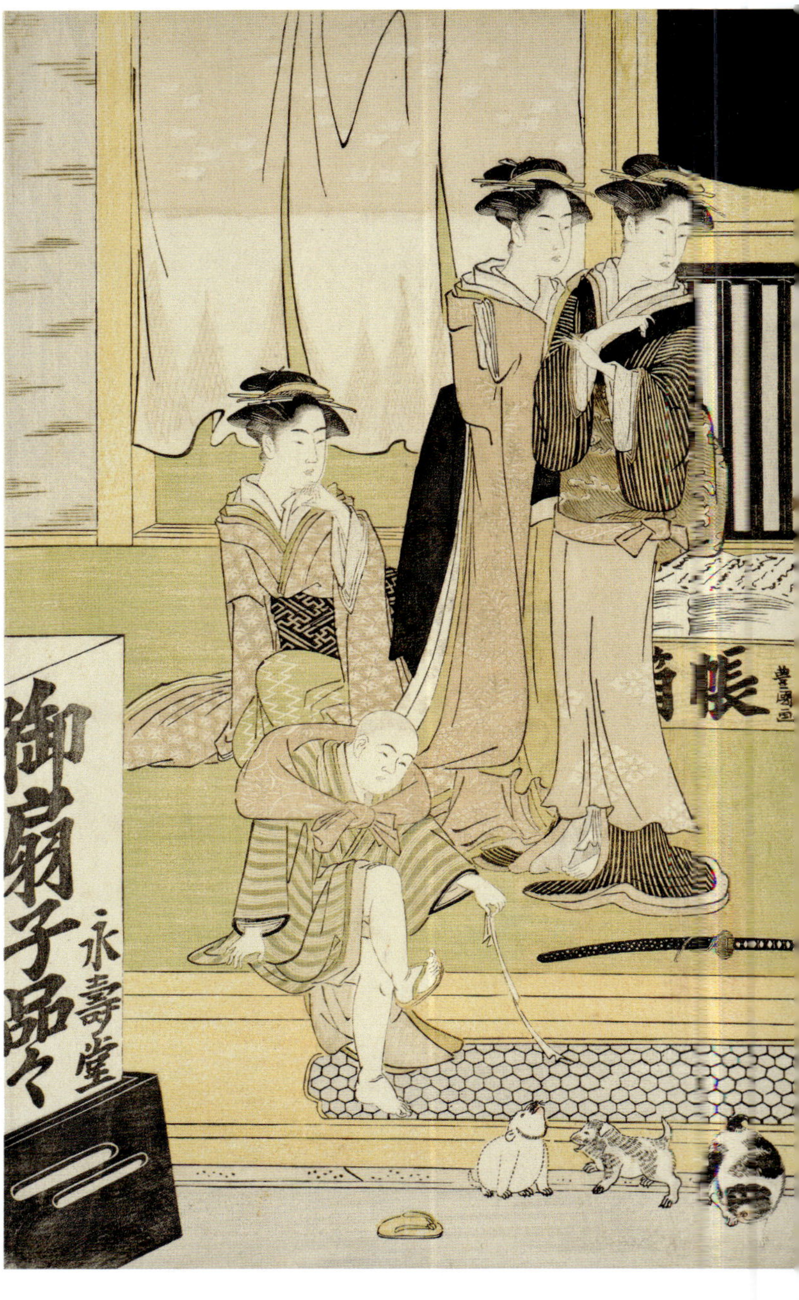

歌川豊国

84
Das Fächergeschäft Eijudô
The Fan Store Eijudô
Utagawa TOYOKUNI I

A lantern reading “Eijudô: Fans and Other Merchandise” stands at the entrance to a shop in which elegantly dressed customers look at folding fans and fan-shaped paintings for sale. Nishimuraya Yohachi was a publisher of woodblock prints, but did not specialize in fans, or, as far as anyone knows, operate a business such as this one. Inscribed on the large decorative fan partially visible on the back wall is the actual name of the store, the Mieidô, a well-known fan shop in Kyoto. The prominently placed “Eijudô” sign and the implied association with a fashionable clientele, however, make the print an effective advertisement for the publishing house.

The work contains interesting genre details: a young boy plays with a litter of puppies, and a sword and tobacco-pouch and pipe (belonging to a well-dressed young man examining a fan) lie just within the store proper. Additionally, a different fan admired by the woman on the right features an image of an actor from the Ichikawa Danjûrô line in a Shibaraku performance, a reminder that Toyokuni was also a renowned designer of actor prints.

CM

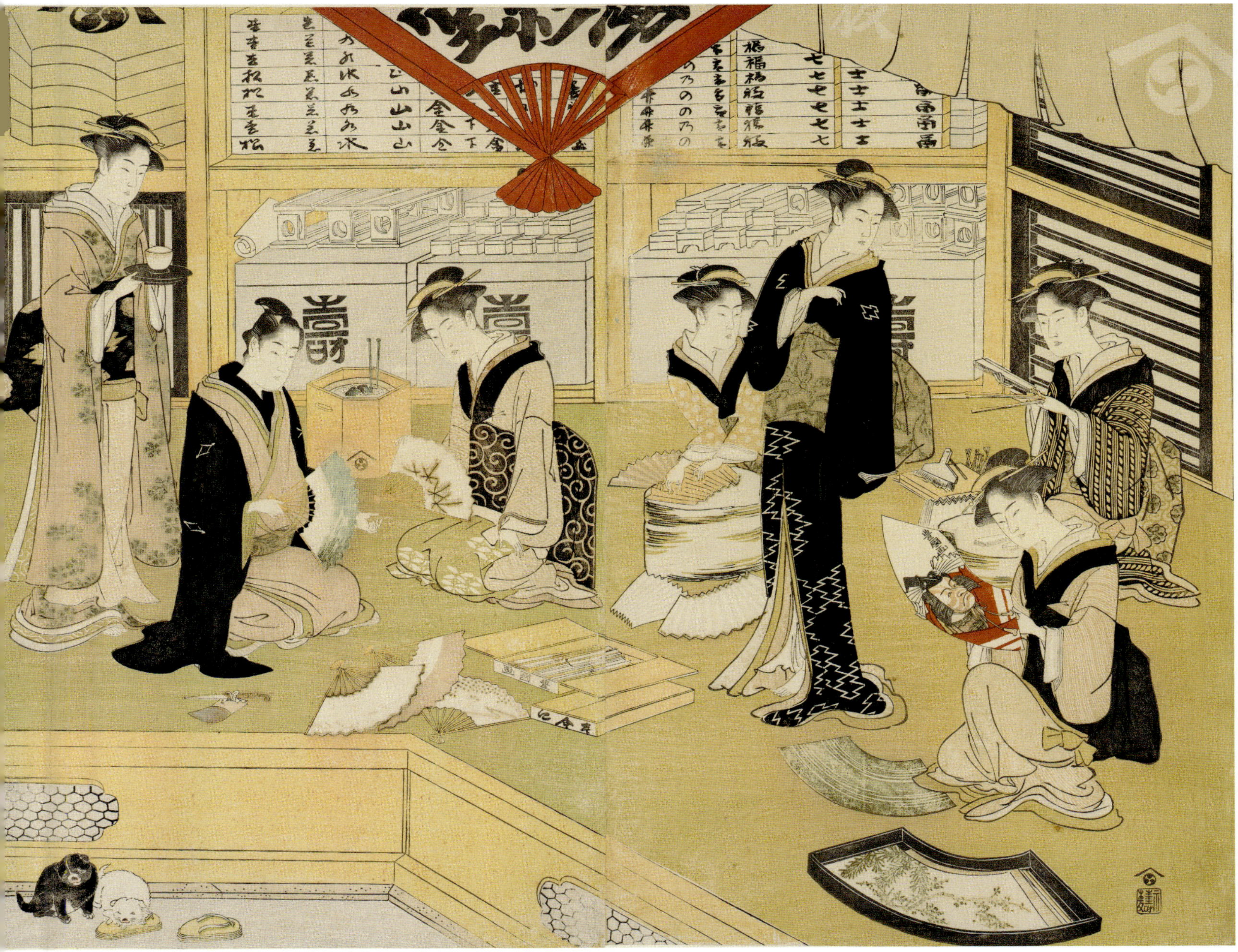

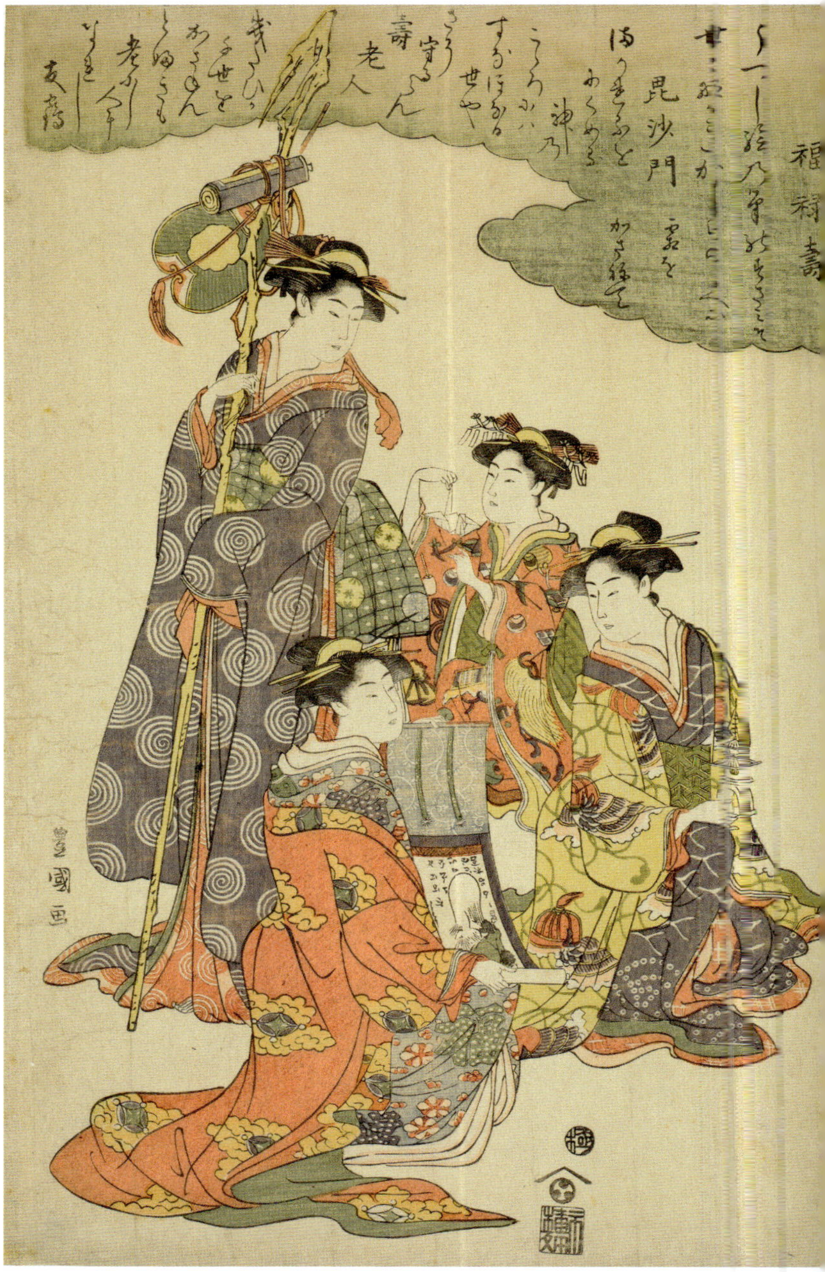

歌川 豊国

85
Kurtisanen in der Gestalt der Sieben Glücksgötter
Courtesans as the Seven Deities of Good Fortune
Utagawa TOYOKUNI I

Dieser Druck parodiert ein beliebtes volkstümliches Thema, die «Sieben Glücksgötter», die hier in Gestalt von Kurtisanen auftreten. Jede der Gottheiten ist an eindeutigen Attributen zu erkennen: Benzaiten, die Siegesgöttin, an ihrer Laute; Daikoku, der Repräsentant des Wohlstands, an Reisweinfässern und einem Holzhammer; Ebisu, der den Erfolg verkörpert, an einer Angelrute und einem Fisch im Korb; Hotei, der Gott der Landwirtschaft, an einem grossen Sack; Bishamonten, der kriegerischen Heldenmut symbolisiert, an einer Pagode; Fukurokuju, das Sinnbild des Glücklichseins, an einem Rollbild, das ihn mit seinem lang gestreckten Schädel zeigt; und Jurôjin, Symbol für langes Leben, an seinem Wanderstab, an dem eine Schriftrolle befestigt ist.

Ausser Ebisu waren alle diese Gottheiten chinesischen Ursprungs. Viele von ihnen spielen in den Pantheons des Buddhismus und des Daoismus eine wichtige Rolle. Gleichzeitig nahmen sie in Japan neue Bedeutungen an. Fukurokuju zum Beispiel hatte seine Wurzeln in drei verschiedenen chinesischen Gottheiten, von denen jede einem eigenen Stern zugeordnet war, bevor sie im japanischen Volksglauben zu einer einzigen Figur verschmolzen.

This print parodies a popular folk subject, the Seven Deities of Good Fortune, depicted as courtesans. Each deity can be identified by their attribute. Benzaiten, representing victory, is indicated by a lute *(biwa)*; Daikoku, representing wealth, by sake barrels and a mallet; Ebisu, representing success, by a fishing pole and fish in a basket; Hotei, representing agriculture, by a large bag; Bishamonten, representing martial prowess, by a pagoda; Fukurokuju, representing luck, by a hanging scroll depicting the god with his elongated cranium; and Jurôjin, representing longevity, by a walking stick with a scroll attached to it.

Aside from Ebisu, these deities were introduced from China, and many of them feature prominently in the pantheons of Buddhism and Daoism. At the same time, they acquired new significance in Japan; for example, Fukurokuju was originally three separate deities in China, each associated with a different star, but they were combined into a single figure in Japanese folk belief.

SE

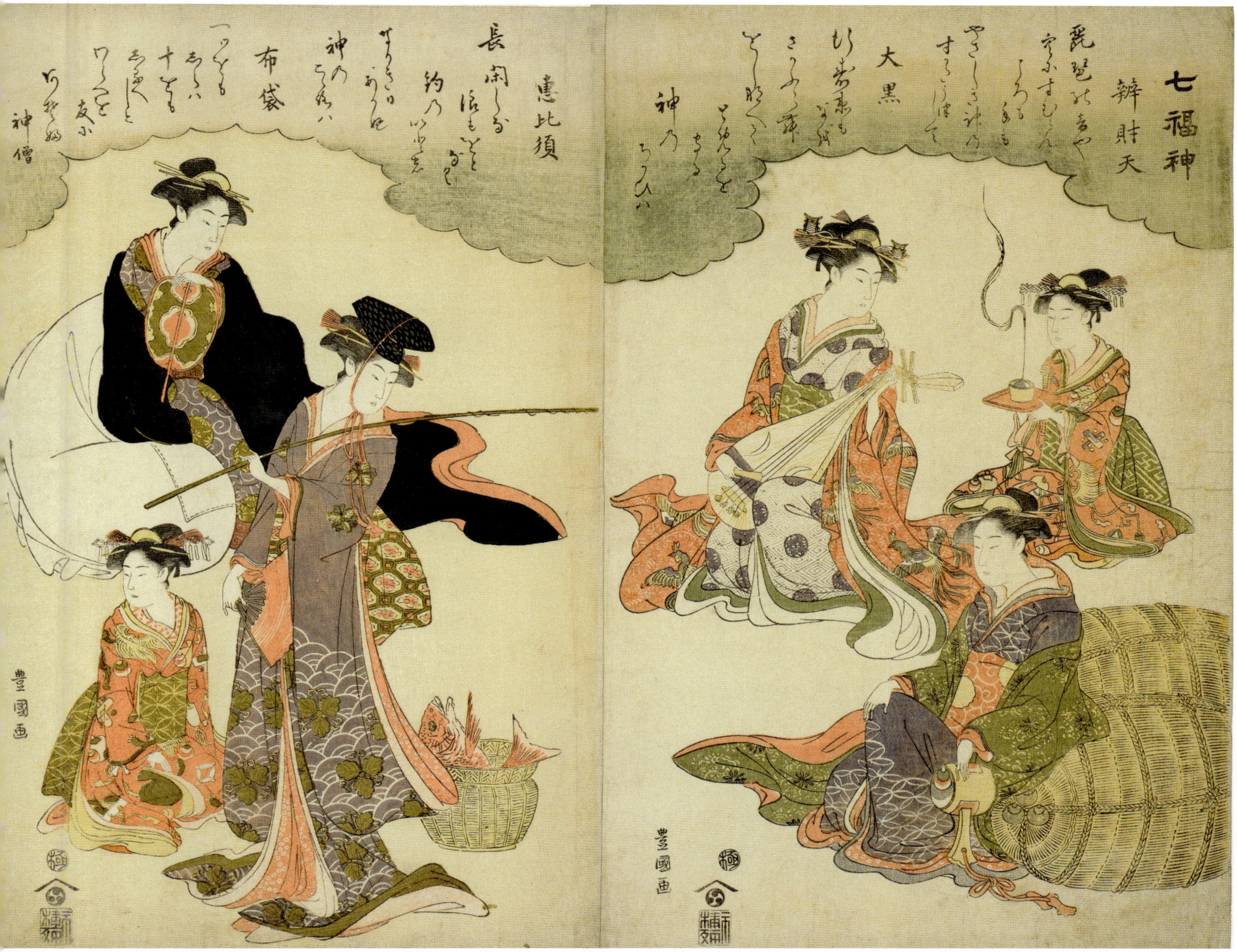
七福神
辨財天
大黒
恵比須
布袋
豊國画
豊國画

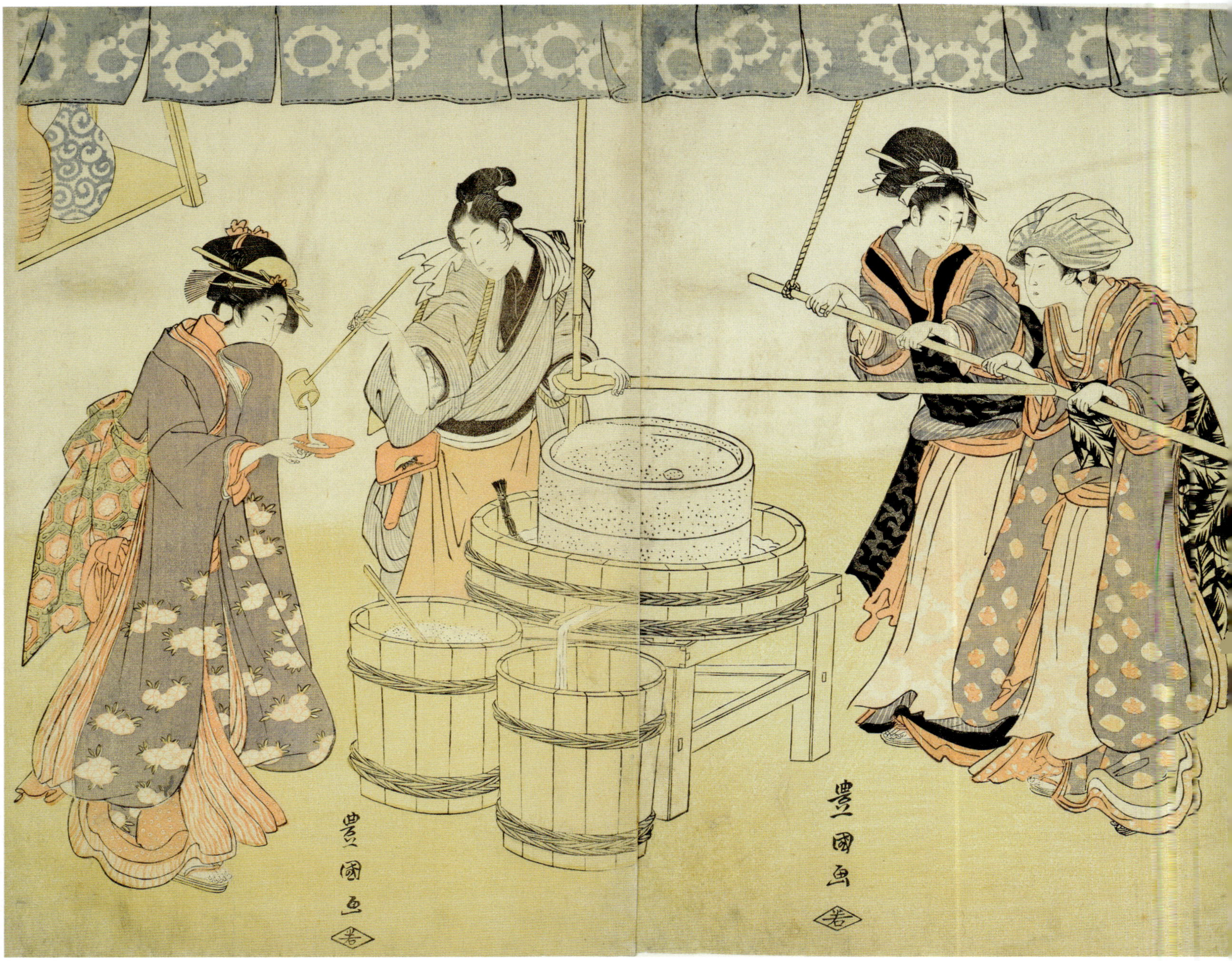
豊國画
豊國画

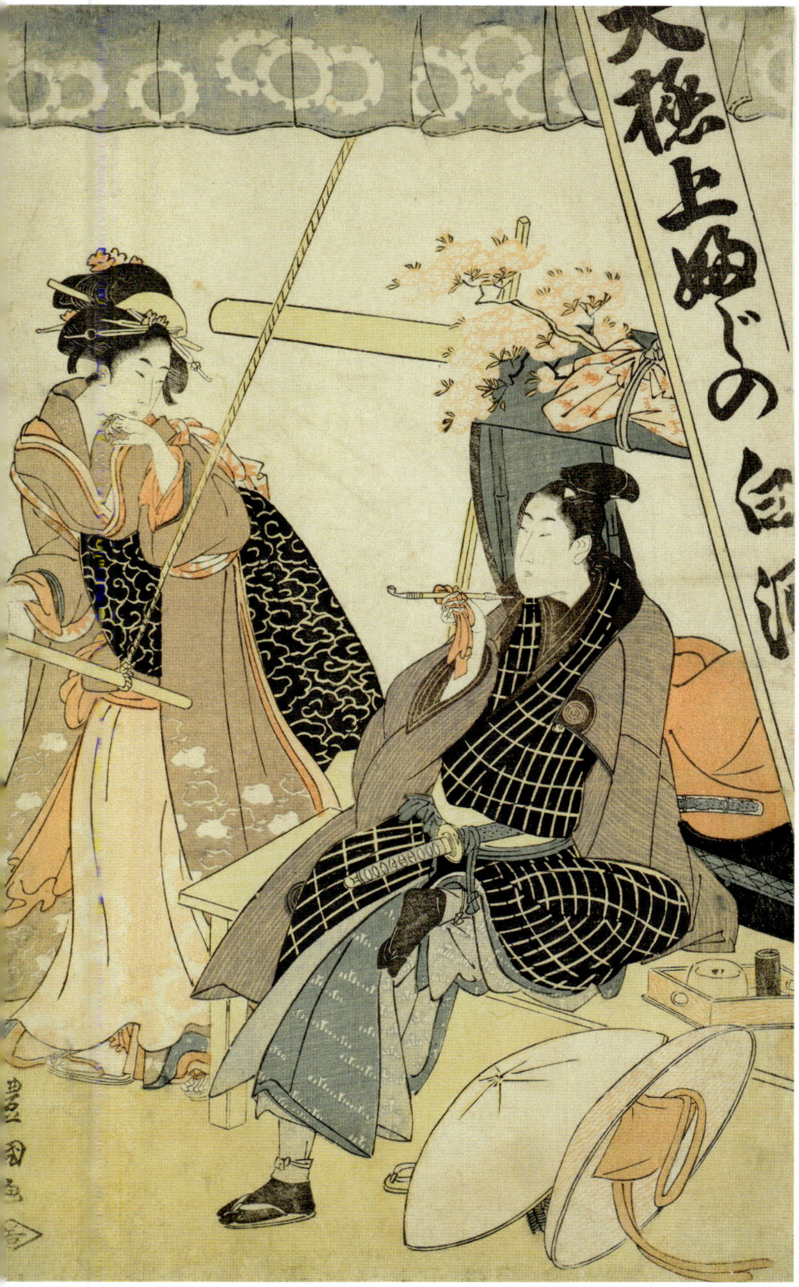

Die Darstellung von Händlern oder Handwerkern bei der Arbeit hat in der japanischen Kunst eine lange Tradition. Der Brauch, die üblicherweise einfachen männlichen Arbeiter durch elegant gekleidete Schönheiten zu ersetzen, konnte dagegen nur im kulturellen Umfeld der «fliessenden Welt» entstehen. Hier abgebildet sind vier Damen, die durch Pressen einer fermentierten Mischung aus gedämpftem Reis und Hefe frischen Sake gewinnen. Ein junger Mann giesst den Reiswein in ein Lackschälchen, das eine der Frauen in der Hand hält. Die Frau wiederum wird das Getränk dem wartenden Herrn servieren, der sich beim Rauchen einer langen Pfeife entspannt. Das Werbebanner ganz rechts aussen preist den hochwertigen Sake zum Verkauf an und nennt den Titel des Drucks. Die gross gewachsenen, statuarischen Figuren erinnern an die stilistischen Vorbilder von Kiyonaga und Utamaro: Wie viele Holzschnittkünstler seiner Zeit stand auch Toyokuni unter dem Einfluss ihrer Schönheitsprinzipien.

The custom of portraying workers engaged in trade or craft has a long history in Japanese art. The convention of substituting elegantly dressed beauties for generally unsophisticated male laborers, however, could have arisen only in the culture of the floating world. Pictured here are four ladies pressing a fermented mixture of steamed rice and yeast to yield fresh sake. A young man pours the sake into a lacquer cup held by one of the women. She, in turn, will serve the waiting gentleman relaxing with a long pipe in his hand. At the far right is a banner advertising the high-grade sake for sale and announcing the title of the print. The figures, tall and statuesque, owe much to the styles of Kiyonaga and Utamaro: like many woodblock artists of his era, Toyokuni was influenced by the canons of beauty promoted by those two artists.

CM

歌川
豊国

86
Herstellung von hochwertigem weissem Reiswein
Making Top Quality White Sake
Utagawa TOYOKUNI I

Sowohl das Triptychon-Format als auch die geometrische Anordnung der würdevollen Figuren in szenischen Gruppen verraten den Einfluss von Kiyonaga, dessen innovative Kompositionen das *ukiyo-e* in den 1780er-Jahren revolutioniert haben. Obwohl Triptychen oft als Anlass genutzt wurden, Holzschnitte als mehrteilige Komposition zu vermarkten, organisierte Eishi jeden einzelnen Druck als eigenständiges Werk (tatsächlich sind heute viele Drucke als Einzelblätter erhalten, die ursprünglich zu einem Triptychon gehörten). Gleichzeitig sorgen die Ausgewogenheit zwischen den drei Frauen bei der Teezubereitung im rechten Druck und den drei Frauen mit Vogelkäfig im Druck links sowie der nach links gerichtete Blick der beiden Frauenfiguren in der Mitte, der von der Frau im linken Bildteil erwidert wird, für eine insgesamt überzeugende kompositorische Geschlossenheit. Die Fortführung der Reisfelder im Hintergrund aller drei Bildteile verstärkt diesen Eindruck. Das winzige Detail einer Gänseformation in der Ferne zeigt an, dass der Herbst beginnt. Aufgrund seiner Abstammung aus einer hochgestellten Samurai-Familie (die er verliess, um als Maler Karriere zu machen) könnte Eishi Szenen wie diese selbst erlebt haben. Für die Stadtbewohner von Edo aber, die das Publikum des Künstlers bildeten, dürfte die nostalgische Abbildung ländlicher Lebensart in erster Linie ein fernes Ideal gewesen sein

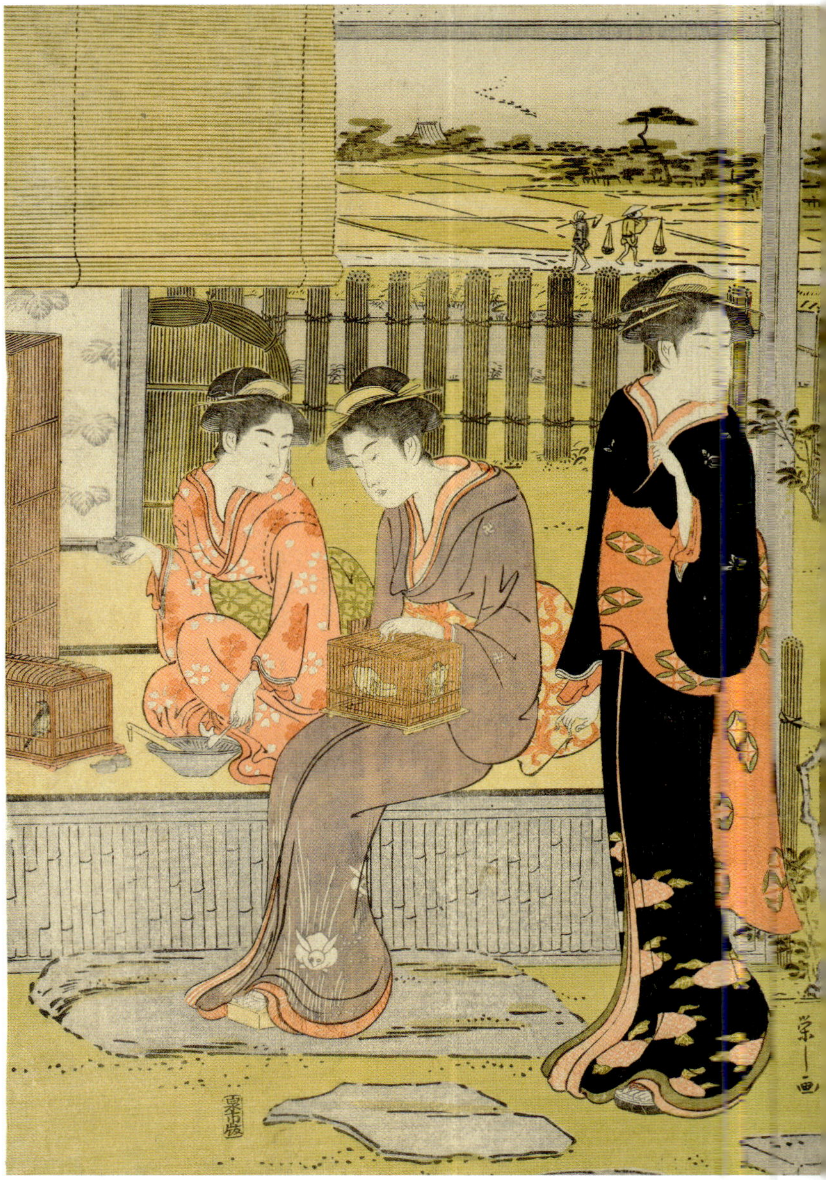

87
Früher Nachmittag in einem Landhaus
Early Afternoon at the Country House
Chôbunsai EISHI
鳥文斎 栄之

Both the triptych format, and the geometric organization of the stately figures in staged groupings reveal the influence of Kiyonaga, whose innovative compositions transformed *ukiyo-e* in the 1780s. Although triptychs expanded marketing possibilities for selling groups of prints, as is often the case, Eishi arranged each print so that it could stand as an independent work (indeed, many prints that were originally parts of triptychs survive today individually). At the same time, the balance between the three women preparing tea in the right print and the three caring for pet birds in the left print, the leftward gazes of the two women in the center, matched by the rightward gaze of the woman standing in the left print, and the continuation of the background landscape of rice paddies across all three prints, establishes a convincing overall coherence. The subtle detail of a line of geese flying in the distance marks the season as autumn. Although Eishi possibly would have had first-hand exposure to such scenes through his upbringing in a high-ranking samurai family (which he abandoned in order to pursue a career as a painter), the nostalgic countryside lifestyle of the subject would have been a distant ideal for the Edo urbanites that made up that artist's audience.

SE

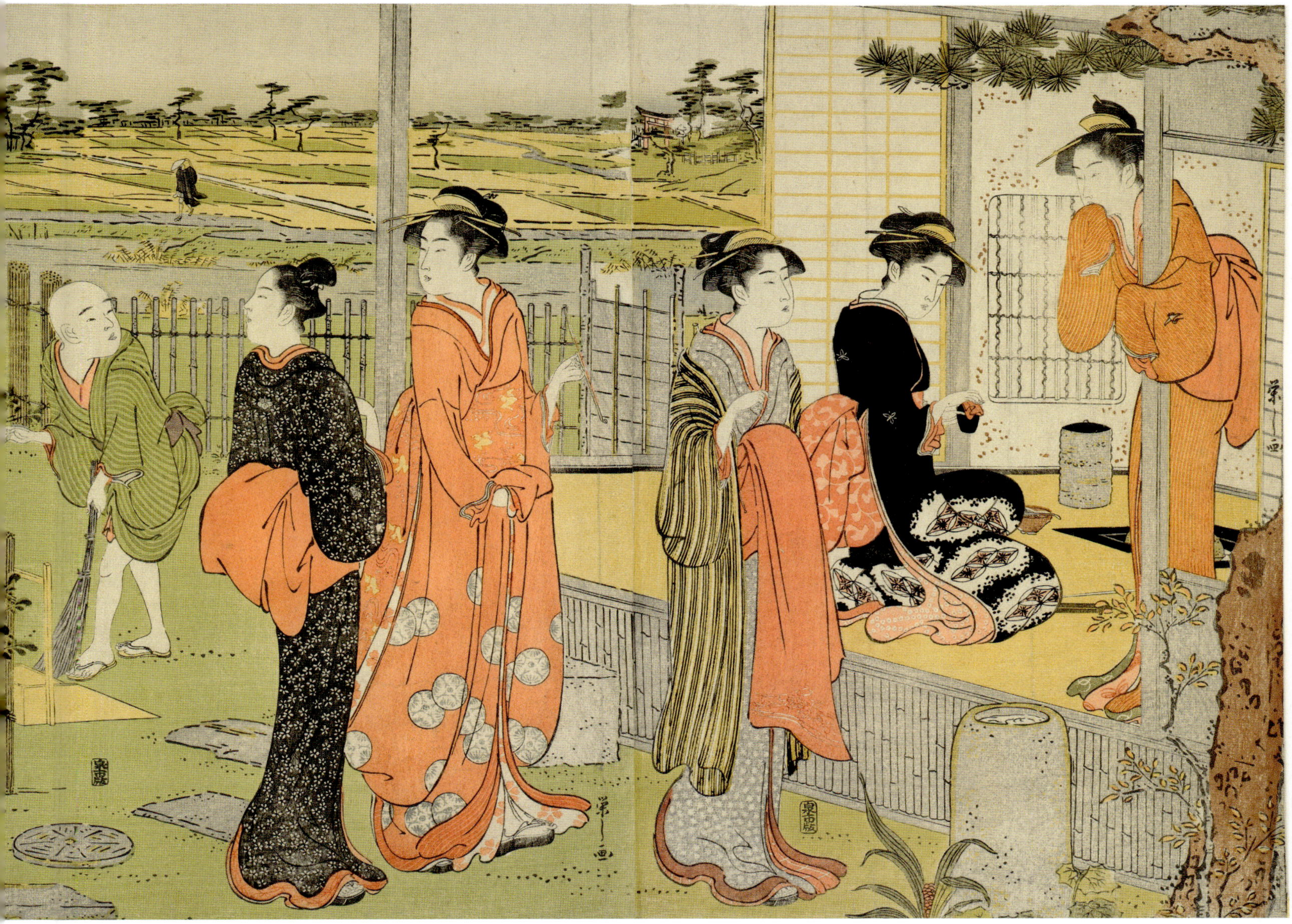

Schöne, gut gekleidete Frauen, die von unerwarteten Wetterkapriolen überrascht werden, sind das Thema dieser beiden Drucke. In Toyokunis Entwurf mühen sich die Kurtisanen, *tanzaku* (Gedichtstreifen) an die Zweige eines blühenden Kirschbaumes zu binden, wie es während der Kirschblütenfeste im Frühling üblich war. Seinen besonderen Reiz bezieht dieser Druck aus dem Nebeneinander von Schönheiten und Blüten (beides «Blumen im Wind»), aber auch aus der verfeinerten Eleganz und dem kapriziösen Unterton des Themas.

Der Mimeguri-Schrein war im Zusammenhang mit Trockenheiten berühmt für seine Wirksamkeit bei Gebeten um Regen und damit ein fester Bestandteil des Lebens in Edo. Einer bekannten Erzählung zufolge hatte der Dichter Takarai Kikaku (1661–1707) ein solches Gebet in Versform verfasst und dem Schrein gewidmet, woraufhin die Trockenheit wie durch ein Wunder endete. Bei Kiyonaga erfährt das Thema eine heitere Wendung. Elegant gewandete Schönheiten werden beim Besuch des Schreins von einem Wolkenbruch überrascht und hasten Schutz suchend durch Regen und Wind. Die Götter, die derweil im Himmel faulenzen, amüsieren sich über das Chaos, das die Erhörung des Gebetes bewirkt hat.

Beautiful, well-dressed women caught unexpectedly in turbulent weather is the subject of these two prints. In Toyokuni's design, courtesans struggle to tie *tanzaku* (poem slips) to the branches of a blossoming cherry. Hanging such paper slips was customary during cherry blossom-viewing parties held in the spring. The charm of this print derives from the juxtaposition of *bijin* and blossoms (both "flowers in the wind") and of the sophisticated elegance and capricious nature of the subject matter.

Drought was a regular feature of Edo life, and prayers for rain the major remedy. Mimeguri Shrine was famous in this context: according to a well-known story, the poet Takarai Kikaku (1661–1707) composed such a prayer in verse and dedicated it to the shrine, an act that miraculously ended the drought. Here, the subject is given a humorous twist. Elegantly dressed beauties visiting the shrine are caught in the sudden downpour and are hurrying through the wind and rain to reach shelter. The gods, lounging about in the heavens, laugh at the havoc the fulfillment of the prayer has wrought.

CM

歌川豊国

88
Blumen im Wind
Flowers in the Wind
Utagawa TOYOKUNI I

鳥居清長

89
Eine plötzliche Windböe am Mimeguri-Schrein
A Sudden Squall at Mimeguri Shrine
Torii KIYONAGA

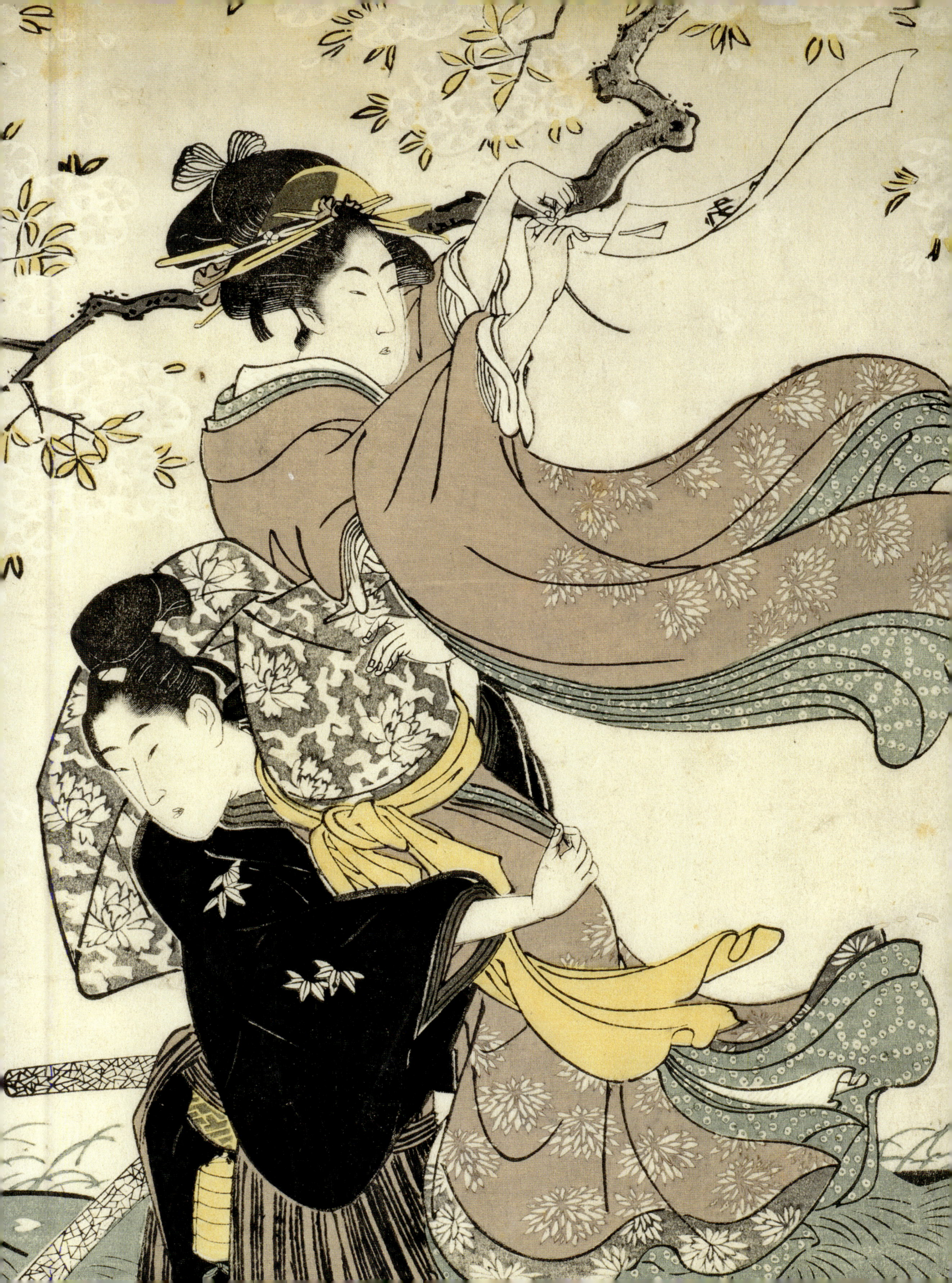

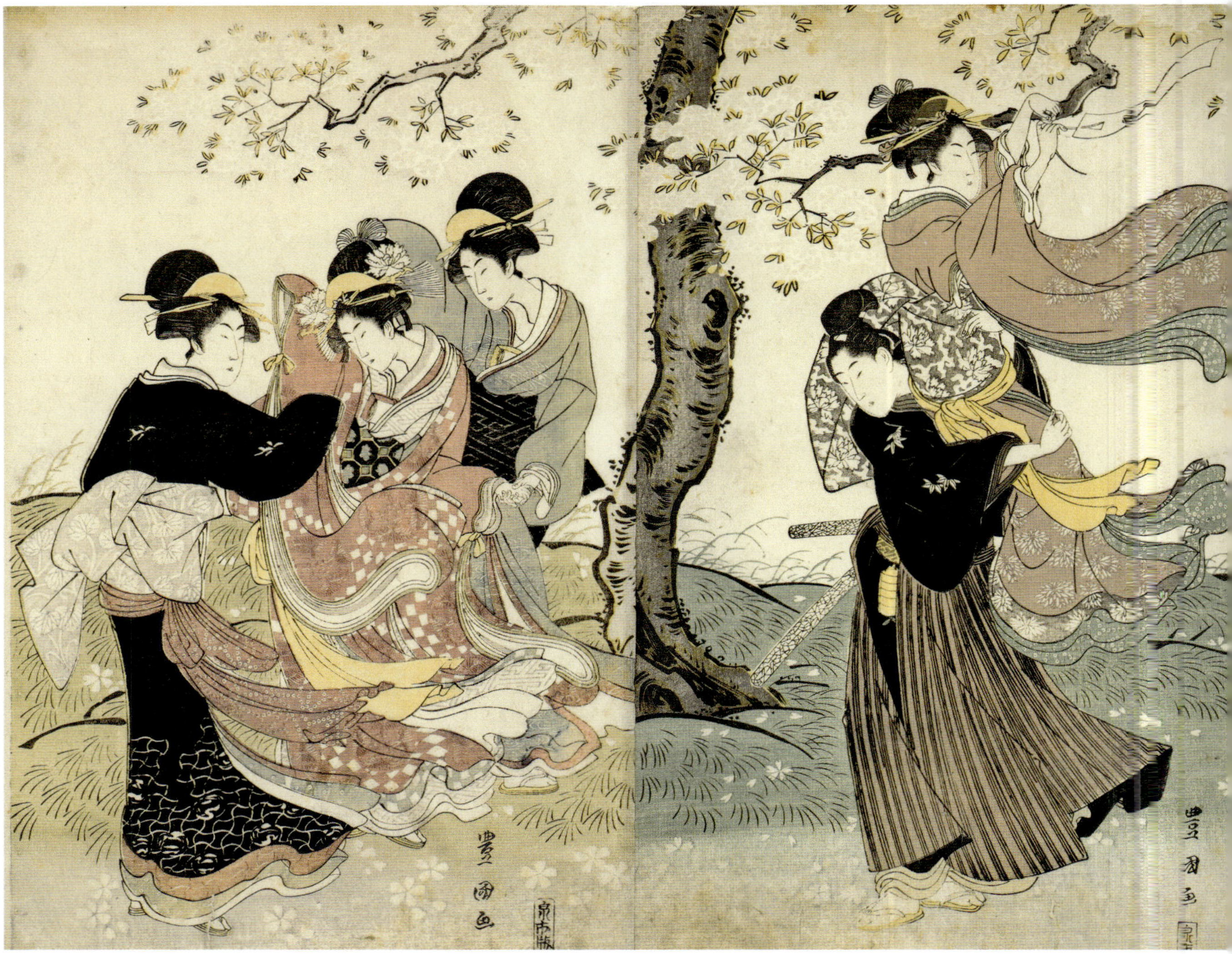

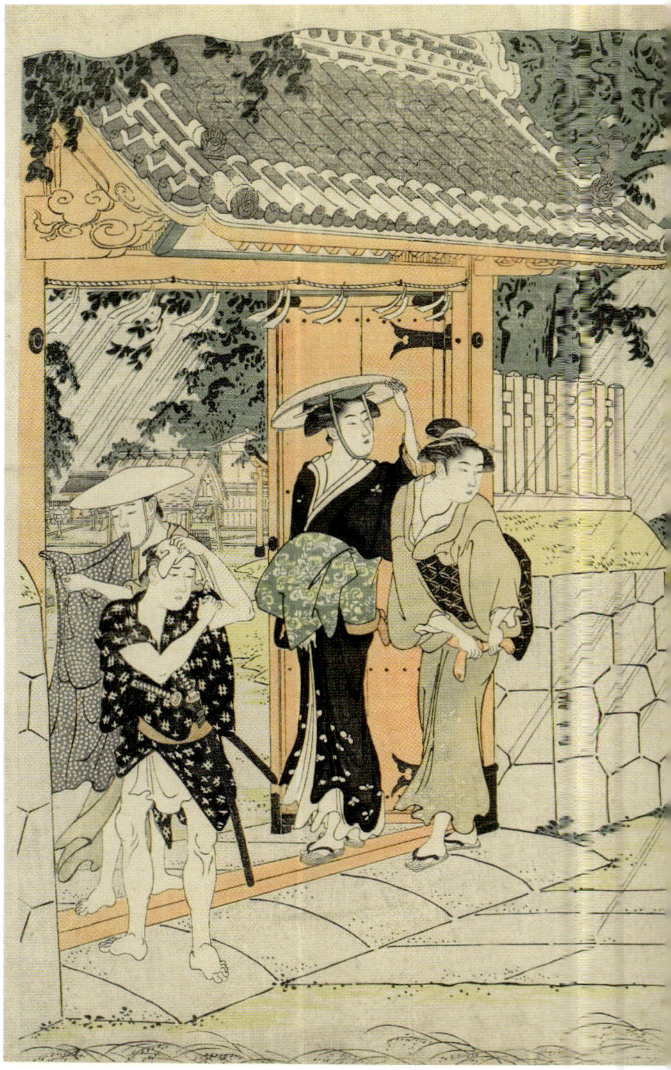

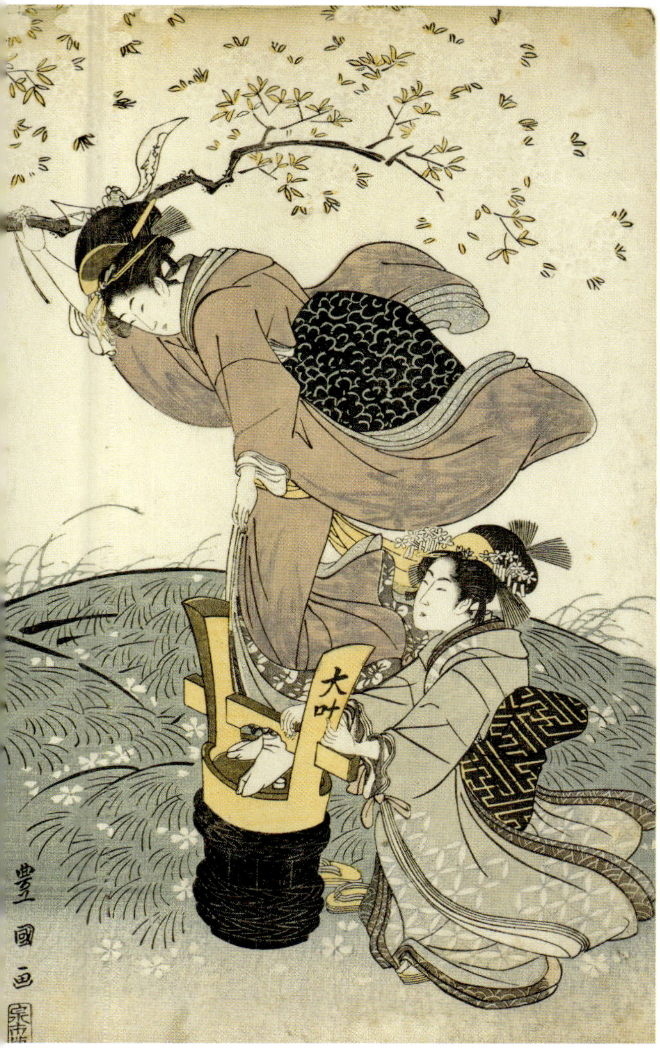
大叶
豊國画

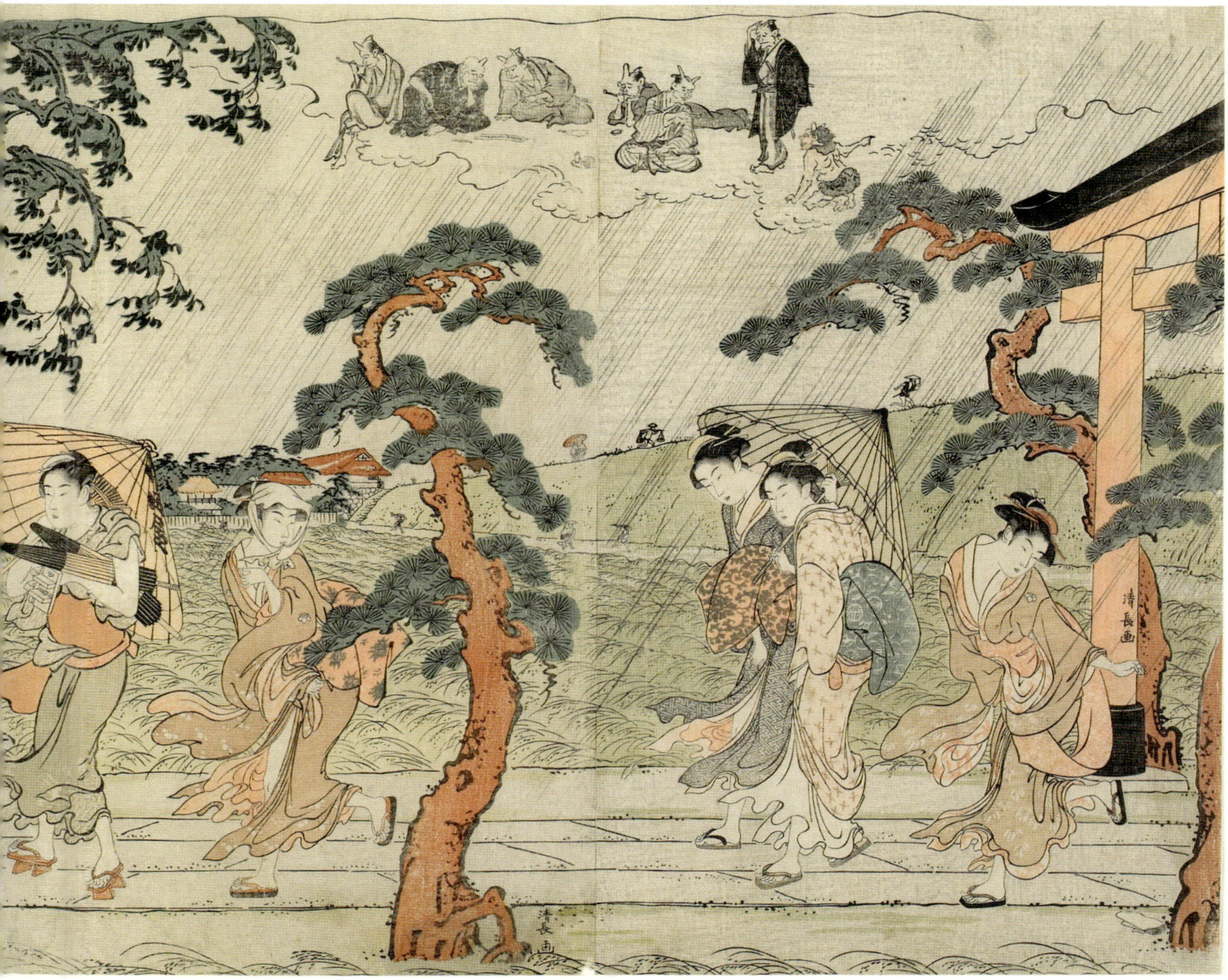
清長画
清長画

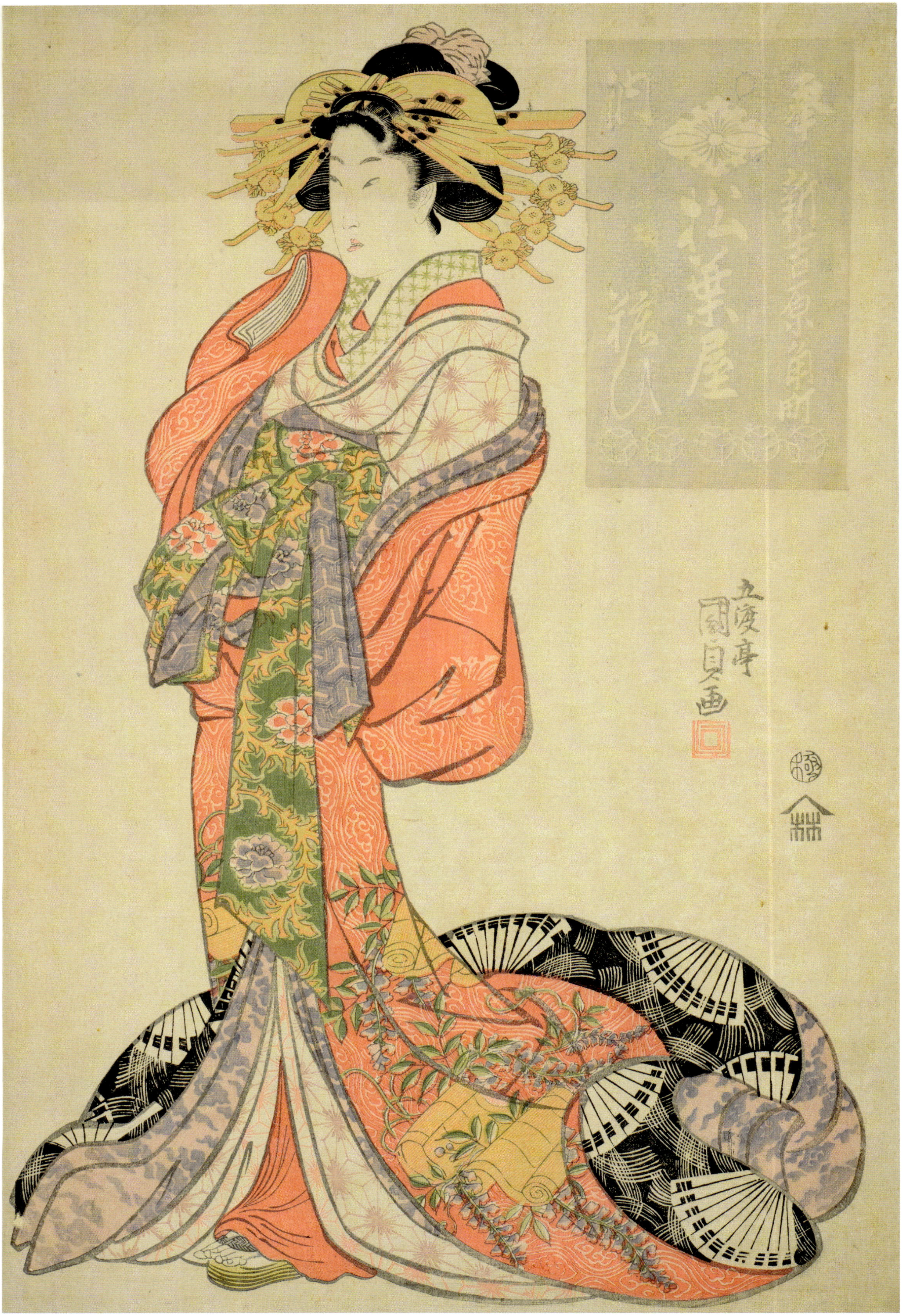
新吉原角町
松葉屋
五渡亭國貞画

Unter dem Einfluss des stark wachsenden Holzschnittmarktes im 19. Jahrhundert sahen sich die Verleger zunehmend genötigt, vermehrt Drucke zu niedrigeren Preisen herauszubringen. Obwohl die Produktionsverfahren immer besser wurden, machten grössere Auflagen den Einsatz detaillierter Schnitttechniken und aufwendiger Materialien wie Glimmerpulver unmöglich. Die im 18. Jahrhundert entwickelte Themenvielfalt, repräsentiert von Utamaros einfühlsamen Darstellungen familiärer Beziehungen und einfacher Teehausmädchen, wurde zugunsten leicht verständlicher Kurtisanenmotive in sich endlos wiederholenden Variationen aufgegeben. Während die dargestellten Frauentypen immer austauschbarer wurden, widmeten sich die Künstler der Gestaltung prächtiger Kimonos und Frisuren, um das Interesse des Publikums zu wecken. Kunisadas Porträt von Yosooi steht mit einer verwirrenden Vielfalt an Stoffmustern in den unzähligen Lagen ihrer Garderobe und mit nicht weniger als 14 Haarnadeln aus Schildpatt und zwei Kämmen im Haar beispielhaft für diesen Trend.

Zur gleichen Zeit belebten Landschaftsdarstellungen, häufig kombiniert mit «Bildern schöner Frauen», den Holzschnitt neu. Beide Entwürfe von Eisen enthalten im oberen Bereich kleine Landschaftsvignetten, von denen eine als Schrein von Miyajima gekennzeichnet ist: An ihrem unteren Rand erkennen wir das ikonenhafte, teilweise im Wasser der Bucht von Hiroshima stehende *torii* (Tor), für das der Schrein berühmt ist.

The market for prints expanded significantly during the nineteenth century, and publishers came under increasing pressure to make available more prints at lower prices. While production techniques continued to improve, larger runs discouraged the use of lavish materials such as mica and finely detailed carving. The variety of subjects developed during the eighteenth century, represented by Utamaro's sensitive portrayals of familial relationships and humble teahouse waitresses, was abandoned in favor of more immediately accessible courtesans in endlessly repetitive variations. As the women depicted in prints became more and more generic, artists turned to elaborately designed kimono and hairstyles for visual interest. Kunisada's portrait of Yosooi is an excellent example of this trend, with a bewildering variety of patterns in the multiple layers of her outfit and no less than fourteen tortoise shell hairpins and two combs in her coiffure.

At the same time, prints found new life in the landscape genre, which was often combined with *bijinga*. Both of the prints by Eisen include small landscape vignettes in their upper registers, one of which is identified as the shrine at Miyajima; the iconic *torii* (gate) partially submerged in Hiroshima Bay, for which this shrine is famous, is visible along the lower edge.

SE

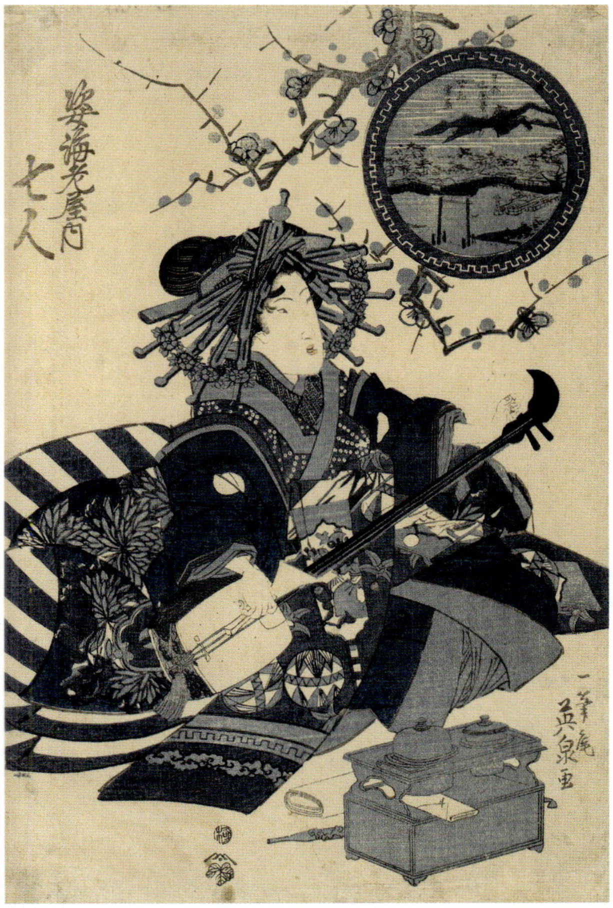

91

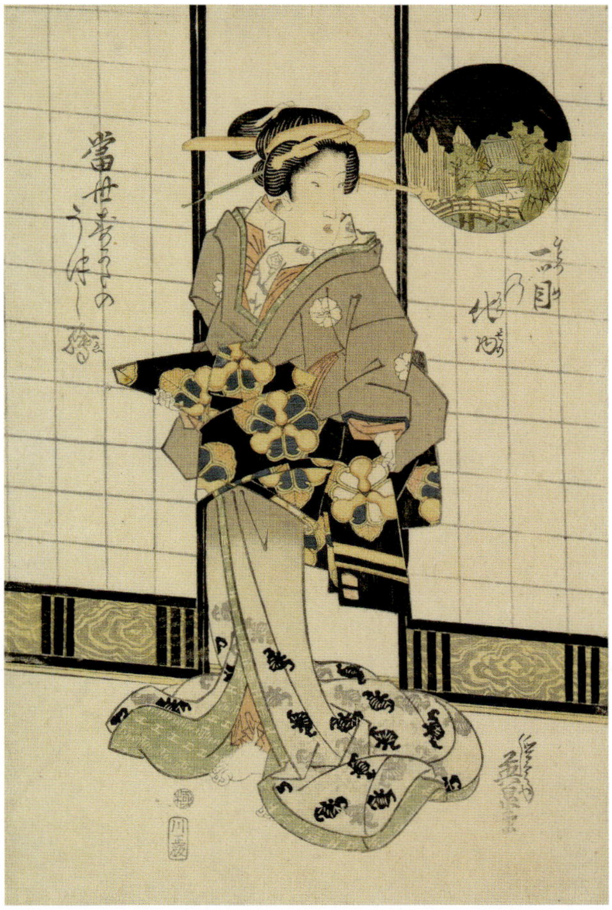

92

歌川国貞

90
Yosooi aus dem Freudenhaus Matsubaya in Shin Yoshiwara Kadomachi – Votivhandtücher
Yosooi of the Matsubaya at Shin Yoshiwara Kadomachi – Votive Hand Towels
Utagawa KUNISADA I

渓斎英泉

91
Miyajima – Nanahito aus dem Sugata-ebiya
Miyajima – Nanahito of the Sugata-ebiya
Keisai EISEN

渓斎英泉

92
Innerhalb des Schrein-Bezirks in Hitotsume – Laternenbild im zeitgenössischen Stil
Inside the Shrine Precincts in Hitotsume – Magic Lantern Slides of Contemporary Styles
Keisai EISEN

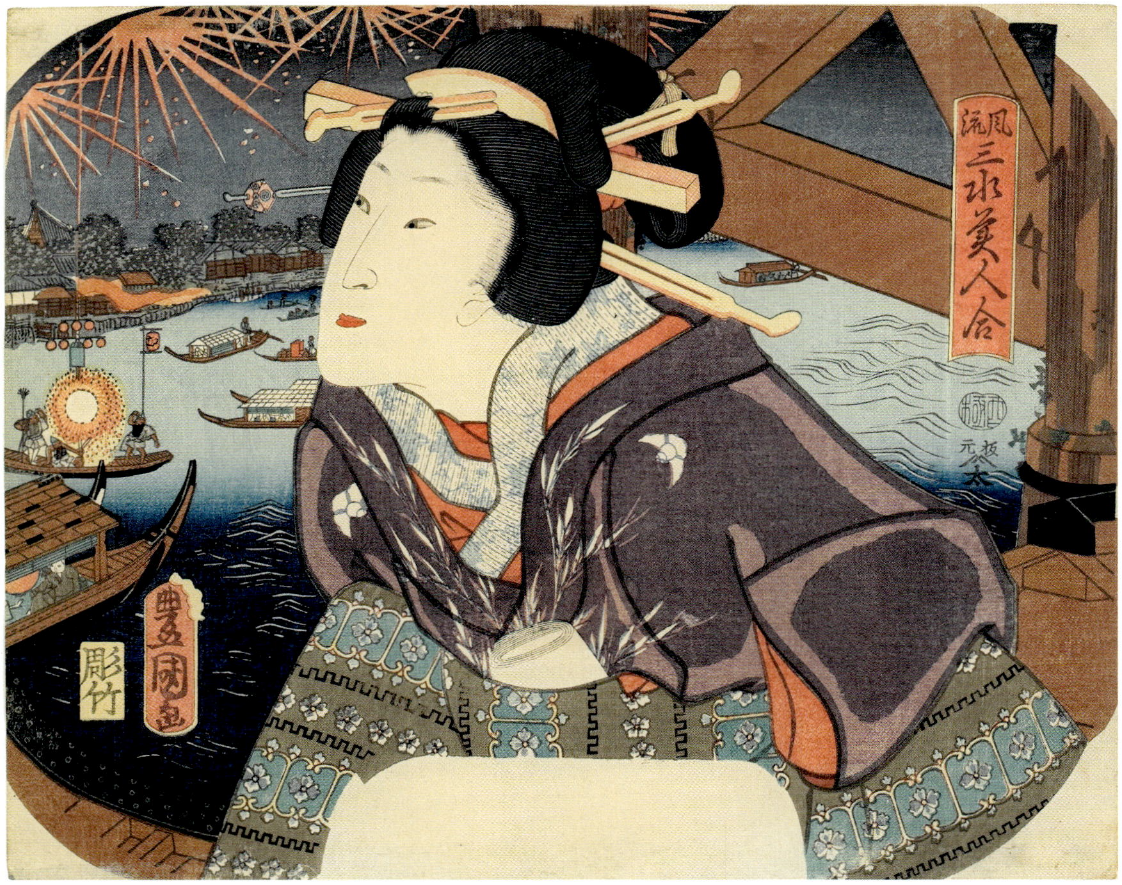

93

93 歌川国貞

Beliebte Kombinationen von Landschaften und Schönheiten

Popular Pairings of Landscapes and Beauties

Utagawa KUNISADA I

94 歌川国貞

Vorbereitungen zum Ausgang – Ein Vergleich von modernen Schönheiten

Preparing to Go Out – Comparison of Modern Beauties

Utagawa KUNISADA I

Zum Ende der Edo-Zeit beherrschten Schönheiten im Stile Kunisadas das *ukiyo-e.* Mit ihren grossen Köpfen, gestreckten Gesichtern und markanten Unterkiefern neigen seine Frauenfiguren zur Gedrungenheit. Ihre oft derbe Sinnlichkeit, die sie mit einem ganz eigenen Charme ausstrahlen, unterscheidet sie von der eleganten Vornehmheit früherer Schönheiten. Schon in den 1830er-Jahren entwickelte Kunisada die Konvention, Kurtisanen vor entfernt liegenden Landschaften im Hintergrund zu platzieren, und unterlief damit das Verbot individueller Kurtisanenporträts, das mit den Reformen von 1840/41 einherging. In diesem fächerförmigen Druck spiegeln die Ausflugsboote und das Feuerwerk am Nachthimmel die Erregung der Frau wider, während sie den Festlichkeiten zusieht.

In Japan galt der Nacken einer Frau als erogene Zone. Hier wird er im Kontext eines alltäglichen Schminkrituals abgebildet. Die Wiederholung des Nackens im Spiegel und die zarte Berührung mit den Fingern der Kurtisane verleihen dem Bild eine erotische Komponente. Die fächerförmige Kartusche am oberen Bildrand zeigt den Kasten einer *shamisen* (japanische Laute) in einem *furoshiki* (Einschlagtuch) und einen Feuerstein, zwei Utensilien, die die Kurtisane für eine gesellige Nacht benötigte: die *shamisen,* um Kunden zu unterhalten, und den Feuerstein, um ihre Ausgehlaterne anzuzünden.

Kunisada's style of *bijin* dominated *ukiyo-e* during the late Edo period. His women tend to be stocky, with large heads, long faces, and prominent jaws. They often project an earthy sensuality different from the elegant refinement of earlier beauties, but with a charm all their own. The convention of placing a courtesan against a distant landscape was developed by Kunisada in the 1830s and helped him circumvent the reforms of 1840–1841 that banned portraits of individual courtesans. In this fan-shaped print, the scene of pleasure boats and fireworks exploding against the night sky reflect the excitement of the woman as she looks out on the evening festivities.

In Japan, the nape of the neck was an eroticized zone of the female body. While it appears here in the context of a woman routinely applying makeup, the doubled depiction and the caressing touch of the courtesan's fingers give the print an erotic charge. The fan-shaped cartouche in the upper section holds a box for a *shamisen* wrapped in a *furoshiki* and a stone flint, both of which the courtesan would need for an evening of parties: the *shamisen* to entertain clients and the flint to light the lantern she would carry on her way.

CM

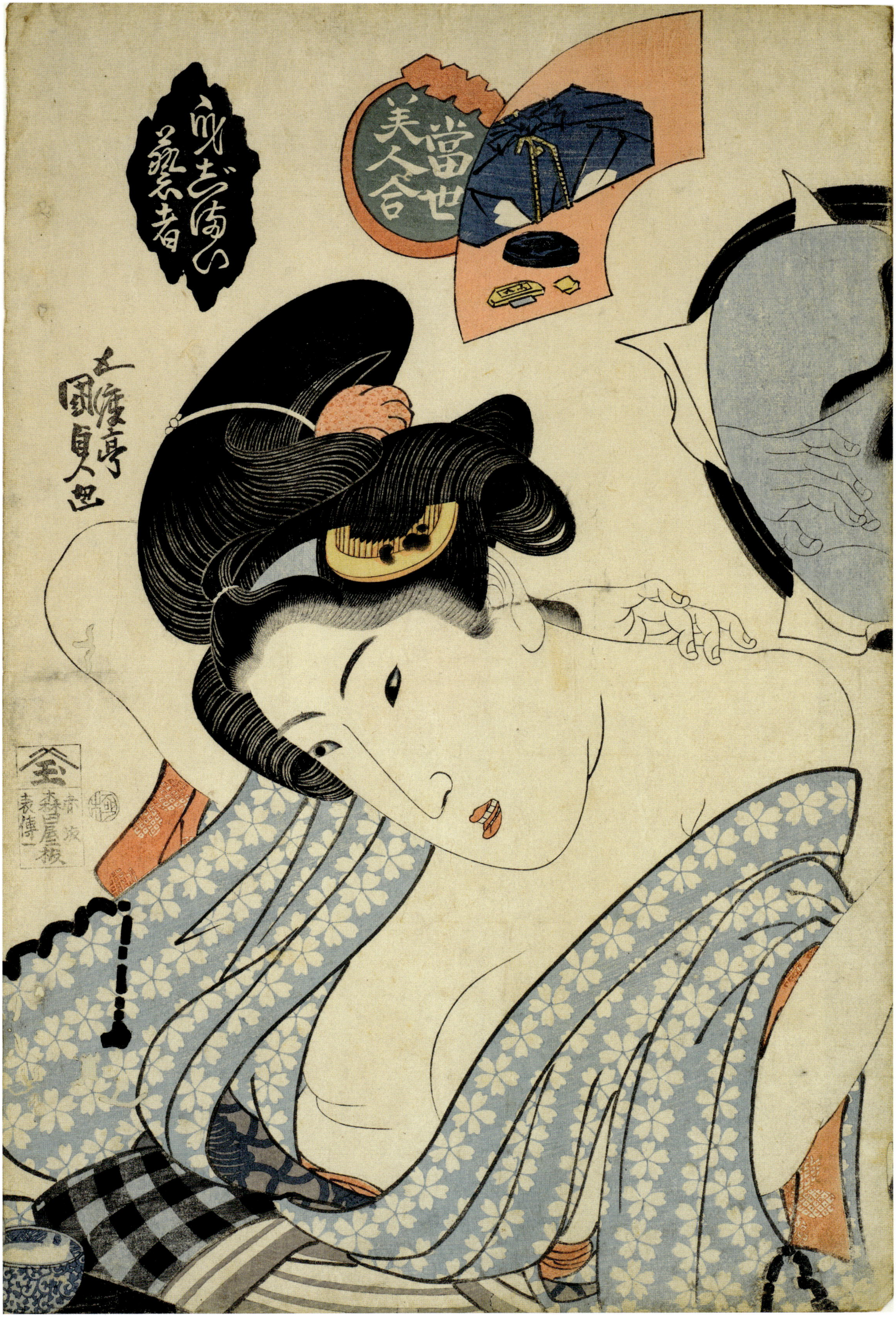
當世美人合
五渡亭國貞画

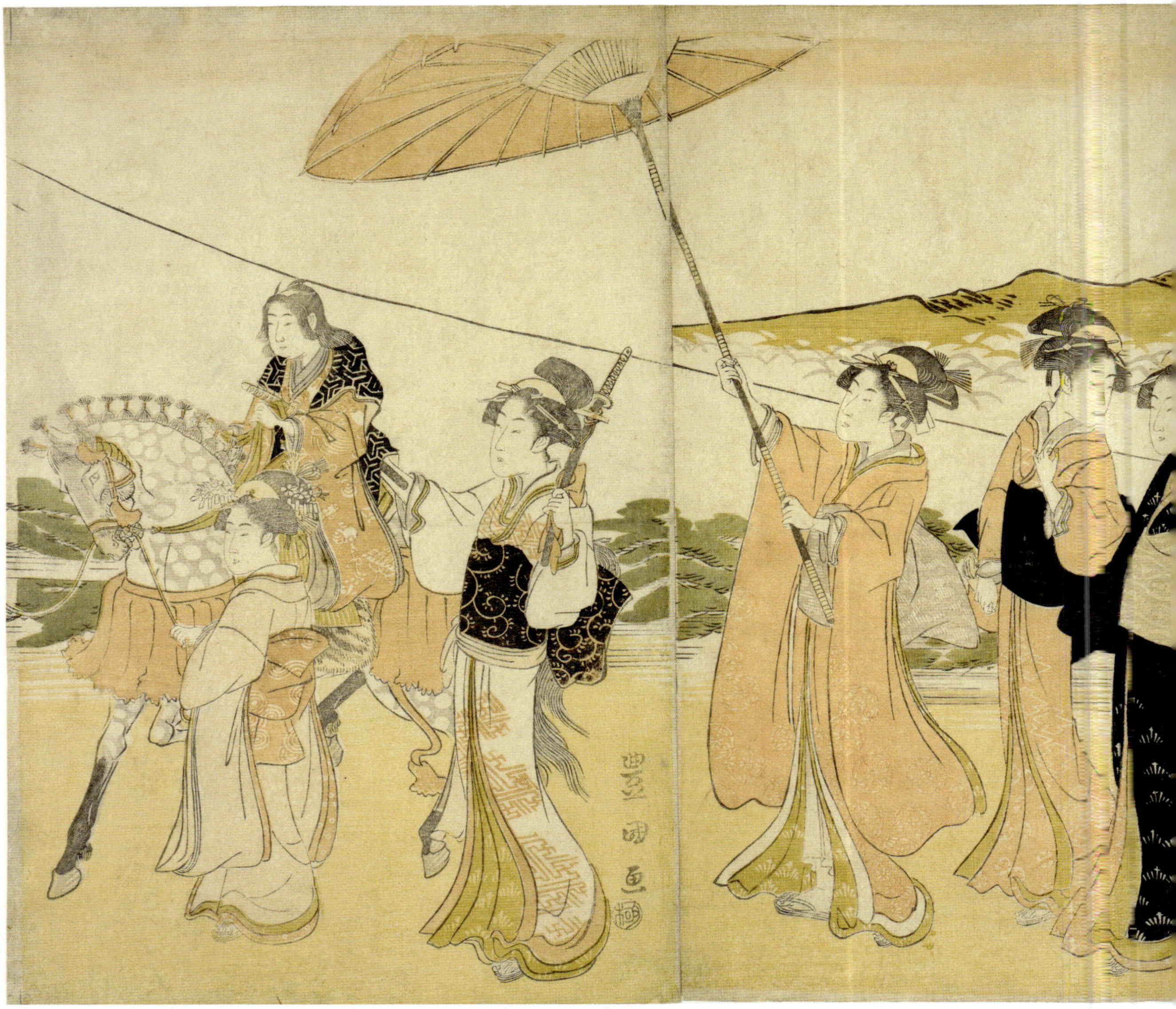

歌川 豊国

95

Eine weibliche Daimyo-Prozession

A Female Daimyo Procession

Utagawa TOYOKUNI I

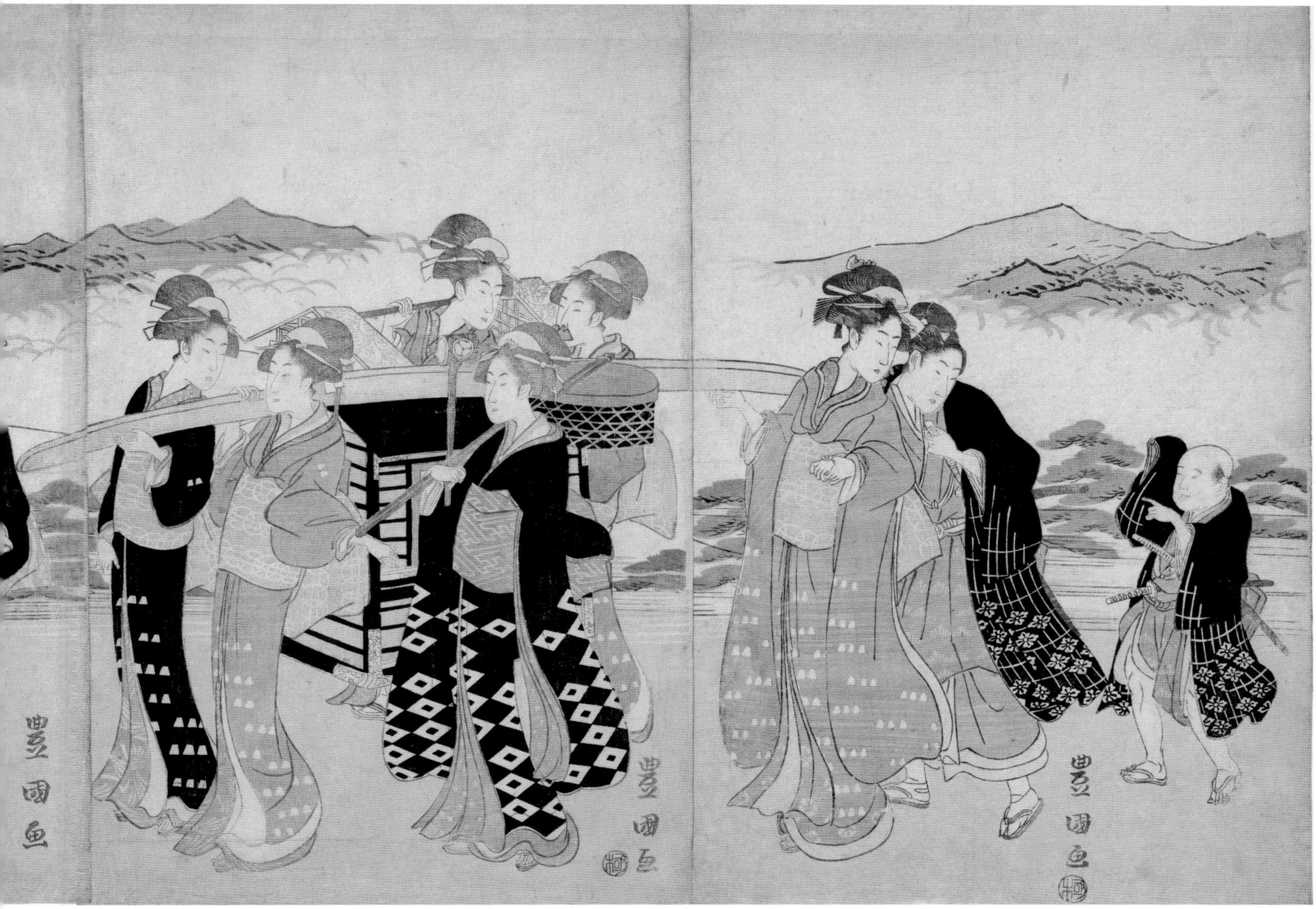

Das von Natur aus subversive *ukiyo-e* nutzte Kurtisanendarstellungen wiederholt, um seriöse Themen zu parodieren, von buddhistischen Gottheiten und Volksgöttern wie etwa in Toyokunis *Kurtisanen in der Gestalt der Sieben Glücksgötter* (KAT. 85) bis hin zu dieser skandalösen Parade von Kurtisanen, die das Gefolge eines *daimyo* (Feudalfürsten) imitieren. Um die *daimyo* zu kontrollieren, ordnete die Tokugawa-Regierung an, dass sie Residenzen sowohl auf ihren Lehensgütern als auch in Edo unterhielten. *Daimyo*-Prozessionen vom Land in die Stadt und umgekehrt waren daher ein vertrautes Bild. In dieser beeindruckenden, acht Einzelblätter umfassenden Komposition präsentiert der Künstler eine Gruppe eleganter Kurtisanen, die nicht durch Yoshiwara stolzieren, sondern vor der Kulisse eines im Hintergrund sanft ansteigenden Fuji über Land ziehen, als stellten sie einen *daimyo* mit seinen Gefolgsleuten auf dem Weg nach Edo dar. Das Werk ist voll von subtil humorvollen Details wie der Frau, die nur mit Mühe den grossen Sonnenschirm über dem Haupt des jungen Herrn balancieren kann, der zu Pferd die Prozession anführt (gestützt von einer weiblichen Begleiterin, deren mütterliche Hand unter seine Gewänder greift, damit er nicht herunterfällt). Oder den fragilen Schönheiten, die eine Sänfte so vorsichtig tragen, dass sie von allein zu schweben scheint.

Inherently subversive, *ukiyo-e* often took advantage of its depictions of courtesans to parody more respectable subjects, from Buddhist and folk deities (for example, see Toyokuni's *Courtesans as the Seven Deities of Good Fortune,* CAT. 85), to this scandalous portrayal of courtesans imitating the entourage of a *daimyo* (lord). In order to control *daimyo,* the Tokugawa government required them to maintain residences in both their fiefdoms and the capital of Edo, and as a result processions of *daimyo* to and from the capital were a regular sight. In this impressive composition spreading over eight prints, the artist shows an elegant group of courtesans parading not through the Yoshiwara, but rather across the countryside as if they were a *daimyo* and his retainers journeying to Edo, with Mount Fuji extending in a long slope across the background. The work is rich in subtly humorous details, from the woman struggling to hold up a large parasol over the young lordling who leads the procession on horseback (with a female attendant extending her motherly hand inside his robes to keep him from falling off), to the fragile beauties delicately supporting the palanquin, which seems to float on its own.

SE

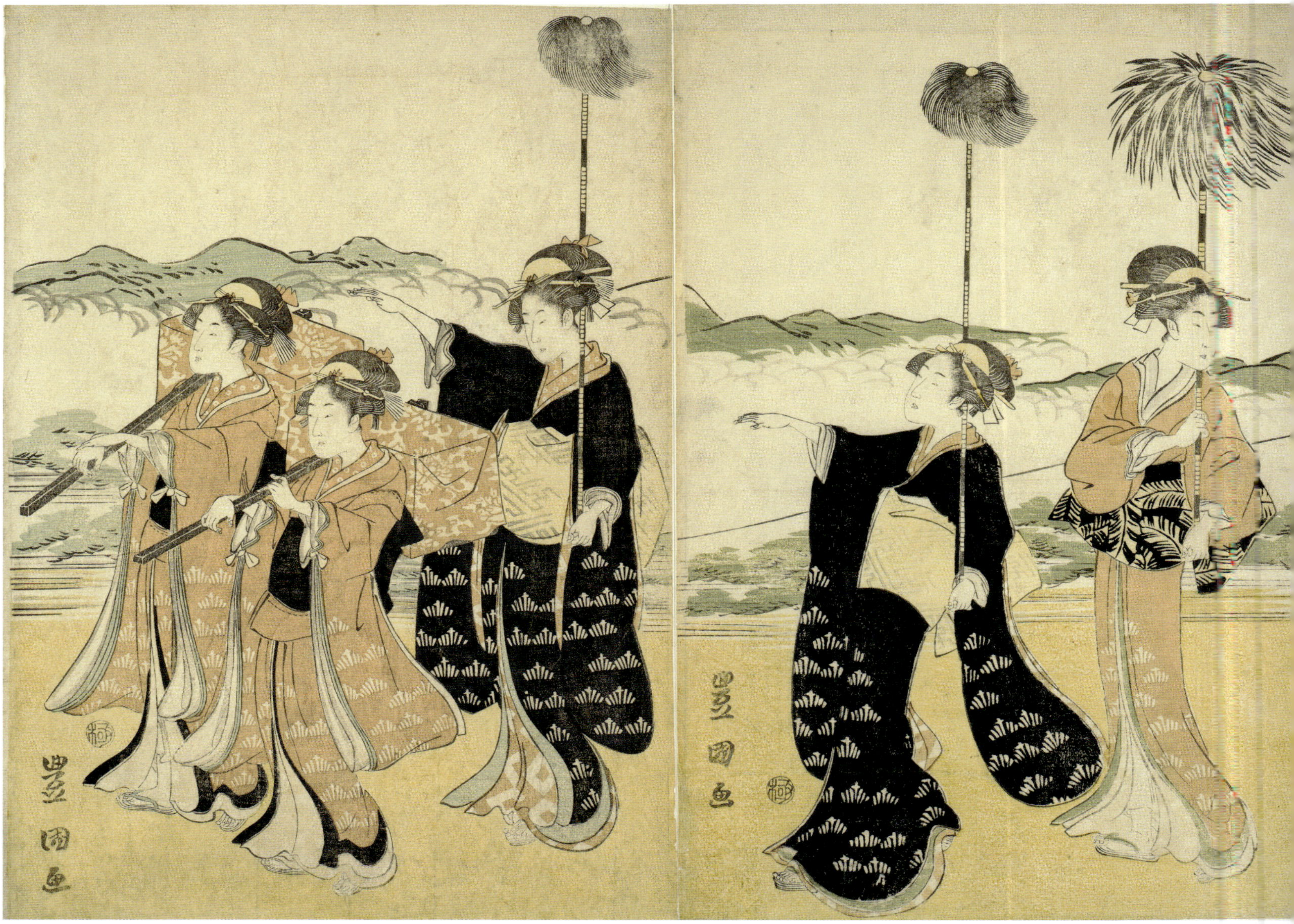
豊国画
豊国画

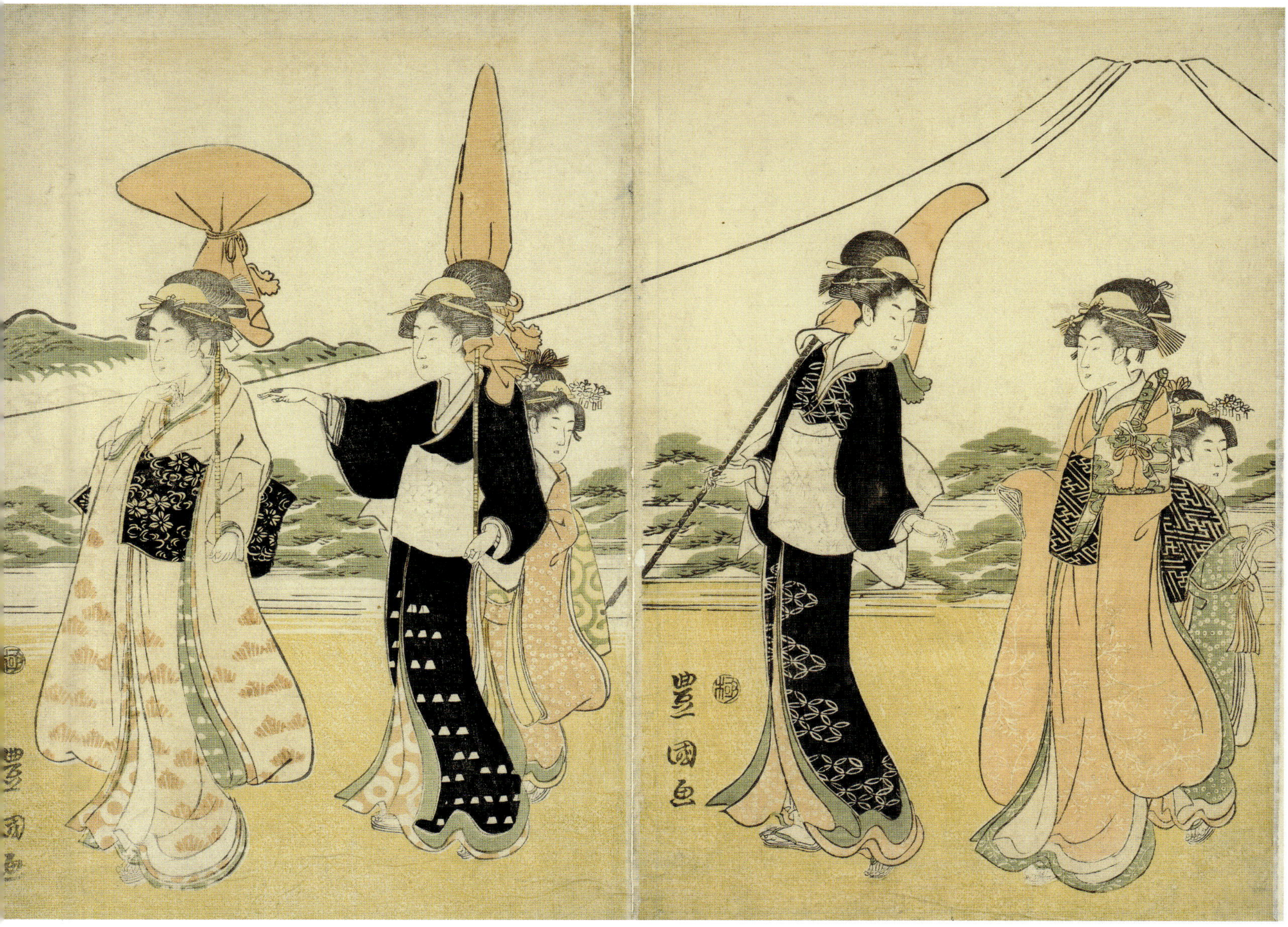

豊国画
豊国画

public conVENience von/by Tabaimo

MARIE KAKINUMA

In ihrer Videoinstallation *public conVENience* zeigt die Künstlerin Tabaimo mithilfe der traditionellen Farbpalette und der Ausdrucksform des *ukiyo-e* Frauen des heutigen Japan. Im japanischen Originaltitel ihrer Arbeit, 公衆便女 *(kôshû benjo)*, verwendet Tabaimo anstelle der richtigen Schriftzeichen für Toilette 便所 *(benjo)* die homonymen Schriftzeichen 便女, die wörtlich übersetzt «Bequemlichkeits-Frau» bedeuten und die im Jargon der japanischen Pornoszene Frauen meinen, die sich allen Männern anbieten. Auch wenn Tabaimo die Schriftzeichen 便女 nicht als Anspielung auf den Jargon, sondern nur als harmloses Wortspiel gewählt hat, fordert dieser Titel den Betrachter heraus, das Bild der Frauen in der Gesellschaft zu hinterfragen.

Der Ort der Handlung dieser Videoinstallation ist eine öffentliche Toilette, also für alle Personen zugänglich, und doch sollen die dünnen Trennwände der Kabinen Räume für sehr Persönliches und Intimes schaffen. In der Arbeit *public conVENience* schaut man vier Frauenfiguren in einer Damentoilette bei körpernahen, vertrauten, aber auch geheimnisvollen Handlungen zu, die deren Wünsche, Obsessionen und Ängste offenbaren. Die auf drei Wände eines Raumes vollflächig projizierte Installation beseitigt dabei die Distanz zu den Zuschauenden und macht sie selbst zu Anwesenden am Handlungsort.

In einer Kabine, deren Tür offen steht, drückt eine Frau immer wieder auf die Spülung einer Hocktoilette; darin reckt eine Schildkröte den Hals und kämpft angestrengt gegen den Wasserstrom an. Das Wasser ist zu feinen Linienbündeln abstrahiert und erinnert an stilisierte Wellenformen im traditionellen Holzdruck (KAT. 28). In Japan symbolisiert die Schildkröte männliche Potenz, und die japanischen Schriftzeichen für den Schildkrötenkopf bezeichnen auch die Eichel des Penis. Die

In her video installation *public conVENience,* the artist Tabaimo uses the traditional color palette and forms of expression of *ukiyo-e* to show women of today's Japan. In the original Japanese title, 公衆便女 *(kôshû benjo)*, rather than the correct characters for toilet 便所 *(benjo)*, Tabaimo uses the homonym characters 便女, which translated literally means "comfort-woman," and in the Japanese porno scene means women who offer themselves to all men. Although Tabaimo selected the characters 便女 as a harmless wordplay rather than in allusion to the slang expression, the selected title challenges the viewer to question society's image of women.

The site of action of the video installation is a public toilet, accessible by all, although the thin partition walls of the cabins are meant to create spaces for something very personal and intimate. The work *public conVENience,* looks at four female figures in a women's toilet engaging in familiar, but also mysterious acts closely related to the body, which reveal their wishes, obsessions, and fears. The installation is projected full screen onto three walls of a room, thereby eliminating any distance from the viewers, making them personally present at the scene of action.

A woman in a cabin with an open door presses again and again on the flush of a squat toilet in which a turtle stretches out its neck and fights laboriously against the current of water. The water is abstracted to fine, bundles of lines and recalls stylized wave forms in traditional woodblock printing (CAT. 28). In Japan, the turtle symbolizes male potency and the Japanese symbol for the turtle's head also identifies the penis' glans. The toilet walls are covered with shield-shaped tiles, which again take up the pattern of the turtle's shell and thereby the sexual connotations. Perhaps this woman wants to flush away her thoughts about male desire.

束芋

public conVENience
TABAIMO

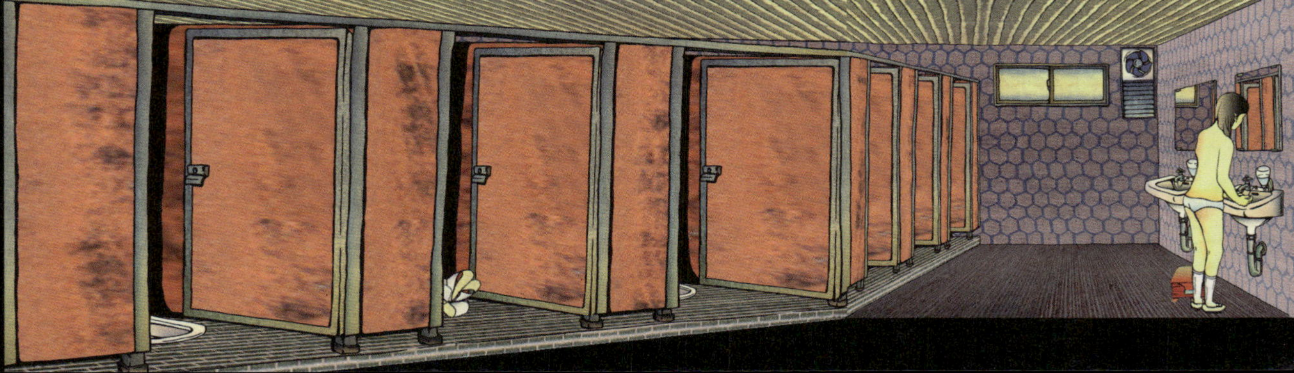

Toilettenwände sind mit schildförmigen Fliesen bedeckt, die das Muster des Schildkrötenpanzers und damit die sexuellen Konnotationen wieder aufnehmen. Möglicherweise möchte diese Frau ihre Gedanken an männliche Begierde wegspülen.

Eine andere, fast nackte junge Frau mit Schultornister wäscht sich am Waschbecken immer wieder die Hände. Motten, die aus Männerhänden freigelassen wurden, fliegen durchs offene Fenster in die Damentoilette, und ihre Augen verwandeln sich in Kameraobjektive. Während sie um das halb nackte Schulmädchen herumflattern, hört man immer wieder das Verschlussgeräusch von Kameras. In seiner Naivität bemerkt das Mädchen offenbar nicht, dass es dem Voyeurismus ausgesetzt ist. Auch in den «Bildern der fliessenden Welt» des Holzdrucks geht es oft um das Thema Voyeurismus, wie beispielsweise in KAT. 64, wo ein am Boden kauernder Mann seinen begehrlichen Blick ins Zimmer einer Kurtisane richtet.

In einer neuen Szene der Videoinstallation zieht sich eine weitere Frau, nachdem ihr Mobiltelefon in die Toilette gefallen ist, ohne zu zögern einen Badeanzug an und bindet sich ein Rettungsseil um den Körper. Sie springt mit Schwung in die Toilette und taucht hinab, um das Mobiltelefon, ihre Nabelschnur zur Welt, zurückzuholen. Wie das Telefonnetz und das Internet bilden auch die schmutzigen Abwasserrohre der Kanalisation ein Netz und führen in eine andere Welt.

Eine vierte Frau kommt vor Schmerzen gekrümmt in die Toilette und befreit sich von einem Kind, das in ihrer Nase steckt. Sie setzt das Kind auf dem Rücken der Schildkröte in der Toilette aus und dreht beide in die andere Richtung. Schon beim ersten Spülen werden auf diese Weise Schildkröte und Neugeborenes in den Abfluss gezogen. Mit diesem deutlich gesellschaftskritischen Unterton weist Tabaimo auf verdrängte und unbequeme Dinge hin, die sich im schmutzigen Abwasser ansammeln und in eine andere Welt fliessen. Diese Andeutung wird durch den tiefen, widerhallenden Ton der Wassergeräusche verstärkt.

Eindrucksvoll endet der Film wieder mit dem voyeuristischen Blick einer Motte, die zum letzten Mal auf den Auslöser drückt. Doch die Frauen sind schon längst hinter den geschlossenen Türen der Toiletten verschwunden. Nun wird der Betrachter der Videoinstallation fotografiert.

Another, nearly naked young woman with a book bag continually washes her hands at the sink. Moths, which are set free from men's hands, fly through an open window into the women's toilet, and their eyes transform into camera lenses. As they flutter around the seminaked school girl, one hears again and again the click of the cameras' shutters. In her naivety the girl apparently does not notice that she is the object of voyeurism. The "images of the floating world" of woodblock prints also frequently take the theme of voyeurism, for example, in CAT. 64, where a man crouching on the floor directs his lustful glance into a courtesan's room.

In a new scene in the video installation, a woman, after her cell phone falls into the toilet, does not hesitate in putting on a bathing suit and tying a safety rope around her body. She jumps boldly into the toilet and dives down to retrieve her cell phone, her umbilical cord to the world. Like the telephone network and the Internet, the dirty sewage pipes of the sewerage system also form a network and lead into another world.

A fourth woman arrives at the toilet doubled over in pain and frees herself of a child that is stuck in her nose. She abandons the child on the back of the turtle in the toilet and turns both around in the other direction. Already with the first flush, both the turtle and the newborn are drawn down the drain. With these clearly socio-critical undertones, Tabaimo refers to repressed and uncomfortable things that gather in the filthy sewage water and flow into another world. The deep, echoing sound of the water noises reinforces this insinuation.

The film ends impressively with the voyeuristic view of a moth pressing the shutter for the last time. Yet the women have long disappeared behind the toilets' closed doors. Now it is the viewer of the video installation that is photographed.

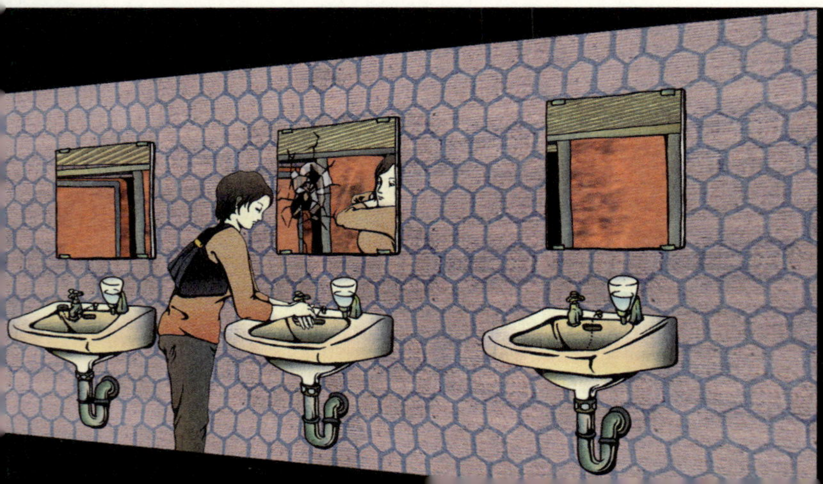

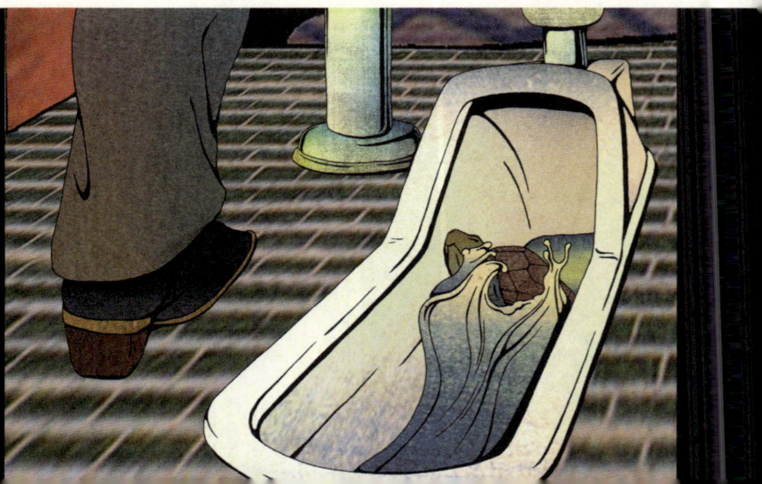

Japanisches Badehaus – Männer von Tabaimo
Japanese Bathhouse – Gents by Tabaimo

MARIE KAKINUMA

東芋

S./pp. 156–157
Japanisches Badehaus – Männer
Japanese Bathhouse – Gents
TABAIMO

Das moderne Badehaus *sentô* hat seinen Ursprung im älteren, traditionellen Badehaus *yuya,* «Heisswasser-Bad», dessen Besuch seit der Edo-Zeit (1603–1868) beim einfachen Volk sehr beliebt war. Damals durften noch beide Geschlechter gemeinsam baden, was heute nicht mehr gestattet ist. Da durch den Einbau von Bädern in privaten Wohnungen seit den 1970er-Jahren die Zahl der Badehäuser stark zurückgegangen ist, weckt das moderne *sentô* nostalgische Gefühle.

In dieser Videoinstallation von Tabaimo betreten die Ausstellungsbesucher durch eine japanische Schiebetür den für Männer bestimmten Bereich des Badehauses. An die Wände projiziert sieht man dann einen Umkleideraum für Männer mit den typischen Requisiten eines *sentô:* Holzschliessfächer, Körbe für Kleidung, Ventilator, Waage, Massagesessel – und eine alte Dame, die auf einem erhöhten Platz in der Mitte der getrennten Baderäume für Frauen und Männer sitzt und von den Besuchern die Gebühren einkassiert. Im Badebereich hinter dem gekachelten Becken erscheint auf der Wand der berühmteste Berg Japans, der Fujisan. Bis heute gilt das Bild des Fujisan als volkstümliches Symbol für das *sentô.* Doch während es seit Beginn des 20. Jahrhunderts üblich ist, den Fujisan in Männerbädern im westlichen Malstil abzubilden, verwendet Tabaimo ganz bewusst eine bestimme Darstellung aus dem *ukiyo-e,* nämlich *Klare Morgendämmerung bei Südwind* aus der Farbholzschnittserie *Sechsunddreissig Ansichten des Berges Fuji* von Katsushika Hokusai (1760–1849).

Am Anfang des Videofilms wird der Männerumkleideraum vom Dampf des heissen Badewassers gefüllt, dann beginnt der Raum sich zu drehen. Ein Badegast betritt mit einem gelben Kübel in der Hand das Badehaus und gibt einer alten Aufseherin eine kleine 100-Yen-Münze. Die im Bad schwimmenden Schildkröten sind ein Symbol für männliche Potenz und demonstrieren bildlich, dass es hier zunächst um eine reine Männerwelt geht. Obwohl man eigentlich nackt zur Entspannung und zum Pflegen sozialer Kontakte ins Bad geht, baden Büroangestellte stillschweigend in Anzug, Krawatte und mit Brille. Sie machen dadurch ihr Unwohlsein deutlich, da sie ihre berufliche Rolle auch im Bad weiterspielen. Dann klettern mit einem Mal nackte Frauen über die Trennwand und dringen, befreit von den Zwängen gesellschaftlicher Konventionen, in das Männerbad ein. Ein Schüler in blauer Schuluniform zieht nicht nur seine Kleidung, sondern auch seine Haut aus, als ob sich eine

The modern bathhouse *sentô* has its origins in the older, traditional bathhouse *yuya,* "hot water bath," which was a favorite among the common people from the Edo era onward (1603–1868). Back then, men and women were allowed to bath together, which is no longer allowed today. Since the number of bathhouses has fallen drastically due to the building of baths in private homes since the 1970s, the modern *sentô* stirs a sense of nostalgia.

In this video installation by Tabaimo, exhibition visitors walk through a Japanese sliding door, entering the area of the bathhouse designated for men. There, one sees a men's changing room projected onto the wall, with the typical *sentô* furnishings: wooden lockers, baskets for clothing, ventilator, scale, massage chair—and an elderly woman sitting on an elevated area in the middle of the two separate bathing areas for women and men, collecting money from the guests. In the bathing area, appearing on the wall behind the tiled tubs is Japan's most famous mountain, Fujisan. Until today, the image of Fujisan is considered the folkloric symbol for the *sentô.* Although it has been common since the early twentieth century to depict the Fujisan in a western painterly style, Tabaimo quite consciously uses a particular representation from the *ukiyo-e,* namely, *South Wind, Clear Sky* from the color woodblock series *Thirty-Six Views of Mount Fuji* by Katsushika Hokusai (1760–1849).

At the beginning of the video, the men's changing room is filled with steam from the hot bathwater, then the room begins to turn. A bath guest enters the bathhouse with a yellow bucket in his hand and gives an elderly attendant a small, 100-yen coin. The turtles swimming in the bath are a symbol of male potency and graphically demonstrate that first and foremost, here, we are dealing with a purely male world. Although one actually enters the bath naked to relax and to cultivate social contacts, office employees bath silently in their suits and ties, with glasses on. They thereby make their unease clear, as they continue playing their professional role also in the bath. Then, all at once, naked women climb over the separating wall; free of the constraints of social convention, they penetrate the men's bath. A school boy in a blue uniform takes off not only his clothes, but also his skin, as though a silkworm was shedding its skin. Before this scene, there is a caption that says that the boy strips off the "skin of responsibility." This theme, namely, the inability or excessive demand to take responsibility for one's own actions, is also shown, among others, in the scene where

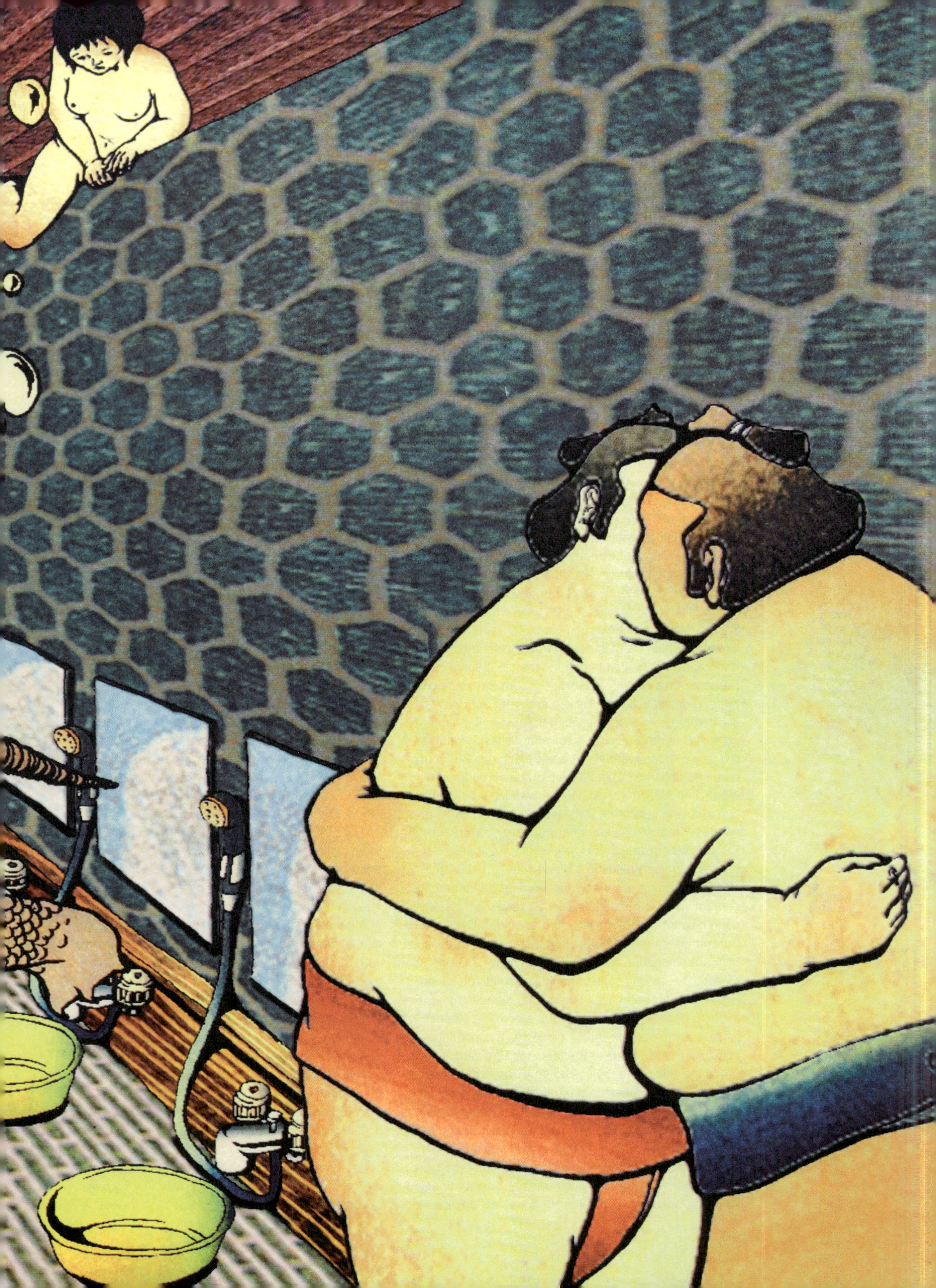

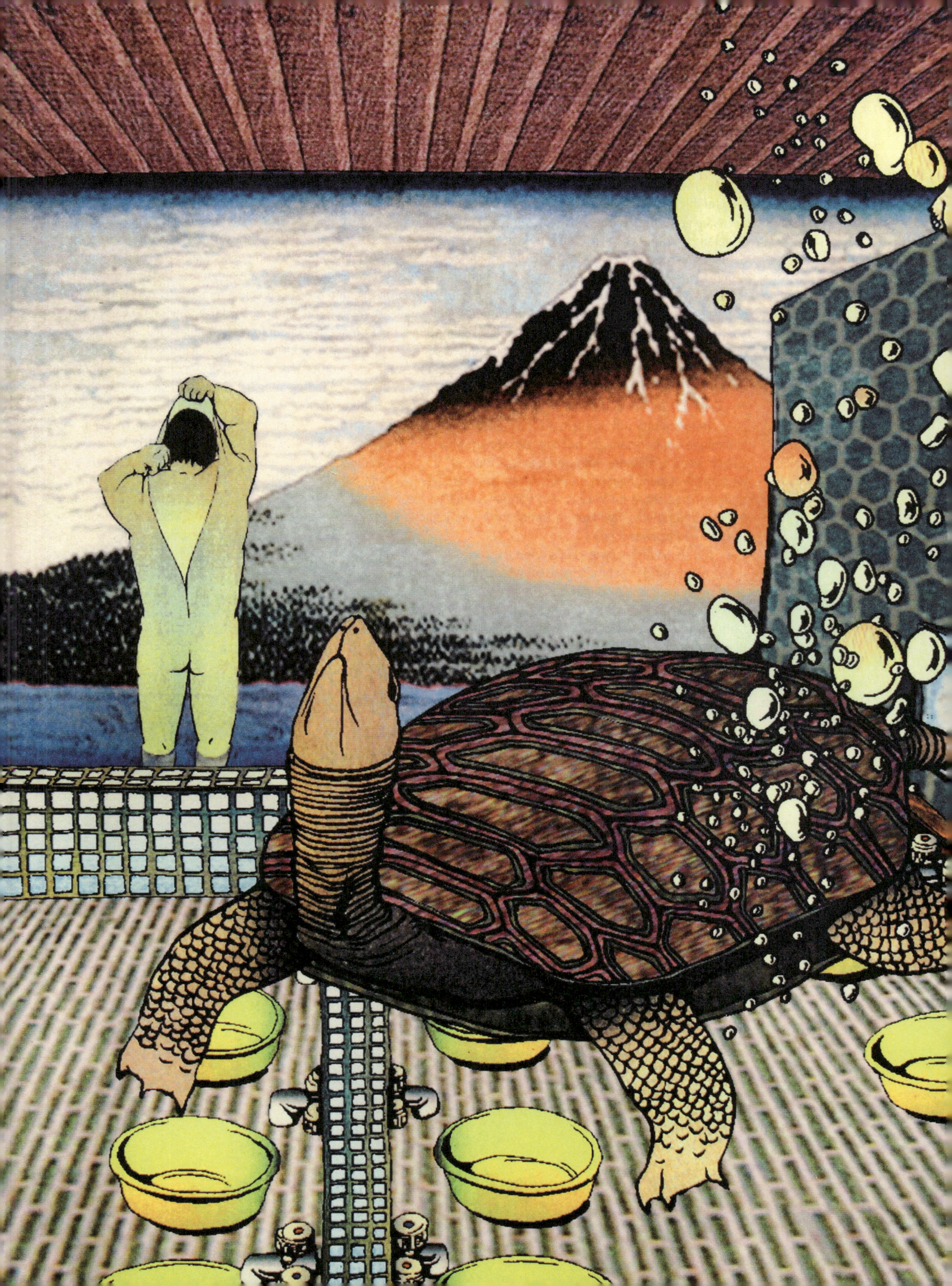

Seidenraupe häuten würde. Dieser Szene geht ein Zwischentitel voraus, der besagt, dass der Junge die «Haut der Verantwortung» abstreife. Dieses Thema, nämlich die Unfähigkeit oder Überforderung, die Verantwortung für das eigene Tun zu übernehmen, zeigt sich unter anderem auch in der Szene, wo eine Frau ihr Baby im Schliessfach deponiert. Anschliessend kämpfen zwei Sumô-Ringer zunächst unentschieden. Der wirtschaftliche Terminus M & A (Mergers & Acquisitions) wird auf den Bildschirm projiziert. Der darauf folgende Kampf ist ein Kuss, bei dem es einem der Sumô-Ringer gelingt, den Gegner aufzusaugen. Tabaimo veranschaulicht so in einem eindrücklichen Bild einen unheimlichen Aspekt der modernen Wirtschaft. Mit ihrer raffinierten Bildsprache versucht Tabaimo, das stereotype Bild von Japan zu verfremden und auf problematische gesellschaftliche Umstände aufmerksam zu machen. Aus einem Müllwagen werden mehrere Abfalltüten in das Becken entsorgt, trotzdem bleiben die Männer in Geschäftskleidung ganz gelassen im Wasser. Ein Polizist erschiesst die Aufseherin und verschwindet im Badedampf, womöglich um sich «reinzuwaschen».

Mit der Aufforderung «Let's drain the dirty water» fliesst nicht nur das schmutzige Badewasser ab, sondern auch die nostalgischen Bilder des Umkleideraums, die sich mit dem Wasserstrudel drehen. Alles verschwindet. Damit wird die japanische Redewendung «ins Wasser fliessen lassen» versinnbildlicht, was so viel bedeutet wie zwischenmenschliche Spannungen lösen oder Probleme der Vergessenheit überlassen. Im Allgemeinen bedient sich die japanische Gesellschaft gerne dieser inaktiven Haltung, um Konflikten auszuweichen.

a woman puts her baby into a locker. Afterwards, two Sumô wrestlers battle; at first, the match is undecided. The business term M & A (mergers & acquisitions) is projected onto the screen. The fight that follows is a kiss in which one of the Sumô wrestlers successfully sucks up his opponent. Tabaimo thus makes clear in an impressive image, an uncanny aspect of the modern economy. With her ingenious visual language, Tabaimo attempts to alienate the stereotypical image of Japan and draw attention to problematic social situations. Several bags of garbage are taken from a garbage truck and disposed of in the bath, but the men in business suits still remain entirely composed in the water. A police officer shoots the attendant and disappears in the bath steam perhaps, to "clean himself."

With the summons "Let's drain the dirty water," not only does the dirty bath water flow away, but also the nostalgic image of the changing room, which swirls along with the whirlpool. Everything disappears. This hereby typifies the Japanese expression "let flow in the water." The phrase means to dissolve tensions among people, or let problems be forgotten. Japanese society, in general, favors this passive position of dodging conflicts.

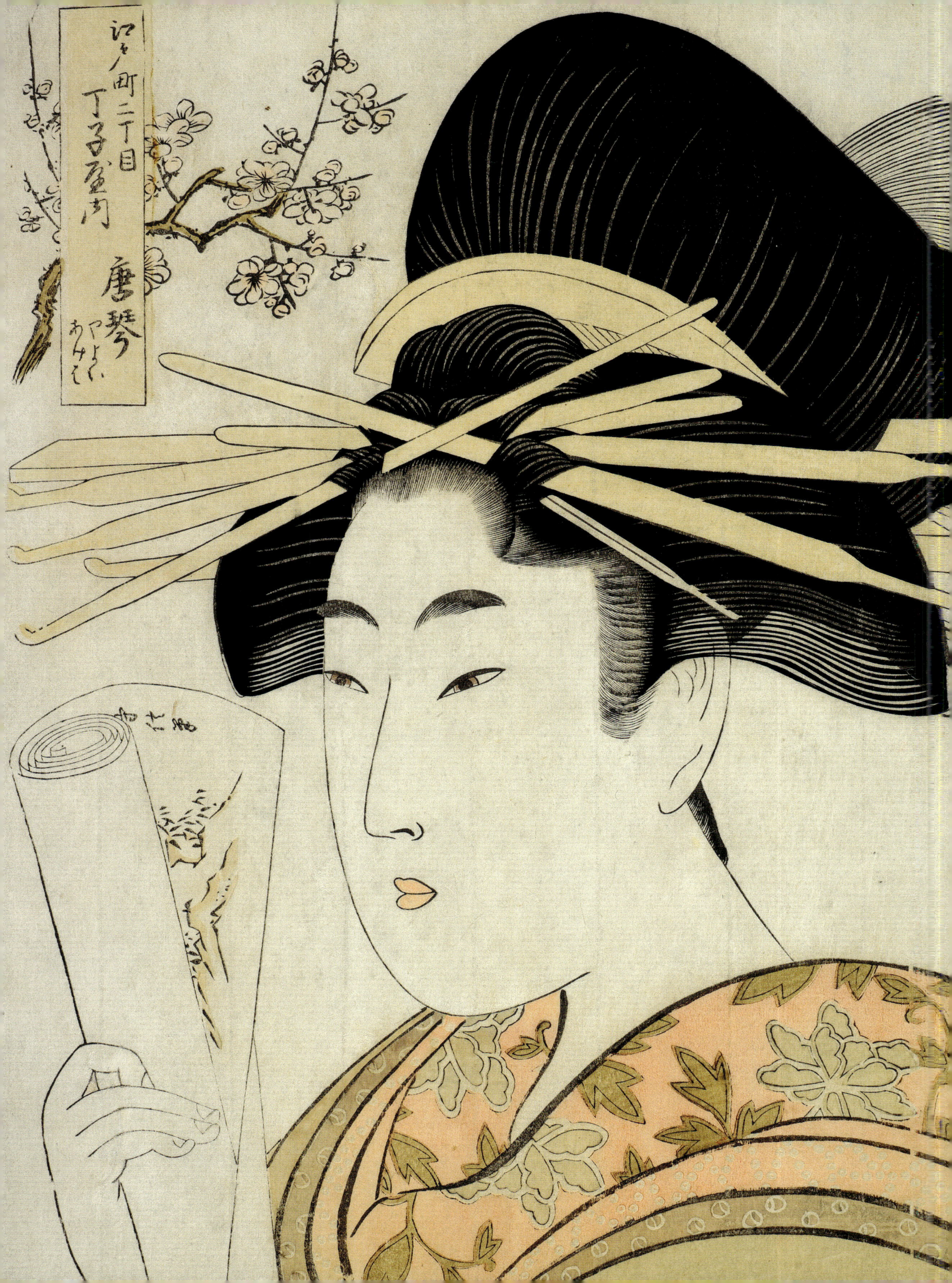
江戸町二丁目
丁子屋内
唐琴
やよい

Künstlerbiografien
Artists' Biographies

JEANNE EGLOFF

ANMERKUNGEN ZUR NAMENSGEBUNG JAPANISCHER KÜNSTLER

Während der Edo-Zeit (1603–1868) herrschte eine strenge Unterscheidung zwischen dem Familiennamen *(uji)* und dem gewöhnlichen Namen/Vornamen *(zukoshô/zukomyô)* einer Person. In Künstlerkreisen geschah es häufig, dass talentierte Schüler von ihren Lehrern adoptiert wurden, um die Familientradition aufrechtzuerhalten. Auf diese Weise wurde der Name eines bekannten Meisters zum Inbegriff einer Schule (z. B. Torii oder Utagawa). Neben dem Familiennamen wurde zusätzlich ein Bestandteil aus dem Vornamen des Lehrers weitergegeben (z. B. die Schüler von Utagawa «Toyo*kuni*» hiessen «*Kuni*sada» und «*Kuni*yoshi»). Sowohl der Familienname als auch der Vorname eines Künstlers sagen somit darüber etwas aus, in welcher Tradition ein Künstler ausgebildet war. Ergänzend zum Familien- und Vornamen führten viele Künstler ein selbst gewähltes Pseudonym *(gagô)*, das sie während ihres Lebens beliebig oft wechseln konnten. Dieses Pseudonym wurde häufig als Signatur verwendet und bezog sich in seiner Bedeutung meist auf eine besondere Lebensphase des Künstlers (z. B. signierte Kunisada in seiner frühen Schaffenszeit mit *gototei,* «Pavillon der fünften Fähre», womit er auf das Fährunternehmen seiner Eltern anspielte).

Wie in Japan üblich stehen in den folgenden Kurzbiografien die Vornamen hinter den Familiennamen. Um Verwechslungen innerhalb derselben Künstlerfamilie zu vermeiden, waren japanische Künstler unter ihren Vornamen meist besser bekannt als unter ihren Familiennamen. Aus diesem Grund dient der Vorname oder manchmal auch das Pseudonym als Hauptname eines Künstlers, weshalb dieser im Titel jeweils in Grossbuchstaben gesetzt ist.

NOTES ON THE NOMENCLATURE OF JAPANESE ARTISTS

A strict distinction between a person's family name *(uji)* and common or first name *(zukoshô/zukomyô)* prevailed during the Edo period (1603–1868). In artist circles, teachers often adopted their talented students to maintain the family tradition. In this way, the name of a famous master came to be the embodiment of a school (e.g., Torii or Utagawa). A component of the first name of the teacher was also passed on along with the family name (e.g., students of Utagawa "Toyo*kuni*" were called "*Kuni*sada" and "*Kuni*yoshi"). An artist's family name and first name thus both provide information about the tradition in which the artist was trained. Supplemental to the family and first names, many artists also had pseudonyms *(gagô)* that they chose themselves and could change as often as they liked during their lifetime. These pseudonyms were frequently used as a signature and their meanings usually referred to a particular phase in the life of the artist (e.g., Kunisada signed his works *gototei,* "pavilion of the fifth ferry," in an early period of his career, whereby he alluded to his parents' ferry business.)

In the following short biographies, first names come after family names as is common in Japan. Japanese artists are usually better known under their first names than under their family names to avoid confusion within the same artist family. For this reason, the first name or sometimes also the pseudonym serves as an artist's main name, which is why this appears in uppercase in the headings below.

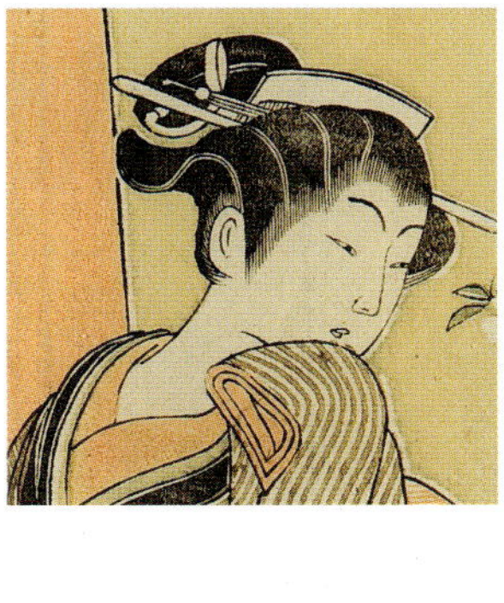

Ippitsusai BUNCHÔ 一筆斎 文調 tätig/active ca. 1755–1790

Bunchôs künstlerisches Schaffen trug entscheidend zur Weiterentwicklung des Farbholzschnitts bei. Ursprünglich studierte er die Malerei der Kanô-Schule, bevor er zum Holzdruck wechselte. Zusammen mit Shunshô (1726–1793) begründete er die Gattung des Schauspielerporträts – sie wurden Bunchôs Spezialität. Als Bunchôs Hauptwerk gilt das *Bilderbuch mit Bühnenfächern (Ehon butai ôgi)*, das er 1770 zusammen mit Shunshô herausgab und das die ersten realistischen Schauspielerbildnisse enthält. Später wurde Bunchô vor allem von den Werken Harunobus beeinflusst. Zuletzt nahmen Bilder von hübschen Mädchen und Kurtisanen den grössten Teil seiner Arbeiten ein. In seinen Werken gelang ihm die Verbindung der realistischen Manier Shunshôs mit der lyrischen Art und attraktiven Farbigkeit Harunobus. Wie viele *ukiyo-e*-Künstler war Bunchô ebenfalls als Dichter tätig.

Bunchô's artistic oeuvre contributed decisively to the further development of color woodblock printing. He originally studied the painting of the Kanô School before switching to woodblock printing. Together with Shunshô (1726–1793), he founded the genre of actor portraits, which became Bunchô's specialty. The *Picture Book of Stage Fans (Ehon butai ôgi)*, which he published in 1770 together with Shunshô, is considered Bunchô's main work. It contains the first realistic portraits of actors. Bunchô was later influenced mainly by the works of Harunobu. In the end, images of beautiful women and courtesans took up the greatest share of his works. In his prints, he successfully combined Shunshô's realistic manner with Harunobu's lyrical style and attractive colorfulness. Like many *ukiyo-e*-artists, Bunchô was also active as a poet.

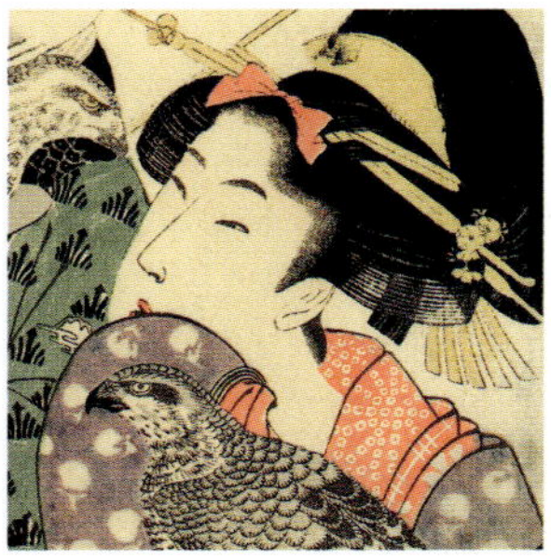

BUNRÔ 文浪 tätig/active 1801–1810

Bis heute liegen kaum Informationen über Bunrôs Leben vor. Er war als Holzschnittkünstler in Edo tätig und konzentrierte sich neben der Produktion von «Bildern schöner Frauen» *(bijinga)* auch auf Alltagsszenen (*fûzokuga,* «Bilder über Sitten und Gebräuche»). Seine Arbeit scheint massgeblich von den eleganten Frauenporträts Utamaros beeinflusst zu sein, was vermuten lässt, dass Bunrô zu dessen Schülern gehörte. Hauptverleger seiner Entwürfe war Ezakiya Kichibei, der um 1805 unter anderem auch Aufträge an Utamaro, Toyokuni und Eisen erteilte.

Until today, there is hardly any information available about Bunrô's life. He was active as a woodblock artist in Edo, and concentrated on everyday scenes (*fûzokuga,* genre paintings) in addition to the production of "images of beautiful women" *(bijinga)*. His work appears to be influenced considerably by Utamaro's elegant portraits of women, which makes it seem likely that Bunrô was among his students. The main publisher of his designs was Ezakiya Kichibei, who also gave commissions to Utamaro, Toyokuni, and Eisen, among others, in ca. 1805.

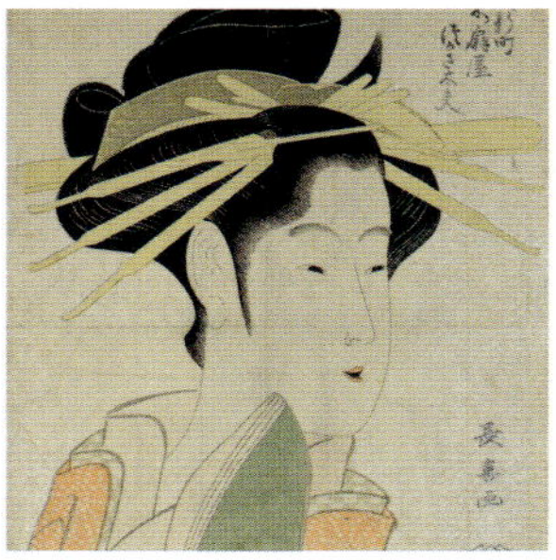

Eishôsai CHÔKI 栄松斎 長喜 tätig/active ca. 1780–1809

Wie Utamaro begann auch Chôki seine Lehre bei Toriyama Sekien (1712–1788), einem Buchillustrator in Edo. Der Schwerpunkt seines künstlerischen Schaffens lag in der Produktion von «Bildern schöner Frauen» *(bijinga)*. Unter dem Namen Shikô entwarf er Drucke im Stil Harunobus und Kiyonagas. Seine späteren, mit Chôki unterzeichneten Drucke weisen Parallelen zu Werken von Utamaro und Eishi auf. Chôkis Schönheiten strahlen oft eine neugierige Freude aus. Ihre hellwachen Gesichter zeigen ein sanftes Lächeln und scheinen sichtlich zufrieden. Dieser Ausdruck stand im Gegensatz zu den sozialen Umstände der damaligen Zeit. Leider sind uns nur wenige Werke von Chôki erhalten, darunter luxuriöse Blätter mit Glimmerhintergrund (KAT. 73). Neben «Bildern schöner Frauen» schuf Chôki auch einzelne Schauspielerporträts *(yakusha-e)*, «Pfostenbilder» *(hashira-e)* und «Blumen- und Vogelbilder» *(kachôga)*. Dank seines Erfolgs arbeitete Chôki für renommierte Verleger wie Tsutaya Jûzaburô, der die meisten seiner Seriendrucke produzierte.

Like Utamaro, Chôki also began his training under Toriyama Sekien (1712–1788), a book illustrator in Edo. The main focus of his artistic oeuvre was the production of "images of beautiful women" *(bijinga)*. Under the name Shikô, he drafted prints in the style of Harunobu and Kiyonaga. His later prints, signed as Chôki, show parallels to works by Utamaro and Eishi. Chôki's beautiful women often radiate an inquisitive joy. Their alert faces display a gentle smile and appear visibly satisfied. This expression countered the social ills of the era at the time. Unfortunately, only a few works by Chôki have been preserved, including luxurious sheets with mica backgrounds (CAT. 73). Along with "images of beautiful women," Chôki also created individual actor portraits *(yakusha-e)*, "pillar prints" *(hashira-e)*, and "images of birds and flowers" *(kachôga)*. Due to his success, Chôki worked for renowned publishers, such as Tsutaya Jûzaburô, who produced most of his print series.

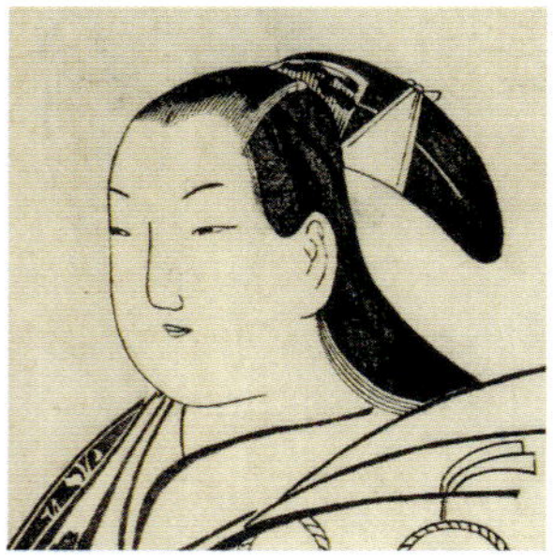

Kaigetsudô DOHAN 懐月堂 度繁 tätig/active 1710–1736

Dohan studierte Malerei unter Kaigetsudô Ando, dem Gründer der Kaigetsudô-Schule. Von den wenigen heute noch erhaltenen Drucken dieser Schule hat Dohan die grösste Anzahl angefertigt. Neben Drucken existieren einzelne Malereien von ihm. Charakteristisch für Dohans Schönheiten sind die feine Ausarbeitung der dekorativen Kimonomuster sowie das elegant über die Schulter gelegte Haar. Wie in allen Bildern der Kaigetsudô-Schule benutzt auch Dohan einen sehr expressiven Pinselduktus mit an- und abschwellenden Konturlinien. Die Schriftzeichen für «Dohan» können ebenso als «Norishige» gelesen werden, was auch schon zu Verwechslungen führte.

Dohan studied painting under Kaigetsudô Ando, founder of the Kaigetsudô School. Of the few prints currently still available from this school, Dohan produced the greatest number. Existing along with the prints are also a few of his paintings. Characteristic for Dohan's beauties are the detailed elaboration of their decorative kimono patterns, and their hair, lying elegantly over the shoulder. Like in all paintings from the Kaigetsudô School, Dohan, too, used a very expressive brush style with rising and fading contour lines. The lettering for "Dohan" can just as easily be read as "Norishige," which already in and of itself leads to confusion.

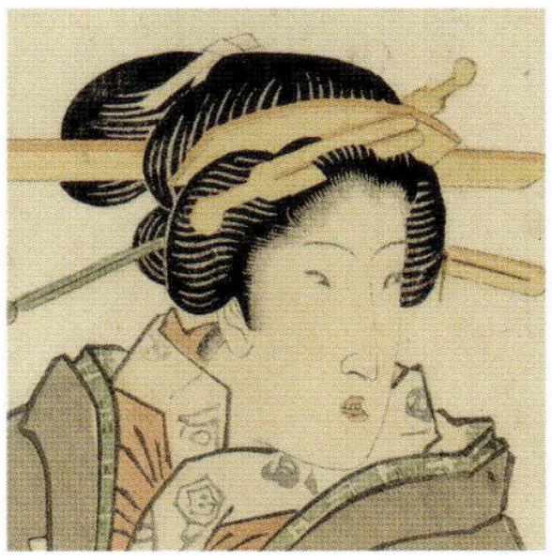

Keisai EISEN 渓斎 英泉 1790–1848

Nach Utamaro und Eizan führte Eisen die Tradition der *bijin*-Künstler fort. Eisen stammte aus einer angesehenen Familie der Fujiwara-Sippe in Edo. Sein Vater Shigeharu war Dichter und Künstler. Nach dem frühen Tod seiner Eltern begann Eisen eine Lehre bei Eizan. Neben Einzelblättern schuf er ab 1811 zahlreiche Buchillustrationen, darunter viele mit erotischem Inhalt. Unter den Namen Chiyoda Saiichi und Ippitsuan Kako ist er auch als Verfasser humoristischer Novellen bekannt. Anschliessend trat er in die Lehre des Kanô-Meisters Hakkeisai (tätig im frühen 19. Jahrhundert). Eisen soll ein ausschweifendes Leben geführt und zeitweise ein Bordell betrieben haben. In seinem Buch *Aufzeichnungen eines namenlosen alten Mannes (Mumeiô Zuihitsu)* beschreibt er sich selbst als einen rücksichtslosen Trinker und häufigen Besucher von Yoshiwara, dem Freudenviertel in Edo. Neben seinen erotischen Bildern und voluminösen Frauenfiguren wurde Eisen auch mit Landschaftsbildern populär. Die Serie *Stationen der Kisôkai-Strasse (Kisokaidô)* wurde von Eisen begonnen und von Utagawa Hiroshige (1797–1858) abgeschlossen.

Following Utamaro and Eizan, Eisen continued the tradition of *bijin* artists. Eisen came from a respected family of the Fujiwara clan in Edo. His father, Shigeharu, was a poet and artist. After the early death of his parents, Eisen began an apprenticeship with Eizan. Along with individual sheets, from 1811 he created numerous book illustrations, among them, several with erotic content. He is also known as the author of humorous novels under the names Chiyoda Saiichi and Ippitsuan Kako. Subsequently, he entered an apprenticeship with the Kanô master Hakkeisai (active in the early nineteenth century). Eisen is said to have led an extravagant life and have run a brothel for a time. In his book *Miscellany of the Old Man with No Name (Mumeiô Zuihitsu)*, he describes himself as a reckless drinker and frequent visitor to Yoshiwara, the pleasure quarter in Edo. Along with his erotic images and voluminous women's figures, Eisen also became well known for his landscape pictures. Eisen began the *The Sixty-nine Stations of the Kisokaidô (Kisokaidô)* series, which was completed by Utagawa Hiroshige (1797–1858).

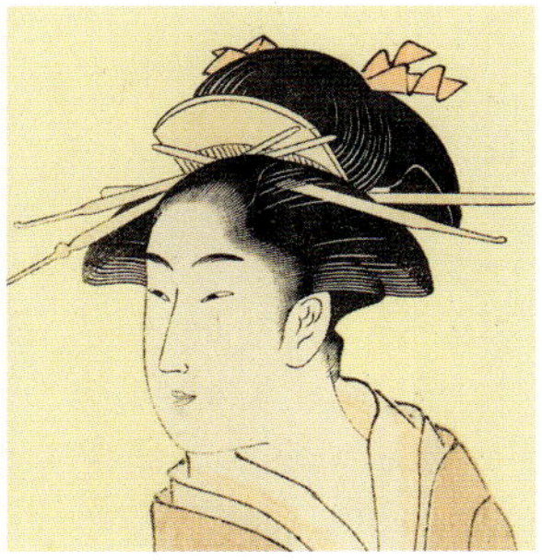

Chôbunsai EISHI 鳥文斎 栄之 1756–1829

Eishi stammte aus einer wohlhabenden Samurai-Familie in Edo. Nach seinem Studium der Malerei unter Kanô Eisen'in Michinobu (1730–1790) trat er eine Stelle als Hausbeamter und Hofmaler im Dienste des Shôguns Ieharu (1737–1786) an. Trotz dieser gesellschaftlich angesehenen Position wandte er sich im Alter von 30 Jahren vom Hofe ab und konzentrierte sich auf den volkstümlichen Farbholzschnitt. Wie Utamaro liebte Eishi die Darstellung von Frauen, entweder von idealisierten Mädchen in idyllischer Umgebung oder von Kurtisanen aus dem Freudenviertel. Seine Frauen strahlen Eleganz und aristokratische Noblesse aus. Erotische Bilder gehörten jedoch ebenso zu seinem Repertoire wie Holzdrucke, die berühmte Legenden thematisierten – z. B. sein Triptychon *Eine Parodie des Ushiwakamaru und der Prinzessin Jôruri* (*Mitate Ushiwaka Jôruri-hime,* KAT. 79). Zu Eishis Vorbildern gehörten Kiyonaga und später Utamaro. Im Jahr 1800 beendete er seine Karriere als Holzschnittkünstler und wandte sich wieder der Malerei zu. Seine Bilder wurden so sehr geschätzt, dass eines seiner Werke in die Sammlung von Kaiserin Go-Sakuramachi (1740–1813) aufgenommen wurde. Zur gleichen Zeit erhielt Eishi den Ehrentitel *jibukyô.*

Eishi came from a wealthy Samurai family in Edo. After painting studies under Kanô Eisen'in Michinobu (1730–1790), he entered a position as royal court painter at the service of Shôgun Ieharu (1737–1786). Despite this socially respected position, he left the court at the age of thirty, and concentrated on folkloric color woodblock printing. Like Utamaro, Eishi loved the depiction of women, either idealized girls in idyllic surroundings or courtesans from the pleasure quarter. His women radiate elegance and aristocratic noblesse. His repertoire includes erotic images as well as woodblock prints thematizing famous legends—e.g., his triptych *A Visual Parody of Ushiwakamaru and Princess Jôruri* (*Mitate Ushiwaka Jôruri-hime,* CAT. 79). Among Eishi's role models were Kiyonaga and later, Utamaro. In 1800, he ended his career as woodblock artist and again turned to painting. His paintings were so highly admired that one of his works was included in the collection of Empress Go-Sakuramachi (1740–1813). At the same time, Eishi received the honorary title *jibukyô.*

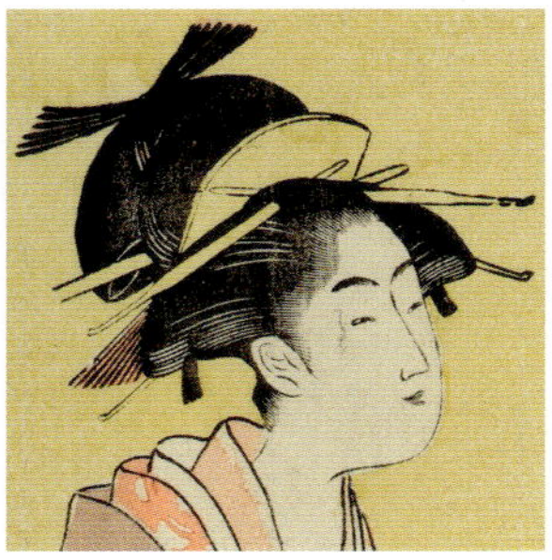

Chôkôsai EISHÔ 鳥高斎 栄昌 tätig/active ca. 1795–1801

Eishô gilt als bedeutendster und produktivster Schüler Eishis. Zwar ist uns sein Œuvre bekannt, zu seinem Leben sind aber keine Informationen überliefert. Er entwarf mindestens 20 Serien zum Thema der schönen Frauen von Yoshiwara und war für 14 Verleger tätig, hauptsächlich für Yamaguchiya Chûsuke. Seine Werke wirken weniger elegant als die seines Meisters, sie sind dafür authentischer und kraftvoller im Ausdruck. Brustbildporträts *(ôkubi-e)* von Schauspielern gehörten ebenso zu seiner Spezialität. Um 1800 entwarf er vorwiegend Buchillustrationen und fertigte einzelne Malereien auf Handrollen an.

Eishô was considered Eishi's most important and productive student. While his oeuvre is known, no information about his life has been handed down. He designed at least twenty series on the theme of beautiful women from Yoshiwara (Edo's pleasure quarter) and worked for fourteen editors, mainly for Yamaguchiya Chûsuke. His works seem less elegant than those of his master, they are, however, more authentic and powerful in their expression. Bust portraits of actors *(ôkubi-e)* were also among his specialties. In ca. 1800, he designed predominantly book illustrations and produced a few paintings on handscrolls.

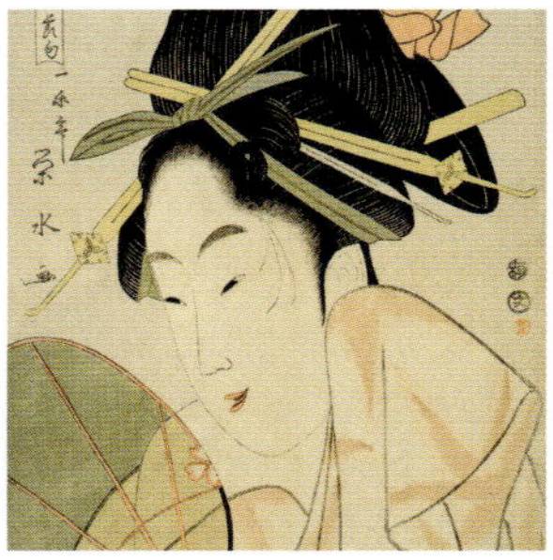

Ichirakutei EISUI 一楽亭 栄水 tätig/active ca. 1795–1823

Die wenigen überlieferten Werke von Eisui zeigen vorwiegend «Bilder schöner Frauen» *(bijinga)* von herausragender Qualität. Leider besitzen wir nur wenige Informationen über sein Leben. Er favorisierte Brustbildporträts *(ôkubi-e)* von berühmten Kurtisanen in der Manier von Utamaro und Eishô. Die Beschriftung seiner Porträts mit den Namen und Adressen der abgebildeten Damen gab seinen Werken ein individuelles Gepräge. Zeitweise signierte er mit dem Namen «Hosoda Eisui», abgeleitet vom Namen seines Lehrers Hosoda Eishi. Zu seinen berühmtesten Werken gehört die Serie *Schönheiten der fünf jahreszeitlichen Feste* (*Bijin gosekku,* KAT. 83), bei der Eisui die Abbilder berühmter Kurtisanen den fünf grossen Feiertagen in Japan zuordnete.

The few works from Eisui that have been handed down show primarily "images of beautiful women" *(bijinga)* of outstanding quality. Unfortunately, we have little information about his life. He favored bust portraits *(ôkubi-e)* of famous courtesans in the manner of Utamaro and Eishô. The signing of his portraits with the names and addresses of the depicted women gave his works an individual imprint. At times, he signed with the name "Hosoda Eisui," derived from the name of his teacher Hosoda Eishi. Among his most famous works is the *Beauties of the Five Festivals* (*Bijin gosekku,* CAT. 83) series, in which Eisui arranges images of famous courtesans thematically according to the five major holidays in Japan.

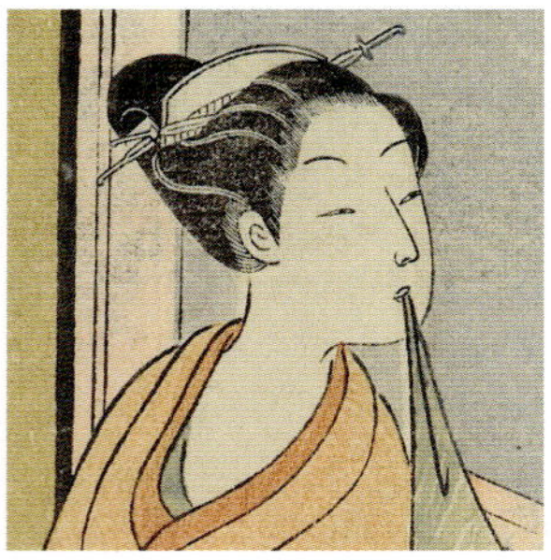

Suzuki HARUNOBU 鈴木 春信 1725?–1770

Harunobu gehörte zu den bedeutendsten Holzschnittkünstlern seiner Zeit. Er trug entscheidend zur Entwicklung des Vielfarbendrucks *(nishiki-e)* bei, der um 1765 seinen Höhepunkt erreichte. Über Harunobus Geburtsort und seine ersten Lebensjahre wissen wir nur wenig. Es wird angenommen, dass Harunobu seine Ausbildung zunächst unter Nishimura Shigenaga in Edo begann. Ebenfalls übte wohl Kyoto-Meister Sukenobu starken Einfluss auf sein Werk aus. Er war ein Maler der «schönen Frauen», der *bijinga.* Harunobu stellte sowohl Damen der Halbwelt, bürgerliche Frauen im Alltagsleben als auch Frauen in mythologischen Szenen dar. Er wählte gerne berühmte Schönheiten aus dem Freudenviertel Yoshiwara als Modelle. Seine Damen weisen stets schlanke Hälse, lieblich-mädchenhafte Gesichter und zierliche Gliedmassen auf. Ihre s-förmig geschwungenen Körper wirken jugendlich, fast knabenhaft. Die Szenerien wirken wie aus einem Traum entnommen, betont durch ein Wolkenband, das häufig als Kartusche am oberen Rand der Bilder zu sehen ist. 1764 erhielt Harunobu den Auftrag, Entwürfe für Bildkalender *(egoyomi)* zu liefern, die später von dem Verleger Shokakudo in den Handel gebracht wurden. Danach folgten Aufträge von verschiedenen Dichter- und Künstlerzirkeln in Edo für die Produktion von Neujahrs- und Glückwunschkarten. Er verwendete dabei kostbare Materialien und trieb die Entwicklung des Vielfarbendrucks voran: Anstatt zwei oder drei Farben benutzte Harunobu eine ganze Farbpalette für seine Bilder. Als die Nachfrage nach Bildkalendern zurückging, richtete Harunobu seinen Fokus auf die Produktion von «Bildern mit Parodien» *(mitate-e)*. In den Beispielen KAT. 18 und KAT. 10 bediente er sich des beliebten Themas der «Sechsunddreissig Unsterblichen der Dichtkunst» *(Sanjû rokkasen)* und ersetzte jeden Dichter durch eine Kurtisane aus Yoshiwara. Daneben beschäftigte er sich mit erotischen Szenen *(shunga)*, Schauspielerporträts *(yakusha-e)*, Buchillustrationen *(e-hon)* und fertigte auch Malereien an.

Harunobu was among the most significant woodblock artists of his era. He contributed decisively to the development of the multicolor print *(nishiki-e)*, which had its heyday in 1765. We know little about Harunobu's place of birth and the first years of his life. It is assumed that Harunobu began his education under Nishimura Shigenaga in Edo. Kyoto master Sukenobu, a painter of "beautiful women," *bijinga,* also certainly had a strong influence on his work. Harunobu depicted women of the underworld, bourgeois women in everyday life, as well as women in mythological scenes. He liked to choose famous beauties from Yoshiwara, Edo's pleasure quarter, as models. His women always have slender necks, smooth, girl-like faces and dainty limbs. Their S-shaped, curved bodies appear youthful, almost boyish. The scenes seem as though taken from a dream, emphasized by a band of clouds, often visible as a cartridge on the upper edge of the pictures. In 1764, Harunobu was commissioned to deliver designs for calendar pictures *(egoyomi)*, which were later brought to the market by the publisher Shokakudo. Afterward, he received commissions from various poet and artist circles in Edo for the production of New Year's and greeting cards. He used valuable materials for this, and pushed forth the development of multicolor print: rather than two or three colors, Harunobu used an entire palette of colors for his pictures. When the demand for picture calendars waned, Harunobu turned his focus to the production of "pictures of parodies" *(mitate-e)*. In the examples, CAT. 18 and CAT. 10, he used the favorite theme of the "Thirty-six Immortal Poets" *(Sanjû rokkasen)* and replaced every poet with a courtesan from Yoshiwara. In addition, he was occupied with erotic images *(shunga)*, actor portraits *(yakusha-e)*, and illustrated bound images *(e-hon)*, as well as painting.

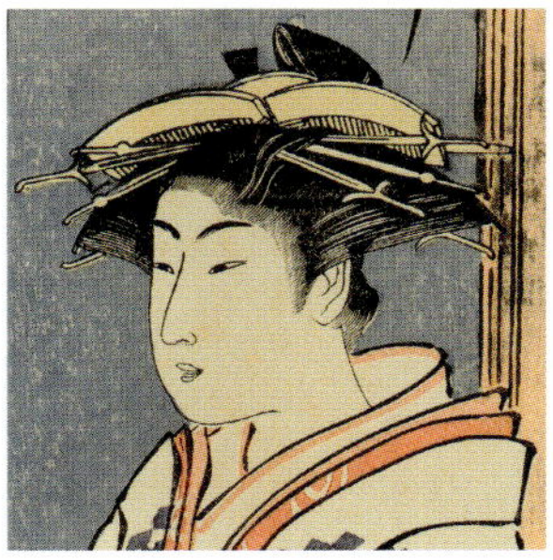

Torii KIYONAGA 鳥居 清長 1752–1815

Als Sohn eines Buchhändlers interessierte sich Kiyonaga bereits mit 14 Jahren für die Druckkunst. Seine Ausbildung begann unter Torii Kiyomitsu (1735–1785), der zur dritten Generation der Torii-Schule, der führenden Werkstatt von Theaterplakaten und Schauspielerporträts, gehörte. Am Anfang seiner Karriere konzentrierte sich Kiyonaga vorzugsweise auf die Darstellung von *kabuki*-Schauspielern, die er während seiner häufigen Besuche der nahen Theaterhäuser Ichimura und Nakamura porträtierte. Ebenso fertigte er ab 1771 zahlreiche Illustrationen für Theaterprogrammhefte *(e-banzuke)* an. Obwohl die Nachfrage an Theaterplakaten und Schauspielerporträts enorm stieg und sie zu Kiyonagas Spezialität gehörten, richtete er sein Augenmerk im Verlauf seiner weiteren Karriere auf die Produktion von «Bildern schöner Frauen» *(bijinga)*. Während der 1780er-Jahre wurde Kiyonaga zum führenden Künstler dieser Gattung und schuf Ganzkörperporträts auf Einzelblättern im *hashira*- und *ôban*-Format und später auch mehrteilige Kompositionen als *ôban*-Diptychen und -Triptychen. Seine Schönheiten waren von hochgewachsener Statur mit eher klein proportionierten Köpfen. Der allgemeine Trend zu mehr Naturalismus und grösseren Figurengruppen in einer realistischen Raumkulisse ist in seinen Werken deutlich spürbar (KAT. 47). Nach dem Tod seines Lehrers Kiyomitsu übernahm Kiyonaga dessen Werkstatt und widmete sich wieder stärker der Gestaltung von Theaterplakaten. In seinen letzten 20 Schaffensjahren, als Utamaro das Feld der Holzschnittkunst dominierte, beendete Kiyonaga die Produktion von grossformatigen Einzeldrucken und beschränkte sich nur noch auf Gedichtblätter *(surimono)*, Malereien und Buchillustrationen.

Kiyonaga, the son of a book dealer, was already interested in print art at the age of fourteen. His training began under Torii Kiyomitsu (1735–1785), who belonged to the third generation of the Torii School, the leading workshop for theater posters and actor portraits. At the start of his career, Kiyonaga chose to concentrate on the depiction of *kabuki*-actors, whom he portrayed during his frequent visits to the close-by theater houses Ichimura and Nakamura. Beginning in 1771, he also completed numerous images for illustrated theater programs *(e-banzuke)*. Although the demand for theater posters and actor portraits increased enormously and they were among Kiyonaga's specialties, in the course of his further career, he turned his attention to the production of "images of beautiful women" *(bijinga)*. During the 1780s, Kiyonaga became the leading artist in this genre and created full body portraits on individual sheets in *hashira* and *ôban* formats and later, also multipart compositions as *ôban* diptychs and triptychs. His beauties were of tall stature with rather small proportioned heads. The general trend to more naturalism and larger figure groups in a realistic, three-dimensional setting is clearly noticeable in his works (CAT. 47). After the death of his teacher Kiyomitsu, Kiyonaga took over his workshop and again dedicated himself more to the design of theater posters. During his last twenty years of production, a time when Utamaro dominated the field of woodblock art, Kiyonaga ceased producing large-format individual prints and restricted himself to poem sheets *(surimono)*, paintings, and book illustrations.

Isoda KORYÛSAI 礒田 湖龍斎 1735–1790

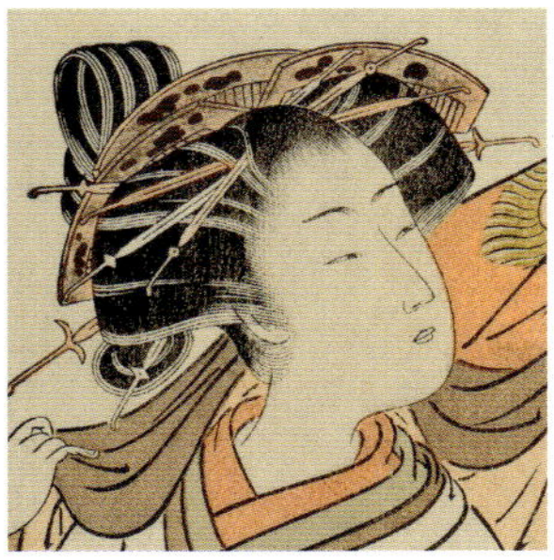

Koryûsai stammte aus einer angesehenen Samurai-Sippe. Erst 1768, nach dem Tod seines Lehensfürsten, liess er sich als *rônin,* «herrenloser Samurai», in Edo nieder und wandte sich der *ukiyo-e*-Kunst zu. Bis 1771 nannte er sich Haruhiro, was auf eine enge berufliche Beziehung zwischen ihm und dem Künstler Harunobu hindeutet. Von seinen ca. 600 Holzdrucken beschäftigen sich die meisten mit Kurtisanen- und Schauspielerporträts. Gegen Ende der 1770er-Jahre schuf er seine typischen Modeblätter im grossen *ôban*-Format mit dem Sujet eines sehr urbanen realistischen Frauentyps. Seine imposante Serie *Neue Muster, so frisch wie junge Blätter* (*Hinagata wakana no hatsu moyô,* KAT. 33) mit über 140 Seiten zeigt berühmte Kurtisanen des Freudenviertels Yoshiwara mit ihren jungen Begleiterinnen. Die Betonung der Gewänder, kunstvolle Frisuren und eine kraftvolle Zeichnung der Figuren auf leerem Grund sind charakteristisch für sein Spätwerk. Von allen japanischen Holzschnittkünstlern hat Koryûsai die meisten «Pfostenbilder» *(hashira-e)* gestaltet, schmale Hochformate, mit denen man die Holzpfeiler der Häuser schmückte.

Koryûsai came from a prestigious Samurai clan. First in 1768, after the death of his feudal master, he settled down as a rônin, "masterless Samurai," in Edo and turned to *ukiyo-e* art. Until 1771 he called himself Haruhiro, which indicates his close professional relationship to the artist Harunobu. Most of his roughly 600 woodblock prints are courtesan and actor portraits. Towards the end of the 1770s, he created his typical fashion sheets in large *ôban* format with the figure of a very urban, realistic woman as subject. His imposing series *Models for Fashion: New Designs as Fresh as Young Leaves* (*Hinagata wakana no hatsu moyô,* CAT. 33) with more than 140 sheets, showed famous courtesans from Yoshiwara, Edo's pleasure quarter, with their young companions. The emphasis on clothing, elaborate hair-dos, and a powerful drawing of the figures against an empty background are characteristic of his later work. Koryûsai was the most productive of the Japanese woodblock artists in designing "pillar prints" *(hashira-e)*, a narrow tall format with which one decorated the wooden pillars of houses.

Utagawa KUNIMASA I 歌川 国政 1773–1810

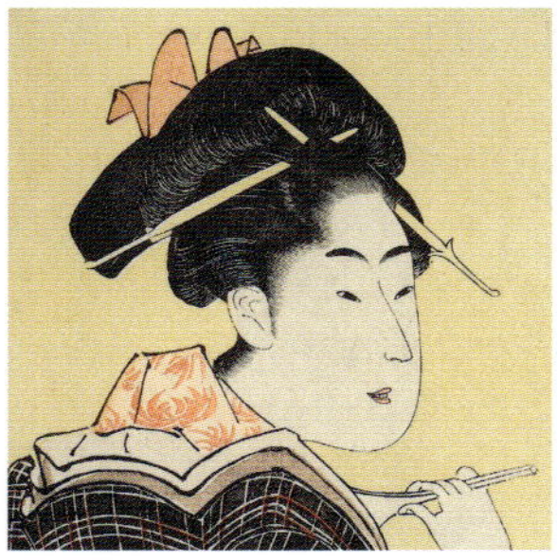

Ursprünglich absolvierte Kunimasa eine Lehre als Färber in Edo, bevor er im Alter von 15 Jahren einer der ersten Schüler Toyokunis wurde. Neben «Bildern schöner Frauen» *(bijinga)* und Buchillustrationen *(e-hon)* entwarf er auch Schauspielerporträts *(yakusha-e)*. Besonders eindrücklich sind seine Brustbildporträts *(ôkubi-e)* aus der Zeit um 1795, herausgegeben vom bekannten Verleger Uemura Yohei. Diese Porträts scheinen die ausdrucksstarke Kraft und Intensität der Bilder von Sharaku und die Feinheit der Figuren Toyokunis zu vereinen. Gegen Ende seiner Karriere fertigte er Schnitzvorlagen für Masken des *kabuki*-Theaters an.

Kunimasa completed his training as a dyer in Edo before becoming one of Toyokuni's first students at the age of fifteen. Along with "images of beautiful women" *(bijinga)* and illustrated bound works *(e-hon)*, he also designed actor portraits *(yakusha-e)*. Particularly impressive are his bust portraits *(ôkubi-e)* from ca. 1795, printed by the well-known publisher Uemura Yohei. These portraits seem to unite the expressive power and intensity of Sharaku's images with the fineness of Toyokuni's figures. Towards the end of his career, Kunimasa made cutting patterns for *kabuki* theater masks.

Utagawa KUNISADA I 歌川 国貞 1786–1865

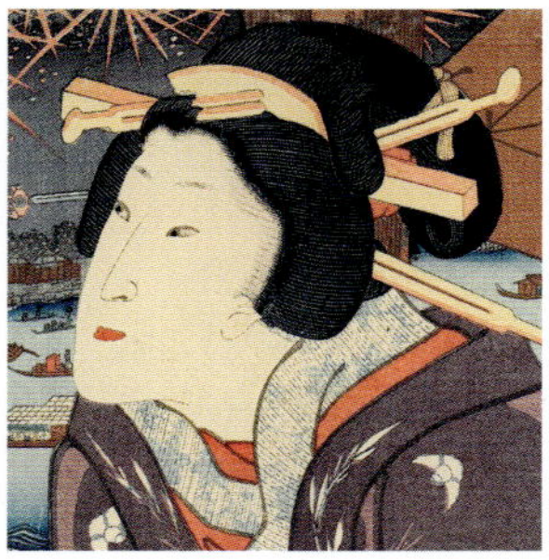

Mit mehr als 20 000 Entwürfen gehört Kunisada zu den produktivsten und kommerziell erfolgreichsten Vertretern des japanischen Farbholzschnitts. Unter seinem Lehrer Toyokuni I (1769–1825) erlernte er das Genre der *kabuki*-Illustrationen und der Schauspielerporträts. Ab 1844 signierte er fortan unter dem Namen seines verstorbenen Lehrers Toyokuni (III) und leitete insgesamt über 40 Jahre die Utagawa-Schule. Obwohl *bijin*-Drucke nur etwa ein Fünftel seines Gesamtwerkes ausmachen, war ihre Gesamtzahl weit höher als bei jedem anderen Künstler seiner Zeit. Im Einklang mit dem jeweils aktuellen Publikumsgeschmack entwickelte er seinen Stil entweder weiter oder änderte ihn radikal. Viele damalige japanische Holzschnittkünstler orientierten sich an seinen stilistischen Vorgaben. Als Zeichen der Anerkennung seines Schaffens wurden zu seinem Tod gleich vier Gedächtnisbilder von verschiedenen Verlegern herausgegeben. Seine Schüler, darunter Kunichika, Kunisada II, Sadahide oder Kunihisa II, führten seine Drucktradition in der nachfolgenden Meiji-Zeit (1868–1912) fort.

With more than 20,000 designs, Kunisada was among the most productive and commercially successful representatives of Japanese color woodblock printing. Under his teacher Toyokuni I (1769–1825), he learned the genres of *kabuki* illustrations and actor portraits. After 1844, he continued to sign under the name of his deceased teacher

Toyokuni III and altogether ran the Utagawa School for more than forty years. Although *bijin* prints comprise only roughly a fifth of his oeuvre, their total number is much greater than for any other artist of his era. In keeping pace with the tastes of his audience, he either further developed or radically changed his style. Many Japanese woodcut artists at the time oriented themselves on his stylistic standards. Upon his death, four commemorative images were printed by different publishers as a sign of recognition of his work. His students, among them Kunichika, Kunisada II, Sadahide, and Kunihisa II, continued his printing tradition in the subsequent Meiji period (1868–1912).

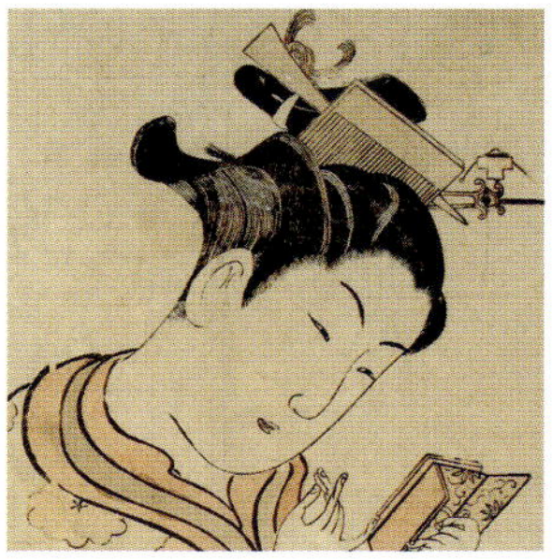

Okumura MASANOBU 奥村 政信 1686–1764

Masanobu war der Begründer der von ihm benannten Okumura-Schule, die für den Holzschnitt seiner Zeit von zentraler Bedeutung war. In Masanobus Schaffenszeit fällt die Entwicklung des Holzschnitts vom Schwarzdruck *(sumizuri-e)* bis hin zum Vielfarbendruck *(nishiki-e)*, die er im Laufe von 50 Jahren massgeblich beeinflusste. Darüber hinaus gilt Masanobu als Erfinder der «Pfostenbilder» *(hashira-e)*, eines schmalen Hochformats. Er studierte Dichtung unter Tachiba Fukaku (1662–1753) und arbeitete zuerst als Buchverleger und Grosshändler, bis er sich der Malerei zuwandte. Sein Werk widmet sich den verschiedensten Themen: Heldensagen, Theater, Leben in den Freudenhäusern, Tiere und Landschaften. Seine «Perspektivbilder» *(uki-e)*, die wohl der Betrachtung in einem Guckkasten dienten, zeigen in der besonderen Betonung der Perspektive einen europäischen Einfluss. Unter seinen vielen Entwürfen galten die «Bilder schöner Frauen» als überaus modisch und populär, sodass sie häufig mit gefälschter Signatur nachgeahmt wurden. Masanobu versuchte sich mit besonders ausführlichen und langen Signaturen seiner Bilder dagegen zu wehren (KAT. 4).

Masanobu was the founder of the Okumura School, which was named for him, and was seminal in the area of woodblock printing. During Masanobu's productive years woodblock developed from black-ink print *(sumizuri-e)* to multicolor print *(nishiki-e)*, a change that Masanobu influenced significantly over the course of fifty years. Beyond that, Masanobu was considered the inventor of the "pillar print" *(hashira-e)*, a tall, narrow format. He studied poetry under Tachiba Fukaku (1662–1753) and worked initially as a book publisher and retailer, until he turned to painting. His work is devoted to extremely diverse themes: hero legends, theater, life in the brothels, animals, and landscapes. His "perspective prints" *(uki-e)*, which were probably used for viewing in a zograscope, display a European influence in their special emphasis on perspective. Among his many designs, the "images of beautiful women" are considered extremely fashionable and popular; they are thus frequently copied with forged signatures. In an effort to protect his pictures from this, Masanobu used especially elaborate and long signatures (CAT. 4).

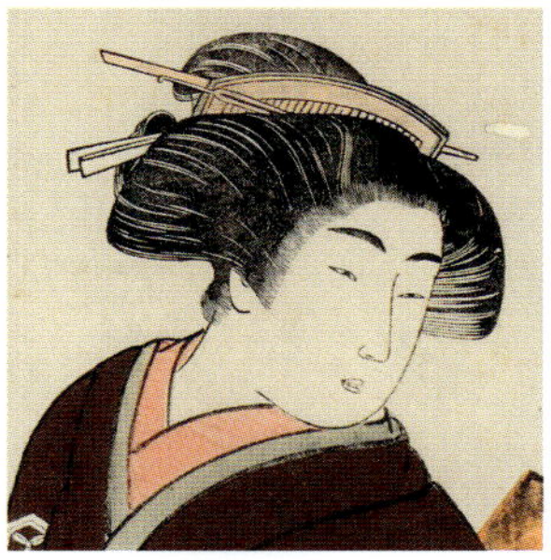

Kitao SHIGEMASA 北尾 重政 1739–1820

Der Vater von Shigemasa war Suharaya Mohei, ein bekannter Buchhändler und Verleger im Nihonbashi-Viertel von Edo. Shigemasa erlernte die Kunst der Malerei im Selbststudium, bevor er in die Lehre bei Nishimura Shigenaga eintrat. Seine ersten Zweifarbendrucke *(benizuri-e)* weisen Parallelen zu den Werken von Torii Kiyomitsu auf. Shigemasas frühe Frauenporträts zeigen Bezüge zu den Werken von Harunobu und Koryûsai, später entwickelte er jedoch einen eigenständigen Stil. Seine Karriere wurde insbesondere durch seine zahlreichen Buchillustrationen geprägt, die er teilweise in Kollaboration mit Shunshô und dem renommierten Verleger Tsutaya Jûzaburô produzierte. Berühmtestes Beispiel ist sein Werk *Auswahl von Schönheiten aus Yoshiwara: der Vergleich ihres Aussehens im Spiegel* (*Seirô bijin awase sugata kagami,* 3 Bd. 1776). Dieses Werk gilt als eines der frühesten gedruckten «Bücher mit Illustrationen» *(e-hon)* in der Tradition der «Bilder der fliessenden Welt» *(ukiyo-e)*.

Shigemasa's father was Suharaya Mohei, a well-known book dealer and publisher in the Nihonbashi quarter of Edo. Shigemasa learned the art of painting in self study before embarking on an apprenticeship with Nishimura Shigenaga. His first two-color prints *(benizuri-e)* reveal parallels to works by Torii Kiyomitsu. Shigemasa's early portraits of women show references to works by Harunobu and Koryûsai, however he later developed his own independent style. His career was shaped especially by his numerous book illustrations, which he produced, in part, in collaboration with Shunshô and the renowned publisher Jûzaburô. The most well-known example is his work *A Mirror Reflecting the Forms of Fair Women of the Green-Houses* (*Seirô bijin awase sugata kagami,* 3 vol. 1776). This work is considered one of the earliest printed "illustrated bound books" *(e-hon)* in the "images of the floating world" *(ukiyo-e)* tradition.

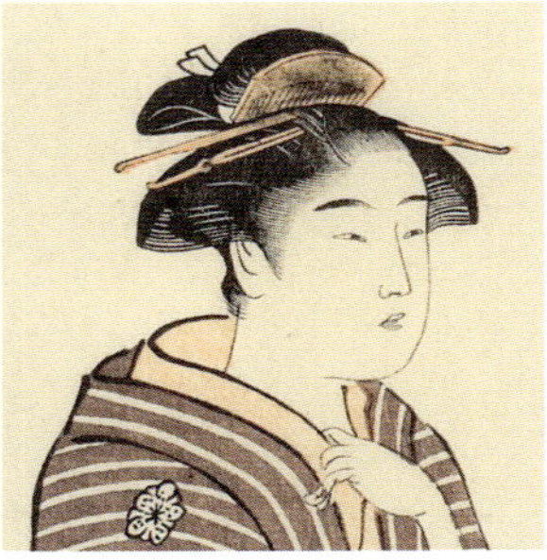

Katsukawa SHUNCHÔ 勝川 春潮 tätig/active ca. 1781–1801

Als Schüler von Shunshô (1726–1793) trat Shunchô in jungen Jahren in die Katsukawa-Schule ein. Ungewöhnlich für ein Mitglied dieser Schule produzierte Shunchô aber keinerlei Schauspielerporträts, sondern vorwiegend *bijinga,* «Bilder schöner Frauen». Unter seinen Werken stechen besonders seine zahlreichen Triptychen und «Pfostenbilder» hervor. Seine dargestellten Frauen zeigen in ihrer Statur und Eleganz starke Ähnlichkeit zu denjenigen des Künstlers Kiyonaga. Neben Frauenporträts schuf Shunchô zahlreiche Erotika *(shunga)*, «Buchillustrationen für Scherzgedichte» *(kyôka-bon)* und «satirische Erzählungen» *(kibyôshi)*.

As Shunshô's (1726–1793) student, Shunchô entered the Katsukawa School at a young age. Unusual for a member of this school, Shunchô did not produce any actor portraits, but instead, mainly *bijinga,* "images of beautiful women." Prominent among his works are, especially, his numerous triptychs and "pillar prints." The women he depicted show a resemblance to those of the artist Kiyonaga in terms of their stature and elegance. Along with portraits of women, Shunchô also created numerous erotica *(shun-ga)*, "book illustrations for joke poems" *(kyôka-bon)* and "satirical tales" *(kibyôshi)*.

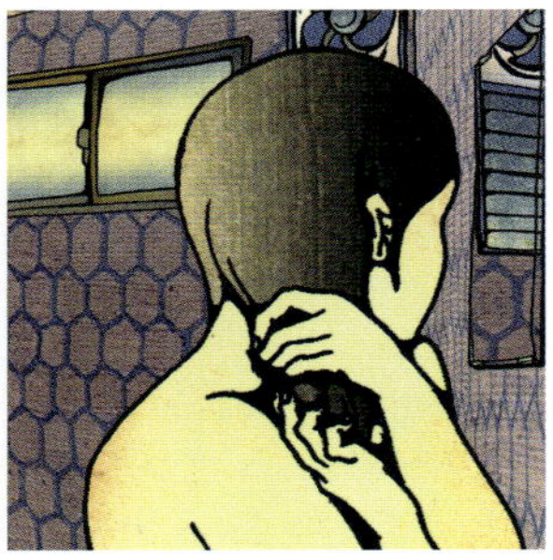

TABAIMO 束芋 geb./b. 1975

Tabaimo ist der Künstlername, unter dem Tabata Ayako, die zweite Tochter einer Keramikerin, bekannt geworden ist. Dieser Name geht zurück auf ihren Spitznamen aus der Schulzeit und ist eine Kontraktion aus ihrem Familiennamen *Taba*ta und dem japanischen Wort für jüngere Schwester, *imo*to.

Tabaimo malte bereits im Alter von sechs Jahren buddhistische Bilder. Ihre unverkennbare zeichnerische Begabung bewog sie dazu, an der Universität Kyoto für Kunst und Design bei Tanaami Keiichi (geb. 1936) Informationsdesign zu studieren. Für ihre Diplomarbeit, die Videoinstallation *Japanese Kitchen* von 1999, wurde sie mit namhaften Preisen ausgezeichnet. Mit Einzelausstellungen in Paris, New York und Stockholm hat sich Tabaimo in den letzten zehn Jahren als international anerkannte Künstlerin etabliert. An der 54. Kunstbiennale von Venedig 2011 war sie die offizielle Vertreterin Japans im Länderpavillon.

In ihren Arbeiten bevorzugt Tabaimo Schauplätze, die in der japanischen Alltagskultur wichtige Berührungspunkte zwischen dem öffentlichen und dem privaten Leben darstellen, wie z. B. den Pendlerzug, das öffentliche Badehaus oder die öffentliche Toilette, wobei die Verschlossenheit oder Gleichgültigkeit des modernen Menschen in solchen Situationen thematisiert wird. Mit ihrer seltsamen, fast unheimlichen Bildsprache und ihrem unübersehbar gesellschaftskritischen Ansatz scheinen Tabaimos Videoinstallationen auf den ersten Blick zur Tradition des *ukiyo-e* in Kontrast zu stehen. Und doch ist Tabaimo eine der wenigen zeitgenössischen Künstlerinnen, deren Auseinandersetzung mit dem *ukiyo-e* bezüglich Farbgebung und Textur besonders augenfällig ist.

Zuerst zeichnet sie jedes einzelne Motiv von Hand, anschliessend werden mehrere Tausend Zeichnungen eingescannt und mithilfe einer *ukiyo-e*-Farbpalette – beispielsweise basierend auf einer Serie von Katsushika Hokusai (1760–1849) – koloriert. Daraus entsteht eine Reihe digital bearbeiteter Zeichnungen, die sich zu einem Zeichentrickfilm zusammenfügen. Die mit Sorgfalt und Ausdauer erarbeiteten Werke Tabaimos stützen sich auf die charakteristischen und subtilen Farbtöne des *ukiyo-e,* die aus pflanzlichen und mineralischen Farbstoffen hergestellt wurden. So wird dann z. B. ein leichtes, helles Orange der Abenddämmerung des *ukiyo-e* (KAT. 64) für die Hauttöne der Menschen verwendet oder eine blaue Gradation einer Wasseroberfläche (KAT. 93) für ein Kleidungsstück, für Möbel oder den Hintergrund. Mit ihrer Vorliebe für traditionelle japanische Farben aus der Natur versucht Tabaimo, den Bildern eine wärmere Textur zu verleihen, die im (japanischen) Betrachter eine gewisse Nostalgie und Sehnsucht nach der Vergangenheit hervorruft.

Die Kombination der traditionellen Farbpalette des *ukiyo-e* mit den merkwürdigen Handlungen des modernen Menschen erzeugt einen Verfremdungseffekt, der für Tabaimos Arbeiten charakteristisch ist.

Tabaimo is the artist's name under which Tabata Ayako, the second daughter of a ceramicist, has attained fame. This name goes back to the nickname she had in her school days and is a contraction of her family name, *Taba*ta, and the Japanese word for little sister, *imo*to.

Tabaimo painted Buddhist images already at the age of six. Her unmistakable drawing talent inspired her to study information design under Tanaami Keiichi (b. 1936) at the University of Kyoto for Art and Design. Her undergraduate thesis, the video installation *Japanese Kitchen,* 1999, earned her several prestigious awards. Over the past ten years, Tabaimo has established herself as an internationally renowned artist with solo exhibitions in Paris, New York, and Stockholm. At the 54th Venice Biennale in 2011, she was Japan's official representative in its national pavilion.

In her works, Tabaimo prefers scenes that represent important contact points between public and private life in everyday Japanese culture, for example, the commuter train, public bath houses, or toilets, whereby she thematizes the modern person's reticence or indifference in such situations. With her strange, almost uncanny visual language and her clearly socio-critical approach, at first glance, Tabaimo's video installations seem to contrast with the *ukiyo-e* tradition. Yet Tabaimo is one of the few contemporary artists whose confrontation with *ukiyo-e,* in terms of coloring and texture, is particularly striking.

She first draws every single motif by hand, then several thousand drawings are scanned in and colored using an *ukiyo-e* color palette—for example, based on one of Katsushika Hokusai (1760–1849)'s series. From that, a series of digitally processed drawings emerges, which coalesce to an animated cartoon. Tabaimo's carefully and patiently crafted works, are based on the *ukiyo-e*'s characteristic, subtle color tones, which were produced from plant and mineral dyes. A light, pale orange of dusk in *ukiyo-e* (CAT. 64), for example, is thus used for the skin tones of people; or a shade of blue on the water's surface (CAT. 93) for a piece of clothing, furniture, or the background. With her preference for traditional Japanese colors from nature, Tabaimo attempts to lend the images a warmer texture, which evokes a certain nostalgia and yearning for the past in the (Japanese) beholder.

The combination of a traditional *ukiyo-e* color palette with the modern person's peculiar behavior generates an alienating effect, which is characteristic of Tabaimo's works.

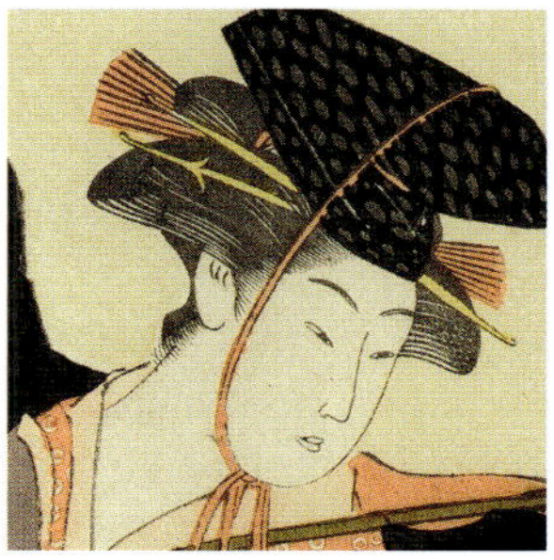

Utagawa TOYOKUNI I 歌川 豊国 1769–1825

Toyokuni war um 1800 der unübertroffene Meister der Schauspielerporträts *(yakusha-e)*. Als Sohn eines Puppenschnitzers begann er seine künstlerische Karriere unter Utagawa Toyoharu (1735–1814), dem Begründer der Utagawa-Schule. Mit seiner zwischen 1794 und 1796 veröffentlichten Serie *Lebensnahe Bilder von Schauspielern auf der Bühne (Yakusha butai no sugata-e)*, die Schauspieler sowohl auf wie auch hinter der Bühne zeigt, hatte er durchschlagenden Erfolg und verhalf der Utagawa-Schule endgültig zur Monopolstellung in der Produktion von Theaterdrucken. Erste Darstellungen weiblicher Schönheiten erschienen von Toyokuni bereits im Jahr 1790. Es dauerte jedoch einige Jahre, bis er auf diesem Gebiet seinen typischen Stil entwickelte. In seinen späteren Drucken (KAT. 84) verschwand die strenge Linienführung, und seine Frauen wirken lebendig und lebensnah. Unter seinen zahlreichen Schülern waren vor allem Kunisada und Kuniyoshi bedeutend.

Toyokuni was the unsurpassable master of actor portraits *(yakusha-e)* around 1800. As the son of a puppet carver, he began his artistic career under Utagawa Toyoharu (1735–1814), founder of the Utagawa School. He had sweeping success with his series published between 1794 and 1796, *Pictures of Actors on the Stage (Yakusha butai no sugata-e)*, which depicted actors both on and behind the stage, and thereby helped the Utagawa School to finally reach a monopoly position in the production of theater prints. Toyokuni's first depictions of women beauties appeared already in 1790. However, it took several years until he developed his characteristic style in this area. In his later prints (CAT. 84), the strict, classical lines disappear and his women seem lively and realistic. Eminent among his numerous students were Kunisada and Kuniyoshi.

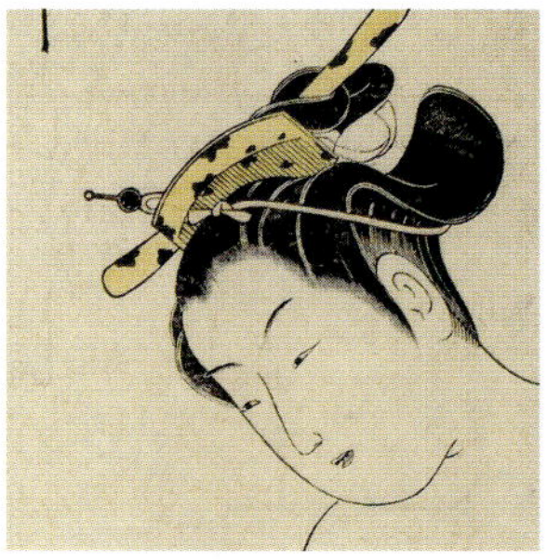

Ishikawa TOYONOBU 石川 豊信 1711–1785

Toyonobu gehört zu den repräsentativen Künstlern des Zweifarbendrucks *(benizuri-e)* zwischen 1740 und 1765. Er war Schüler von Shigenaga, der neben Masanobu den grössten Einfluss auf sein Schaffen ausübte. Seine künstlerische Karriere begann in der Kanpô-Ära (1741–1744) mit Entwürfen für «Lackdrucke» *(urushi-e)* häufig in Form von handkolorierten «Pfostenbildern». Die weiblichen Figuren in seinen frühen Werken zeichnen sich durch runde Körperformen und klassische Gesichter aus. Seine Zweifarbendrucke bestechen durch einen feinen Grün-Grundton. Bilder nach 1760 offenbaren eine Tendenz hin zu schlankeren und kleineren Frauentypen. Liebesszenen, Kurtisanen, Schauspieler und Puppenspieler gehörten zu seinen beliebtesten Motiven. Wie sein Lehrer experimentierte auch Toyonobu mit der Darstellung des nackten Körpers. In sogenannten «gewagten Drucken» *(abuna-e)* stellt er spärlich bekleidete Damen dar wie z. B. in den Bildern von Frauen nach dem Bad (KAT. 3). Seine Karriere endete schlagartig mit dem Aufkommen des Vielfarbendrucks *(nishiki-e)* in der Meiwa-Ära (1764–1772) und dem Erfolg der Bilder des Künstlers Harunobu.

Toyonobu was among the representative artists of two-color prints *(benizuri-e)* between 1740 and 1765. He was a student of Shigenaga, who in addition to Masanobu, had the greatest influence on his production. His artistic career began in the Kanpô period (1741–1744) with designs for "lacquer pictures" *(urushi-e)* frequently in the form of

hand-colored "pillar prints." The female figures in his early works are distinguished by their round body forms and classical faces. His two-color prints captivate through a fine green base tone. Images after 1760 reveal a tendency toward more slender and smaller women characters. Love scenes, courtesans, actors, and puppeteers are among his favorite motifs. Like his teacher, Toyonobu also experimented with the depiction of the naked body. In so-called "risqué pictures" *(abuna-e)*, he depicted sparsely clad women, for example, in the images of women after the bath (CAT. 3). His career ended abruptly with the rise of the multicolor print *(nishiki-e)* in the Meiwa period (1764–1772) and the success of images by the artist Harunobu.

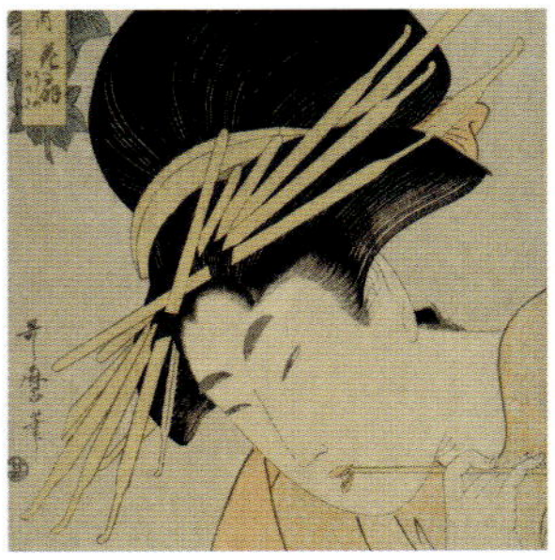

Kitagawa UTAMARO 喜多川 歌麿 1753–1806

Kein anderer Holzschnittkünstler hat sich so konsequent und mit solchem Erfolg der Darstellung von Frauen gewidmet wie Utamaro. Nach dem Tod des Vaters zog Utamaro aus der Provinz Musashi nach Edo, wo er 1775 in der Werkstatt des Stadtmalers Sekien seine Lehre zum Holzschnittkünstler begann. Zunächst fertigte er Illustrationen zu *kabuki*-Stücken und zu Gedichten an, später folgten Schauspielerporträts im Stil Shunshôs. Der bedeutende Verleger Tsutaya Jûzaburô erkannte seine Begabung und nahm ihn 1780 in sein Haus am Eingang des Stadtteils Yoshiwara auf, das zum Treffpunkt von Künstlern und Dichtern wurde. Kiyonaga, einer von Utamaros Zeitgenossen, hat ihn am meisten beeinflusst. Utamaro versuchte, die Psyche der dargestellten Frauen in seine Porträts einfliessen zu lassen, und versah sie mit einem Hauch Erotik. Herausragend sind seine Abbilder berühmter Kurtisanen von Yoshiwara. Auf diesen Blättern war ein anmutiger, äusserst schlanker und eleganter Frauentypus mit herabfallenden Gewändern zu sehen (KAT. 52). Nicht nur die raffinierten Bildkompositionen, sondern auch der gekonnte Umgang mit der Technik, z. B. die Kombination verschiedener Druckverfahren, kennzeichnen die hohe Qualität seiner Werke. Utamaro verwendete mit Vorliebe frische, helle Farben, häufig auf Glimmergrund und mit Gold- oder Perlmuttstaub bestreut (KAT. 70). Frauen im Alltag, beim Schminken, Baden oder Frisieren, beim Spaziergang im Garten, Mütter mit Kindern, Kurtisanen oder Liebespaare waren seine bevorzugten Motive. Ausserdem gestaltete er viele Alben, darunter hervorragende naturkundliche Bilderbücher mit Insekten, Muscheln, Pflanzen, Vögeln und Landschaften, sowie zahlreiche erotische Buchillustrationen. Kurz vor seinem Tod kam Utamaro 1804 in Konflikt mit der Zensur. Wegen eines Triptychons mit historischen Motiven, in denen man eine Satire auf das Leben am Hof der Shôgun zu entdecken glaubte, geriet er in Haft und erhielt 50 Tage Hausarrest mit Handschellen. Neben Hokusai gehörte Utamaro zu den ersten japanischen Künstlern, die auch in Europa bekannt wurden. Der Maler Toulouse-Lautrec war einer seiner Bewunderer. 1891 veröffentlichte der französische Schriftsteller und Kunstkritiker Edmond de Goncourt in Paris die erste Monografie über ihn.

No other woodblock artist was so consistently and successfully devoted to the depiction of women as Utamaro. After the death of his father, Utamaro moved from the Musashi province to Edo, where he began his apprenticeship as a woodblock artist in the workshop of city painter Sekien in 1775. At first he made illustrations for *kabuki* plays and poems, later he produced actor portraits in the style of Shunshô. The distinguished publisher Tsutaya Jûzaburô recognized his talent and in 1780 took him into his house at the entrance to the Yoshiwara quarter, which had become a meeting point for artists and poets. Kiyonaga, one of Utamaro's contemporaries, was his greatest influence. Utamaro attempted to allow the psyche of the depicted women to flow into his portraits, and furnished them with a slightly erotic touch. His portrayals of famous courtesans from Yoshiwara are outstanding. Visible on these sheets was a more graceful, extremely slender, and more elegant woman character with falling garments (CAT. 52). Hallmarks of his work's high quality are the refined pictorial composition, and also the skilful handling of technology, for example, the combination of various printing processes. Utamaro preferred to use fresh, light colors, often with a mica base and strewn with gold or mother of pearl dust (CAT. 70). His favorite motifs included women in everyday life, putting on makeup, bathing, or having their hair done, taking a walk in the garden, mothers with children, courtesans, and lovers. Apart from that, he designed several albums, among them, outstanding natural-history illustrated volumes with insects, plants, birds, and landscapes, as well as numerous erotic book illustrations. Shortly before his death, Utamaro came into conflict with the censors in 1804. Because of a triptych with historical motifs, in which a satire of life in the court of the Shôgun was supposedly discovered, he ended up in prison and was handcuffed and put on house arrest for fifty days. Together with Hokusai, Utamaro was among the first Japanese artists who also achieved fame in Europe. His admirers included the painter Toulouse-Lautrec. In 1891, French writer and art critic Edmond de Goncourt published the first monograph on Utamaro in Paris.

Objektliste
List of Works

The prints originated in Japan during the Edo period (1603–1868). Unless otherwise mentioned, all are woodblock prints, ink and color on paper. Special techniques are indicated. All works were photographed by Tim Siegert and Scott T. Kubo.

Die Drucke entstanden in Japan während der Edo-Periode (1603–1868). Alle Drucke sind Holzdrucke, mit Tusche und Farbe auf Papier. Spezielle Techniken werden angegeben. Alle Objekte wurden von Tim Siegert und Scott T. Kubo fotografiert.

TABLE OF APPROXIMATE PRINT SIZES
TABELLE DER UNGEFÄHREN DRUCKFORMATE
Height × Width [Höhe × Breite]

ôban	39 × 27 cm	hashira-e	73 × 12 cm
hosoban	33 × 15 cm	ôtanzaku	17 × 39 cm
chûban	26 × 19 cm	shikishiban	22 × 19 cm
aiban	33 × 23 cm		

KEY
LEGENDE

Title (Japanese Romanized)
Titel
Series Title (Japanese Romanized)
Serientitel
Artist [Künstler], Date [Lebensdaten]
Date of Origin [Entstehungsdatum]
Special Technique [Spezielle Technik]
Size in cm (Height × Width) [Grösse in cm]
Provenance [Provenienz]
Honolulu Museum of Art (No.)

1 *Courtesan (Tachi bijin zu)*
Kurtisane
Kaigetsudô DOHAN, active 1710–1736
ca. 1710
sumizuri-e
57.3 × 31.8 cm
Gift of James A. Michener, 1991
(24453)

2 *Girl Playing Shamisen (Shamisen wo hiku onna)*
Ein Mädchen spielt Shamisen
Anonymous/Anonym
early 1720s
hand-colored/handkoloriert
32.8 × 15.7 cm
Gift of James A. Michener, 1991
(21667)

3 *Lingering Scent (Utsuriga)*
Schwebender Duft
Ishikawa TOYONOBU, 1711–1785
1740s–1750s
hand-colored/handkoloriert
65.4 × 16.1 cm
Gift of James A. Michener, 1971
(16086)

4 *Spying on a Dandy (Wakashû to monomimado)*
Beäugen eines eitlen Jünglings
Okumura MASANOBU, 1686–1764
ca. 1745
60.2 × 25.7 cm
Gift of James A. Michener, 1991
(21886)

5 *Beauty with a Mirror (Kagami wo miru bijin)*
Schöne Frau mit einem Spiegel
Okumura MASANOBU, 1686–1764
mid 1740s
urushi-e
70.7 × 25.4 cm
Gift of James A. Michener, 1991
(21888)

6 *Courtesan Walking (Yûjo)*
Gehende Kurtisane
Okumura MASANOBU, 1686–1764
mid 1740s
urushi-e
67.7 × 24.7 cm
Gift of James A. Michener, 1991
(24457)

7 *Girl with Umbrella (Kasa wo motsu shôjo)*
Mädchen mit Schirm
Ishikawa TOYONOBU, 1711–1785
ca. 1750
68.8 × 14.8 cm
Gift of James A. Michener, 1991
(23308)

8 *Girl with Umbrella (Kasa wo motsu shôjo)*
Mädchen mit Schirm
Ishikawa TOYONOBU, 1711–1785
late 1740s
hand-colored/handkoloriert
70 × 15.5 cm
Gift of James A. Michener, 1991
(23307)

9 *Evening Snow at Yamashita (Yamashita no bosetsu)*
Schnee am Abend in Yamashita
The Eight Views of Edo's Pleasure Quarters
(Edo irozato hakkei)
Acht Ansichten von Edos Freudenvierteln
Isoda KORYÛSAI, 1735–1790
ca. 1770
26.1 × 18.9 cm
Gift of James A. Michener, 1970
(15994)

10 *Nakatsukasa (Nakatsukasa)*
Nakatsukasa
Thirty-six Immortal Poets (Sanjû rokkasen)
Die Sechsunddreissig Unsterblichen der Dichtkunst
Suzuki HARUNOBU, 1725?–1770
ca. 1767–1768
28.5 × 21 cm
Gift of James A. Michener, 1959
(14836)

11 *Discovering the Address of a Husband's Sweetheart*
(Yoshiwara saiken)
Entdeckung des Namens der heimlichen Geliebten
A Collection of Humorous Poems (Haifû yanagidaru)
Eine Sammlung humorvoller Gedichte
Torii KIYONAGA, 1752–1815
1790
24.7 × 18.4 cm
Gift of James A. Michener, 1970
(15969)

12 *Righteousness (Gi)*
Aufrichtigkeit und Gerechtigkeit
The Five Cardinal Virtues (Gojô)
Die fünf Kardinaltugenden
Suzuki HARUNOBU, 1725?–1770
1767
27.2 × 20.8 cm
Gift of James A. Michener, 1959
(14654)

13 *The Sakuragawa Teahouse (Mizujaya Sakuragawa)*
Das Sakuragawa-Teehaus
Isoda KORYÛSAI, 1735–1790
ca. 1770
71.7 × 12.3 cm
Gift of James A. Michener, 1987
(20056)

14 *Osen of Kasamori Shrine (Kasamori Osen)*
Osen des Kasamori-Schreins
Ippitsusai BUNCHÔ, active ca. 1755–1790
ca. 1770
33 × 15.4 cm
Gift of James A. Michener, 1991
(21567)

15 *Osen of the Kagiya Teahouse (Kagiya no Osen)*
Osen aus dem Kagiya-Teehaus
Ippitsusai BUNCHÔ, active ca. 1755–1790
ca. 1772–1781
32.6 × 14.9 cm
Gift of James A. Michener, 1991
(24466)

16 *Osode of the Sakaiya Teahouse (Sakaiya misesaki Osode)*
Osode aus dem Sakaiya-Teehaus
Suzuki HARUNOBU, 1725?–1770
ca. 1769
29 × 14.3 cm
Gift of James A. Michener, 1973
(16385)

17 *Two Beauties by the Water's Edge (Mizube ni bijin)*
Zwei Schönheiten am Flussufer
Suzuki HARUNOBU, 1725?–1770
ca. 1765
26.7 × 41.8 cm
Gift of James A. Michener, 1991
(21727)

18 *"Harvest Moon," Minister Minamoto no Saneakira*
(Meigetsu. Minamoto no Saneakira [Ason])
«Herbstmond», Minister Minamoto no Saneakira
Suzuki HARUNOBU, 1725?–1770
ca. late 1760s
27 × 20 cm
Gift of James A. Michener, 1959
(14833)

19 *"Autumn Wind," after the poem by Fujiwara no Toshiyuki*
(Fujiwara no Toshiyuki. Akikaze)
«Herbstwind», nach einem Gedicht von Fujiwara no Toshiyuki
Suzuki HARUNOBU, 1725?–1770
late 1760s
27.8 × 21.1 cm
Gift of James A. Michener, 1991
(21735)

20 *Lady Rokô (Rokômusume Tokonatsu)*
Lady Rokô, genannt Tokonatsu
Flowers of Beauty from the "Floating World"
(Ukiyo bijin hananiyosu)
Blumen der Schönheit aus der «Fliessenden Welt»
Suzuki HARUNOBU, 1725?–1770
ca. 1768–1769
27.6 × 19.5 cm
Gift of James A. Michener, 1959
(14485)

21 *Sixth Month (Minazuki)*
Sechster Monat
Popular Versions of Immortal Poets in the Four Seasons
(Fûzoku shiki kasen)
Populäre Darstellungen der Gedichte der Unsterblichen der Dichtkunst in den vier Jahreszeiten
Suzuki HARUNOBU, 1725?–1770
ca. 1768
28.5 × 21.5 cm
Gift of James A. Michener, 1959
(14839)

22 *Tenth Month (Kannazuki)*
Zehnter Monat
Popular Versions of Immortal Poets in the Four Seasons
(Fûzoku shiki kasen)
Populäre Darstellungen der Gedichte der Unsterblichen der Dichtkunst in den vier Jahreszeiten
Suzuki HARUNOBU, 1725?–1770
ca. 1768
28 × 21.7 cm
Gift of James A. Michener, 1959
(14482)

23 *Second Month, Plum Tree at the Water's Edge*
(Nigatsu, Mizube no ume)
Zweiter Monat, Pflaumenbaum am Flussufer
Fashionable Versions of Immortal Poets in the Four Seasons
(Fûryû shiki kasen)
Modische Darstellungen der Gedichte der Unsterblichen der Dichtkunst in den vier Jahreszeiten
Suzuki HARUNOBU, 1725?–1770
ca. 1768
27.5 × 20.7 cm
Gift of James A. Michener, 1991
(21738)

24 *Princess Sannomiya, the Third Princess from the "Tale of Genji"*
(Genji Monogatari Onna Sannomiya)
Prinzessin Sannomiya, die dritte Prinzessin aus der «Geschichte vom Prinzen Genji»
Suzuki HARUNOBU, 1725?–1770
ca. 1766
28.7 × 21.7 cm
Gift of James A. Michener, 1991
(21737)

25 *Lovers Sharing an Umbrella (Setchû aiaigasa)*
Liebespaar unter einem Schirm
Suzuki HARUNOBU, 1725?–1770
late 1760s
70.5 × 12.7 cm
Gift of James A. Michener, 1991
(20031)

26 *Lovers Sharing an Umbrella (Setchû aiaigasa)*
Liebespaar unter einem Schirm
Suzuki HARUNOBU, 1725?–1770
ca. 1766–1767
26.9 × 19.9 cm
Gift of James A. Michener, 1991
(21736)

27 *The Wind God's Sudden Squall (Fûjin ga okosu yûdachi)*
Der Windgott schickt eine überraschende Sturmböe
Suzuki HARUNOBU, 1725?–1770
ca. 1769
69 × 11.6 cm
Gift of James A. Michener, 1987
(20034)

28 *Parody of Act 7 of the "Chûshingura"*
(Mitate Chûshingura nanadanme)
Parodie des 7. Aktes des «Chûshingura»
Ippitsusai BUNCHÔ, active ca. 1755–1790
ca. 1760s–1770s
25.5 × 19.3 cm
Gift of Anna Rice Cooke, 1934
(10144)

29 *Woman Disguised as a Komusô (Komusô sugata no onna)*
Dame als Bettelmönch verkleidet
Isoda KORYÛSAI, 1735–1790
ca. 1770
63.8 × 11.7 cm
Gift of James A. Michener, 1987
(20050)

30 *Beauty Reading a Letter Outside Mosquito Netting*
(Kaya no soto de fumiyomu bijin)
Schönheit ausserhalb des Moskitonetzes, einen Brief lesend
Suzuki HARUNOBU, 1725?–1770
ca. 1769
70.6 × 12 cm
Gift of James A. Michener, 1970
(15558)

31 *Woman Feeding Her Pet Rat (Nezumi ni esa wo yaru bijin)*
Dame füttert ihre zahme Ratte
Isoda KORYÛSAI, 1735–1790
ca. 1768
72.1 × 13.1 cm
Gift of James A. Michener, 1991
(23658)

32 *Somenosuke of the Matsubaya Brothel House*
(Matsubaya no uchi Somenosuke)
Somenosuke aus dem Freudenhaus Matsubaya
Models for Fashion: New Designs as Fresh as Young Leaves
(Hinagata wakana no hatsu moyô)
Modelle für die Mode: Neue Muster, so frisch wie junge Blätter
Isoda KORYÛSAI, 1735–1790
ca. 1778
37.1 × 25.2 cm
Gift of James A. Michener, 1973
(16400)

33 *Michinoku with Attendants (Sadoya no uchi Michinoku)*
Michinoku mit Begleiterinnen
Models for Fashion: New Designs as Fresh as Young Leaves
(Hinagata wakana no hatsu moyô)
Modelle für die Mode: Neue Muster, so frisch wie junge Blätter
Isoda KORYÛSAI, 1735–1790
ca. 1778
38.9 × 25.6 cm
Gift of James A. Michener, 1991
(21562)

34 *Beauty Hanging a Mosquito Net (Kaya wo tsuru bijin)*
Schöne Frau beim Aufhängen eines Moskitonetzes
Isoda KORYÛSAI, 1735–1790
ca. 1772
69 × 12 cm
Gift of James A. Michener, 1971
(16005)

35 *After the Bath (Yuagari bijin)*
Nach dem Bad
Torii KIYONAGA, 1752–1815
1781
69.4 × 11.6 cm
Gift of James A. Michener, 1986
(19665)

36 *A Young Woman Watching a Youth*
(Wakashû to mado no musume)
Eine junge Frau beobachtet einen Jüngling
Torii KIYONAGA, 1752–1815
1783
69.2 × 12.3 cm
Gift of James A. Michener, 1986
(19667)

37 *Summer Twilight on the Banks of the Sumida River*
(Sumidagawa no yûsuzumi)

Sommerliche Morgendämmerung am Ufer des Sumida-Flusses
Torii KIYONAGA, 1752–1815
1784
37.2 × 25.6 cm
Gift of James A. Michener, 1991
(21799)

38 *A Group of Women at a Shrine Gate (Torii mae no onnatachi)*
Frauen vor dem Tor eines Schreins
Torii KIYONAGA, 1752–1815
1788
38.2 × 25.2 cm
Gift of James A. Michener, 1958
(14246)

39 *A Geisha on Her Way to Work (Kayoi no geisha)*
Eine Geisha auf dem Weg zur Arbeit
Kitao SHIGEMASA, 1739–1820
ca. 1770s
38.3 × 25.8 cm
Gift of James A. Michener, 1971
(16148)

40 *A Geisha and Her Servant (Geisha to hakoya)*
Eine Geisha und ihre Dienerin
Kitao SHIGEMASA, 1739–1820
ca. 1777
39.2 × 26.7 cm
Gift of James A. Michener, 1991
(21756)

41 *Beauties of the East in Nakachô. Onaka and Oshima (Tôhô no bijin Nakachô Onaka, Oshima)*
Schönheiten des Ostens im Stadtviertel Nakachô. Onaka und Oshima
Beauties of the East, West, North, and South (Tôzainanboku no bijin)
Schönheiten des Ostens, Westens, Nordens und Südens
Kitao SHIGEMASA, 1739–1820
ca. 1775
39.5 × 26.6 cm
Gift of James A. Michener, 1991
(21758)

42 *Departing Geisha (Geisha no okuri)*
Heimgehende Geisha
Torii KIYONAGA, 1752–1815
1781
63.7 × 12.3 cm
Gift of James A. Michener, 1986
(19663)

43 *Thinking More of Yourself Than of Your Husband (Otto wo karoshime ware wo tate)*
Mehr an sich selbst denken als an den Ehemann
A Textbook for Young Girls (Jijo hôkun onna imagawa)
Lehrbuch für junge Mädchen
Torii KIYONAGA, 1752–1815
1784
26.2 × 19.6 cm
Gift of James A. Michener, 1970
(15562)

44 *The Takashimaya Teahouse (Takashimaya misesaki)*
Das Takashimaya-Teehaus
Eishôsai CHÔKI, active ca. 1780–1809
early 1800s
32.8 × 22.8 cm
Gift of James A. Michener, 1957
(14178)

45 *Asakusa (Asakusa)*
Im Stadtbezirk Asakusa
Ten Summer Scenes in the Eastern Capital (Tôto natsu jikkei)
Zehn Sommerszenen in der Östlichen Hauptstadt
Torii KIYONAGA, 1752–1815
1787
25.2 × 18.4 cm
Gift of James A. Michener, 1976
(16791)

46 *Morning Snow at the Brothel House (Seirô yuki no asa)*
Schnee am Morgen vor dem Freudenhaus
Torii KIYONAGA, 1752–1815
1789
38 × 50 cm
Gift of James A. Michener, 1991
(21800)

47 *Street Traffic at Nihonbashi (Nihonbashi no ôrai)*
Menschen auf der Strasse in Nihonbashi
Torii KIYONAGA, 1752–1815
1786
37.7 × 50 cm
Gift of James A. Michener, 1991
(21801a–b)

48 *Segawa with Sasano and Takeno of the Matsubaya Brothel House (Matsubaya Segawa)*
Segawa mit den Schülerinnen Sasano und Takeno aus dem Freudenhaus Matsubaya
Models for Fashion: New Designs as Fresh as Young Leaves (Hinagata wakana no hatsu moyô)
Modelle für die Mode: Neue Muster, so frisch wie junge Blätter
Torii KIYONAGA, 1752–1815
1782
39.2 × 26.3 cm
Gift of James A. Michener, 1957
(13824)

49 *Seyama of the Matsubaya Brothel House (Matsubaya no uchi Seyama)*
Seyama aus dem Freudenhaus Matsubaya
Katsukawa SHUNCHÔ, active ca. 1781–1801
late 1780s
39.1 × 25.6 cm
Gift of James A. Michener, 1971
(16069)

50 *Utaura of the Kadotamaya Brothel House (Kadotamaya no uchi Utaura)*
Utaura aus dem Freudenhaus Kadotamaya
Chôbunsai EISHI, 1756–1829
1789
36.1 × 24.3 cm
Gift of Anna Rice Cooke, 1932
(06441)

51 *Seventh Month, Evening Send-Off (Shichigatsu, Yoru no okuri)*
Siebter Monat, abendlicher Abschied
Twelve Months in the South (Minami jûnikô)
Zwölf Monate im Süden
Torii KIYONAGA, 1752–1815
1784

38 × 50.7 cm
Gift of James A. Michener, 1991
(24452)

52 *The Hour of the Cock (Tori no koku)*
Die Stunde des Hahnes
Twelve Hours in the Yoshiwara (Seirô jûnitoki tsuzuki)
Zwölf Stunden im Freudenviertel Yoshiwara
Kitagawa UTAMARO, 1753–1806
ca. 1795–1796
38.3 × 25.5 cm
Purchase C. Montague Cooke, Jr. Memorial Collection, 1953
(13253)

53 *The Hour of the Snake (Mi no koku)*
Die Stunde der Schlange
Twelve Hours in the Yoshiwara (Seirô jûnitoki tsuzuki)
Zwölf Stunden im Freudenviertel Yoshiwara
Kitagawa UTAMARO, 1753–1806
ca. 1794
36.3 × 24.1 cm
Gift of James A. Michener, 1991
(21878)

54 *Picture of the Upper Class (Jôbon no zu)*
Darstellung der Oberschicht
Three Ranks of Young Women According to Their Fashions (Fûzoku sandan musume)
Junge Frauen aus drei gesellschaftlichen Schichten, erkennbar an ihrer Kleidung
Kitagawa UTAMARO, 1753–1806
ca. 1794–1795
38.3 × 25.4 cm
Gift of James A. Michener, 1991
(21879)

55 *Geisha with Shamisen (Shamisen wo motsu bijin)*
Eine Geisha mit Shamisen
Utagawa KUNIMASA I, 1773–1810
ca. 1796
39 × 25.3 cm
Gift of James A. Michener, 1972
(16261)

56 *Tomimoto Toyohina (Tomimoto Toyohina)*
Tomimoto Toyohina
Kitagawa UTAMARO, 1753–1806
ca. 1790s
36 × 24.2 cm
Gift of James A. Michener, 1969
(15488)

57 *Karagoto of the Brothel House Chôjiya in Edochô Nichôme (Edochô Nichôme Chôjiya no uchi Karagoto)*
Karagoto aus dem Freudenhaus Chôjiya in Edochô Nichôme
A Comparison of Courtesan Flowers (Tayû hanamitate)
Kurtisanen verglichen mit Blumen
Kitagawa UTAMARO, 1753–1806
1801
36.7 × 24.6 cm
Gift of James A. Michener, 1959
(14539)

58 *Teahouse Maidens under a Wisteria Trellis (Fujidana shita no chaya musume)*
Teehausmädchen unter einem Glyzinienspalier
Kitagawa UTAMARO, 1753–1806
ca. 1795
36.6 × 23.9 cm
Gift of James A. Michener, 1973
(16516)

59 *Vulgarly Called the Wanton (Zokuni iu bakuren)*
Gewöhnlich als leichtes Mädchen bezeichnet
A Parent's Moralizing Spectacles (Kyôkun oya no megane)
Durch die moralisierende Brille der Eltern gesehen
Kitagawa UTAMARO, 1753–1806
ca. 1802
36.7 × 23.5 cm
Gift of James A. Michener, 1957
(13788)

60 *Lover of Loud Noises (Sawagizuki)*
Kind findet Gefallen an lauten Geräuschen
The Eight Views of Popular Things (Tôsei kôbutsu hakkei)
Die acht Darstellungen von beliebten Dingen
Kitagawa UTAMARO, 1753–1806
ca. 1800
37.7 × 24.3 cm
Gift of James A. Michener, 1987
(20013)

61 *Mother and Child with Puppies (Hahako to koinu)*
Mutter und Kind mit Welpen
Kitagawa UTAMARO, 1753–1806
ca. 1800
37.4 × 24.3 cm
Gift of James A. Michener, 1987
(20012)

62 *Two Beauties. One Holding a Pipe, the Other a Round Fan (Kiseru to uchiwa)*
Zwei Schönheiten. Die eine hält eine Pfeife, die andere einen Rundfächer
Kitagawa UTAMARO, 1753–1806
ca. 1797
38.8 × 25.4 cm
Purchase, 1951
(13063)

63 *A Weakness for Love (Iro ni fukeru kuse)*
Eine Schwäche für Liebe
Everyone Has Faults (Nakute nanakuse)
Jeder hat seine Fehler
Kitagawa UTAMARO, 1753–1806
ca. 1804
38.9 × 26.2 cm
Gift of James A. Michener, 1970
(15580)

64 *Morning at the Temporary Lodgings (Karitaku no asa)*
Morgenstimmung in einem Freudenhaus am Fluss
Kitagawa UTAMARO, 1753–1806
1801
37.4 × 74 cm
Gift of James A. Michener, 1977
(17153)

65 *Falconer and Maid (Takajô to musume)*
Falkner und Mädchen
BUNRÔ, active 1801–1810
ca. 1800–1810
34 × 22.2 cm
Gift of James A. Michener, 1991
(21837)

66 *Agemaki and Sukeroku (Agemaki Sukeroku)*
Agemaki und Sukeroku
Kitagawa UTAMARO, 1753–1806
ca. 1800
65.6 × 14.9 cm
Gift of James A. Michener, 1991
(23688)

67 *Fan Dancer, Country Maiden Autumn Dancer, and Full Moon Blossom (Maiôgi natorizuki, inaka-musume aki no teodori, ominaeshi sakari no Mochizuki)*
Fächertänzerin, Landmädchen als Herbsttänzerin und Tänzerin als Vollmond
Geisha Dancers from the Niwaka Festival (Seirô Niwaka onna geisha)
Geisha-Tänzerinnen vom Niwaka-Fest
Kitagawa UTAMARO, 1753–1806
ca. 1790
39.1 × 26 cm
Gift of James A. Michener, 1970
(15571)

68 *Okita and Ohisa in a Tug-of-War with a Sash Looped Around Their Necks (Nibijin kubihiki)*
Okita und Ohisa beim Kräftemessen mit einer Schärpe um den Hals
Kitagawa UTAMARO, 1753–1806
ca. 1793–1794
25.7 × 38.6 cm
Gift of James A. Michener, 1957
(13909)

69 *Flower Arrangement Contest between Okita and Ohisa (Okita, Ohisa no hana awase)*
Wettstreit im Blumenstecken zwischen Okita und Ohisa
Kitagawa UTAMARO, 1753–1806
ca. 1789
25.2 × 37.6 cm
Gift of James A. Michener, 1957
(14039)

70 *Three Beauties of the Yoshiwara (Seirô san bijin)*
Drei Schönheiten aus dem Freudenviertel Yoshiwara
Kitagawa UTAMARO, 1753–1806
1793
38.6 × 26 cm
Gift of James A. Michener, 1991
(21877)

71 *Takashima Ohisa (Takashima Ohisa)*
Takashima Ohisa
Kitagawa UTAMARO, 1753–1806
ca. 1790–1791
32.4 × 14.8 cm
Gift of James A. Michener, 1991
(21881a–b)

72 *Hanaôgi of the Ôgiya Brothel House at Edochô Itchôme (Edochô Itchôme Ôgiya no uchi Hanaôgi)*
Hanaôgi vom Freudenhaus Ôgiya in Edochô Itchôme
A Comparison of Courtesan Flowers (Tayû hanamitate)
Kurtisanen verglichen mit Blumen
Kitagawa UTAMARO, 1753–1806
1801
36.8 × 24.1 cm
Gift of James A. Michener, 1991
(24515)

73 *Tsukasa Dayû of Higashi Ôgiya in Osaka's Shinmachi District (Ôsaka shinmachi higashi no Ôgiya Tsukasa Dayû)*
Tsukasa Dayû aus dem Freudenhaus Higashi Ôgiya in Osakas Shinmachi-Viertel
Eishôsai CHÔKI, active ca. 1780–1809
ca. 1800
38.8 × 26.2 cm
Gift of James A. Michener, 1991
(21760)

74 *Cooling off under Ryôgoku Bridge (Ryôgoku nôryôsen no zu)*
Abkühlung unter der Ryôgoku-Brücke
Eishôsai CHÔKI, active ca. 1780–1809
ca. 1800
38.2 × 74.2 cm
Gift of James A. Michener, 1991
(22061)

75 *Misayama of the Chôjiya Brothel House in Her Dressing Room (Tokogi no zu, Chôjiya Misayama)*
Misayama aus dem Freudenhaus Chôjiya in ihrem Ankleidezimmer
Beauties in the Pleasure Quarters (Seirô bijin awase)
Schönheiten in den Freudenvierteln
Chôbunsai EISHI, 1756–1829
ca. 1795
37.7 × 25 cm
Gift of James A. Michener, 1954
(13425)

76 *The Doll Festival (Hinamatsuri)*
Das Mädchenfest
The Elegant Five Festivals (Fûryû gosekku)
Die fünf eleganten jahreszeitlichen Feste
Chôbunsai EISHI, 1756–1829
ca. 1795
35.6 × 23.3 cm
Gift of James A. Michener, 1991
(21704)

77 *Kisegawa of the Matsubaya (Matsubaya Kisegawa)*
Kisegawa aus dem Freudenhaus Matsubaya
Six Beautiful Flowers of the Pleasure Quarters (Seirô bijin rokkasen)
Sechs schöne Blumen aus den Freudenvierteln
Chôbunsai EISHI, 1756–1829
ca. 1795
38.6 × 25.7 cm
Gift of James A. Michener, 1973
(16378)

78 *Somenosuke of the Matsubaya (Matsubaya Somenosuke)*
Somenosuke aus dem Freudenhaus Matsubaya
Courtesans Modeling the New Year's Fashions (Wakana hatsuishô)
Kurtisanen führen die Neujahrsmode vor
Chôbunsai EISHI, 1756–1829
ca. 1800
39.4 × 26.2 cm
Gift of James A. Michener, 1958
(14204)

79 *A Visual Parody of Ushiwakamaru and Princess Jôruri (Mitate Ushiwaka Jôruri-hime)*
Eine Parodie des Ushiwakamaru und der Prinzessin Jôruri
Chôbunsai EISHI, 1756–1829
ca. 1789–1801
37.6 × 72.5 cm

Gift of James A. Michener, 1991
(22056)

80 *Minister Narihira's Coming of Age (Narihira Ason uikôburi yatsushi)*
Minister Narihira wird volljährig
Chôkôsai EISHÔ, active 1795–1801
ca. 1790s
37.1 × 74.9 cm
Gift of James A. Michener, 1991
(22064)

81 *Catching Fireflies on a Raft (Batsu no hotarugari)*
Glühwürmchenjagd auf dem Floss
Chôbunsai EISHI, 1756–1829
ca. 1790s
36.7 × 23.9 cm
Gift of James A. Michener, 1958
(14207)

82 *Mosquito Smudge (Kayaribi)*
Rauch gegen Mücken
Utagawa KUNIMASA I, 1773–1810
1800
23.7 × 26.4 cm
Gift of James A. Michener, 1991
(21752)

83 *Somenosuke of the Matsubaya Brothel House, Who has the Kamuro Wakahi and Wakaha (Matsubaya no uchi Somenosuke, Wakahi, Wakaha)*
Somenosuke aus dem Freudenhaus Matsubaya, deren Begleiterinnen Wakahi und Wakaha hiessen
Beauties of the Five Festivals (Bijin gosekku)
Schönheiten der fünf jahreszeitlichen Feste
Ichirakutei EISUI, active ca. 1795–1823
ca. 1800
37.4 × 24.3 cm
Gift of Anna Rice Cooke, 1933
(09804)

84 *The Fan Store Eijudô (Eijudô sensu mise)*
Das Fächergeschäft Eijudô
Utagawa TOYOKUNI I, 1769–1825
ca. 1800
38.4 × 76.8 cm
Gift of James A. Michener, 1991
(22057)

85 *Courtesans as the Seven Deities of Good Fortune (Shichifukujin)*
Kurtisanen in der Gestalt der Sieben Glücksgötter
Utagawa TOYOKUNI I, 1769–1825
ca. 1800
38.8 × 75.7 cm
Gift of James A. Michener, 1957
(13855a–c)

86 *Making Top Quality White Sake (Daigokujô fuji no shirazake)*
Herstellung von hochwertigem weissem Reiswein
Utagawa TOYOKUNI I, 1769–1825
ca. 1795–1801
38 × 75.6 cm
Gift of James A. Michener, 1955
(13707a–c)

87 *Early Afternoon at the Country House (Ryô no hirusagari)*
Früher Nachmittag in einem Landhaus
Chôbunsai EISHI, 1756–1829
ca. 1790
34.4 × 74.2 cm
Gift of James A. Michener, 1991
(22068)

88 *Flowers in the Wind (Hana no kaze)*
Blumen im Wind
Utagawa TOYOKUNI I, 1769–1825
ca. 1795–1825
37.8 × 75.9 cm
Gift of James A. Michener, 1955
(13633a–c)

89 *A Sudden Squall at Mimeguri Shrine (Mimeguri no yûdachi)*
Eine plötzliche Windböe am Mimeguri-Schrein
Torii KIYONAGA, 1752–1815
1787
37.8 × 75.4 cm
Gift of James A. Michener, 1991
(21633)

90 *Yosooi of the Matsubaya at Shin Yoshiwara Kadomachi (Hônô Shin Yoshiwara Kadomachi Matsubaya Yosooi)*
Yosooi aus dem Freudenhaus Matsubaya in Shin Yoshiwara Kadomachi
Votive Hand Towels (Hônô tenugui)
Votivhandtücher
Utagawa KUNISADA I/TOYOKUNI III, 1786–1865
ca. 1816
38.1 × 26.4 cm
Gift of James A. Michener, 1957
(13959)

91 *Miyajima (Miyajima)*
Miyajima
Nanahito of the Sugata-ebiya (Sugataebiya no uchi Nanahito)
Nanahito aus dem Sugata-ebiya
Keisai EISEN, 1790–1848
ca. 1830s
37.6 × 25.5 cm
Gift of Anna Rice Cooke, 1928
(06208)

92 *Inside the Shrine Precincts in Hitotsume (Hitotsume no keidai)*
Innerhalb des Schrein-Bezirks in Hitotsume
Magic Lantern Slides of Contemporary Styles (Tôsei sugata no utsushie)
Laternenbild im zeitgenössischen Stil
Keisai EISEN, 1790–1848
ca. 1830s
38.6 × 26.1 cm
Gift of Anna Rice Cooke, 1928
(06209)

93 *Popular Pairings of Landscapes and Beauties (Fûryû sansui bijin awase)*
Beliebte Kombinationen von Landschaften und Schönheiten
Utagawa KUNISADA I/TOYOKUNI III, 1786–1865
1861
22.5 × 28.8 cm
Gift of Anna Rice Cooke, 1927
(05055)

94 *Preparing to Go Out (Mijimai Geisha)*
Vorbereitungen zum Ausgang
Comparison of Modern Beauties (Tôsei bijin awase)

Ein Vergleich von modernen Schönheiten
Utagawa KUNISADA I/TOYOKUNI III, 1786–1865
ca. 1830–1831
37.8 × 25.7 cm
Purchase, 1927
(05087)

95 *A Female Daimyo Procession (Onna daimyô gyôretsu)*
Eine weibliche Daimyo-Prozession
Utagawa TOYOKUNI I, 1769–1825
ca. 1795–1825
33.5 × 89.3 cm, 32.4 × 90 cm
Gift of James A. Michener, 1991
(22059a–d, 22058a–d)

Abbildungsverzeichnis
List of Figures

1 *A Kiss (Kuchizuke)*
Ein Kuss
Suzuki HARUNOBU, 1725?–1770
ca. 1766
with embossing/**mit Blinddruck**
19 x 27 cm
Gift of Julius Mueller
Museum Rietberg RJP 1936
Photo/**Foto**: Rainer Wolfsberger

2 *Scene from "Tales of Ise" (Ise monogatari musashino)*
Szene aus den «Erzählungen von Ise»
Kitagawa UTAMARO, 1753–1806
ca. 1796
mica print of the full moon/**Glimmerdruck für den aufgehenden Vollmond**
38 × 25.5 cm
Gift of Julius Mueller
Museum Rietberg RJP 2734a–c
Photo/**Foto**: Rainer Wolfsberger

3 *The Ide Tama River in Yamashiro (Yamashiro ide no tamagawa)*
Der Ide-Tama-Fluss in Yamashiro
Fashionable Views of the Six Tama Rivers (Fûryû mu tamagawa)
Populäre Ansichten der sechs Tama-Flüsse
Kikukawa EIZAN, 1787–1867
ca. 1815
39.3 × 26.8 cm
Gift of Julius Mueller
Museum Rietberg RJP 3115
Photo/**Foto**: Rainer Wolfsberger

4 *Beauties Representing Jôruri Narrative Music*
Schönheiten, die Jôruri-Gesänge repräsentieren
Modern Pine Needles (Tôsei matsu no ha)
Moderne Kiefernnadeln
part of a triptych/**Teil eines Triptychons**
Keisai EISEN, 1790–1848
ca. 1830
38 × 79.5 cm
Gift of Julius Mueller
Museum Rietberg RJP 3012
Photo/**Foto**: Rainer Wolfsberger

5 *Imported and Domestic Goods: Playful Picture Comparing the Handiness of Tools and Means (Hakurai wamono tawamure dôgu chôhô kurabe zu)*
Importierte und regionale Ware: Lustiges Bild, auf dem die Handlichkeit von Werkzeugen verglichen wird
Utagawa YOSHIFUJI, 1828–1887
ca. 1870s
36 × 72.3 cm
Teishin Sôgô Hakubutsukan collection

6 *High-ranked Courtesan (Oiran)*
Hochrangige Kurtisane
Anonymous/**Anonym**
ca. 1890s–1900s
sepia-toned, hand-colored photograph/**Sepia-Fotografie, handkoloriert**
9.1 × 13.4 cm
Nagasaki University Library Collection
ID 3622, Cabinet 72-84-0

7 *Portrait of Three Geisha: Kayo of Kyoto, Ikkaku of Osaka, and Kokichi of Tokyo (Saikyô geiko Kayo, Osaka geiko Ikkaku, Tokyô geisha Kokichi)*
Porträt dreier Geishas: Kayo aus Kyoto, Ikkaku aus Osaka und Kokichi aus Tokio
Kobayashi KIYOCHIKA, 1847–1915
ca. 1877
37.9 × 25.2 cm
Gift of Carl Holmes
Los Angeles County Museum of Art (M.71.100.47)
© 2012. Digital Image Museum Associates/LACMA/Art Resource NY/Scala, Florence

8 *Woman in Summer Kimono (Natsugoromo no onna)*
Frau in einem Sommerkimono
Hashiguchi GOYÔ, 1880–1921
1920
45.1 × 29.5 cm
Honolulu Museum of Art (20688)
Photo/**Foto**: Tim Siegert

pp./**S.** 153–154
公衆便女
public conVENience
TABAIMO, b./**geb.** 1975
2006
Still images from the 3-Channel Video Installation with Sound, 6 min. 5 sec. loop/**Standbilder aus der 3-Kanal-Videoinstallation mit Ton, 6 Min. 5 Sek. Loop**
© Tabaimo/Courtesy of Gallery Koyanagi

pp./**S.** 156–157 (gatefold/**Ausklapper**)
にっぽんの湯屋（男湯）
Japanese Bathhouse—Gents
Japanisches Badehaus – Männer
TABAIMO, b./**geb.** 1975
2000
Lithograph for the 3-Channel Video Installation with Sound, 7 min. 21 sec. loop/**Lithografie für die 3-Kanal-Videoinstallation mit Ton, 7 Min. 21 Sek. Loop**
© Tabaimo/Courtesy of Gallery Koyanagi

Bibliografie
Bibliography

Aono 2006
Aono, Kazuko. "Tabaimo through the Looking Glass." In *Tabaimo: Yoro Yoron.* Ed. by/hrsg. vom Hara Museum of Contemporary Art, p./S. 14–17. Tokyo/Tokio: Hara Museum of Contemporary Art, 2006.

Asano and/und Clark 1995
Asano, Shugô, and/und Timothy Clark. *The Passionate Art of Kitagawa Utamaro.* Tokyo/Tokio: Asahi Shinbun, 1995.

Brown and/und Goodall-Cristante 1996
Brown, Kendall, and/und Hollis Goodall-Cristante. *Shin-Hanga: New Prints in Modern Japan.* Los Angeles: Los Angeles County Museum of Art, 1996.

Chiba 2007
Chiba Bijutsukan (ed./Hrsg.). *Torii Kiyonaga: The Birth of Venus in Edo.* Chiba: Chibashi Bijutsukan, 2007.

Clark 1995
Clark, Timothy T. "Utamaro and Yoshiwara: The 'Painter of the Green Houses' Reconsidered." In *The Passionate Art of Kitagawa Utamaro.* Ed. by/hrsg. von Timothy T. Clark and/und Asano Shûgô. 2 vols./Bde., text volume/Textband, p./S. 35–46. London: British Museum Press, 1995.

Clark 2001
Clark, Timothy T., Anne Nishimura Morse and/und Louise Erica Virgin. *The Dawn of the Floating World, 1650–1765: Early Ukiyo-e Treasures from the Museum of Fine Arts, Boston.* London: Royal Academy of Arts, 2001.

Collia-Suzuki 2009
Collia-Suzuki, Gina. *The Complete Woodblock Prints of Kitagawa Utamaro: A Descriptive Catalogue.* Weston-super-Mare: Nezu Press, 2009.

Fahr-Becker 1994
Fahr-Becker, Gabriele (ed./Hrsg.). *Japanese Prints.* Cologne/Köln: Taschen, 1994. [German edition/Deutsche Ausgabe: *Japanische Farbholzschnitte.* Cologne/Köln: Taschen, 1993.]

Genshoku 1982
Genshoku ukiyo-e daihyakka jiten henshû iinkai (ed./Hrsg.). *Genshoku ukiyo-e dai hyakka jiten (Encyclopedia of Ukiyo-e in Full Color/Lexikon des Ukiyo-e in Farbe).* Vol./Bd. 6 & 7. Tokyo/Tokio: Taishûkan Shoten, 1982.

Hamanaka and/und Newland 2000
Hamanaka, Shinji, and/und Amy R. Newland (eds./Hrsg.). *The Female Image: 20th Century Prints of Japanese Beauties.* Tokyo/Tokio, Leiden: Abe; Hotei, 2000.

Hashimoto 2010
Hashimoto, Mari. "Artist Interview Tabaimo." In *Bijutsu Techo,* p./S. 160–167. Tokyo/Tokio: Bijutsu Shuppan-Sha Co. Ltd., 2010.

Hempel 1986
Hempel, Rose. *Japanische Farbholzschnitte I: Von Moronobu bis Hiroshige.* Hamburg: Museum für Kunst und Gewerbe, 1986.

Hockley 2003
Hockley, Allen. *The Prints of Isoda Koryûsai: Floating World Culture and its Consumers in Eighteenth-Century Japan.* Seattle, London: University of Washington Press, 2003.

Kawabata 1975
Kawabata, Yasunari. *Beauty and Sadness.* New York: Charles E. Tuttle Company, 1975. [German edition/Deutsche Ausgabe: *Schönheit und Trauer: Roman.* Munich/München: Deutscher Taschenbuch Verlag, 1990.]

Kobayashi 2005
Kobayashi, Tadashi. "The Kanbun *Bijin:* Setting the Stage for *Ukiyo-e Bijinga.*" In *The Hotei Encyclopedia of Japanese Woodblock Prints.* Ed. by/hrsg. von Amy Reigle Newland. Vol./Bd. 1, p./S. 83–86. Amsterdam: Hotei Publishing, 2005.

Lewinsky-Sträuli 1989
Lewinsky-Sträuli, Marianne (ed./Hrsg.) *Japanische Dämonen und Gespenster: Geschichten aus zwölf Jahrhunderten.* München: Eugen Diederichs Verlag, 1989.

Link 1980
Link, Howard A. *Primitive Ukiyo-e from the James A. Michener Collection in the Honolulu Academy of Arts.* Honolulu: The University Press of Hawaii, 1980.

Kobayashi and/und Link 1994
Kobayashi Tadashi, and/und Howard A. Link. *Edo Beauties in Ukiyo-e: The James A. Michener Collection.* Honolulu: Honolulu Academy of Arts, 1994.

Marks 2010
Marks, Andreas. *Japanese Woodblock Prints: Artists, Publishers and Masterworks, 1680–1900.* Rutland, Vermont: Tuttle Publishing, 2010.

Marks 2011
Marks, Andreas. *Publishers of Japanese Woodblock Prints: A Compendium.* Leiden, Boston: Hotei Publishing, 2011.

Meech and/und Oliver 2008
Meech, Julia, and/und Jane Oliver (eds./Hrsg.). *Designed for Pleasure: The World of Edo Japan in Prints and Paintings, 1680–1860.* Seattle and/und London: University of Washington Press, 2008.

Meech-Pekarik 1987
Meech-Pekarik, Julia. *The World of the Meiji Print: Impressions of a New Civilization.* New York: Weatherhill, 1987.

Merritt 1990
Merritt, Helen. *Modern Japanese Woodblock Prints: The Early Years.* Honolulu: University of Hawaii Press, 1990.

Michener 1954
Michener, James A. *The Floating World.* New York: Random House, 1954.

Michener 1959
Michener, James A. *Japanese Prints: From the Early Masters to the Modern.* Rutland, Vermont and/und Tokyo/Tokio, Japan: Charles E. Tuttle Company, 1959. [German edition/Deutsche Ausgabe: *Japanische Holzschnitte von den frühen Meistern bis zur Neuzeit.* München: Bruckmann, 1961.]

Newland 2005
Newland, Amy Reigle (ed./Hrsg.). *The Hotei Encyclopedia of Japanese Woodblock Prints.* Amsterdam: Hotei Publishing, 2005.

Ooba 1986
Ooba, Osamu. *Monogatari monono kenchikushi. Furo no hanashi.* Tokyo/Tokio: Kajima Institut Publishing Co. Ltd., 1986.

Saikaku 1992
Saikaku, Ihara. "Shoen Ôkagami," *Taiyaku Saikaku Zenshû.* Vol./Bd. 2. Tokyo/Tokio: Meiji Shoin, 1992.

Seigle 1993
Seigle, Cecilia Segawa. *Yoshiwara: The Glittering World of the Japanese Courtesan.* Honolulu: University of Hawaii Press, 1993.

Seigle 2004
Seigle, Cecilia Segawa. *A Courtesan's Day: Hour by Hour.* Amsterdam: Hotei Publishing, 2004.

Swinton 1995
Swinton, Elizabeth de Sabato. *The Women of the Pleasure Quarter: Japanese Paintings and Prints of the Floating World.* Ed. by/hrsg. vom Worcester Art Museum, Equitable Gallery and/und Kimbell Art Museum. New York: Hudson Hills Press, 1995.

Tabaimo and/und Yoshida 2009
Tabaimo and/und Shuichi Yoshida. "Dialog: Tabaimo × Yoshida Shuichi. Why the Danmen no Sedai (DANMEN Generation)?" In *Tabaimo: Danmen no Sedai.* Ed. by/hrsg. vom Yokohama Museum of Art and/und The National Museum of Art, Osaka, p./S. 16–23. Kyoto: Seigensha Art Publishing, Inc., 2009.

Thompson and/und Harootunian 1991
Thompson, Sarah E., and/und Harry D. Harootunian. *Undercurrents in the Floating World: Censorship and Japanese Prints.* New York: Asia Society Galleries, 1991.

Uematsu 2009
Uematsu, Yuka. "Tabaimo: Outside-In." In *Tabaimo: Danmen no Sedai.* Ed. by/hrsg. vom Yokohama Museum of Art and/und The National Museum of Art, Osaka, p./S. 106–111. Kyoto: Seigensha Art Publishing, Inc., 2009.

Uragami 1983
Uragami, Toshiro. *The Beauty of Ukiyo-e: From Harunobu to Kiyochika.* Yamaguchi: TYS Terebi Yamaguchi, 1983.

Bibliografie
Bibliography

Aono 2006
Aono, Kazuko. "Tabaimo through the Looking Glass." In *Tabaimo: Yoro Yoron.* Ed. by/hrsg. vom Hara Museum of Contemporary Art, p./S. 14–17. Tokyo/Tokio: Hara Museum of Contemporary Art, 2006.

Asano and/und Clark 1995
Asano, Shugô, and/und Timothy Clark. *The Passionate Art of Kitagawa Utamaro.* Tokyo/Tokio: Asahi Shinbun, 1995.

Brown and/und Goodall-Cristante 1996
Brown, Kendall, and/und Hollis Goodall-Cristante. *Shin-Hanga: New Prints in Modern Japan.* Los Angeles: Los Angeles County Museum of Art, 1996.

Chiba 2007
Chiba Bijutsukan (ed./Hrsg.). *Torii Kiyonaga: The Birth of Venus in Edo.* Chiba: Chibashi Bijutsukan, 2007.

Clark 1995
Clark, Timothy T. "Utamaro and Yoshiwara: The 'Painter of the Green Houses' Reconsidered." In *The Passionate Art of Kitagawa Utamaro.* Ed. by/hrsg. von Timothy T. Clark and/und Asano Shûgô. 2 vols./Bde., text volume/Textband, p./S. 35–46. London: British Museum Press, 1995.

Clark 2001
Clark, Timothy T., Anne Nishimura Morse and/und Louise Erica Virgin. *The Dawn of the Floating World, 1650–1765: Early Ukiyo-e Treasures from the Museum of Fine Arts, Boston.* London: Royal Academy of Arts, 2001.

Collia-Suzuki 2009
Collia-Suzuki, Gina. *The Complete Woodblock Prints of Kitagawa Utamaro: A Descriptive Catalogue.* Weston-super-Mare: Nezu Press, 2009.

Fahr-Becker 1994
Fahr-Becker, Gabriele (ed./Hrsg.). *Japanese Prints.* Cologne/Köln: Taschen, 1994. [German edition/Deutsche Ausgabe: *Japanische Farbholzschnitte.* Cologne/Köln: Taschen, 1993.]

Genshoku 1982
Genshoku ukiyo-e daihyakka jiten henshû iinkai (ed./Hrsg.). *Genshoku ukiyo-e dai hyakka jiten (Encyclopedia of Ukiyo-e in Full Color/Lexikon des Ukiyo-e in Farbe).* Vol./Bd. 6 & 7. Tokyo/Tokio: Taishûkan Shoten, 1982.

Hamanaka and/und Newland 2000
Hamanaka, Shinji, and/und Amy R. Newland (eds./Hrsg.). *The Female Image: 20th Century Prints of Japanese Beauties.* Tokyo/Tokio, Leiden: Abe; Hotei, 2000.

Hashimoto 2010
Hashimoto, Mari. "Artist Interview Tabaimo." In *Bijutsu Techo,* p./S. 160–167. Tokyo/Tokio: Bijutsu Shuppan-Sha Co. Ltd., 2010.

Hempel 1986
Hempel, Rose. *Japanische Farbholzschnitte I: Von Moronobu bis Hiroshige.* Hamburg: Museum für Kunst und Gewerbe, 1986.

Hockley 2003
Hockley, Allen. *The Prints of Isoda Koryûsai: Floating World Culture and its Consumers in Eighteenth-Century Japan.* Seattle, London: University of Washington Press, 2003.

Kawabata 1975
Kawabata, Yasunari. *Beauty and Sadness.* New York: Charles E. Tuttle Company, 1975. [German edition/Deutsche Ausgabe: *Schönheit und Trauer: Roman.* Munich/München: Deutscher Taschenbuch Verlag, 1990.]

Kobayashi 2005
Kobayashi, Tadashi. "The Kanbun *Bijin:* Setting the Stage for *Ukiyo-e Bijinga.*" In *The Hotei Encyclopedia of Japanese Woodblock Prints.* Ed. by/hrsg. von Amy Reigle Newland. Vol./Bd. 1, p./S. 83–86. Amsterdam: Hotei Publishing, 2005.

Lewinsky-Sträuli 1989
Lewinsky-Sträuli, Marianne (ed./Hrsg.) *Japanische Dämonen und Gespenster: Geschichten aus zwölf Jahrhunderten.* München: Eugen Diederichs Verlag, 1989.

Link 1980
Link, Howard A. *Primitive Ukiyo-e from the James A. Michener Collection in the Honolulu Academy of Arts.* Honolulu: The University Press of Hawaii, 1980.

Kobayashi and/und Link 1994
Kobayashi Tadashi, and/und Howard A. Link. *Edo Beauties in Ukiyo-e: The James A. Michener Collection.* Honolulu: Honolulu Academy of Arts, 1994.

Marks 2010
Marks, Andreas. *Japanese Woodblock Prints: Artists, Publishers and Masterworks, 1680–1900.* Rutland, Vermont: Tuttle Publishing, 2010.

Marks 2011
Marks, Andreas. *Publishers of Japanese Woodblock Prints: A Compendium.* Leiden, Boston: Hotei Publishing, 2011.

Meech and/und Oliver 2008
Meech, Julia, and/und Jane Oliver (eds./Hrsg.). *Designed for Pleasure: The World of Edo Japan in Prints and Paintings, 1680–1860.* Seattle and/und London: University of Washington Press, 2008.

Meech-Pekarik 1987
Meech-Pekarik, Julia. *The World of the Meiji Print: Impressions of a New Civilization.* New York: Weatherhill, 1987.

Merritt 1990
Merritt, Helen. *Modern Japanese Woodblock Prints: The Early Years.* Honolulu: University of Hawaii Press, 1990.

Michener 1954
Michener, James A. *The Floating World.* New York: Random House, 1954.

Michener 1959
Michener, James A. *Japanese Prints: From the Early Masters to the Modern.* Rutland, Vermont and/und Tokyo/Tokio, Japan: Charles E. Tuttle Company, 1959. [German edition/Deutsche Ausgabe: *Japanische Holzschnitte von den frühen Meistern bis zur Neuzeit.* München: Bruckmann, 1961.]

Newland 2005
Newland, Amy Reigle (ed./Hrsg.). *The Hotei Encyclopedia of Japanese Woodblock Prints.* Amsterdam: Hotei Publishing, 2005.

Ooba 1986
Ooba, Osamu. *Monogatari monono kenchikushi. Furo no hanashi.* Tokyo/Tokio: Kajima Institut Publishing Co. Ltd., 1986.

Saikaku 1992
Saikaku, Ihara. "Shoen Ôkagami," *Taiyaku Saikaku Zenshû.* Vol./Bd. 2. Tokyo/Tokio: Meiji Shoin, 1992.

Seigle 1993
Seigle, Cecilia Segawa. *Yoshiwara: The Glittering World of the Japanese Courtesan.* Honolulu: University of Hawaii Press, 1993.

Seigle 2004
Seigle, Cecilia Segawa. *A Courtesan's Day: Hour by Hour.* Amsterdam: Hotei Publishing, 2004.

Swinton 1995
Swinton, Elizabeth de Sabato. *The Women of the Pleasure Quarter: Japanese Paintings and Prints of the Floating World.* Ed. by/hrsg. vom Worcester Art Museum, Equitable Gallery and/und Kimbell Art Museum. New York: Hudson Hills Press, 1995.

Tabaimo and/und Yoshida 2009
Tabaimo and/und Shuichi Yoshida. "Dialog: Tabaimo × Yoshida Shuichi. Why the Danmen no Sedai (DANMEN Generation)?" In *Tabaimo: Danmen no Sedai.* Ed. by/hrsg. vom Yokohama Museum of Art and/und The National Museum of Art, Osaka, p./S. 16–23. Kyoto: Seigensha Art Publishing, Inc., 2009.

Thompson and/und Harootunian 1991
Thompson, Sarah E., and/und Harry D. Harootunian. *Undercurrents in the Floating World: Censorship and Japanese Prints.* New York: Asia Society Galleries, 1991.

Uematsu 2009
Uematsu, Yuka. "Tabaimo: Outside-In." In *Tabaimo: Danmen no Sedai.* Ed. by/hrsg. vom Yokohama Museum of Art and/und The National Museum of Art, Osaka, p./S. 106–111. Kyoto: Seigensha Art Publishing, Inc., 2009.

Uragami 1983
Uragami, Toshiro. *The Beauty of Ukiyo-e: From Harunobu to Kiyochika.* Yamaguchi: TYS Terebi Yamaguchi, 1983.

Inhaltsverzeichnis
Table of Contents

Impressum
Imprint

Dieses Buch begleitet die Ausstellung *Die Schönheit des Augenblicks – Frauen im japanischen Holzdruck,* Museum Rietberg Zürich, 7. Juli bis 14. Oktober 2012.

This book accompanies the exhibition *The Beauty of the Moment—Women in Japanese Woodblock Prints,* Museum Rietberg Zürich, 7 July to 14 October 2012.

In Zusammenarbeit mit dem Honolulu Museum of Art
In collaboration with the Honolulu Museum of Art

Konservierung ermöglicht durch die Robert F. Lange Stiftung
Conservation funded by the Robert F. Lange Foundation

UMSCHLAGBILDER VORNE, INNEN VORNE, INNEN HINTEN, HINTEN, BILD S. 160/
ILLUSTRATIONS FRONT COVER, INSIDE FRONT COVER, INSIDE BACK COVER, BACK COVER, ILLUSTRATION P. 160
Kat./Cat. 73, 72, 94, 83, 57

ISBN 978-3-85881-357-2

Verlag Scheidegger & Spiess AG
Niederdorfstrasse 54
CH-8001 Zürich
Schweiz/Switzerland
www.scheidegger-spiess.ch

Mit Unterstützung von/Supported by

R. BRUNNER
JTI

PUBLIKATION
PUBLICATION

KONZEPT UND REDAKTION / CONCEPT AND EDITING
Katharina Epprecht, Zürich

GESTALTUNG UND SATZ / DESIGN AND TYPOGRAPHY
Hitomi Murai, Zürich

LEKTORAT DER ENGLISCHEN TEXTE /
COPY EDITING OF THE ENGLISH TEXTS
Julie Pickard, London

ÜBERSETZUNG INS DEUTSCHE /
TRANSLATION OF THE ENGLISH TEXTS
Claudia Kotte, Berlin (Essays)
Kurt Rehkopf, Hamburg (Katalogeinträge/Catalogue Entries)

ÜBERSETZUNG INS ENGLISCHE /
TRANSLATION OF THE GERMAN TEXTS
Lisa Rosenblatt, Wien/Vienna

KORREKTORAT DEUTSCH / PROOFREADING GERMAN
Marco Morgenthaler, Zürich

KORREKTORAT ENGLISCH / PROOFREADING ENGLISH
Lisa Rosenblatt, Wien/Vienna

LITHOGRAFIE, DRUCK UND BINDUNG /
LITHOGRAPHS, PRINTING AND BINDING
DZA Druckerei zu Altenburg GmbH, Altenburg, Thüringen

AUSSTELLUNG
EXHIBITION

KONZEPT / CONCEPT
Katharina Epprecht

AUSSTELLUNGSASSISTENZ / EXHIBITION ASSISTANTS
Christof von Waldkirch, Laura Beyer

AUSSTELLUNGSGESTALTUNG / DESIGN AND INSTALLATION
Martin Sollberger

BELEUCHTUNG / LIGHTING
Rainer Wolfsberger

REGISTRARIN / REGISTRAR
Andrea Kuprecht

AUSSTELLUNGSGRAFIK UND WERBEGESTALTUNG /
GRAPHIC DESIGN
Jacqueline Schöb, Frédéric Tischhauser

MARKETING UND KOMMUNIKATION / MARKETING
Christine Ginsberg, Andrea Stefanoni

MEDIAPLANUNG UND EVENTS / ADVERTISING AND EVENTS
Monica Stocker